MW00534832

# The Colony that Rose from the Sea

The Norwegian–American Historical Association

*Lawrence O. Hauge,* PRESIDENT

BOARD OF PUBLICATIONS

*Odd S. Lovoll,* EDITOR
*Carl H. Chrislock*
*Jon Gjerde*
*Steven J. Keillor*
*Ann M. Legreid*
*Terje I. Leiren*
*Deborah L. Miller*
*Todd W. Nichol*
*Janet E. Rasmussen*

# The Colony that

# Rose from the Sea

## Norwegian Maritime Migration and Community in Brooklyn, 1850–1910

*David C. Mauk*

PUBLISHED BY The Norwegian-American Historical Association   1997

DISTRIBUTED BY The University of Illinois Press

Photographs on pages iv and v
Group photo of Nordmaendenes Sangforening. From the private collection of
    Bertha and Gudrun Kartevold, Brooklyn.
A seaman lifts his glass to a woman in a bar. Lithograph from *Harper's New Monthly
    Magazine*, July 1873.
Norwegian Seamen's Home.
Two Women in hats. Private collection of Bertha and Gudrun Kartevold,
    Brooklyn
Grimstad, showing the sea, ca. 1900.

Copyright © 1997
NORWEGIAN-AMERICAN HISTORICAL ASSOCIATION
ISBN 0-87732-086-1
Published with support of the Norwegian Research Council

*For the good people of Norwegian Brooklyn, Manhattan,
Staten Island, and New Jersey; for my wife;
and for the generations of seamen
who made this history a reality.*

# Preface

*The Colony that Rose from the Sea* continues the Association's effort to document the urban experience of Norwegian immigrants. It is only the second monograph dedicated to the story of the Norwegians who formed enclaves and colonies in America's large metropolitan areas. When the first such study, *A Century of Urban Life: The Norwegians in Chicago before 1930*, appeared in 1988, the Association's editor from 1960 to 1980, Kenneth O. Bjork, graciously stated that he felt the Association had been given new life. It is a field of inquiry that the Association plans to pursue vigorously in years to come. The investigation must move beyond the big city to take a closer look at life in smaller urban centers, in towns, and villages. Vibrant Norwegian-American communities in these settings deserve to be given historical interpretation as well.

The present volume calls the reader's attention not only to the emergence of a "Little Norway" in Greater New York, but to Norwegian settlement on the eastern seaboard in general. Separation from the midwestern heartland of Norwegian settlement and a greater interaction with the homeland than occurred there created unique characteristics and developments in the East. The Association is pleased to publish the unfolding story of the international nature of early Norwegian settlement in the port city of New York and the emergence of a permanent immigrant colony in the Red Hook district of Brooklyn; it is a rich story of sailors deserting ship, of employment in the yards and docks of the city, of benevolent institutions, and of residential patterns. It is well documented social history delineating the formative years, 1850–1910, of an urban colony that was destined to become the largest urban concentration of Norwegians outside Norway itself.

David C. Mauk, born in Lima, Ohio, is Associate Professor in American Civilization in the Department of English at the Norwegian University of Science and Technology in Trondheim. *The Colony that Rose from the Sea* is based on his doctoral dissertation of the same name; his degree from New York University was conferred in 1991. Mauk intends to continue his studies of the urban history of Norwegian Americans.

The Association wishes to express its appreciation to the University of Illinois Press for marketing the book, thereby giving it a broad audience beyond the Association's membership. The Association's assistant secretary Ruth Hanold Crane expedited an accelerated production schedule. The volume marks the twenty-fifth publication since 1980 where Mary R. Hove has served as my dedicated, capable, and always cheerful assistant in preparing manuscripts for publication. My deep gratitude and respect for her invaluable contributions to the Association's program cannot be adequately expressed; a simple thank you will have to suffice. She is, as in past publications, responsible for the index.

Odd S. Lovoll
*St. Olaf College*
*The University of Oslo*

# Acknowledgments

This history of the Norwegians in Brooklyn and New York City has been long in coming. Theodore Blegen and Knut Gjerset, America's leading scholars in Norwegian-American studies in the 1930s, and Norway's premier historian of the emigration to America, Ingrid Semmingsen, in the 1950s voiced a need for works dealing with the ethnic group's urban communities. In 1988, Odd S. Lovoll realized a goal set by the Norwegian-American Historical Association in 1928 by publishing the first such study, *A Century of Urban Life: The Norwegians in Chicago before 1930*. Though it comes nearly a decade later, this second and very different story of Norwegians in a large city indicates a continued interest in this aspect of Norwegian immigrant experience.

Many people and institutions have helped me bring to fruition a work that began over a decade ago and developed through a series of research periods in Norway and the United States. At the project's inception no one was more inspiring and helpful in providing access to a variety of primary materials and colony veterans than the then editor of *Nordisk Tidende*, Brooklyn's remaining Norwegian-American newspaper, Sigurd Daasvand, and his wife Synnøva. From the same period dates the invaluable guidance and encouragement of David M. Reimers and Paul R. Baker, among the best NYU had to offer; the vital interest of Steinar Bryn (then an apprentice journalist with a future in the Norwegian Broadcasting System); the patience and infinitely detailed knowledge of Ed Wozny (the wise man of the census records in the Kings County Clerk's Office); and the open-hearted hospitality of Bjørn Jacobsen (President of the Norwegian Singing Society) and his wife Kitty who filled my schedule with dates to speak at community affairs where dozens of colony veterans agreed to give me interviews about their life experiences—which often were the truest guide for interpreting the public record of the past. These generous contributors are named in the appendix. Among the many who deserve my gratitude, none unfolded the tapestry of a family past more copiously rich in historical documents and moving anecdotes than Gudrun and Bertha Kartevold. My thanks too to the many churches and organizations that listened to my pleas and shared their group archives and protocols. The tables and the maps, which transfer and make visible the findings of analyzed data, have benefited greatly from Architect Marit Dale's clearheadedness and technical skills.

And then there are the librarians, archivists, museum directors and local historical organizations without whom all would have been lost more often than one wants to remember: in New York City at NYU's Elmer Holmes Bobst and Tamiment Labor Libraries, the New York Public Library's Research and Special Collections, The New York Historical Society Library, the Archives of the City of New York, the New York Department of Docks and Ferries, maritime historian and librarian Norman Brouwer at the Herman Melville Library of the South Street Seaport Museum, the American-Scandinavian Foundation Library and its Brooklyn Collection, the James A.Kelly Institute for Local Historical Studies at St. Francis College, the Long Island (Brooklyn) Historical Society, the Kings County Clerk's Office's census and public documents rooms, the Brooklyn Borough Office and New York City Register, the Brooklyn Office of the New York City Department of Buildings; in the Midwest at the Norwegian-American Historical Association Archives and Rølvaag Library at St. Olaf College, Luther College Library, and Vesterheim the Norwegian-American Museum; in Norway at the National Archives in Oslo and the Regional Archives at Kristiansand, Bergen and Trondheim; the University of Oslo Norwegian-American Collection, the University of Trondheim Library at Kalvskinnet, the Norsemen's Federation, *Arbeiderbevegelsenarkiv*, the library of the Norwegian Foreign Ministry, Aust-Agder Archives, The Norwegian Emigration Center (and the former Cleng Peerson Institute) in Stavanger, the Norwegian Emigrant Museum at Hamar, and the Maritime Museums of Oslo, Bergen and Trondheim.

Grants from New York University, the Scandinavian American Foundation, the Norwegian Foreign Ministry, an endowment at the

University of Oslo, and the Faculty of the Humanities of the University of Trondheim, now the Norwegian University of Science and Technology (NTNU), made burrowing into all of the above-listed institutional collections possible. In Norway during the years that my knowledge of Norwegian Brooklyn matured, two scholars listened and encouraged, critiqued and suggested, always opening their offices, homes, and minds. I will always owe Ingrid Semmingsen and Dorothy Burton Skårdal an unpayable debt of thanks for providing at once the support I needed and a standard I could reach for when motivating aspiring scholars in my turn.

I was fortunate indeed, when the field work and other basic research was done and my understanding of it was committed to paper, to have insightful, honest readers: my wife Marit, my colleagues Robert Weiss, Ole Moen, Orm Øverland, the anonymous readers for the NAHA, David Reimers, Elliott Barkan, and most of all Odd S. Lovoll and his editorial assistant, Mary Hove, after whose excellent work only my incorrigible errors in judgment remain.

David C. Mauk
*Norwegian University of Science*
*and Technology*

# Contents

# The Colony that
# Rose from the Sea

# 1

# The Colony that
# Rose from the Sea

Most studies of Norwegian immigration to the United States focus on the movement of peasants from inland fjord districts and upland valleys to America's northern plains states. Part of the vast folk movement and land-taking that demanded indigenous peoples' territory in order to create European-style farmlands not only in North America but elsewhere on the globe, this rural-to-rural migration accounts for most Norwegian immigration until the late nineteenth century. Jon Gjerde's *From Peasants to Farmers*, perhaps the most noted recent example of such studies, attracted special attention because it analyzes the evolution of rural Norwegian societal and agricultural customs under the influence of American farming conditions—and thus provides a complement to a variety of research that traces the adjustments of European peasants to urban industrialism in the United States.[1]

But Norwegian emigration, like that from most countries, was multifaceted because it reflected the interplay of specific regional variations in natural resources, economic development, and social traditions. In the last century Norway's inland ecotypes included mining and logging communities. On its central and arctic mountain plateaus the Same lived according to the age-old traditions of their reindeer-herding culture. Along the country's long serrated coast were fishing and shipping towns, as well as rural districts where many families combined farming with fishing and seafaring. Emigration took place from these subcultures but in contexts that differed from Norway's—and Europe's—better known agricultural exodus.[2]

As historians have often pointed out, the great expansion of commercial shipping between the Americas and Europe from 1850 to the early 1920s played a crucial role in the rising volume of immigration to the United States. The Atlantic trade contributed to the dissemination of information about America. It also determined the migratory path and often the permanent residence of immigrants, and, in response to the swelling tide of immigration, it developed a branch of shipping that specialized in transporting and recruiting immigrants.

The often neglected aspects of this story are the effects of expanding trade on the migration of *merchant seamen*, on emigration from Europe's coastal shipping areas, and on the development of maritime ethnic communities or sub-communities in America's and, indeed, the world's port cities.[3] The origins and evolution of Brooklyn's Norwegian *koloni*—ethnic settlement or neighborhood—illustrates all three of these understudied facets of the Atlantic migration. By 1850 Norway was posed to become a major shipping nation, and by 1880 it boasted of the world's third largest commercial fleet. Shippers' and officials' warnings about a growing manpower migration from the country's vessels grew in stridency in the second half of the century. And with good cause: One analysis of Norwegian government reports shows that the country's merchant marine lost nearly 70,000 seamen through legal and illegal immigration between 1866 and 1915.[4]

Today, poor third-world peoples provide the itinerant cheap labor on the world's shipping fleets. Scholars ought to investigate whether significant numbers of these workers, like the Norwegian merchant seamen of an earlier era, are using their maritime trades as a means of easing legal and illegal immigration. Much has changed in shipping conditions and in immigration and maritime law, but ships' crews still experience the lure of much higher wages in more developed nations and extraordinary chances for international migration.

Brooklyn's *Little Norway* was but the largest of several similar maritime Norwegian settlements in the United States and other countries that appeared primarily because of expanded trade across the Atlantic. The historical sources that throw light on the Brooklyn colony's origins and development not only reveal these other Norwegian colonies but also indicate that international migration from other major maritime nations' merchant fleets occurred through a similar constellation of historical processes and circumstances. The margins of research notes for this study continually became cluttered with evidence that Swedish, British, German, Spanish, and Italian seamen, among others, migrated and very likely contributed to the growth of overseas ethnic communities in much the same fashion as Norwegian sailors did.[5]

Concentrating on the factors that gave the Norwegian colony in Brooklyn's Red Hook section a strong maritime orientation, one could only wonder how exactly the patterns there resembled those that molded the harbor-related parts of other ethnic communities. That significant immigration from many nations' merchant marines *had* occurred, however, was clear. Thus, a work planned as a community study of an apparently unique Norwegian colony became instead, like Gjerde's *From Peasants to Farmers*, a specifically Norwegian example of a more general aspect of transatlantic migration and adjustment to American conditions.

Dependent on a cheap, portable work force, the long trade boom between the Americas and Europe brought hundreds of thousands of foreign merchant seamen to North American harbors. In the nineteenth century, moreover, ships' crews commonly stayed in port for one or more weeks while incoming cargoes were unloaded and new cargoes were negotiated and stowed on board. Not infrequently seamen completed work contracts in a foreign port and so stayed for some days or weeks before signing on another ship that took them out of the harbor. As a result, cities like New York developed dockside "sailortowns" where more or less shady entrepreneurs offered a variety of legal and illegal services, entertainments, and goods for temporarily resident seafarers with time to kill and money to spend. Municipal authorities and foreign consulates, shipping companies and maritime tradesmen, boardinghouse keepers and shopkeepers, social reformers, religious charities, and ethnic communities—all were concerned with the social problems and economic possibilities related to a port city's transient marine workforce.[6]

**International Migration and the Atlantic Trade Expansion**

While ashore between voyages, many foreign sailors considered the advantages of making an occupational change when they learned about opportunities on land or in other nations' merchant fleets. Maritime wage scales as well as working and living conditions on board varied greatly from ship to ship and nation to nation.[7] Major port cities and their hinterlands offered perhaps the world's largest and most diverse job markets. Encouraged by their relatively short-term contracts and the itinerant nature of deep-sea sailing, seamen felt that they took only a very limited economic risk when they tried their hands at new lines of work or life in different countries. Desertions and emigration remained constant problems for shipping companies primarily because the demand for crewmen continued until the shipping crisis of the 1920s.[8] In other words, sailors knew they could move from one country's merchant marine to another or experiment with work on land because the home fleet would always welcome them back if they decided to return. Seamen who sailed back and forth between a small number of foreign

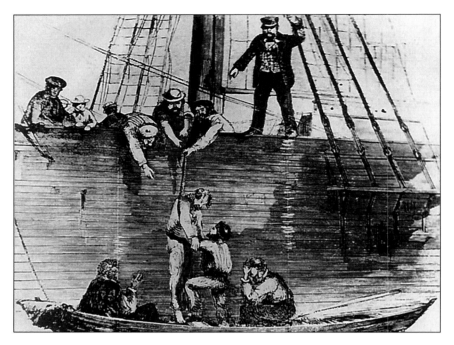

THE COFFIN-SHIPS.

Some men took berths on ships with the intention of emigrating, while others jumped ship after considering their options at sea or because they objected to shipboard working and living conditions. Yet others found tempting opportunities or made personal obligations ashore.

•

Drawing of a sailor being hoisted unconscious on board a ship. From Leah Rousmaniere's *Anchored within the Vail: A Pictorial History of the Seamen's Church Institute.*

•

"The Coffin-Ships" from *Punch*, March 15, 1873.

harbors year after year were especially likely to settle abroad because the probability of making lasting personal ties or finding long-term employment in one of those port cities increased with each visit.

And, as long as international trade flourished, mariners who drifted into more or less long-term residence in foreign ports faced few legal obstacles to their migration. Because the period's technology and commercial organization required itinerant workers on board ship, governments seldom saw regulating their movements as an appropriate goal of immigration laws. By the last three decades of the century, the crews of most merchant ships were polyglot mixtures of foreign contract laborers of various ancestries, who not infrequently changed their transitory presence to more permanent residence. Yet politicians did not take the legislative action that would clearly determine the borders separating foreign mariners' legal status as transients, or sojourners, or permanent residents—even though government reports provided statistical proof that foreign contract workers comprised a steadily rising percentage of the Atlantic nations' merchant seamen as the century progressed. In the United States, for example, legislation banning the use of foreign contract labor *on land* was passed in the mid-1880s, but no law placed time limits on the "temporary" residence of foreign seamen—the key provision needed to prevent undocumented maritime immigration—until forty years later, when a surplus of seamen appeared for the first time in the Atlantic economy.[9]

Until the 1920s seamen also benefited from lax enforcement of the few restrictions concerning their movements that were common among Atlantic nations. Legally, a seaman could take work in another nation's fleet in a foreign harbor as long as he had satisfied the terms of his contract with a home-country ship first. International agreements prohibiting and punishing breach of contract through ship-jumping went into force in some parts of Europe in the late 1820s and included that whole continent and North America after mid-century. In theory, these laws were draconian. Typically, they provided that deserters were to be apprehended with the assistance of the local police and brought back in chains to their ships, where captains would confiscate their sea chests, dock their wages, and transport them home to serve a jail sentence.[10]

In practice, however, maritime desertion laws were unenforceable. Foreign police forces seldom cooperated effectively. Captains, painfully aware that every extra day in port was costly for shipowners, had little time to pursue deserters. Instead, they found replacements for missing crew members with the assistance of sailortown boardinghouse keepers, or "crimps" as they were commonly known. Crimps encouraged desertions because sailors on the run from the authorities became in effect a private manpower pool whose market value they controlled. Many sailors found falling into crimps' clutches unavoidable because of their monopoly over affordable dockside flophouses, willingness to extend credit to pleasure-starved mariners on a spending spree, and strict blacklisting of men who did not repay their debts by signing onto the ship the boardinghouse keeper chose. Faced with these realities, governments gave up on general enforcement of desertion laws and settled for occasionally making examples of a few ship-jumpers. Laws against desertion commonly made the authorities' inability to control the situation obvious by including a provision guaranteeing sailors who returned voluntarily to their home fleet amnesty from punishment.[11]

In the last third of the century, the United States did make some effort to limit the number of foreigners in its merchant marine. By the early 1880s sailors on American ships had to claim residence in the American port where they signed on. Later in the decade, the authorities required that crewmen claim an American birthplace. But a variety of evidence suggests that these rules were easily circumvented. Statistics from the U. S. Commissioner of Navigation showed that the number of foreign or foreign-born sailors on American vessels continued to rise through the beginning of World War I. In 1916, for instance, 70 percent of the seamen registered for service on American ships were foreign-born and, of these, only 13 percent were naturalized citizens.[12]

Judging from the histories of Atlantic shipping, reports of the Commissioner of Navigation, newspaper articles, and the career paths, testimony, and memoirs of Norwegian sailors used in this study, official measures did not restrict the movement of foreigners into the American fleet for four main reasons: The number of native-born Americans who chose seafaring declined steadily from mid-century because employment opportunities on land were more attractive. Pressed by captains facing a combination of maritime manpower shortages, desertions, and a crimp-controlled labor market, many harbor officials did not question the addresses and birthplaces on lists of crew members presented to them. Foreign sailors were often recruited for work on American ships when those vessels touched land abroad, where American requirements for hiring on did not apply. Most important, wages on American ships remained higher than those offered in European fleets for much of the period, especially in the Port of New York, which made work in the United States merchant marine attractive for men who wanted to accumulate a nest egg before returning home or who sought a low-risk way of trying their luck as immigrants.[13]

## The Extent and Causes of Norwegian Maritime Migration

If the history of Norwegian maritime emigration is in any degree representative, the large numbers of seamen who visited and the minority who took up more permanent residence in foreign ports played significant roles in the founding of harbor-related immigrant colonies in America and elsewhere. The overwhelming majority of Norwegian sailors remained loyal to their homeland's fleet. Only an estimated 4 percent left permanently by jumping ship or emigrating between 1866 and 1915. As noted earlier, however, these men represented a net maritime manpower loss of almost 70,000 over half a century. To this total

we must add another 20,000 deserters or sojourners who eventually returned to Norway, and therefore were not included in the tally of manpower loss, as well as an unknown number of seamen not recorded by
Norwegian authorities in those categories because they had *legally*
served in other nations' fleets for a time after completing their contracts
in a foreign port.[14] With these figures in focus it is not surprising that
the expansion of Norwegian shipping resulted in maritime colonies first
in European cities, then in North America's ports, and finally in the
shipping centers of South America, South Africa, and Australia. Maritime immigration, often illegal or little documented, decisively influenced the development of small Norwegian enclaves in such diverse
cities as Boston, Baltimore, Pensacola, New Orleans, San Francisco, and
Brooklyn.[15]

Several factors suggest that Norwegian sailors may have had better
reason to jump ship or emigrate than seamen from most other Western
countries. Along with Ireland and Italy, Norway lost a larger portion of
its population to emigration than the rest of Europe because its rate of
population growth, its relative poverty, and the lateness of its industrialization left people who wanted to maintain or improve their status few
other alternatives. Still, seafarers and their families felt the brunt of these
macroeconomic factors less than most until the mid–1880s, when
steam-driven vessels drove Norwegian sailing ships from many freight
markets. During the thirty-year crisis of the country's shipping industry
that followed, emigration from Sørlandet, the south coast counties of
Agder and Rogaland which were most dependent on shipping, moved
from near the bottom to the top of the national statistics.[16] But those
records were compiled from lists of people departing as declared emigrants. Few of the men who settled abroad through the processes of
maritime emigration are included in Norway's emigrant protocols, and
the large majority of them based their choices on a set of factors specifically related to conditions in the homeland's merchant marine.

Comparative wages and working conditions were probably the
most important elements in Norwegian maritime emigration. Although
Norwegian sailors' pay scales improved steadily between 1870 and 1920,
in the 1850s and 1860s they were consistently the lowest of those offered by North Atlantic nations. And in New York they did not reach a
par with competing western nations until well into the 1890s, when
Norwegian companies began paying "American" wages to men who
manned steamships used exclusively in the trade between the United
States and Latin America. Most Norwegian ships even after 1890, however, were wooden sailing vessels that specialized in other kinds of trade.
Touching land in Norway only infrequently, the largest part of this fleet
moved between the major European exporting nations and the United
States.[17] Thus, while receiving the lowest wages available, the majority
of Norwegian sailors were among the mariners most tempted to settle
abroad both because they were frequently exposed to seamen who were

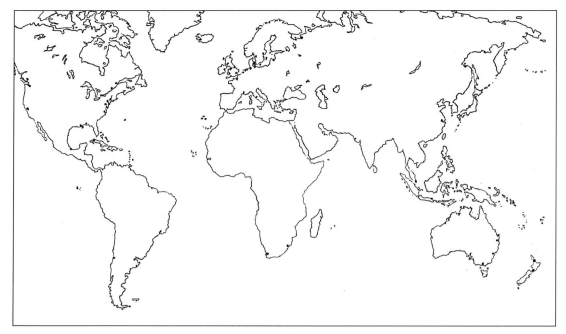

## Some Locations of Norwegian Maritime Settlement
## Around the World, 1850–1940

| Europe | | North America | Central America | Asia |
|---|---|---|---|---|
| Gothenberg | Hull | New York | Vera Cruz | Singapore |
| Riga | London | Baltimore | **South America** | **Austral–Asia** |
| Hamburg | Glasgow | Norfolk | Rio Di Janiero | Brisbane |
| Amsterdam | Cardiff | Mobile | La Plata | Sydney |
| Rotterdam | Dublin | New Orleans | Buenos Aires | Melbourne |
| Antwerp | Reykjavik | SanFrancisco | Santiago | Auckland |
| Le Havre | **North America** | Seattle | **Africa** | Wellington |
| Marsielle | Quebec | Vancouver | Cape Town | |
| Rome | Montreal | | Durban | |

Sources: "Nordmenn jorden rundt" in *Nordmanns-Forbundets Tidsskrift,* 1908–1936. See especially G. H. Gottenborg, "Det utflyttede Norge jorden rundt" (Kristiania, 1914), 7:316–339, and Ragnvald Jønsberg, "Hvor mange nordmænd bor utenfor Norge?" (Oslo, 1924), 17:417–423. "Port Cities" (*Havnebyer*) Archives of the Norwegian Seamen's Mission Society, Norwegian Regional Archives, Bergen, Norway. Vilhelm Vilhelmsen, *Den norske sjømannsmisjon i 75 år, 1864–1939.* Bergen, 1939.

better paid and because they seldom had opportunities to return home. This situation alone may have been sufficient to cause a relatively high emigration rate from Norway's merchant marine, but other circumstances played important roles too.

Compared with most other Atlantic countries, Norway was a capital-poor nation with a small import-export market. To take advantage of the trade boom, its shipping industry had to concentrate on carrying other nations' goods with a minimum of investment and operating overhead. Somehow Norwegian shippers had to squeeze a profit out of a situation in which lower freight rates were the best argument for convincing foreign businessmen to use their vessels. Before the conversion to steam, Norway competed internationally through a unique combination of natural advantages. The country had a wealth of timber close to an enormously long coast with a multitude of inlets appropriate for shipbuilding and a disproportionately large population with seafaring and shipbuilding traditions. After the lifting of Britain's Navigation Acts opened new freight markets at mid-century, Norway's rush to take advantage of these new opportunities became a grass-roots affair, especially around the southern tip of the country, which was geographically best placed for the competition with British and continental shippers. Local families and communities pooled their funds and skills, with the result that officers and crew often included neighbors and relatives who had financial shares in the vessel they sailed on.[18]

Some Norwegian historians have argued that these ties to a local community resulted in better treatment by officers and a willingness to tolerate lower wages from crewmen who stood to share in the profits of the voyage. That may have been true in the 1850s and 1860s, particularly on trade routes between European nations, but Norwegian government reports indicate that ship-jumping became a serious problem almost as soon as the country's vessels began docking in American ports in appreciable numbers. American wages double their own or more were Norwegian mariners' main grievance, but they also complained to home-country officials about longer watches, extra duties handling cargo and making ship repairs in port, poorer food, less satisfactory living quarters in the forecastle, and rougher treatment from their officers.[19] Discipline on board very likely grew stricter with the crews' increasing temptation to desert as they compared their lot with that of American merchant sailors, but the rest of these complaints are traceable to shipowners' decision to cut costs.

In any case, the growing competition from faster and larger steamships from around 1870 forced a consolidation of ownership that reduced seamen's stake in profits from shipping and led owners to pare overhead to the bone in order to maintain their profit levels. The results of these processes were living and working conditions that were considerably worse than those in the other Atlantic commercial fleets. Vitamin deficiency diseases were more frequent on Norwegian vessels. Explosions and other accidents related to such dangerous cargoes as grain, oil, and coal also more commonly sent Norwegian ships to the bottom.[20] That fact may have resulted in part from delayed ship repairs, but more likely it stemmed from a specialization in freight that shippers in other nations were reluctant to carry.

The percentage of Norwegian ships lost through sinkings tripled between 1870 and the mid-1890s, when it was the highest among the Atlantic nations. To a degree the rapid increase arose from continued specialization in risky cargoes and faulty safety precautions, but mostly it came from the addition of older, less seaworthy vessels to the Norwegian fleet. In the last third of the century Norwegian shippers bought wooden sailing vessels at low prices from other countries that considered them outmoded.[21] In short, shipowners were willing to sacrifice not only seamen's health but their very lives if that seemed necessary to ensure their own financial survival. Such brutal self-interest was far from unknown in other maritime nations, but Norway's particular economic situation probably made consequent maritime emigration more likely.

## Maritime Variations on Common Themes in Immigration History

In spite of the conditions outlined above, Norwegians were not the largest group of foreign sailors working in America's commercial fleet around the turn of the century. A somewhat larger contingent of Germans and over twice as many British seamen—many of them probably "Liverpool Irishmen"—sailed on American ships. After 1910 Spaniards were the largest foreign group, and the numbers of Russians and Filipinos were rising rapidly.[22] What is the most helpful term to describe these men's status? Were they transients, sojourners, or immigrants? Asking the question directly focuses attention on the need to distinguish the migratory patterns of seamen—"maritime migration"—from the processes we usually call international migration.

Foreign sailors working in the American merchant marine ought to be called sojourners. Like millions of other foreigners working on land, many of them probably intended to save some money and return home. But for most seamen sojourning was the *second* stage in the migratory process. Transient residence—the time spent in port between voyages on foreign ships—was usually the initial stage of maritime migration. Unlike other sojourners or immigrants, a sailor did not have to base a decision to migrate on learning about his adopted country from afar. He might choose to leave his home country's fleet the first time he touched land abroad, but he could also visit it over a number of years without any change in his legal status. This particular kind of "transience" also altered the character of other phases in seamen's migratory patterns. For mariners, sojourning and even taking out immigration papers were much less binding on them than on other immigrants because, in practice, these were steps easily entered into and easily reversed. All a man had to do was take a berth on one of his homeland's ships at the next opportunity and his return migration was started—with his wages paying the cost of the trip.

The occupational histories of Norwegian sailors who were subjects of this study suggest that several flexible phases of sojourning in maritime migration can be categorized according to the likelihood that they would lead to immigration. Working as a sailor on an American oceangoing ship, often the first phase, least often resulted in permanent settlement. Employment on coastal vessels and harbor craft suggested stronger tendencies to settle and frequently functioned as intermediate second and third phases. Norwegians called the turning-point in sailors' sojourning, or immigration, "going on land," leaving the sea for work on shore. Many former mariners spent the rest of their careers in America working on the docks or in firms such as ship chandleries that directly served incoming ships. According to colony old-timers, however, the surest sign that a sojourner had become an immigrant came when he moved out of the harbor economy. When that indicator became unreliable because carpentry work developed into a popular form of sojourning for seamen, the only sure indication of the intention to immigrate was establishing a family in Brooklyn.[23]

An initial period of transience followed by several easily reversible stages of sojourning made maritime migration a more indeterminate and lengthy process than that usually involved for migrating workers on land. In some ways the migration of Mexicans, French-Canadians, and Cubans may be seen as roughly similar to seamen's. Because these nationality groups could, for various reasons, enter and leave the United States easily during the period, they often "commuted" or migrated seasonally before settling into more permanent residence. Official approval or toleration of these "irregular" movements, as in the case of sailors, resulted from the need for workers in specific labor markets. In a broad sense, their long periods of temporary residence may also have affected their premigration experience and community formation in America in similar ways.[24]

Maritime transients and sojourners, rather than immigrants, were the trailblazers of migration from the coastal shipping areas of southern Norway to America's port cities. From seamen's letters and firsthand testimony, families from these areas learned to make changes in the traditional practice of combining farming with seafaring. By the 1860s and early 1870s, the higher wages that sojourning fathers and brothers earned in the United States merchant marine became an accepted way for some families to solve financial difficulties or fund goals, such as buying more land or building boats and barns. Wives adjusted to their men being at sea for longer periods than earlier, usually because Norwegian shipping had expanded to more distant markets but also because of this increasing practice of sojourning. It became common for them to take the responsibility for managing family finances and running farms with the help of younger children. Even for the large majority of families whose men did not sojourn on American or other nation's ships in these years, that alternative became a natural part of calculations about what to do if the times took a turn for the worse.[25]

Then, Norwegian maritime emigration through desertion in American ports more than doubled, surging to its first peak in the latter 1870s and early 1880s, as seamen anticipated the coming economic triumph of steamships over sailing vessels. Roughly five years later, desertions in Canadian, Latin American, and British harbors also reached unprecedented levels. The point here is that this dramatic rise in unregulated migration resulted not only from changing economic conditions in Atlantic shipping but from the pathfinding experience of sojourning seamen who had prepared coastal Norwegian families to use work in foreign merchant fleets as a way of maintaining their socioeconomic status at home. A related point is that transient and sojourning seamen's prior knowledge of maritime labor shortages and high wages in the United States contributed greatly to the fact that the first and preferred goal of departing Norwegian mariners was work in America. In Britain, for example, where wages for seamen were closest to those offered in the United States, less than half as many men jumped ship during the peak years.[26]

Large numbers of people from Norway's southern shipping districts did not begin to settle in Brooklyn and other American port cities until the ten-year period after the peak of desertions. After the shipping crisis caused widespread maritime unemployment at home in the mid-1880s, the main purpose of working on American ships changed. Instead of serving as a short-term solution for coastal families in difficulty, it became a *modus operandi* for mass emigration from a whole region. In the thirty years that followed, especially in Sørlandet where the exodus was greatest, a particular kind of chain migration developed. Transient mariners continued to desert in American ports but increasingly did so after finding a berth on another country's ship abroad.[27] Together, the accumulated body of maritime sojourners and deserters in American ports formed an amateur corps of *in situ* travel agents who facilitated emigration from coastal Norway. Sailors sojourning in the United States sent for their families. At home, seamen and maritime craftsmen boarded immigrant ships after contacting seafaring relatives or friends in America to ask for temporary lodgings and help finding work on arrival. When the continuing crisis in shipping depressed other sectors of the economy in the southern coastal districts, people in a wide range of occupations used the links in a network of maritime connections to assist their passage to America and ease their adjustment to conditions there. By the turn of the century Brooklyn's Norwegian colony had become one of the most rapidly growing communities in Norwegian America primarily through this maritime chain migration.[28]

Thus, at every step of the research the unfolding nature and effects of merchant sailors' migration forced a rethinking of basic concepts and processes. Understanding the mechanisms involved in community formation that resulted from maritime migration presented no exception. From the early 1860s to the mid-1880s, formal community structures in the Brooklyn colony derived from a model that defined the settlement as a haven for maritime transients rather than as an immigrant enclave. All but one of the Norwegian organizations in the Red Hook section were what might be termed "transplanted institutions." That is, their staffs, organizational models, notions of charity, and much of their financial support were imported from mother organizations and their supporters in Norway. Their founding purpose and rules of operation aimed primarily at improving the morals, health, or living conditions of transient seamen serving on the homeland's ships. Their leaders were either emissaries sent on tours of duty from headquarters in Norway or sojourners asked to come into the organizations by old-country officials already in place in Brooklyn or Manhattan. Because of the conditions of their employment, these leaders shared the old-country concept of the colony as a way station for sailors between voyages, saw themselves as the proper guardians of the whole community's development, and gently but firmly informed the more settled elements of the colony that transient mariners had to receive first priority in their institutions.

As long as maritime transients far outnumbered them, the colony's sojourners and immigrants were content with this situation. Using the transplanted institutions as handy substitutes spared them the effort and cost of creating organizations focused on their particular needs. Adjusting to their second-class status, they channeled their limited resources into the organizations for transients. A combination of mixed emotions strengthened their willingness to put off the establishment of an independent associational life: sympathy for the plight of transient countrymen, their own intention to return to Norway in a few years, a feeling that the transplanted institutions were more genuinely Norwegian than Norwegian-American organizations could ever be, and a need to justify their demands on organizations not meant for them. So dependent had immigrants become on this arrangement that they tried and sometimes managed to seize power from the emissary leaders before reluctantly founding separate institutions in the late 1880s. A few years later the shipping crisis at home had resulted in an immigrant population large enough to produce a settled community with a keen sense of its own importance, a network of informal housing and employment patterns based on maritime chain migration, and a dozen or so Norwegian-American institutions in which seafaring transients took second priority.

This study is organized to strike a balance between an examination of the Brooklyn colony's various backgrounds and an exploration of the ways these molded the enclave's development from a haven for transient seamen to a settled immigrant community. Chapters 2 and 3 explore the roots of maritime migration in Norway and the Atlantic shipping economy, placing these in the broader perspectives of European and Norwegian emigration history and commercial development. Chapter 4 functions as a pivot by directing attention to the ways that conditions in the United States, the port of New York, Manhattan, and Brooklyn intersected with developments in Norway and Europe to bring thousands of transient Norwegian seamen to Red Hook and lay the foundations for an immigrant colony there.

The next three chapters trace different aspects of the settlement's evolution from a stopping place for transients to a harbor-oriented immigrant community. The transplanted institutions play a key role in the discussion of the haven for transients; where their benevolence mixed with paternalistic notions of Christian charity, relations to shipowners in a modified "company-town economy" and a tendency to inhibit settlement and accommodation to americanizing influences are central issues. Chapter 5 culminates in an analysis of the open conflicts between emissary and immigrant leaders that resulted from ambivalent loyalties and resistance to change on both sides. In the next chapter, the focus switches to the ground swell of informal cooperation among sojourners and immigrants that arose from the need to find work, lodgings, and means of stabilizing family life in a multicultural industrial city. Here, comparisons between the residential and occupational patterns of Brooklyn's Norwegians and other immigrant communities throw light on the dynamics of cultural maintenance in a small ethnic group with a disproportionately large population of transients and sojourners. Chapter 7 weighs the influence of maritime migration and earlier stages of community formation on the flowering of Norwegian-American institutions that occurred between 1890 and 1910. Underscoring the organizational energies released by emissary leaders' diminishing authority, this discussion also emphasizes the occasional strains in colony life that developed from the simultaneous appearance of cultural forms from coastal Sørlandet and a diversity of religious, class, and political interests.

Because the transition to immigrant dominance was complete by 1910, the study does not closely analyze events after that date. The conclusion does, however, discuss the continuing importance of patterns established by then on the colony's evolution up to World War II. Throughout the volume there is a recognition that urbanization and technological change dynamically affected Norwegian migration to and settlement in Brooklyn. Where it seems enlightening, there is also an effort to place that movement in comparative contexts—with maritime migration generally and the experience of other American ethnic groups.

# 2

---

# The Norwegian
# Background
# of Brooklyn's
# Red Hook Colony

The background for Norwegian emigration to Red Hook illustrates not only the well-known contours of European and Norwegian migration but also the variety of conditions and aspirations that lay behind one of the most important processes in modern history. Although international migration did not become a mass movement in their homeland until 1866, Norwegians joined the general exodus earlier than their Scandinavian neighbors. The intensity of their emigration, once well under way, was surpassed only by the Irish during the rest of the century.[1]

Norwegian emigration crested three times between 1814 and 1915. The two largest waves of departures, between 1880 and 1893 and from 1900 to World War I, accounted for over seventy percent of the country's emigrants in the period. Norwegians migrated to all parts of the globe, but, compared to the United States, which received 96 percent of the emigrants, the three next most frequent destinations—Canada, Australia, and South Africa—attracted only a small number, despite repeated attempts to direct the stream of emigrants to these and other nations.[2]

In 1910 three-fourths of the Norwegians in the United States

●
Emigrants came to Brooklyn city streets much like this at the turn of the century.
New York City Municipal Archives.

lived in the north-central region, from Illinois through the Dakotas. The Northeast and the West, although they became the most popular destinations after 1890, contained, respectively, only ten and fifteen percent of the Norwegian-born population twenty years later. Nonetheless, settlement patterns around the turn of the century clearly show a turning point in the character of Norwegian emigration. Between 1890 and 1910 the absolute number of Norwegians in America's rural areas declined for the first time, while the percentage in cities doubled, rising to over 40 percent. Even if one allows for Norwegian Americans leaving the farm for the city and deaths among the older rural population, the disproportionate growth of the urban population indicates that much larger numbers of new arrivals were settling in cities. Urban colonies on the east and west coasts grew most rapidly, and among these only Seattle experienced a larger increase in its Norwegian population than Brooklyn.[3] Thus, the colony investigated in this study represents a distinct, later phase of Norwegian emigration. In fact, most Brooklyn Norwegians differed not only in the timing of their emigration and their destination but also in their regional Norwegian background, occupations, and motivations for leaving the old country.

Changing settlement patterns in the United States resulted from a sequence of developments in Norway that altered the factors behind the impulse to emigrate. As elsewhere in Europe, rapid population growth was fundamental for Norwegian internal and overseas migration. Mushrooming by 59 percent between 1800 and 1850, the Norwegian population maintained its rate of increase during the next fifty years, despite the country's unusually intense emigration. The urban portion of the population, however, grew only from 10 percent in 1800 to 28 percent a hundred years later. Even in the decade from 1855 to 1865, when Norway's cities experienced their highest growth rate (3.11 percent), in *absolute numbers* the population increase in rural areas was almost twice as large. The effects of the demographic explosion, therefore, were felt first and most acutely in the countryside.[4]

**Rural Population Growth and Social Geography**

    Patterns of rural adjustment, among them the timing and importance of emigration, differed tremendously because of the disparities of Norwegian cultural geography. Sliced into pieces by fjords, broken up along an irregular coast with island archipelagoes, divided into numerous narrow valleys and highland plateaus by mountain ranges, and stretched over a length equal to the distance from Oslo to Rome, rural Norwegian culture naturally developed a high degree of diversity. As late as 1850, there seemed to be as many different rural cultures as there were rural communities, each with its distinctive dialect, folk costume, building style, and socioeconomic configuration. The various rural areas were not entirely isolated. Growing internal migration and commerce strengthened their interdependence. Yet, these long-term processes also contributed to an evolving geographic division of labor that accentuated local dissimilarities as much as it increased contact between parts of the country.[5]

To emphasize the contours of adjustment to demographic change, the following discussion divides rural communities according to the convenient categories established by Norwegian historians. Along the Atlantic coast, winters are short and mild, allowing early planting and late harvests. With one exception, however, mountains and waterways cut the *coastal* rural districts into areas too small for large-scale farming. The only sizable plain bordering the sea is Jæren, a rock-strewn peninsula south of Stavanger. Interior areas have colder, longer winters but warmer summers, creating a hectic growing season between late thaws and early snows. Most inland agricultural areas are *highland or mountainous* districts, where the terrain and climate are appropriate for subsistence farming supplemented by stock-raising and logging. Only the *flatland* rural districts around the Oslo and Trondheim fjords are sufficiently extensive for farming based on grain production. As each type of rural district evolved methods of coping with changing demographic conditions, climate and topography formed the basis for the development of communities with divergent cultural norms and socioeconomic structures.[6]

As a whole, Norwegian agriculture responded to the population explosion with improvements in productivity that not only kept pace with the domestic demand for food but also provided the basis for expanded employment and an improved living standard. Agricultural areas near growing cities supported their expanding populations through food production for urban markets. While keeping their land holdings undivided through a system of primogeniture, farmers in other such areas increased grain production by clearing more fields, investing in improved farm machinery and methods, and hiring day laborers and cotters (*husmenn*). These flatland farm owners secured a stable labor force through agreements that gave cotters minimal wages for their farmwork but allowed them to supplement their families' diet by cultivating marginal land "nearest the forest's wild animals." In this way these central agricultural districts boosted production and the growing surplus population found a means of survival, but the social consequence was the sharpening of class differences between a burgeoning agrarian proletariat and well-to-do commercial farmers, who were often in debt for modern machinery and buildings.[7]

To maximize the use of mountainside fodder and support their expanding populations, higher altitude inland areas turned increasingly to animal husbandry, selling butter, cheese, and livestock to other districts in exchange for grain and fish. Low profits in relation to the work required to find fodder for animals, as well as transportation difficulties, however, forced most of these upland farmers to rely chiefly on subsistence agriculture and feed their growing families a diet heavily dependent on potatoes. Farms became quite small because fathers divided land

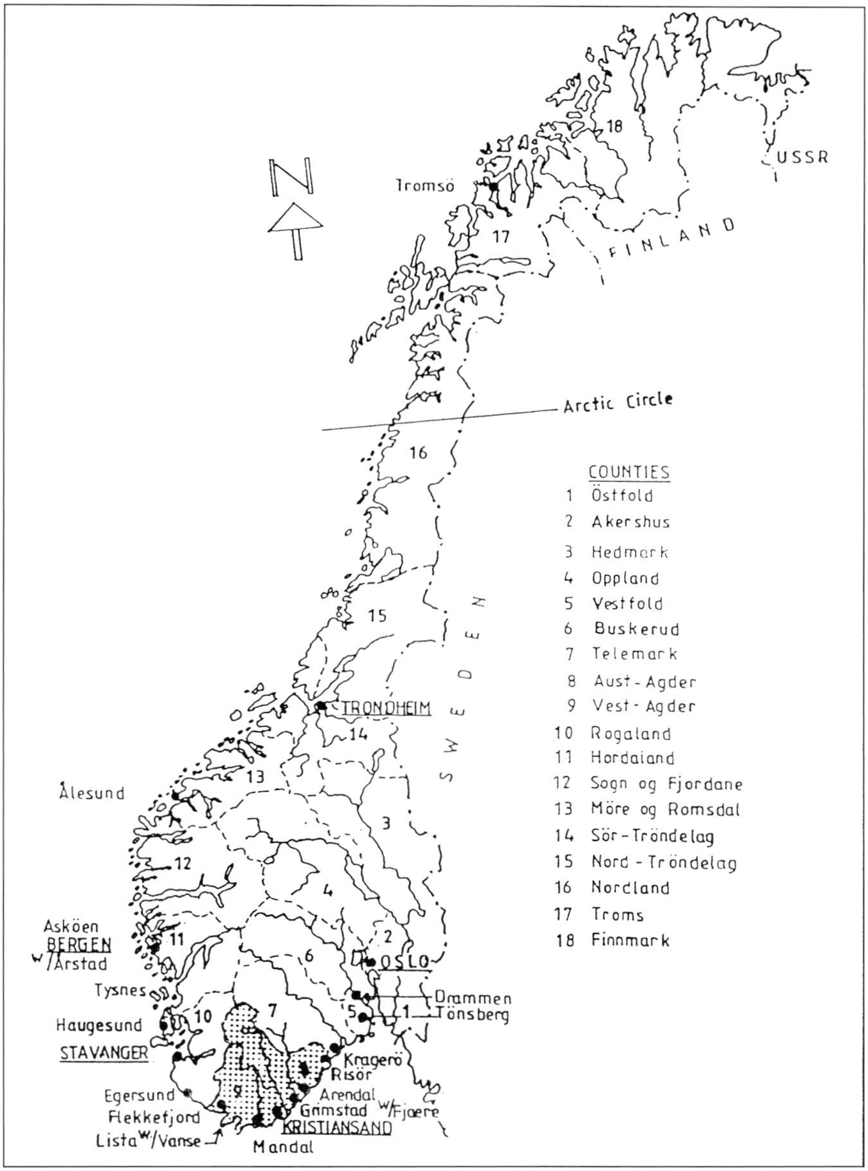


Map of Norway with main coastal cities, counties, and Arctic Circle marked and Agder counties shaded.

among their male heirs, the extended families often living in clustered farmhouses. As poverty was general and class differences minimal, a sense of closely-knit, democratic community developed.[8]

Coastal districts such as those in Agder and Rogaland counties showed yet another pattern of development. Here too, the cotter class grew and farmers parceled out land to their sons, creating ever smaller agricultural units. The crucial difference was that the sea's resources made families much less dependent on income from farming. Most cotters also earned a living as fishermen and *owned* a small piece of land where their families raised vegetables for their own consumption. Herring and potatoes formed the staples of a poor man's diet along the coast. Farm owners too were often fishermen, and thus farm size was not so important as in inland districts. Because Norwegian fisheries expanded throughout the century, the coastal agrarian population, especially in western Norway, experienced good times that depended little on agricultural production.[9]

Around the southern tip of the country, especially in the Agder counties, shipbuilding and seafaring offered abundant additional sources of income because of the great expansion of Norwegian shipping from the 1850s to the 1880s. Since fathers and sons worked as ship's carpenters and seamen while wives managed the family farm, women assumed a position of greater economic importance and independence in the South. Shipyards sprouted up not only in southern port cities but all along the coast. A wide range of rural working people, including farmers, pooled their capital and labor to buy shares in and build vessels that carried freight to all parts of the world. Successfully completed voyages brought rich dividends to large sections of the coastal population during the South's golden age.[10]

Especially in these coastal areas shipping and fishing sustained a rural society with widely spread prosperity and cosmopolitan experience. Supplementary income from other work relieved families of dependence on farming and thus evened out socioeconomic differences. Fishing increased the men's familiarity with the nearby towns and cities where they sold their fish. The long shipping boom in time made many southern men feel more at home in the port districts of European and American cities than they did in their homeland's urban areas. Meanwhile, as we shall see, southern women not only handled their own and men's traditional tasks, but found another route to extra income and urban experience through work as domestics in coastal towns and cities.

**Internal Migration, the Prelude to Emigration**

It was in the areas most dependent on agriculture that population growth first outstripped the available economic opportunities and forced unpleasant changes in social traditions. The crux of the problem was that here adjustments in farming methods and markets could not provide members of the younger generation with sufficient land to maintain the social status and life-style their parents had enjoyed. And in these districts social prestige and the traditional succession of family roles depended almost entirely on the ownership of land.[11]

By mid-century, however, there was no more land to be cleared. Even the poorest marginal areas were under cultivation, and therefore even logging, the only other means of supporting a family, offered few chances of saving to buy farmland. Meanwhile, the decline in infant mortality and the increase in longevity continued. Thus, with growing frequency young people had to choose between a lowered social status and migration. Staying at home not only meant a loss of status but the alteration of rural household traditions. Fathers felt pressure to retire prematurely. Sons put off marriage, decided to marry and raise a family while still living on the family farm, or joined the growing ranks of seasonal migrants, combining agricultural work with fishing, peddling, or handicrafts to support their families. Unmarried daughters increasingly found employment as milkmaids on other farms or as domestics in urban areas.[12] In southern inland Norway one dependable sign of spring was seeing flocks of children walking east to distant farms where they spent the summer working as goatherds. The rural population's reluctance to resort to more drastic changes in life-style or residence was mirrored in the unprecedented growth of the cotter class, rising farm debt, and widening class divisions in the lowlands and deepening poverty and migratory work patterns in the upland areas.[13]

As the strain on the inland rural social fabric deepened, economic need overwhelmed family and district loyalties with increasing frequency. By the 1860s permanent migration to other parts of the country or to America had assumed the irresistible force of mass movements. In general, internal migration showed the movement of agricultural population from inland south and central Norway to the far north, the coasts, and the towns. Clearing farmland north of the Arctic Circle meant adjusting to a shorter growing season and months without sunshine, but was less expensive than emigration and offered a chance of reestablishing traditional landowning rural culture within national boundaries. As a result, Arctic Norway experienced the nation's highest rate of population increase between 1845 and 1900.[14]

The attraction of migrating from inland to coastal areas lay chiefly in opportunities to combine farming with other occupations. For many, earlier seasonal migration had revealed the advantages of the coastal districts' mixed economies, which allowed families to shift from farming to fishing, shipbuilding, or shipping and thus both extend the work year and alleviate the economic disaster of a poor harvest.[15] Between 1845 and 1875, according to the Norwegian Bureau of Statistics, the annual population increase in coastal rural districts was four times that of the inland countryside. In the same thirty-year period districts relying primarily on agriculture showed an annual growth of 0.48 percent, while fishing and shipping districts expanded at almost three times that rate.[16]

Fishing in the North Sea, the expansion of shipping along the coasts, and the Arctic North functioned as "alternate Americas" for Norwegians who rejected, or put off,the more radical solutions of emigration or accommodation to urban life. Although growth centers shifted, the rural population's overall rate of increase remained around one percent per year until 1865. During the next ten years, however, it plummeted to 0.25 percent. For the rest of the century the rural population explosion was defused by mass emigration to America and internal migration to the cities.[17]

## Cultural Contrasts and Delayed Migration to the City

Many people from Norway's inland regions reached the decision to accept city life only after having exhausted the opportunities for rural migration. They first left mountainous inland areas for lower-lying inland plains, then moved on to the rural coasts, and thus arrived in cities as third-time migrants who were accustomed to adjusting their occupations and living arrangements—or at least as members of families who had made these accommodations over two generations. People who migrated directly to the city usually came from the cities' partially urbanized hinterlands. Their proximity to the city undoubtedly resulted in an increased awareness of urban opportunities and eased the difficulties of adjustment.[18] The unusually wide chasm between urban and rural Norwegian culture in the nineteenth century offers at least a partial explanation for the stages of internal migration that for many preceded arrival in the city.

With good reason, many farmers viewed the cities' leading classes as representatives of foreign influence. From the late Middle Ages to the early nineteenth century, foreign merchants—mainly Germans from the Hanseatic states, Danes, and Swedes—immigrated to Norway's cities and took control of the country's international commerce. As late as 1700, around 40 percent of the urban bourgeoisie were foreign-born. A century later the descendants of these commercial immigrants still controlled a large part of Norway's economic life. Although the class expanded from the bottom to include the newly prosperous—and thus became mainly Norwegian-born—it continued to adopt the views and the foreign, or at least international, culture of the educated administrative class.[19]

Families of Danish or mixed Dano-Norwegian ancestry dominated this class. Establishing their political expertise during four centuries of Danish rule, they continued to supply the majority of Norway's politicians and civil servants after 1814, when the country won limited self-government and its own constitution after being ceded to the king of Sweden. The *sine qua non* for belonging to this class was higher education, a university degree. The official class therefore also included lawyers, doctors, military officers, teachers at institutions of higher learning, and state-church clergymen, who belonged to the class not only by reason of their education but by virtue of their responsibilities as civil servants. Since the first Norwegian university did not open its doors until 1811, most men holding positions of authority in the first half of the nineteenth century had been educated in Copenhagen. In this way, even those of purely Norwegian ancestry had acquired the language, manners, dress, and loyalties of urban Danish culture common to their class.[20]

The disproportionate concentration of the official class in the cities is obvious when one considers that by mid-century only thirteen percent of the total population, but about half of the upper class, was urban.[21] Scattered over the countryside as local administrators and parish priests, the other half lived in isolation, maintaining their status as representatives of a national class rather than adapting to local customs. Their vital cultural contacts came through correspondence, newspapers and literature, and occasional visits to exclusive urban clubs. Long before migrating to the city, the common farming population had been made to feel the gulf separating them from their betters.[22]

Although their interests did not always coincide, the commercial and the educated elites understandably seemed a single class to ordinary rural people excluded from their ranks. The merchant class looked upon the officials as their natural representatives in public life. The educated class, which grew slowly and relied on public funds for income, was dependent on the bourgeoisie for both economic support and the replenishment of its numbers. Provided with the money for higher education, merchants' sons constituted an important part of the recruiting base for administrative positions. For example, between 1820 and 1860 over a third of those trained to be clergymen came from the bourgeoisie. Associating with each other officially and socially, the two elites assisted each other economically and intermarried so frequently that class and family ties became almost identical. Their common culture set the tone of urban life.[23]

The result was a striking dividing line between city and country. According to the Norwegian clergyman and pioneer sociologist Eilert Sundt, an acute contemporary observer who nonetheless could not escape the value judgments of his class, at mid-century a short walk beyond Bergen's city gate was equivalent to leaving civilization many miles behind. A generation earlier, in his view, the contrast had been as great around Oslo. If country people came to the capital, their appearance "exposed them to the ridicule of small boys, and they felt unwell until they got home again." Sundt felt that migration from Oslo's hinterland had changed all this by mid-century, because by then rural visitors met so many relatives and country people in town that they no longer felt isolated in the city.[24]

Partially because of the contrasts in Norwegian social geography, large cities developed relatively late. Most nineteenth-century cities and built-up areas included in the Norwegian census were extremely small. In 1875, for example, fifty-three "urban" areas contained fewer than 500 people and only nine cities had more than ten thousand inhabitants.

The relative scale of Norwegian cities is clearer if one remembers that Oslo, the country's largest and most steadily expanding city, had 100,000 inhabitants in 1875 and 250,000 in 1900. Bergen, the next largest city at the turn of the century, was only one third as big as the capital.[25]

Relative to their former number and size, however, urban areas experienced an explosive growth during the century. Oslo's population trebled between 1845 and 1875 and then, as the figures above show, grew by 250 percent in the last quarter of the century. Stavanger, expanding even more rapidly than Oslo in the first half of the century, quintupled its population by 1855.[26] Even more startling by Norwegian standards, new cities and towns sprouted up. Official statistics categorized them according to the branch of commerce that was most important for their local economies. Lumbering cities, concentrated on the southeast coast, thrived by exporting timber floated down from the eastern valleys. Farther west, around the country's southern tip, shipping centers sprang up from sleepy seaside villages. All along the North Sea coast, but especially in Rogaland—the so-called "herring county"—cities arose on profits from the export of fish. Although they were fewer and grew less rapidly, administrative market centers developed inland. In 1885 state statisticians mentioned two "factory cities," Moss and Skien, which continued to expand when most other urban areas began to decline, but did not consider such cities significant enough to warrant a separate urban category.[27]

The cities' growth came largely from in-migration. The urban death rate was twice that of the countryside at mid-century, and only when this difference evened out in the 1880s did natural increase contribute significantly to the urban population. Economic opportunity determined the importance of in-migration for individual cities, and therefore Norwegian historians have customarily distinguished between "expanding" and "stagnating" urban areas. A booming local economy attracted many new inhabitants from the countryside or other cities. Between 1850 and the middle 1880s, for example, the average portion of migrants in the cities was 50 percent. In expanding southern shipping cities such as Arendal and Grimstad, however, they constituted a majority of inhabitants, while in stagnating Bergen and Kristiansand the native-born made up over two-thirds of the population.[28]

The majority of those who settled in cities joined the swelling ranks of the working population. As late as 1875 women outnumbered men in urban areas because the cities' largest occupational group, domestic servants, consisted mostly of women from the countryside. This female population was unstable. Going into service was a normal stage in the life cycle of farmers' daughters, who, if they lived near a city, served there a few years, experiencing a more sophisticated world and accumulating a dowry before they married. Young men who came to the city more often stayed there and became part of the largest male job category, day laborers. As the century progressed, rural antagonism to urban culture lessened, and people arrived directly from areas far inland. Most of these were men who entered the pool of laborers immediately.[29]

In fact, day laborers and their families made up the bulk of the urban population born outside these areas. To escape constant economic insecurity and the likelihood of unemployed winters, many day laborers grasped opportunities to learn trades. The resourceful and ambitious tried their luck at small businesses. These two groups were the backbone of a nascent urban middle class that steadily grew in importance during the last two-thirds of the century.[30] The broad base of the occupational pyramid, of course, assumed a different character according to the chief economic activity of each city. If sawmill workers assumed the foreground in pictures of the typical working man in the southeast, ship's carpenters, seamen, and fishermen represented their class farther south and west.[31]

Generally, the cities showed a rising growth curve until the last third of the century, when international competition and technological change posed a progressively more serious threat to the nation's economy. Norway was particularly vulnerable to international economic developments because of its small domestic market, dependence on the export of fish and lumber, and shipping based on carrying other nations' products. As market saturation and cheaper timber from Canada and the Baltic countries undermined lumber exports in the mid-1870s, employment opportunities at sawmills flattened out until the 1890s when Norway made the changeover to paper and cellulose production. The expensive transition from small wooden sailing ships to large metal steam freighters plunged the nation's shipping into a depression that produced bank failures and massive unemployment in southern shipping cities in the mid-1880s and lasted until Norway became a major neutral carrier during World War I. Only by shifting export products, markets, and technologies throughout the period did the export fisheries sustain rising job opportunities. Fishermen suffered periods of dislocation and underemployment during these rapid changes, but because most were farmers who fished seasonally, they avoided extreme hardship.[32]

Both general surveys of Norwegian history and more detailed studies of single districts report a reliable rule of thumb that accounts for important variations in the timing and intensity of Norwegian migration: A city and its hinterland experienced low emigration as long the urban economy was expansive. Movement to the city was often the last choice of internal migrants, but for many it was also just the final stage before international migration. Cities generally grew from in-migration until the 1870s. From then on the intensity of emigration from urban areas not only outpaced that from the countryside, but continued to rise while rural emigration declined. The turning point varied in time according to a city's primary economic base but, as a rule, declining employment opportunities first led to slackening in-migration and then to emigration. Urban areas dependent on a single industry, such as the southern shipping cities, were hardest hit by "America fever." As early as the 1870s, however, even cities with varied economic activity, such as Oslo, conformed to the typical pattern of demographic change. When the cities suffered industrial downturns, many urbanized migrants from the countryside swelled the flood of emigrants leaving for America.[33]

**Destination Brooklyn, New York, and the First Phase of Emigration**

Only about ten percent of Norwegian emigration to the United States before World War I occurred during the introductory "pioneer" phase, which lasted from 1825 to 1865. Whatever their destinations within America, these pioneers assumed an importance out of proportion with their numbers because their trailblazing precedents established the patterns on which later settlement developed.

The overwhelming majority of early Norwegian emigrants came from isolated inland mountain, valley, and fjord districts. They constituted a dissenting minority within rural folk cultures because they decided that the chances of preserving traditional ways of life were greater in the American Midwest than in Norway's urban areas or even in its other rural districts. Historians have rightly cited a higher frequency of emigration among internal migrants to show that geographic mobility made the decision to emigrate easier. These figures may also suggest that internal migration did not always satisfy the needs of people who wanted to reproduce their traditional culture in a new location. Typically, the emigrants were established farm couples who traveled together with their children after having sold their land, homes, and household goods. Not infrequently, organized groups of relatives and neighbors set out for a rural colony site in America after receiving detailed advice from a leader who had emigrated earlier. Having based their agricultural economy primarily on self-sufficiency rather than raising crops for market, most decided to pull up stakes for the New World after bad harvest years, when letters and visits from earlier emigrants seemed to offer a practical solution to pressing local problems. Their transplanted agricultural communities laid the foundations for more broadly based rural emigration later in the century. In the 1850s and early 1860s, these Norwegians did not pass through New York City on their way to the Midwest, but traveled instead from Liverpool to Quebec on Norwegian ships whose participation in the lumber trade was made possible by the repeal of the British Navigation Acts in 1849.[34]

Judging from the meager source materials available, Norwegian emigration to Brooklyn and New York was most unlike the country's emigration in general during the early period. At a time when most emigrants came from inland rural areas, almost all the Brooklyn pioneers documented in colony histories and newspapers departed from southern and eastern coastal cities, such as Drammen, Kragerø, Arendal, Farsund, and Stavanger. These people's exact geographical origins are known because they later became prominent members of the community. Their biographies, however, often reveal that on arrival their occupations were the common ones among Norwegians who settled in the city. The overwhelming majority came as seamen, captains, or ship's carpenters and, unlike the few remembered in local histories, continued in the same line of work.[35]

Since Norway's shipping was located primarily around its southern tip and eastern coast, these people departed from districts which lost few inhabitants through emigration until the 1880s. As Helge Ove Tveiten has documented, between 1843 and 1860 there was a wave of emigration from the southern county of East Agder, for example, but less than a third of those who left came from coastal areas, whether these were rural or urban. Instead, although coastal areas were already more densely populated than inland districts, they continued to attract migrants. Most of those voyaging to America were typical of the agricultural family emigration described above. Farmers and agricultural workers made up 57 percent of the emigrants from East Agder between 1843 and 1860. The largest occupational groups that emigrated to Brooklyn or New York, seamen and ship's carpenters, accounted, respectively, for only 10 and 13 percent of the adult emigrants in Tveiten's study.[36]

The predominant process behind the settlement of Norwegians in Brooklyn and New York was anomalous during this period. It is probable that many emigrants who settled in the cities at this time did not appear to have emigrated at all, at least in the usual sense. As we shall see in succeeding chapters, many were not recorded in the emigration records kept in Norwegian ports or in the passenger lists of immigrant vessels arriving in America because they deserted in the port of New York and then drifted into more or less permanent residence. Mostly members of the maritime working class, they came from cities or coastal areas when these places experienced high rates of in-migration and little emigration. Few among them chose to emigrate before leaving Norway; only later in the century did service in the merchant marine become an important form of concealed emigration. And usually they came as individuals, rather than in families or organized parties, and had no preconceived plan of preserving an old-world sense of cultural community.[37] Their distinctive pattern of emigration proved as fundamental for the kind of community that grew up in Brooklyn as the factors that conditioned the development of the very different Norwegian farming communities in the Midwest.

As Norwegian emigration rose to its nineteenth-century peak, it showed several trends that differentiated it from the earlier, introductory phase. First, the scale of the movement reached unprecedented proportions. While the country had lost roughly 78,000 people to emigration during the forty-year "pioneer" phase, about 112,000 boarded ships for America during the first eight-year wave—1866–1873—of mass emigration. A host of factors—among them letters from relatives containing prepaid tickets, recruiting by emigration agents, improvements in do-

**The First Two Waves of Mass Emigration: 1866–1873 and 1880–1893**

mestic and international transportation, the end of the American Civil War, cheap land and industrial expansion in America—made emigration a less daunting idea for ever wider sections of Norwegian society. By the early 1880s, when more departed in four years, 1880–1883, than in the first phase's four decades, the movement seemed to surge forward under its own power.[38]

A number of other tendencies in emigration after 1865 become clearer if one contrasts the characteristics of the people in the two large waves of emigrants. Family groups still dominated in the first wave, but by the 1890s most of the emigrants were unmarried, and married men often traveled alone, sending for their families later. In general, fewer children and adults over twenty-five left in the second wave, while the number of unattached young adults between 15 and 25 increased. Despite the inaccuracy of government statistics on emigrants' occupations for both the 1860s and the 1880s, this increasing youthfulness inevitably meant more individuals came from lower occupational levels. Footloose and less established, these young people had little capital for starting a new life abroad. In the 1880s most emigrants still came from inland rural areas, but fewer were farm owners. The agricultural population that was poor or threatened with poverty—cotters and their grown children, day laborers, and farmers' sons and daughters—swelled the emigrant stream to a greater degree in the 1880s and later. When they got to America, they would sell their labor and, unlike the earlier emigrants, most would spend years as urban workers or farm laborers before they could buy land.[39]

The mass exodus starting in the 1880s also revealed the growing importance of the international economy as a decisive factor behind the decision to emigrate. Because Norwegian agriculture had become more market-oriented in the 1870s, the bulk of the agrarian population departing in the next decade reacted not to poor harvests but to the general depression that set in after 1877 and affected rural districts as much as areas directly involved in international commerce. Whereas emigration had affected primarily the southwestern interior in the earliest period and then both that region and the southeastern inland districts in the 1860s, almost no region escaped a population loss during the 1880s, because the nation as a whole had become dependent on the global economy. The decisive factor in the timing of rural emigration was now the same as that which caused urban emigration to rise from only four percent in the mid-1850s to 34 percent in the mid-1880s: a falling international demand for Norway's products and services. As a result, the emigrant flood of the 1880s included people from all occupations and classes, not only large groups from agricultural areas but growing numbers of fishermen, seamen, industrial workers, craftsmen, and even professionals and members of the upper classes.[40]

Important regional differences in the intensity of emigration still existed, but these variations were less pronounced than earlier. The most significant deviations, the rising intensity of urban and coastal emigration, resulted from the crisis in Norwegian shipping brought on by the transition to steam-driven vessels. From 1885 onward, emigrants from shipping areas were primarily responsible for maintaining the high rate of urban emigration. Moreover, as the pioneer immigration historian Ingrid Semmingsen noted, the intense emigration from both rural and urban shipping areas signaled the beginning of a new epoch in Norwegian emigration history, a period lasting to World War I, when the crisis in shipping—specially in the Agder counties—played an essential role in Norwegian emigration.[41]

The slow growth of the New York area colonies through the 1860s suggests that the gradual accretion of Norwegians there continued chiefly through the indirect processes of maritime settlement that were common before the Civil War. By 1855 Brooklyn and Manhattan contained no more than around 400 Norwegians. Only near the end of the 1866–1873 wave of emigration did the settlements begin to grow rapidly. Some of the urban settlers may have arrived on Norwegian emigrant ships, which after 1870 regularly docked in New York instead of Quebec. Such bona fide immigrants to the city were still rare, however. According to observers in the colonies, the vast majority stayed only long enough to arrange transportation to the Midwest.[42]

Yet, in the 1870s Brooklyn's Norwegian population nearly tripled and Manhattan's more than doubled. The increasing numbers of Norwegian merchant ships frequenting the harbor and the soaring desertions from these ships seem to offer the best explanation for the swelling size of the settlements. New York was the logical home port for these men, since their chances of steady employment on American or other nations' ships were best in the nation's busiest port. Seeking contacts with countrymen, they gravitated to the colonies, whose residents operated saloons and boardinghouses suited to sailors' needs. Some sent for their families in Norway or found wives in the city and thus became more committed to a settled life. Such processes were probably the primary means by which the cities' Norwegian population grew during the 1870s.

During the 1880s the Brooklyn colony quintupled in size. Then between 1890 and 1910 it more than tripled its population, reaching a total of over 15,000. From 1880 onward it seems likely that passengers on emigrant ships supplemented the irregular in-migration of seamen to a considerable degree. In part, the newcomers were family members joining men who had settled during the 1870s, but most—especially after 1885—came because of the collapse of shipping and shipbuilding along Norway's southern coast. Although most people from this coastal area arriving in New York had been directly employed in these depressed industries, others left because of the deepening economic decline started by severe cutbacks at the region's largest shipping firms. As

**1880–1914: Brooklyn Becomes a Typical Goal for Norwegians**

Norwegian immigrants in New York City and vicinity came mostly from
Norway's southern shipping towns or the surrounding rural coastal districts.

- A view of Arendal harbor, circa 1905. The Norwegian-American Historical
Association.
- A residential street in coastal Farsund. The Norwegian-American Historical
Association.

all classes repeatedly pared their family budgets, the job market for craftsmen, laborers, store clerks, domestic servants, and others in the bottom half of the occupational scale shrank again and again. Young, single, underemployed or jobless, these people gradually became typical of the emigrant population during the next thirty years. If a single-minded concentration on shipping and seafaring had proved catastrophic for the area's economy by the mid-1880s, it had also accustomed the local population to the presence of foreigners in the region's harbors and familiarized seamen, the region's largest occupational group, with the employment opportunities in the world's great ports. When the crisis came, emigration held fewer terrors for them than it did for many others who departed from Europe.[43]

In Norway the period from the 1880s to the First World War was a difficult time for such people all over the country because of a series of economic downturns and increasing competition from cheap mass-produced foreign goods. Carpenters and other skilled workers migrated to cities because of building booms in the 1870s and 1890s but emigrated in the following decades when abrupt economic contractions left many of them unemployed. Whether they worked in the countryside or in cities, a whole series of craftspeople—shoemakers, tailors, dressmakers, milliners, blacksmiths, to name a few—discovered that Norwegians chose less expensive imported factory products, especially when their incomes were reduced. Even the entrepreneurs who attempted to industrialize these crafts found foreign competition prohibitive and, in general, the growth of industry in Norway slowed in the 1880s. Though the rate of industrialization increased sharply after 1900, even in 1914 Norway could not provide industrial jobs anywhere sufficient to the need for such employment. Often denied even the alternative of becoming factory workers, many craftspeople chose to emigrate. Newly educated engineers and technicians from polytechnical colleges established late in the century also began to emigrate when they found few firms that could pay them well for their expertise. In the United States, rapidly expanding cities offered rich opportunities for employment for all these groups. Brooklyn and New York were prominent among these cities, and thus attracted not only large numbers of people from the southern coastal areas but also smaller groups from other parts of Norway.[44]

According to colony sources, people from Agder and the west coast's southernmost county, Rogaland, have always comprised the dominant regional grouping among Brooklyn Norwegians, mostly because so many mariners settled in the community. By the 1880s the majority had christened one of its most-used intersections and several cafes and saloons with names taken from this region. America letters near the century's end commented on the few colony residents from other parts of the country. A Norwegian observing the local 17th of May Constitu-

**Emigration
from Three
Norwegian
Ports to New
York in 1904**

tion Day celebration in 1908 heard dialects from the whole range of the homeland's coastal cities and rural districts, but found the "buzz" of West Agder pronunciation so overwhelming that he was "tempted to believe that the whole county has emigrated." By the 1920s colony newspapers reported both larger and more numerous associations for people from Rogaland and the Agder counties than for any other region of the country. In 1928 *Nordisk Tidende* surveyed the regional origins of its subscribers and, finding that 45 percent came from coastal cities in these counties, confirmed its long-standing policy of serving as their special newspaper. A canvass of all *Nordisk Tidende*'s obituaries in 1926 and 1934 which gave an indication of the deceased's regional ties showed that 55 percent had connections to Rogaland or East or West Agder. Without exception, the local residents interviewed for this study, who arrived between 1904 and 1940, asserted that emigrants from southern coastal areas formed the largest component in the community's population.[45]

The Brooklyn colony's mainly southern origin, which contributed greatly to many aspects of its development, is evident from the information in police protocols from three of Norway's largest emigrant departure points, Kristiansand, Bergen, and Trondheim, during 1904, when all three cities' records include exact notations of emigrants' destinations, occupations, and a range of personal information about them.[46]

In 1904, Norway was just one year past the peak of a huge wave of emigration that had begun in 1900 and would continue through 1914. While most other northwest European countries experienced ebbing emigration during those years, Norway lost 241,000 people to America, only 15,000 fewer than it had in the 1880s and early 1890s. More than 22,000 Norwegians left for foreign lands during 1904, over nine-tenths of them voyaging to the United States and most of the rest to Canada. Somewhat under half (43 percent) of the total emigrant stream departed from Kristiansand, Bergen, and Trondheim during the year, and 3,196 or 14 percent of these reported their specific destination as New York or Brooklyn. Few years in the entire history of Norwegian emigration could match 1904's lancing of the country's life blood, and only three years surpassed it.[47]

The proportion of those going to New York-Brooklyn from each of the three ports varies widely and indicates the attraction of the metropolitan area for southerners in particular and for Norwegians from coastal areas in general. High emigration from Agder and coastal areas was typical for Norwegian migration during the year,[48] but the metropolitan area did not exert an equal appeal in all regions of the country. Fully two-thirds of the emigrants leaving from Kristiansand were on their way to the New York City colonies. Over nine-tenths of these New York-bound emigrants gave the Agder counties as their last residence in Norway, and 79 percent of them came from the coast. Although the research for this study did not include an analysis of Oslo's emigrant protocols, data from Peter Rinnan and Rolf Østrem's study of the capital's emigrants suggests that, after people from the southern coastal counties, people from Oslo were most attracted to the metropolitan area. A third of the capital's emigrants departed for New York City in 1907. Only 18 percent of the people departing from Bergen three years earlier gave New York or Brooklyn as their destination. Over half of these emigrants came from the city itself or coastal areas in its immediate hinterland, Hordaland county. Of those leaving from Trondheim, only 9 percent, most of whom came from fjord and coastal areas in middle and northern Norway, journeyed to New York–Brooklyn. The predominance of southerners and coastal Norwegians among people emigrating to New York–Brooklyn seems clear.[49]

Crisis conditions in Norway's economy and glowing reports of good times in America combined in classic fashion to motivate a mass exodus in 1904. In the second half of the 1890s Norway's economy expanded rapidly, creating jobs over the whole country but especially in cities with a diversified economic base, such as Oslo and Bergen. Many in the large generation of young people that matured in the nineties migrated to such booming cities and filled the decade's growing need for labor. Then in 1899 the crash came. The numbers of young people entering the job market remained high during the next decade, but the sluggish economy provided few new employment opportunities, and those created by the expansion in the nineties were still occupied by people in the prime of their working lives.[50]

When profits from international freight rates fell sharply around 1900, maritime countries like Norway quickly experienced an economic contraction. Even shipowners in Bergen and Oslo who had successfully made the transition to steam-powered vessels reacted by cutting their capital investments and reducing their labor costs. As a result, maritime craftsmen, officers, and crews comprised the largest male occupational group among Norway's emigrants in 1904. Both the primacy of shipping on the south coast and New York's special pulling power for southerners is obvious in the emigration statistics for the year. While maritime workers made up about 17 percent of the nation's male emigrants, they comprised more than 48 percent of the men leaving Kristiansand for New York City.

Construction workers abruptly felt the changed economic situation when credit tightened and building activity dropped off rapidly. Among the most dependent on ordinary consumers' purchasing ability, craftsmen soon felt the effects of the downturn in building and shipping. Craftsmen-entrepreneurs laid off help, and large numbers of skilled workers found themselves unemployed as the public bought less clothing, acquired fewer household goods, and made do with cheaper food. Both rural and urban craftsmen, moreover, were already facing hard times because of the pressure of imported goods and the smaller number of workers needed for factory production. Of the male emigrants who left Kristiansand for New York, only maritime and farm workers comprised larger groups than skilled and semi-skilled workers. Interestingly, less than one percent of these were laborers, while over 15 percent of the nation's emigrants were in this category. On the other hand, significantly more construction workers departed from the southern city, probably because some maritime craftsmen reported their line of work in general terms, telling the police they were carpenters, for example, instead of saying ship's carpenters.[51]

Agricultural laborers experienced a situation similar to craftsmen's as mechanization progressed in Norwegian farming, especially in the flat lands of Trøndelag county and the southeastern valleys. When increasing numbers of these hired hands became redundant around 1900, their chances of finding other work were small indeed. Considering the inappropriateness of mechanized agriculture for the predominantly small, rock-strewn farms along the southern coast, it is surprising that farm laborers made up a slightly larger part of the emigrants leaving Kristiansand than from all the rest of Norway. One plausible answer is that many farmers in the region were also sailors. As Karen Løvland and other historians have noted, rural families from this area could seldom make a living from farming alone. At an early age most men went to sea for years at a time and left their wives to run the farm with the help of the younger children.[52]

As one might expect from the range of occupations affected by the depression, men made up about six-tenths of those emigrating in 1904, both for the nation as a whole and also among people departing for New York City. The women hoping for a new start in America felt equally pressing economic necessity. Earlier, farmers' daughters had usually reduced the mouths to feed among their families by going into domestic service in nearby cities, but now they found that few city households could afford to pay for their services. During the current depression these young women found few chances of turning to clerical or factory work. In the sample year many emigrated instead, making domestic servants the largest occupational category among departing women. The subsistence economy of most of the small family farms, combined with failing supplementary income from men's earnings at sea, may suggest why in 1904 domestics comprised over 48 percent, two and a half times the national rate, of the female emigrants leaving Kristiansand. The largest group of single women with no occupation among emigrants departing from the city that year, moreover, were farmers' daughters, who in better times would probably have become domestics. It seems likely that both groups of young women earned wages as household help in Brooklyn, since over two-thirds of Norwegian working women there in 1892 were employed in this way, and most other Norwegian working women then—and at the next state census—were cooks, housekeepers, or laundresses. For them, emigration was not much different from their earlier internal migration. They still served families from a higher socioeconomic class in an urban setting but, according to former domestics interviewed in Brooklyn, got higher wages, more respect for their work, and the adventure of living abroad.[53]

In 1904 about 64 percent of Norwegian emigrants were from rural areas, and the urban third of the emigrants included considerable numbers of people who had been born in the countryside. The largest age group among both men and women, between fifteen and twenty-nine, represented the young who found little chance of entering an employment market that had shrunk in both cities and country districts. The emigrants traveling to New York-Brooklyn followed the national trends in somewhat exaggerated form. They were by about five percent both more urban and more concentrated in the 15 to 29 age group. The rural young discovered the hard way that migration to Norway's coastal cities, especially those in the shipping-oriented South, no longer offered a solution.

In 1904 the high rate of emigration from the nation's coastal areas, both urban and rural, reflected the lack of sufficient economic opportunities in two of Norway's traditional "internal Americas." Only mining in the far northern counties and fishing now offered domestic lands of promise, and these gave work to just two occupational groups. Met with underemployment or joblessness which forced them to go on relief or return to the inland countryside, thousands of young people escaped need by booking passage for the real America overseas, which still seemed to crave their energies. By 1904, many of those departing from the southern ports and from Oslo were headed for the New York colonies.

The emigrant protocol from Bergen conclusively documents the irregular drifting-in of mariners discussed earlier. Its comments column in 1904 describes three-quarters of those leaving for the New York colonies—all but seven of them seamen—either generally as employed maritime workers or as sent to specific Norwegian ships in United States waters. Tore L. Nilsen confirms that these men were probably not in the usual sense emigrants at all but maritime workers whose presence in New York was conditional on their term of employment with Norwegian shipping companies. While they did not officially announce their intention to emigrate, working in New York harbor gave them the chance to jump ship or to settle if their job kept them in or near the city over a period of years. These men represent one more indication of Norwegian shipping's importance for the colonies in New York and Brooklyn even in the early twentieth century when large numbers of men and women were arriving through the normal processes of emigration.[54]

Few family groups stood waving farewell on the decks of emigrant ships leaving Norway's ports at the turn of the century. In a group so pronouncedly young that is not surprising. Only one-fifth of all emigrants in 1904 were married. The percentage of married people sailing

•

Young men and women emigrants in 1906 toast each other on the beginning of bold adventure on the deck of a ship that has just left Oslo harbor. Norwegian Emigrant Museum.

•

The famous Norwegian photographer Anders Wilse titled this picture "the beginning of the emigration journey." Norwegian Emigrant Museum.

•

The *Thingvalla,* built in 1874 in Copenhagen for the Thingvalla Line that docked in Brooklyn at the turn of the century, brought many Norwegian immigrants to the city's "Little Norway." Vea, Schreiner, and Seland, *Den norske amerikalinje, 1910–1960.*

for New York was about the same, but a closer examination of the protocols revealed that fewer than one in fourteen of these left with relatives, even when that was defined to include grandparents, siblings, or in-laws. Most married men traveled alone, and would likely send for their families once they were established in the city. The largest category among family groups was unaccompanied mothers and children with prepaid tickets. After the standard data about these mothers, the protocol often includes the comment, "husband in America." Clearly, the practice of bringing one's family to New York after a period of adjustment was not new. Single women could not have lacked for male attention during the voyage, since on average six-tenths of the passengers were men. For most there was the companionship of others sharing a similar age and situation. And even if some felt lonely and homesick, there were relatives at home they could write to and usually the consolation of knowing that family members or friends would meet them and assist their adjustment after the ship docked in New York.[55]

When asked about their own or their parents' departures at the turn of the century, old-timers in the Brooklyn colony tell cherished family stories about wives, sometimes with several children, managing the trip without their husbands' help—but able to leave because their men had sent them prepaid tickets. Time and again, women claim that they, or their mothers, were used to managing alone because in Agder and Rogaland husbands were usually at sea and sons followed suit as soon as they were confirmed. Even people who had been young and single when they left tell of seafaring friends and relatives meeting them at Ellis Island.[56]

America letters, diaries, and fiction written by Norwegian immigrants in Brooklyn at the turn of the century confirm the evidence in the protocols and interviews through their near constant repetition of the same regional and maritime origins in Norway. These various narrative sources present a unanimous picture of a special kind of "chain" migration. Brooklyn became the destination of choice for these emigrants because their seafaring friends or relatives had been in the Port of New York once or many times. On coming home, they had told of its opportunities for work—and of Norwegian mariners who had successfully made the transition from transient or sojourning seamen to settled workers on shore.[57]

The interviews, moreover, commonly reveal pre-emigration family histories that conform to the demographic patterns previously noted here. In most cases, the immigrants' parents or grandparents were born on farms along Norway's coasts, where the family combined subsistence farming with fishing and seafaring. When asked what line of work parents and grandparents followed, old-timers often reveal that their forebears were farmers or farm workers in inland districts before moving to coastal areas. Few recall more than one generation of experience in port towns or cities. Those who do explain that female relatives in previous generations moved to town when they became housemaids or note a change in family fortunes when men took up skilled crafts in urban areas.[58]

Some interviews and one collection of diaries and letters reveal resentment toward upper-class ministers in port cities and irritation at finding representatives of that class in Red Hook. On the other hand, even the immigrants that arrived directly from coastal farms resist admitting that adjusting to an American city was difficult. More than stubborn pride born of defending a decision to emigrate lies behind these assertions that conditions in Brooklyn did not seem completely foreign. As the old-timers repeatedly remark, even if they did not live in Norwegian cities before they left, their seafaring brothers and fathers frequented Norway's seaports. More important, *all* the colony veterans, even those with unusual regional origins, say they had known "all about" Brooklyn for years because "nearly everyone at home knew sailors who'd been there."[59]

# 3

# Getting There and Coming Ashore:

## Maritime Transience, Desertion, and Settlement in Manhattan

The first Norwegian immigrants came to the New York area with the Dutch in the seventeenth century. Their nineteenth-century descendants probably had no significant contacts with new waves of Norwegian immigrants.[1] Nevertheless, colonial immigration invites comment, since it offers a paradigm for the later settlements in Manhattan and Brooklyn. The earliest settlers migrated first to Holland. By the early 1600s the expansion of European commerce resulted in trade wars, an acute shortage of seamen and maritime craftsmen, and a European maritime labor market. Merchants on the coasts of Germany and Holland, for example, established economic ties in the 1500s with many harbor centers in southern Norway, which first exported raw materials and then provided manpower for the European nations' navies and commercial fleets. In the 1600s, faced with harsh naval discipline and mortal danger because of their nation's union with Denmark, growing numbers of seamen from southern Norway thus knew of an alternative career. Legally or through desertion, they left the Danish navy and sought the steady work, good pay, and largely peaceful opportunities for advancement on Dutch merchant vessels. In time, many of these men

41

New Amsterdam's *Stadt Huys* and surrounding buildings in lower Manhattan, drawn by a traveler in 1679 after the English had conquered the colony and re-named it New York. Very likely Norwegian sailors who emigrated to the Nether-lands to avoid naval warfare in the Baltic were among the early harbor workers in New Amsterdam. Brooklyn Historical Society.

settled in Holland, established families, and moved into trades in harbors or on land.[2]

When they joined the Dutch colonization of the Hudson River valley, these migrants took part in the European occupation of the Americas, sharing in the golden promises of a New World that stirred the European imagination and devastated the continents' native cultures. Although most of the first contingents settled farther northwest, where the Rensselaerwyck colony formed the knife edge of contact with Indian society, by the late 1600s New Amsterdam had accumulated a small population of Norwegian seamen and captains, fishermen, and shipwrights. As they had in Holland, some of these mariners left the sea to become artisans and harbor workers. As Dutch settlement spread, others staked out farms in modern-day Brooklyn and New Jersey. A few eventually assumed membership in New York's eighteenth-century elite, through economic advancement and intermarriage with leading Dutch, and later English, families. When Norwegian immigration resumed with the arrival of the immigrant ship *Restauration* in 1825, a few area place names, such as Norman Avenue and Bergen Street, remained as a legacy of that distant past. Only a small, little-documented trickle of maritime migration connected the two periods of settlement, as a few Norwegian seamen continued to find work on British, or smugglers', vessels in the seventeenth and eighteenth centuries, then came ashore, and settled down.[3]

Although chronologically separated from Norwegian settlement among the Dutch, nineteenth-century Norwegian immigration in New York and Brooklyn repeated several of its paradigmatic features. Like the Rensselaerwyck settlers, most passengers on the *Restauration* and later ships wanted land and so merely passed through on their way to found farming communities farther west. The cities' Norwegian settlements once again grew slowly as latter-day captains and crews increasingly took part in an international labor market and repeated the original pattern, progressing from casual transience to settled residence based on the local economy's opportunities and the establishment of family life. The largest regional groupings in the New York area's Norwegian settlements again came from southern coastal areas, especially the Agder counties, as these regions' many harbors joined in the later, global phase of European expansion that tied the fortunes of local families to fluctuations in a more integrated international economy.[4]

In short, opportunities in international shipping continued to be the main "pull" factor. One crucial difference in the nineteenth century was the increasing strength of the New York area's magnetic attraction for seamen employed in international commerce. As American shipping experienced a golden age between 1820 and 1860, New York captured an ever-increasing part of the United States' coastal and transatlantic trade to become the nation's dominant seaport. The overcrowding of Manhattan's East River dock area spurred development of docking and repair facilities on the Brooklyn coastline, where construction of the huge Atlantic and Erie ship basins reached completion before the Civil War.[5]

The other crucial difference resulted from the Norwegian economy's growing dependence on profits from the international carrying trade. Between 1850 and 1880 Norway rose from eighth to third place among the world's shipping nations. The combination of New York's growing commercial power and the home country's economic development made ever larger numbers of the Norwegian merchant marine familiar with the port's need for skilled manpower. When the bottom fell out of Norway's shipping industry in the late 1870s owing to the country's difficulties in making the changeover to steam-powered vessels, the southern coastal area was least prepared to adjust to new technology. Consequently, the southern provinces experienced severe economic depression in the 1880s and the country's highest emigration rates in the 1890s. Unemployed seamen, ship's carpenters, and dock workers comprised the largest occupational groups among those who departed for America. If they chose the metropolitan area, it soon appeared that their specific destination was more often Brooklyn than Manhattan.[6]

**Evidence of How They got There and Made Themselves at Home**

In 1837 Johannes Nordboe wrote home, describing the easiest way to make contact with New York's Norwegians, which was to go to the waterfront and shout, "Swedish Norwegian man." Soon a sailor would appear and direct the immigrant to colony artisans and boardinghouses. After the Napoleonic wars, Norwegian sailors began arriving in the city on American packet ships and, as early as 1830, the Norwegian government recorded their desertions in the harbor. Scandinavian mariners constituted a majority among the crews on American clipper ships even before 1850. Customshouse records reveal that as early as 1842 a few had advanced to the rank of ship's officers in the East Coast trade. As Norway's shipping expanded toward mid-century, its own merchant vessels visited New York with increasing frequency. Fewer than a half-dozen Norwegian ships, including the *Restauration,* arrived between 1825 and 1837, but after that time, the number multiplied rapidly. Between 1846 and 1850, 212 anchored in New York. By 1879 the city's Swedish-Norwegian consul reported an annual total of 1,128 Norwegian vessels visiting the city.[7]

During the era of mass immigration, American government reports often underestimated the Norwegian population in the metropolitan area because of difficulties in recording mariners' presence. Unlike other immigrants, sailors rarely entered the country through Castle Garden or Ellis Island. Instead, they arrived as transients waiting to hire on another Norwegian ship or as deserters planning to join the American merchant marine.[8] Even after they came to view New York as their home port, their residence in the city often eluded census enumerations because they lived on boats in the harbor or were on sea voyages at census-taking time.

The New York State censuses used for this study counted just a small part of the mariners in port. Because the state's 1892 population count for Brooklyn did not include street addresses, it made no clear distinction between inhabitants on land and on ships. In 1905, however, enumerators' instructions not only required exact addresses but, judging from evidence in the manuscript schedules, also encouraged registering people on craft docked at piers. A search of the schedules indicates that census employees boarded vessels only sporadically and limited their inquiries to the inhabitants of harbor craft. Thus, although 353 Norwegian ships entered the port of New York in 1905, no trace of their crews appeared in the schedules. The information gathered on harbor craft occasionally gave a tantalizing glimpse of Norwegians working in the bay. For instance, one enumerator in Brooklyn went aboard ships at the foot of Degraw Street just north of the Atlantic Basin. There he found one Norwegian, Anton Brechan, working as captain of the barge *Anna S* and three others employed as deckhands on the tugs *Chas. E. Kuper*, *Border City*, and *James West*.[9]

Around the turn of the century, a combination of economic and geographic circumstances made a complete canvass of New York's "floating" population highly impractical, if not impossible. Because larger numbers of vessels entered and left New York harbor than any other American port, the maritime population's turnover rate was the nation's highest. With wharves, industrial plants, and population centers on several islands, the local economy depended to a unusual degree on harbor craft. Starting in the late 1830s, a growing number of railroad lines ended on the Hudson River's west bank, where journeys were completed by water to points around the harbor's 771-mile shoreline. By 1916, well over 6,000 port vessels crisscrossed area waterways carrying passengers as well as food, fuel, raw materials, and finished products between the hinterland and the metropolis.[10]

Not only single men but many families lived on New York's harbor craft. When a census enumerator registered boat people near Brooklyn's Forty-Second Street in 1905, he found one barge captain sharing his boat with a wife and three school-aged children. In his *Norwegians in New York, 1825–1925*, A. N. Rygg described work on boats in the port as a common economic niche for immigrating Norwegian sailors in the nineteenth century. During interviews, elderly Brooklyn Norwegians spoke of relatives and acquaintances who spent their lives on such vessels. According to these old-timers, barge life was a well-known form of family living around the turn of the century. Norwegian bargemen found wives on shore to share their two-room deck houses. There the couples ate, slept, and raised families. Unconcerned about legal formalities, they seldom bothered to apply for American citizenship. When the women were ready to give birth, their husbands brought colony midwives on board. Only years later did grown-up children who had left the barge life wish they had birth certificates. Until the early 1960s, when container ships first dominated marine freight transport, barge life was a natural consequence of Norwegian maritime migration to the port.[11]

The inclusion of people on harbor craft in population counts was a matter of chance. Barges and lighters remained docked only until cargo was loaded or unloaded. A census enumerator could register only people on craft that happened to lie at piers when he arrived. Lighters were flat-bottomed boats that got their name from "lightening" ocean-going vessels of cargo so they could enter the port. Consequently, these ships often operated outside the bay, and their inhabitants were even less likely to appear in census reports. Given the port's huge size, harbor-craft families could be hard to trace from one day to the next. They were free to anchor for the night at the nearest convenient spot, which might be along the New Jersey coast rather than at piers in Manhattan or Brooklyn. In 1891, *Nordisk Tidende*, a Brooklyn Norwegian weekly newspaper, supplied incidental evidence of this fact in its description of a local bargeman's birthday party. According to the newspaper, "Mr. E. Singdahlsen celebrated his thirty-ninth birthday on board his boat, which docked in Weehawken, New Jersey, for the occasion."[12]

Clearly, making an estimate of sailors' contribution to local colonies' growth presents special problems that neither census nor immigration records alone can solve. Although no one has seriously studied Norwegians living on harbor craft, maritime transients and deserters are nothing new to students of Norwegian immigration. In 1928 and 1933, Knut Gjerset published standard works about transient Norwegian sailors in American ports which demonstrated that the expansion of Norwegian shipping after 1850 brought large numbers of the country's seamen to American shores, where they often found employment on American vessels.[13] A few years later, Theodore Blegen called ship-jumping an "irregular" form of immigration for over ten thousand Norwegian men between 1876 and 1890 and presented Norwegian statistics on desertion in American harbors to buttress his claim that American census reports underestimated immigration from Norway. A decade later, Ingrid Semmingsen's *Veien mot vest* cited the most recent Norwegian statistical analyses of total desertions in the United States as an important factor in the rise of the Norwegian communities in American ports. Most later historians have followed her lead without further examination of the accuracy of applying general trends to specific communities, more probing criticism of traditional source materials, or an attempt to understand this form of Norwegian migration as one instance of the larger phenomenon of global maritime migration.[14]

Larger political and economic processes had pronounced effects on Norwegian shipping, and so help explain fluctuations in the city's population of transient Norwegian mariners. The Swedish-Norwegian consul's annual reports give the number of Norwegian ships arriving, distinguish among vessels arriving once and those docking more often, and indicate total desertions from these craft during their periods of time in port. Manpower figures, however, include foreigners employed in Norway's merchant fleet, a growing presence from 1870 on, and for this and other reasons reliable figures on the size of the transient and deserting maritime population require careful calculation and critical interpretation.[15]

In the nineteenth century, Norwegian spokesmen in New York considered the merchant marine the largest element in their communities. Local leaders pointed out that the old country's sailors, unlike the seamen of most other nations, did not usually return home between voyages, but instead sailed back and forth between New York and ports outside their homeland for years. Later historians have supported this contention with documentation showing that Norway based its expanding shipping industry on carrying other nations' freight from the 1850s onward. Manhattan or Brooklyn thus became a second home for increasing numbers of Norwegian mariners.[16]

For that reason, local leaders claimed a much larger population than the census indicated. In 1874, Jørgen Gjerdrum, a visiting Norwegian businessman, reported the assertions of the local consul and a Norwegian Lutheran minister that the New York and Brooklyn colonies were ten times larger than the 1870 census indicated. The two local leaders' claim might appear to be an unfounded boast unless, as seems likely, they did not distinguish between permanent and sojourning or temporary residents. Gjerdrum noted that most countrymen he met were either seamen or tradesmen serving them. Other contemporary observers confirmed his impression that mariners constituted the largest group of Norwegian wage-earners. Since enumerators had difficulty counting a group whose presence in the city was intermittent, a substantially larger population must surely have existed than the census showed.

Official statistics reveal that the settlements' growth rate was high after 1870, although the actual number of Norwegians reported remained small. By 1880 the settlements in Manhattan and Brooklyn had more than doubled their size, growing from 372 and 301 Norwegian-born residents to 893 and 874 respectively. Then the Brooklyn colony expanded much faster than its neighbor, more than quadrupling its population by 1890 and nearly doubling it again to almost 8,000 by the end of the century.

The crews of Norwegian ships undoubtedly swelled the population of the settlements. During the period most critical for the growth of these communities—from the mid-1860s through the 1880s—higher wages in the American commercial fleet attracted many Norwegian

Looking into the entrance of the Gowanus Canal, which marked the eastern boundary of Red Hook, from farther south along Brooklyn's shoreline in 1887. Harry Johnson and Frederick S. Lightfoot, *Maritime New York in Nineteenth-Century Photographs*.

A strange floating village in New York City. In 1902 *Leslie's Weekly* included this drawing by E. J. Meeker to document the many families living on barges docked for the winter around New York Bay. South St. Seaport Museum Melville library.

sailors. Whether Norwegian shippers recruited crew at home or abroad, in the 1860s they offered low wages compared to those available in other Atlantic fleets. In most international ports Norwegians' pay rose to parity with that of other nations' sailors by 1870, however, because they demanded the going rate when recruited abroad. But for reasons still incompletely determined, in New York wages on Norway's vessels declined until 1880, and only in the 1890s reached the levels common in the international maritime labor market.[17]

To take advantage of this anomalous situation, some Norwegian mariners declared their immigrant status and joined the American service in New York. Others jumped ship in the harbor and hired on American vessels. Nonetheless, Norway's deep-water fleet suffered a net manpower loss of only four percent through emigration or desertion in all foreign ports between 1866 and 1915. But in absolute numbers that meant legal and illegal emigration amounted to a drain of nearly 70,000 men in those fifty years. At the peak of their economic dissatisfaction in New York in the 1870s, the desertion rate alone rose to four times the overall rate for the period studied when 6,200 left their ships illegally in one decade.[18] If the overwhelming majority of Norwegian seamen resisted the temptation of higher wages and remained in the home country's service, the minority, the maritime migrants, were nonetheless in raw numbers a sizable group that formed the kernel of many harbor-related communities, most notably around New York Bay, but also elsewhere in the United States and the world.

The majority of Norwegian sailors in New York, as elsewhere, lived a transient existence for a few days or weeks and then shipped out on another Norwegian ship. A rough estimate of this transient population's size puts its effects on the local settlements in better focus. In 1893 *Nordisk Tidende* stated that the average crew size was at least ten. But manpower needs varied greatly according to type and size of ship, and not all crewmen were Norwegians. A conservative estimate is that no fewer than five men per ship were Norwegian.[19] Between 1850 and 1861, consular reports from New York showed fluctuations in the volume of Norwegian shipping. The yearly average hovered around fifty vessels, or approximately 250 men per year. In the 1870s, Norwegian ship arrivals traced a sharply rising curve from 320 in 1872, to 500 the next year, and on to the nineteenth-century peak of 1,128 in 1879. That trade expansion increased the annual transient maritime population to a high point of over 5,500. In 1880, Norwegian shipping reversals caused by steamship competition suddenly became apparent. During that year 826 ships or a little over 4,000 seamen came. In 1883, the number of incoming vessels plummeted to around 350 and remained near that level until the next decade, when it sank to under 200 per year. Thus the estimated visiting Norwegian merchant marine on the homeland's ships averaged around 1,700 during the 1880s and 1,400 in the last years of the century.[20]

**TABLE 1: NORWEGIAN SHIPS, SEAMEN, AND DESERTERS**
**IN THE PORT OF NEW YORK, 1872–1902**

| Year | Number of Norwegian ships arriving in NY | Estimated Seamen Arriving | Estimated Deserters |
|---|---|---|---|
| 1872 | 320 | 1,600 | 406 |
| 1873 | 500 | 2,500 | 505 |
| 1874 | 498 | 2,490 | 537★ |
| 1875 | 368 | 1,840 | 411★ |
| 1876 | 484 | 2,420 | 291★ |
| 1877 | 481 | 2,405 | 327 |
| 1878 | 921 | 4,605 | 487 |
| 1879 | 1,123 | 5,640 | 575 |
| 1880 | 826 | 4,130 | 695 |
| 1881 | 624 | 3,120 | 533 |
| 1882 | 420 | 2,100 | 383 |
| SUBTOTALS | 6,565 | 32,850 | 5,150 |
| 1883 | 349 | 1,745 | 358 |
| 1884 | 324 | 1,620 | 223 |
| 1885 | 356 | 1,780 | 235 |
| 1886 | 323 | 1,615 | 232 |
| 1887 | 381 | 1,905 | 386 |
| 1888 | 334 | 1,670 | 210 |
| 1889 | 352 | 1,760 | 201 |
| 1890 | 377 | 1,885 | 208★ |
| 1891 | 380 | 1,900 | 143 |
| 1892 | 339 | 1,695 | – ! |
| SUBTOTALS | 3,515 | 17,545 | 2,196 approx. |
| 1893 | 300 | 1,500 | 30★ |
| 1894 | 199 | 995 | 30★ |
| 1895 | 233 | 1,165 | 85 |
| 1896 | 275 | 1,375 | 85★ |
| 1897 | 281 | 1,405 | – ! |
| 1898 | 287 | 1,435 | 128★ |
| 1899 | 334 | 1,670 | – ! |
| 1900 | 362 | 1,810 | 87★ |
| 1901 | 332 | 1,660 | 75★ |
| 1902 | 296 | 1,480 | 79★ |
| SUBTOTALS | 2,899 | 14,495 | 599 approx. |

*Source:* Annual Reports, Swedish–Norwegian consul in New York. Arriving Norwegian seamen = 5 per ship. Desertion figures adjusted to exclude foreigners except where "★" indicates exact figures for Norwegians. ! = no figure available
See note 20.

In comparison with the New York enclaves' size, even these conservative figures suggest that the local colonies were swamped with transient mariners at the height of Norway's shipping expansion. Assuming that census reports counted the more stable population, in 1880 there were approximately 4,000 visiting sailors to 1,667 resident Norwegians. A decade later the colonies' population was much larger than the transient merchant marine, but there was still more than one visiting sailor for every four local residents. Only at the century's end did the settlements' nearly 10,000 inhabitants far outnumber the 1,400 seamen temporarily in port each year. Even then, Norway's merchant marine continued to be a major economic resource for the settlements. Local Norwegians organized to provide room, board, entertainment, ships' supplies, and social institutions for their transient countrymen. And, of course, a percentage of the Norwegian crewmen frequenting the port eventually made the colonies their permanent home.

Norwegian deserters undoubtedly also settled in the colonies. Between 1850 and 1900, New York showed a higher rate of desertion from Norwegian vessels than any other American port. One important factor was the city's size and commercial preeminence, which made it the easiest place to elude authorities and find another berth. Equally important, New York was the harbor most frequented by Norwegian shipping. How long ship-jumping mariners remained is uncertain. Since they were fugitives from the law, some probably left quickly to avoid detection. Until 1893 Norway punished desertion by imprisonment or fines, depending on whether the seaman returned willingly or was captured. Fear of punishment carried little weight with deserters, however, because few men suffered the prescribed penalties for ship-jumping. In 1872 authorities in New York apprehended only thirteen of 812 seamen deserting Norwegian ships in the harbor. Enforcement of the official statutes was lax because it was prohibitively expensive. Effective punishment required sending offenders home at government cost. Even consuls in European ports seldom gained government approval to do that. When the consul in Le Havre asked permission to send several deserters home in 1877, the Norwegian Department of the Interior agreed, but only "as an exception to make an example" of the men involved.[21]

Deserting Norwegians' initial stay in New York was brief. They were likely to ship out quickly, but primarily because they wanted swift access to higher American wages rather than because they feared capture. Still, entering the United States merchant marine, especially the coastal trade, inevitably meant docking in New York with greater frequency, and so increased the chances that deserters would eventually settle there. The great size of the city's maritime employment market also attracted Norwegians who jumped ship in other North American ports and consequently encouraged additional sailors to locate in area enclaves. Another essential fact to keep in mind is that local and international economic conditions varied tremendously in the last half of the nineteenth century. Therefore, the likelihood that deserters would join New York's Norwegian colonies also fluctuated greatly.

According to contemporary Norwegian officials, alarming numbers of the nation's seamen jumped ship in New York. In 1871, the Director of Norway's Bureau of Statistics, A. N. Kiær, blamed most of the rise in Norwegian desertions, world-wide, on growing trade with just one city—New York. Since some of these runaways may have settled in the area, knowing their actual number would shed light on the populations of local colonies. Unfortunately, determining the runaways' numbers is difficult. "The available statistical records concerning the desertion of Norwegian sailors are very incomplete," the maritime historian Johan Tønnessen remarked, because "desertion was illegal, a concealed form of emigration, which prevented an exact official tally."[22]

On vessels owned in St. John, New Brunswick, crews included men from many nations and frequented ports around the globe between 1863 and 1913. According to Lewis R. Fischer and Helge W. Nordvik, this fleet's rising desertion rate resulted from escalating opportunities to desert in the harbors that offered the greatest economic opportunities. At least a hundred sailors from twelve nations in these polyglot crews jumped ship in twenty different international harbors during the period. The most frequent pattern, however, was the desertion of Norwegian seamen in New York. The city also ranked first in total number of deserters of all nationalities, but when listed by the percentage of desertions among men frequenting each harbor, it ranked second after Liverpool and was followed closely by London, San Francisco, and Melbourne. The global scale of merchant sailors' international migration is thus evident.[23]

The statistics in the annual reports of the Swedish-Norwegian Consulate in New York are too unreliable to give more than a rough idea of total desertions in New York between 1850 and 1900. But these statistics can highlight the relationships between changing economic conditions and the frequency of desertions, and, even if treated cautiously, the calculation of total desertions shows that thousands of ship-jumping Norwegians became probable settlers in the colonies. As might be expected, Norwegian seamen jumped ship when desertion seemed to offer the greatest advantages. The Brooklyn colony experienced its highest growth rates in the years immediately following peaks in the desertion rate.[24]

As a rule, more men jumped ship as the number of vessels in New York increased. At several points during the period, however, the correlation between desertions and ship arrivals was far from exact. At these times, the influence of large-scale historical processes on the local desertion rate becomes apparent. Between 1850 and 1861 each Norwegian ship that entered the port of New York lost, on average, one man through desertion. The first irregularity appeared in 1862. Ship arrivals rose to 207 while desertions fell to 44, or fewer than one man to every four ships. Part of Norwegian shipping's increased volume resulted from the Civil War. When southern raiders and military needs forced the North's merchant marine from the Atlantic trade, the English fleet filled most of the vacuum, but other maritime nations, such as Norway, also expanded their involvement in the American market. Even such a relatively small increase in Norwegian vessels in New York Bay, as we shall see, contributed to the establishment of the first Norwegian institutions in the Red Hook section of Brooklyn. A possible answer to the low de-

**TABLE 2: FREQUENCY OF DESERTION IN NEW YORK (DESERTION RATES)**

|        | total ship arrivals | total deserters | deserters per ship |
|--------|--------------------|-----------------|--------------------|
| 1870   | 320                | 406             | 1.3                |
| 1880   | 826                | 645             | .8                 |
| 1885   | 356                | 253             | .7                 |
| 1890   | 370                | 208             | .6                 |
| 1895   | 233                | 85              | .4                 |
| 1900   | 362                | 87              | .2                 |

*Source:* Desertion rates derived from Worm-Müller, *Den norske sjøfartshistorie* (1870) and the Annual Reports of the Swedish-Norwegian consul in New York. Total desertions adjusted to exclude non-Norwegians. See note 20.

sertion rate could be that few Norwegian sailors wanted to exchange their transient status for service in the Union navy. On the other hand, perhaps more of those deserting during the war years planned to settle in America, since one reward of military service was citizenship. Individual motivations no doubt varied, but the decline in American shipping was probably the deciding factor, because it drastically reduced the opportunities for higher pay on American vessels.[25]

As Norway's shipping in the harbor rose sharply during the early 1870s, the number of her ship-jumping mariners soared. In these years the two overall patterns for the entire period to 1900 become evident: The number of deserters rises with shipping increases (although individual years are exceptions to this trend), and the frequency of desertion begins to fall. According to Fischer and Nordvik's study of sailors' wages, this overall decline in frequency might be the result of decreasing differences in wages in the Atlantic nations' fleets.[26] Runaways were still on the rise in 1874, but during the next year they suddenly began to decline. Specific conditions that varied by individual year and place also played important roles. By 1876, Norwegian sailors chose to jump ship only half as often. Apparently, many men had become aware of New York's exceptionally high unemployment rates following the Panic of 1873. Staying with Norway's fleet now offered more security than the city's depressed job market.[27]

The high tide of Norwegian desertions came in 1880, one year later than the peak of Norwegian trade with New York. The number of arriving ships dropped by more than 300 between 1879 and 1880. Yet, in the latter year, seventy more seamen deserted. Complaining of "more desertions than ever before," the local consul pointedly commented that Norwegian wages were "hardly a quarter of those paid at times here." By the end of the decade, the local economy had recovered, and job-hunting again became attractive for foreign mariners. Yet, despite the consul's sense of events, the rate of desertion had not quite returned to its normal level in good times. Fewer than one man per vessel deserted. In fact, the attraction of American wages was, relatively speaking, somewhat weaker than in 1850 or 1872. Most likely, the high total of desertions resulted instead from the still large number of Norwegian sailors in port during a time of local economic expansion. The consul's reaction was natural, considering the total manpower loss.[28]

After 1880, Norwegian seamen less and less frequently jumped ship in New York. The American economy fluctuated greatly. There were booms around 1890 and 1900 but depressions in the mid-1880s and 1890s. Yet the Norwegian desertion rate fell steadily. The American job market alone was apparently no longer decisive.[29] The sharp decline in the volume of ship arrivals evident by 1885 indicates one factor that reduced desertions in New York. Because Norwegian shipping did not fully recover from the crisis brought on by steamship competition until after 1900, fewer than half as many sailors had the opportunity of choosing to jump ship in the city after the mid-1880s.[30]

During the century's last decade, however, the decline in desertions exceeds the reductions in ship arrivals. Johan Tønnessen's survey of developments in international shipping offers some possible explanations. The new maritime technology permitted shippers to increase their profit margin by carrying larger cargoes on a smaller number of steam-driven vessels. Even though the new ships were larger, their operation required fewer seamen. The maritime job market shrank because of both smaller numbers of ships and reduced manpower requirements. At the same time, the rush to acquire steamship fleets soon met the needs of international trade and put a cap on job opportunities in foreign ports. Perhaps most important, Norway and other maritime nations combatted the problem of runaways with higher wages, intensified waterfront controls, and improved working conditions.[31]

The combination of these factors apparently meant that desertion was seldom attractive or feasible. Facing unemployment at home and limited chances of escaping to other merchant fleets, Norwegian mariners chose instead to emigrate legally. After comparing the statistics of mariners' legal and illegal emigration from 1866 to 1915, Tønnessen notes, "Until the mid-1880s, the Norwegian sailors' migration to other countries and their merchant marines occurred mainly through desertion. Around 1885, there is a clear change in that the migration happens more through emigration."[32]

**Sailors' Irregular Immigration, 1885–1918: A New View**

During this new phase, seamen's settlement in the area continued, although that fact is no longer evident from statistics showing desertions and the arrival of transient crews on Norwegian ships alone. Near the century's end, the number of seamen living in the New York colonies may have increased mostly from legal immigration. However, in New York and elsewhere, Norwegian sailors had other alternatives for escaping the dearth of employment in their homeland's depressed shipping industry. In the late 1880s, one contemporary observer who supplied crews for Norwegian ships in the harbor claimed that he had difficulty

•

As this lithograph of the South Street Seaport area in the 1870s shows, the decks and docks in Manhattan and Brooklyn teemed with crowds into which a runaway sailor could vanish from shipboard authorities in moments. South St. Seaport Museum

placing the hundreds of Norwegian sailors who came to him for berths on *American* vessels. These men had not deserted. They had legally completed their contracts with Norwegian captains on arrival in the port and decided their prospects would perhaps improve if they discarded constant loyalty to Norway's fleet. Other observers, the seamen's pastors in Red Hook, asserted that from 1885 onward more Norwegian mariners began arriving in the port than ever before, but each year fewer of these came on the old country's ships. Between 1885 and 1888, the pastors counted an average of 3,000 Norwegians a year on the combined Scandinavian fleets. On other nations' ships they estimated totals rising above 20,000. Even if these figures are exaggerated—and there are no official statistics with which to compare them—they clearly indicate the continuing exodus of Norwegian mariners. In their experience, the pastors noted, men who had earlier left Norway's fleet for another nation's were more likely to desert or go on land after arrival in the port.[33]

Some seamen continued to jump ship and go on land in the port. The Swedish-Norwegian consul remarked that desertions had dropped to low levels by 1902 in part because by then most Norwegian mariners worked on Norwegian ships under contract with American firms and therefore could quit legally whenever it suited them. Only two years later, however, he began recording rising numbers of desertions. When the total fell precipitously in 1908, the consul explained the change by commenting that men "stayed with their ships more often because of difficulties finding jobs on shore."[34] A sharply rising trend in desertions

**TABLE 3: NORWEGIAN SHIPS, SEAMEN, AND DESERTERS IN THE PORT OF NEW YORK, 1903–1918**

| Year | Number of Norwegian ships arriving in NY | Seamen Arriving | Estimated Deserters* |
|---|---|---|---|
| 1903 | 335 | 1,675 | 73 |
| 1904 | 334 | 1,670 | 118 |
| 1905 | 353 | 1,765 | 121 |
| 1906 | 474 | 2,379 | 158 |
| 1907 | 491 | 2,455 | 146 |
| 1908 | 514 | 2,570 | 33 |
| 1909 | 498 | 2,490 | 45 |
| 1910 | 398 | 1,990 | 74 |
| 1911 | 486 | 2,430 | 87 |
| 1912 | 458 | 2,290 | 58 |
| SUBTOTALS | 4,341 | 21,714 | 913 |
| 1913 | 582 | 2,910 | 118 |
| 1914 | 709 | 3,545 | 137 |
| 1915 | 795 | 3,975 | 255 |
| 1916 | 823 | 4,115 | 397 |
| 1917 | 840 | 4,200 | 188 |
| 1918 | 640 | 3,200 | 266 |
| SUBTOTALS | 4,389 | 21,945 | 1,361 |

*Source:* U.S. Censuses of Population, 1870-1900.    See note 20.   *All desertion figures are exact.

occurred between 1913 and 1918, when the approach of World War I led to dramatic increases in the number of Norwegian ships and crews in port.

Norwegian shipping (at least in New York) was well on the way to recovery from its long depression by the middle of the twentieth century's first decade. Desertions were low, but the number of transient seamen becoming acquainted with opportunities in the harbor again reached the level of the early 1880s. In 1909 and 1910, moreover, the consul complained that the percentage of men who jumped ship, though low in number, was equal to nearly 10 percent of the number of Norwegian seamen who completed work contracts on arrival. Most impressive for measuring the increase in sailors who were likely to settle in the area eventually, he noted that between 645 and 695 took jobs on American or other nations' ships during the same years.[35]

Thus, it appears that neither the increased wages, waterfront controls, and improved working conditions Tønnessen stressed nor the recovery of Norwegian shipping could keep Norwegian sailors from following what they saw as their best interests. The irregular or concealed means of immigration they had used for over half a century remained more common than the authorities would have liked. As Norway's shipowners sent over all the bottoms they could muster to aid in—and profit from—the Allies' war effort, desertions reached a new peak. The consul claimed that the men had misunderstood the terms of America's new law, the La Follette Seamen's Act, that the Norwegian-American leader of the seamen's union, Andrew Furuseth, had at last lobbied to passage. They thought it gave sailors on all Norwegian ships the right to break their contracts in American ports. Perhaps some men did mistake the new law's intention, but the old salts interviewed in Brooklyn thought the Seamen's Act was probably no more than a handy pretext for "just doing what we'd always done," as one man put it.[36]

Comparing the two flood tides of desertion in the port suggests a number of supports for the old-timers' view. First, except for 1908–1912, rising desertions parallel increasing ship arrivals, and during the exceptional years the consul indicated that men went on land legally. Thus, perhaps the most important feature of maritime immigration during the 1870s appeared again: the greater the number of men experiencing the port's opportunities, the greater the number of those leaving the old country's fleet. Second, as in the 1870s, jobs were plentiful on shore when most men deserted during World War I. Veterans of the Brooklyn colony said some men joined the American navy or merchant marine while others got work in wartime industries on land.[37]

Third, desertions reached a peak (the highest or next highest) one year later than the crest of Norwegian shipping. There is reason to believe that seamen sensed the shifts taking place in the fortunes of Norway's maritime industry within a year. They were among the first to feel a decrease in available berths. During the late 1870s, sailors frequenting a

●
From the late 1860s until the advent of container ships in the 1950s, thousands of seamen from a host of nations went ashore in the port of New York. Desertions were a constant. South St. Seaport Museum

major world port like New York could not avoid seeing how metal steamships were driving wooden sailing vessels out of the market. Old-timers in Brooklyn said crewmen knew the freight market would collapse with the end of World War I. Therefore, it seems reasonable to conclude that significant numbers of seamen sensed the hard times coming in both these periods and began looking for other opportunities. The repetition of these three general patterns, in sum, suggests that macroeconomic factors and the men's traditional reactions to them—rather than the Seamen's Act—prompted the wave of desertions during the 1910s.[38]

## Prologue in Manhattan

The first Norwegian settlement in the metropolitan area that resulted from sailors' traditional migratory habits appeared in southeast Manhattan rather than Red Hook, Brooklyn. Before following the course of their story across the East River, therefore, it is necessary to stop—as they did—on the Lower East Side. For, as with seamen's ship-jumping during peak periods of shipping, patterns established there during the 1870s and early 1880s were repeated later in Red Hook. The Manhattan settlement directly preceded and crucially affected the evolution of the Brooklyn community. A large part of the older settlement's population, businesses, and social institutions eventually moved across the East River, but, before that happened, the two areas competed, sometimes bitterly. The most impressive community mobilization in Manhattan, moreover, aimed at solving social problems in the emerging Brooklyn colony.

Throughout its development, the Manhattan colony's main population center remained squarely in the island's sailortown, although members of the elite often lived elsewhere. Early in the century the shipping center was near the Battery, where the largest concentration of Norwegians lived as late as 1855. About that time, sailortown moved farther north and east, occupying a wedge-shaped strip with its narrow western end near Washington and Carlisle Streets and its broad base along the East River from Fulton Market to Corlear's Hook. Between 1855 and 1860 the colony's population center moved to the same area, remaining there until the exodus to Brooklyn's Red Hook district got under way in the late 1870s.[39]

Sailortown's Norwegians were a tiny minority of the city's total population. At the 1855 state census, the eastside shipping center stretched over wards 1, 2, 4, and 7. Irish immigrants dominated the area, constituting over 45 percent of the population in wards 1 and 4, and more than a third in wards 2 and 7. Although much less numerous, Germans averaged around ten percent and English somewhat under five percent in these wards. By contrast, the largest Norwegian cluster, in the first ward, constituted only about half a percent of its population. Italians and Russian Jews poured into the sailortown area after 1870, and by 1900 comprised its largest immigrant groups.[40]

Leaving crowded, smelly tenements and boardinghouses in the

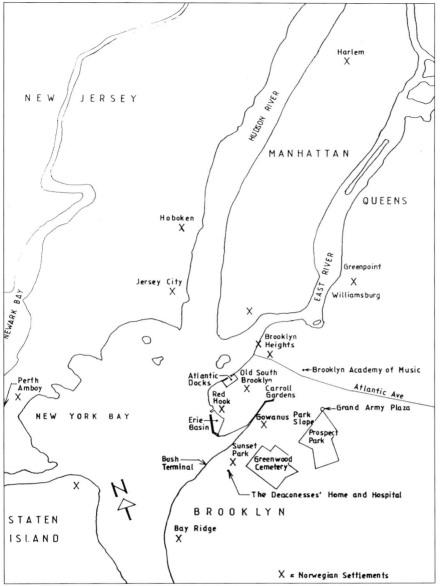

Norwegian settlements in the Metropolitan Area, circa 1890.

morning, waterfront workers and seamen walked to the host of ship-yards, docks, and piers along sailortown's shorelines. By the late 1870s, not only the tenements but also several boardinghouses provided living quarters for Norwegians. If employed on the west side, they had perhaps spent the night at Nicolai Smith's boardinghouse. Many countrymen arriving at Castle Garden stayed there before traveling to the Midwest, because Smith also ran a ticket agency and emigrant bank. Albert Nilsen's combined boardinghouse and saloon for deep-water seamen probably held greater appeal for less sober-minded salts on the west side.[41]

Between the 1850s and the 1880s, however, most Norwegians lived and worked in the east-side center of sailortown on South, Cherry, Market, and Monroe streets. "Here, in the hundreds of drinking dens, dance-halls, tattoo parlours, skittle-alleys, boardinghouses, and tailor shops," wrote Stan Hugill, "were to be found the seamen of all nations, boisteriously endeavoring to live to the fullest their limited hours ashore." In 1874, the area's temptations included "halls" with Norwegian names. By Jørgen Gjerdrum's account, inside these establishments were "women who could speak with Norwegians and employ charms to ensnare them, if possible." Near the East River, a family of Norwegian Baptist teetotalers struggled to win sailors from their sinful ways. After visiting their "New Seaman's Home," Gjerdrum concluded that its abundant good food, clean rooms, and family atmosphere would appeal to "sober and proper folk." On the other hand, he ironically remarked, the six after-dinner hymns—and accompanying sermonettes—were "more value" than lodgers deserved for paying room and board.[42]

In the east-side heart of sailortown, boarding masters and runners preyed on seamen. In the 1860s and 1870s Stavanger-Larsen, Olsen the Swede, and Paddy McCormack had houses on Cherry and Monroe streets. Runners helped them keep rooms occupied and captains supplied with docile manpower. If Stavanger-Larsen's Norwegian employees operated like other runners of the time, they met Norwegian ships entering New York Bay, climbed on board, and, while liberally distributing free liquor, made the crews promise to stay at the Norwegian house before the ship docked. Once on shore, the runners encouraged sailors to run up tabs in the boarding master's name at area dives and shops. When seamen were ready to ship out, the captain paid these debts from their future wages. This vicious system, together with drunken debauches, kept the Manhattan colony filled with destitute mariners.[43]

Reconstruction of the colony's socioeconomic pyramid is problematic. Although seriously flawed by their undercount of seamen, Manhattan census schedules are the only source of detailed occupational information. Transient seamen comprised a clear working-class majority from the 1830s onward. The 1855 New York state census registered few of these men but shows that a high percentage of more permanently resident Scandinavians worked as rivermen, riggers, and ships carpenters. Rygg claims that an assortment of skilled workers made the colony less purely harbor-related from the 1850s onward but gives only one example, the arrival of three piano-makers. Although Robert Ernst's analysis of the 1855 state census lists a group of Scandinavian musical instrument makers, he emphasizes that the building trades showed the largest concentration of non-maritime Nordic workmen. He also finds that the predominant occupations among Scandinavian women in 1855 were domestic servant, seamstress, and dressmaker. The colony's Lutheran pastor during the 1860s and 1870s commented that many Scandinavians had found employment in the leather industry. That must have been a recent development, since Ernst's study showed only four leather workers at mid-century.[44]

The less numerous middle class consisted mostly of small businessmen. Shopkeepers reported in the 1830s and 1840s included a baker, two smiths, and a general merchant. One ambitious Norwegian milkman of the 1840s married the milk dealer's daughter, set up a milk company of his own, and then used his capital to buy property in Wisconsin. The largest Scandinavian middle-class groups in Ernst's 1855 survey were general merchants and retailers, boardinghouse keepers, wine and liquor dealers, and clothiers. Between the 1850s and 1880s, a Norwegian florist, a leather worker, a tailor, and a ship chandler established businesses that endured for several decades, according to Rygg. Sea captains were also a stable middle-class element. The dominant element of the Norwegian *petit bourgeoisie* all through the century, however, was boardinghouse owners and saloonkeepers, two of the groups Ernst found most common among Scandinavian businessmen.[45]

The many capsule biographies in Rygg's *Norwegians in New York* reveal a tiny but colorful group of professionals and successful businessmen at the pinnacle of Manhattan's Norwegian society. Although Rygg's selection takes the form of "rags to riches" success stories and testimonials to the founders of community institutions, it offers a valuable record of the colony elite. Norwegian professionals began settling in the city about mid-century, when a physician and an attorney opened practices and engaged actively in community affairs. The career of the lawyer, James Denoon Reymert, well illustrates the advantages and adventures of the class. Born into a family well connected in both Norway and Scotland, Reymert studied in Edinburgh and then emigrated in 1842. During nearly two decades in Wisconsin, he practiced law and engaged in other activities, such as editing the early Norwegian-American newspaper *Nordlyset*. Then he moved to New York in 1861, organized the Hercules Mutual Life Assurance Society, and built up a local law practice. Later in the decade, Reymert trained his newly-arrived sailor nephew, August, for the law and was instrumental in founding the Norwegian Society, the colony's first voluntary association. August Reymert later became the attorney used by most Norwegian immigrants and ethnic institutions, in both Manhattan and Red Hook.[46]

"Brooklyn Bird's Eye View of the City of New York [from] Williamsburg, 1859,"
a lithograph in colors after John Bachmann publisher. New York Public Library

During the 1860s and 1870s, a colony elite formed that would lead
community affairs for the rest of the century. Christian Børs moved
his import-export business from Boston in the sixties and was the
Norwegian-Swedish Consul General in New York from 1871 to 1889.
Børs and his wife Anna not only made their home and the consulate
the elite's primary social milieu but also drew on their friends' time and
resources to found charitable institutions for less fortunate countrymen,
especially in Brooklyn.[47]

A few skilled craftsmen, captains, and shopkeepers accumulated
sufficient property and capital to share the society and causes of the
consular circle. Two piano-makers, Conrad Narvesen and Lars Ihlseng,
built and successfully maintained an instrument factory on Thirty-third
Street. A leather worker, Hans Reese, established a large, profitable business near Broadway and Ann Street. Gunnerius Gabrielsen, the florist,
did so well with his store at Broadway and Twelfth Street that he became a major donor to colony institutions. Captain A. Thomas Nielsen

entered an importing-house partnership and subsequently became a pillar of Our Savior's Norwegian Lutheran Church. By the early 1890s, James Reymert's nephew August had made a name for himself by negotiating the United States Army's purchase of the Norwegian Krag-Jørgensen rifle and, moreover, took time to champion the interests of poor Scandinavian immigrants who had lost their savings through a bank swindle.[48]

Social gatherings and cultural events gave this well-to-do coterie an intimate sense of community and occasions for discussing colony problems. The Reymerts, Gabrielsens, Ihlsengs, Narvesens, and Børses celebrated New Year's Day and Norwegian Constitution Day together. When entertaining the Reverend Ole Juul from Our Savior's or Peder Larsen, the Norwegian missionary at Castle Garden, they could lay plans for a seamen's mission and emigrant relief society. Pastor Juul probably took their views seriously, since they contributed heavily to his church's finances and comprised the congregation's lay leadership. Larsen must have realized that they were the only local group with sufficient funds to aid waves of newcomers.[49]

Their social affairs sparkled with the presence of Hans Balling, the Norwegian portrait artist who had painted President Lincoln, and Skougaard-Severini, the Norwegian singer and vocal teacher, who often brought his close friend, Alfred Corning Clark of the Singer Sewing Machine family. Because the famous Norwegian violinist Ole Bull often met Ihlseng when visiting James Reymert in 1867, he asked the factory owner to prepare a model for an improved piano. The young August Reymert often carried Bull's violin to concerts in Manhattan. Such familiar contacts with talented countrymen were so conducive to ethnic pride and social confidence that they became the treasured memories of a lifetime.[50]

Unified by its mutual experiences, interests, and social status, the elite was ready to tackle the need for colony-wide institutions by 1870. For almost two decades, a few of its members had been involved in the creation of pan-Scandinavian institutions—two newspapers, a social club, a Lutheran congregation, and the Methodist Bethel Ship, a seamen's mission. By the late 1860s, the number of Norwegians residing in or frequenting the city could support a separate associational life. The colony elite's informal social network articulated group consciousness and fostered the formation of purely national organizations, starting in 1870 with Our Savior's Norwegian Lutheran Church. The Norwegian Society's list of founders from 1871 reads like a directory of the prominent families discussed above. Nordmændenes Sangforening (the Norwegian singing society), founded in 1873, received its banner as a gift from Consul Børs and included many Society members. Finally, in 1878 *Nordiske Blade* provided the colony with its first newspaper. Although located in Brooklyn's Red Hook, this newspaper nonetheless faithfully represented Manhattan colony views until it stopped publication in

1910. As they entered the eighties, the Manhattan Norwegians had become a much more self-sufficient group. The inter-Scandinavian societies continued to exist, becoming for most Norwegians a supplementary resource used when the exceptional amounts of money or manpower required could not be obtained from their own sources of support.[51]

In Manhattan, Our Savior's congregation and the members of the Norwegian Society, representative of the more settled part of the population, accepted the leadership of the most prominent local Norwegians. When Jørgen Gjerdrum visited in 1874, his status as a well-known businessman from the old country gave him easy access to the colony elite, whose institutions he judged by the standards expected at home. His sense of superiority is evident in his remark that, although the Lutheran minister lacked "Latin training after Norwegian conceptions," he was "*mirabile dictu*—in possession of adequate culture to carry on his work." Gjerdrum thought such a small group might easily disperse in the metropolis, so he approved of the Norwegian Society because it formally knit the membership together by providing sick benefits, social affairs, and a Norwegian-language library.[52] Yet, within a decade of Gjerdrum's visit, the dispersion that Gjerdrum feared had occurred, although not for the reason he had predicted. Some of the rank and file of the enclave went north to settle in today's Harlem. Most moved to Red Hook for the same reason that they had once chosen Manhattan, the proximity of work in the harbor or on the docks and the nearness of incoming ships in Norway's fleet.[53]

**The Eclipse of the Manhattan Colony: a Conclusion and a Glance Forward**

The Norwegian population's growth rate soared in the New York area between 1870 and 1890. Even at the beginning of this period, the Manhattan-based ethnic organizations and businesses could scarcely have survived without drawing on the Norwegian population across the East River, but by 1890 the Brooklyn colony was more than three times the size of the Manhattan settlement. Several factors made Brooklyn the new center for the metropolitan area's Norwegians. The Manhattan community's largest working-class groups were identical with those in the Brooklyn colony, a continuity suggesting a number of processes involved in the migration to Brooklyn. Many of the Manhattan workers may simply have moved to Brooklyn, as colony historians claimed. Certainly, transient seamen increasingly touched land on the Brooklyn side of the East River because of the expansion of shipping activity there. But the similar occupational training of new arrivals between 1880 and 1890 seems equally important, since Brooklyn's Norwegian population more than quintupled in size while Manhattan's grew by only sixty percent during that decade. Moreover, if the settled colony had relocated, its best chance of helping newcomers find work would naturally be through the occupational concentrations recently established in Brooklyn rather than in Manhattan.[54]

Disturbed by the seamen's alleged immorality in 1874, Gjerdrum

had found some comfort in the Norwegian Baptist teetotalers' boardinghouse for mariners. In fact, the Methodist Bethel Ship and Our Savior's Lutheran Church, both purely Norwegian by the time of his visit,
were also attempting to reform the morals of Norwegians on the waterfront. The leaders of the Manhattan colony, however, were more familiar than Gjerdrum with local population movements and knew that
most Norwegians who might benefit from religious charity now
touched land on the other side of the East River. In the late 1870s and
1880s, therefore, the Manhattan colony elite led efforts to handle the
mounting problems of unemployment, poverty, and sickness in Red
Hook. By mobilizing the influence and assets of the consulate, the Seamen's Mission Society in the old country, and the Norwegian Lutheran
Synod in the Midwest, they managed to found a variety of social institutions with close links to orthodox state-church Lutheranism and the
shipping interests in Norway. By the 1890s the Brooklyn settlement
contained a seamen's church, a temperance home, and a hiring office to
address the material and spiritual problems of the merchant marine. The
Norwegian Relief Society provided temporary housing and job counseling for Red Hook's needy and homeless. The Deaconess Home and
Hospital concerned itself with the full range of medical, religious, and
social problems across the East River.[55]

Norway's shipping and her sailors' irregular immigration provided
the broad base of customers and working people needed to support the
growth of a Norwegian colony and elite in Manhattan. On May 17,
1889, the Norwegian Society in Manhattan convinced the mayor and
the aldermen to raise its flag over New York's City Hall in honor of
Norwegian Constitution Day. Brooklyn's City Hall would have been a
more appropriate place to raise the flag, since the hub of Norwegian
community life had already moved there, and the influence of the
Manhattan-based organizations was waning.[56]

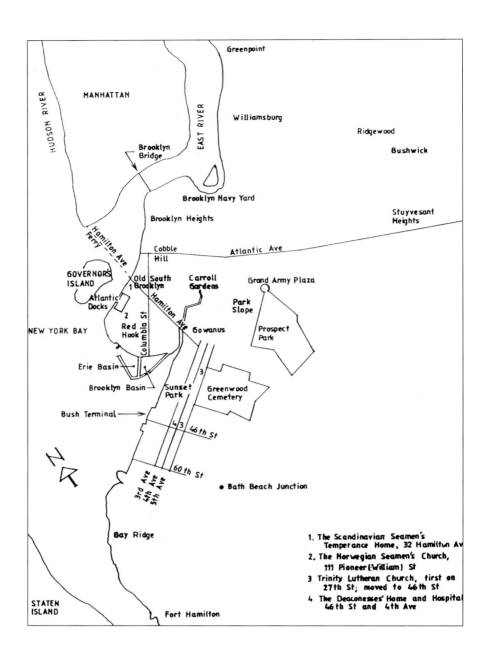

Brooklyn Neighborhoods.

# 4

---

# One Pattern among Many in Brooklyn's Complex and Shifting Fabric

The Norwegians who came to Brooklyn in the nineteenth century found themselves in a city experiencing a series of dramatic transformations. A prospering village in 1830, it had become the nation's third largest city by 1855, and was a metropolis of over one million that sprawled across all of Kings county in 1898 when it became a borough of Greater New York. A significant part of this phenomenal growth came from the annexation of adjacent towns, such as Greenpoint and Williamsburg, but in-migration and subsequent natural increase contributed most to the the city's skyrocketing population figures.[1]

Free blacks came early and constituted the only significant minority in the Village of Brooklyn, forming almost a third of the population in 1790. Groups of native-born Americans, especially Yankees, settled in soon after. By mid-century, Brooklyn was an extension of New England culture, famous for Brooklyn Heights entrepreneurs with fleets of Yankee clippers that sailed to exotic ports. Its other claim to fame was Henry Ward Beecher's Plymouth Church, where Beecher and other leading abolitionists railed against the evils of slavery. Although they were the city's wealthiest elite and its most disadvantaged minority,

**The Urban Context: An Overview 1830–1890**

Yankees and African Americans counted less for Brooklyn's further development by the last decades of the century. By 1870, blacks composed only slightly more than one percent of the population. About the same time, the Yankee leadership surrendered control over city hall to Irish and German Americans, though they experienced a brief revival of influence under Seth Low's mayoralty in the early 1880s.[2]

After 1855, the foreign-born comprised at least a third of Brooklyn's population, and by 1900 a majority of the city's residents were immigrants or their children. The Irish had begun arriving in considerable numbers as early as the late 1820s, yet by 1890 the city's 95,000 German immigrants outnumbered them, even if one counted most of the nearly 6,000 resident Canadians as relocated Irishmen. Until near the end of the century, Irish and German Americans were almost the only ethnic groups that attracted more than sporadic attention from the general public.[3]

The main lines of their meeting with old-stock Americans and each other were not very different from those in many other parts of the country. The usual stereotypes prevailed. Nativists attacked Irish immigrants for their Catholicism and alleged tendency to drunkenness. Ethnocentric Yankees assailed German Americans for keeping *bierstuben* open on Sundays and their apparent unwillingness to embrace America's language and culture. Opposition to the Irish mounted in the 1830s and climaxed in a bloody street battle with the "Native Americans" in 1844. German-American soldiers' participation in the Civil War, and the ease with which many German immigrants entered the city's economic and political mainstream reduced accusations of their ethnic exclusivity. Even in the mid-1890s, however, a *New York Tribune* feature article describing Brooklyn's foreign settlements complained that the German-American community in Williamsburg was self-sustaining and the people there clannish. German Americans' protracted battle with the sabbatarians ended only in 1882 when Mayor Seth Low, of Yankee stock himself, asked Brooklyn's Excise Board to use "common sense" in enforcing the state's blue laws. By that time, Brooklynites had been celebrating the rags-to-riches stories of successful German and Irish Americans for decades.[4]

Ingrained cultural dissimilarities and competition for work resulted in continuous tension but few open clashes between the city's largest ethnic communities. Although an overview conceals a multitude of internal differences, the broad contrasts between the two groups are clear. Irish Americans were overwhelmingly Catholic, loyal members of the Democratic Party, and infamous for their use of machine politics under Boss Hugh McLaughlin to control municipal patronage. Primarily Lutheran, Brooklyn's "little Germany" included groups of freethinkers, Catholic parishes, and by the 1870s, Jewish enclaves. The Republican Party held the allegiance of most German Americans. The best-known German-American politicians were reformers who captured the mayor's office by combining with old-stock Americans to defeat the Democratic machine.[5]

Despite the wide range of occupations within each ethnic community, a few salient employment patterns also characterized the two groups. While women from Ireland dominated the market for domestic servants, fewer women from the German states took paid work and those who did worked in factories more often than did Irish-American women. Many German-American men found work in breweries, sugar refineries, and factories requiring skilled craftsmen. Irish-American men, on the other hand, dominated the work force in the city's transportation network, on the docks, and in the police and fire departments. Workmen in both communities were heavily involved in construction jobs, however, and competition between them for building contracts occasionally grew fierce, especially when large public-works projects were involved. For example, when ethnic rivalry led to rioting between Irish and German Americans working on the construction of the Atlantic Docks in 1846, only a strict 50-50 division of the available jobs could keep the peace.[6]

Immigrants from Great Britain remained the third largest foreign-born group until the turn of the century, but few histories of Brooklyn do more than briefly mention population statistics to describe their role in the life of the city. Studies note that German and Irish Americans lived in all parts of the city and use colorful quotations from contemporary accounts to emphasize the location of Brooklyn's largest Germantown in the Williamsburg tenements and the Irish quarter in the slum area between City Hall and Red Hook. None charts the settlement patterns of the British-born, although one remarks that, unlike natives of Germany, British Americans were not clannish and therefore were evenly spread throughout the city.[7]

The 1890 census gave a somewhat different picture. The British-born were indeed widely dispersed, residing in all wards of the city, but that was also true of the two largest ethnic groups. A few areas of the city, such as Park Slope, Stuyvesant Heights, Bushwick, and Ridgewood, contained districts with concentrated British settlement. Over a quarter of Brooklyn's British Americans lived in the better parts of these four communities, and 57 percent had settled in just seven of the city's twenty-six wards. Immigrants from Scotland carved out their own sub-colonies, always adjacent to, but clearly discrete from, the larger areas where Welsh and English Americans lived. In general, the British-born enjoyed better housing in the healthier parts of town, which they shared with the native-born and immigrants from northwestern Europe.[8]

In Greenpoint and the poorer sections of Bushwick and Stuyvesant Heights, however, British Americans lived in factory-district tenements with a wider variety of peoples, including Jewish newcomers from eastern European and recent Italian immigrants. In middle-class districts of these areas and Gowanus, they shared neighborhoods with

Scandinavian Americans. There were a few prominent trades among the group's working class: hoteliers and highly skilled craftsmen in the porcelain and lace industries. Their diversity of residence suggests both British Americans' wide socioeconomic range and their broad spectrum of occupations.[9]

Despite its contemporary reputation as a bedroom suburb of Manhattan, Brooklyn developed into a commercial-industrial powerhouse in the decades after the Civil War. People moved to the city to find work as often as they settled there to be near New York. In the early 1880s, Brooklyn provided homes for about 40,000 commuters with jobs in Manhattan, but at the same time the value of its annual manufactures made it the fourth most important industrial center in America. The city was nationally important for its production of glass, porcelain, machinery, refined oil and sugar, chemicals, cast iron and steel building elements, ships, books, cordage, hats, and beer. By 1890 Brooklyn's 10,000 factories employed 110,000 workers, and its docks handled most of the heavy freight entering or leaving the country's premier port.[10]

Brooklynites alternately thanked and blamed their larger sister city for this rapid industrial development and population increase. In southern Manhattan, space for large-scale housing, shipping, and manufacturing had already become limited and expensive in the two decades before the Civil War. New York entrepreneurs therefore began to transfer such enterprises across the East River. The Atlantic Docks, for many years the country's largest cargo depot, opened in Old South Brooklyn in 1847. Similar projects formed the basis for a lasting functional relationship between the two cities by the 1870s. Manhattan's more congested commercial area was reserved for the financial center, executive decision-making, the production and sale of the most expensive luxury goods, and piers for both dry goods and the best-known passenger shipping lines. Brooklyn's huge underdeveloped districts and long shoreline provided the necessary room for working-class housing, industry that demanded great amounts of space, and waterfront facilities for both the shipping and the warehousing of bulk cargo.[11]

Perhaps more than any other improvement, the opening of the Brooklyn Bridge in 1883 quickened the pace of the city's development. As speculators had hoped, the bridge relieved the congestion of lower Manhattan by making residence across the East River so convenient and cheap that multitudes left crowded immigrant quarters and settled in Brooklyn. Just seven years after the bridge opened, Brooklyn had more homes than Manhattan. Having boardrooms in Manhattan and factories on the other side of the river also became easier and more profitable. Brooklyn boomed as never before. New industrial districts and residential sections sprang up along the newly rerouted transportation networks that fanned out from the bridge.[12]

The influx from Manhattan, combined with continued immigration that for the first time included large groups from southern and

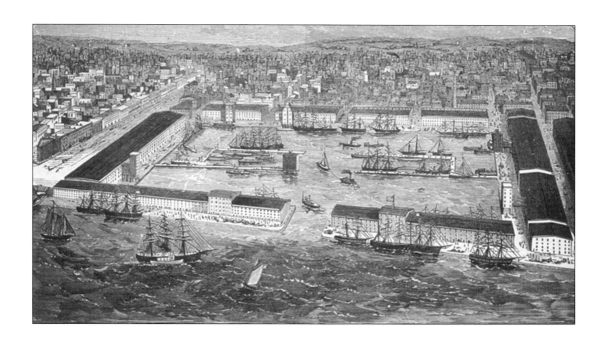

•

Atlantic Docks and Basin: Until 1866, when the Erie Ship Basin was completed
on the south end of the Red Hook Peninsula, the Atlantic Docks and Ship Basin
were an engineering and commercial wonder that completely dominated the area.
Brooklyn Historical Society

eastern Europe, brought a decades-long period of radical change in Brooklyn's ethnic landscape. Significant alterations were already clear by 1890. During the previous decade, not only did the German-born population outstrip the Irish-American community in size, but the Scandinavian immigrant population nearly quadrupled. The 1880 census was the first to reveal that Nordics were the city's fourth largest foreign-born population group, but by the early nineties they had grown to a contingent of over 16,000 that attracted the attention of the city's premier newspaper, *The Brooklyn Daily Eagle*. In 1891 and 1892, for example, the newspaper commented on the city's first Leif Erikson Day Parade, first Norwegian Constitution Day celebrations, and first Scandinavian court interpreter.[13]

Although emigration from the Scandinavian countries reached its highest peak in the early 1880s, the exodus from some Scandinavian cities, especially those involved with international shipping, continued to grow. At the same time, the lack of space in Manhattan's traditional seaport area steadily transferred more of the job opportunities Nordics sought to Brooklyn. As might be expected, that process both caused migration from older settlements in New York and led more newcomers to choose Brooklyn as their first place of residence. Equally important, it meant that Scandinavian sailors, most of whom were Norwegian, came ashore in Brooklyn. Unlike other European countries, except perhaps the United Kingdom, Norway consistently sent many more transient workers than immigrants to the city each year.[14]

The 1865 New York State Census had provided the first official evidence of Scandinavian immigration's sparse beginnings in Brooklyn. That tally of 660 also revealed the approximate relative size of the three nationality groups for the next fifty years. The majority were natives of Sweden, with the Norwegian-born in second place and Danish-born Americans in third. Scandinavian Americans clustered first in Old South Brooklyn near the Atlantic Docks and then spread farther south into the Red Hook-Gowanus area. In 1890, about half the city's Scandinavian Americans lived together in these communities. Swedish and Danish Americans tended to find homes farther in from the coast, which meant that they more often enjoyed the better health that came from living on higher ground. The city's other Scandinavian enclaves were widely scattered. One little working-class group lived not far south of the Brooklyn Navy Yard. A loose string of small Scandinavian settlements, composed mostly of Swedish Americans, followed the course of Atlantic Avenue all the way from Cobble Hill east to Stuyvesant Heights, consistently occupying parts of better residential areas. When the Scandinavian-American Line moved its docks to Brooklyn's new Bush Terminal in 1903, the *Brooklyn Daily Eagle* described Red Hook as "thoroughly Norwegian" and the Atlantic Avenue area farther from the coast as "Swedish."[15]

The state census of 1892 showed Norwegian immigrants grouped closely together, over three-fourths of them concentrated in the contiguous parts of two wards extending from Old South Brooklyn through Gowanus. Four contrasting districts held much smaller, basically Norwegian-American settlements. Along the border between Greenpoint and Williamsburg, about a hundred Norwegians and even fewer Danish Americans lived in a district of tenements and factories near the Poulson and Eger Architectural Iron Works, a factory owned by Danish and Norwegian immigrant partners. Near the wharves at the foot of Brooklyn Heights, a few Norwegian immigrants shared a commercial district's tenements with old-stock Americans and people from the other Scandinavian countries, Ireland, and Germany. Much farther south, small groups of Norwegian Americans had found homes in the streets of new housing immediately north of Greenwood Cemetery and in the thinly populated area following the extension of Third and Fifth avenues to the city line at 60th Street. By 1885, enough Norwegian immigrants had gathered at Bath Beach Junction, south and east of the city, to support a small house for religious meetings and Sunday school. In the mid-twentieth century, that area would be part of Bay Ridge, the home of most latter-day Norwegian Americans.[16]

The composition of the settled Scandinavian-American population gradually shifted after 1890. Danish settlement was steady but small-scale and stagnated after 1900. As successive censuses reported, more Norwegians than Swedes took up residence around the turn of the century, so that by 1920 Norwegian Americans had become the largest of the three groups. Much earlier, the crewmen of Norway's merchant fleet, added to the resident population of immigrants, had given the country a presence in the city that was larger than that of the other Nordic lands. Colony historians asserted that it was precisely Norway's greater involvement in international shipping that caused their group to become the largest.[17]

Around the turn of the century, many spokesmen for the immigration-restriction movement described Scandinavians as the most desirable of foreigners. Stereotyped as blond-haired, blue-eyed, and fair-skinned, they seemed the purest strain of the northwestern European in the 1890s and supplied one of the names, Nordic, for Madison Grant's ideal racial type in *The Passing of the Great Race* in 1916. Their reputed cultural baggage of Protestantism, democratic traditions, industry, and reserved manners, moreover, would supposedly guarantee easy assimilation into American society. Their high literacy rate, noted Henry Cabot Lodge and others, was yet another factor that recommended them. The author of the mid-1890s *Tribune* feature article mentioned earlier apparently believed that all the Scandinavians in Brooklyn were Swedes and complained that they were as clannish as the Germans, but perhaps justifiably so. In 1916, a *Daily Eagle* feature article showed a greater knowledge of the differences among the three Scandinavian groups but repeated the stereotypes supporting their easy assimilability, claimed that

Lithograph showing seamen dancing with women in a bar. Maritime workers, permanently settled in the housing near the docks, frequented waterfront dance-halls and dives between voyages. *Seaport Magazine*, Winter 1992.

they resided "in all localities without regard to nationality," and concluded that they were already breaking into the city's best society.[18]

As the *Eagle* article noted, there was little open animosity between Danish Americans and their sister nationality groups, but antagonism between Swedish and Norwegian Americans had sometimes run high. Between the late 1880s and 1905, tensions between their two homelands gradually mounted until they reached the brink of war in 1905, before Sweden granted her neighbor full independence. That conflict carried over to Brooklyn for a number of reasons. First, being primarily a maritime group, local Norwegians joined their compatriots at home in insisting that Swedish-Norwegian consuls in foreign ports ought to be of their nationality, because they thought that would guarantee a better understanding of their own and the visiting Norwegian fleet's needs.

Second, prominent Norwegian Americans claimed that their homeland was more American in spirit because it lacked an aristocracy, believed in the self-determination of peoples, and had a constitution modeled on America's own. Disagreement about whether Brooklyn immigrants had any right to involve themselves in the matter even caused dissension within Brooklyn's Norwegian-American colony and between it and the Manhattan settlement.[19]

In general, population movements within the city illustrated the classic pattern of residential succession in run-down immigrant tenement districts, although some East European Jews, Finns, and the Norwegians who settled near the southern edge of the city were exceptions to the general pattern. The cultural dissimilarities and antagonisms described above may have played a role in individual situations, but for Norwegian Americans, as for other immigrant groups, there were other at least equally important reasons for moving within the city. For example, as Norwegian-born residents gained a better knowledge of local topography and living conditions, they realized that low-lying Red Hook-Gowanus was relatively unhealthy. In 1897, *Nordisk Tidende* moved farther south to Third Avenue and 22nd Street. About a decade later, remarking on the unhealthy smell of the Gowanus Canal district, the newspaper loudly urged other colony institutions to follow the people and migrate to Sunset Park and Bay Ridge. Naturally, Italians and Poles soon became acquainted with these disadvantages of the area and moved on too.[20]

News about the city's established immigrant quarters traveled back to the sending countries through America letters, and that brought more of the ethnic groups already there. Crowded in cheap housing, newcomers hoped for something better, and neither they nor the owners of buildings, who lived in better districts, spent as much on maintenance as they would have on more valuable property. In the 1890s, most tenements and homes in South Brooklyn and Red Hook were less than forty years old, but many were already in poor condition. Immigrant ghettos were favorite targets for public and private redevelopment projects, especially if they were close to industrial and commercial districts and lay across convenient routes for improvements in the transportation network.[21]

Red Hook and Gowanus were ripe for both kinds of change near the beginning of the twentieth century, as the northwestern part of Sunset Park was not too many years later. In the 1890s, elevated railroads cut a strip south through the district connecting Fifth Avenue with approaches to the Brooklyn Bridge. Around 1900, the Brooklyn Rapid Transit Company electrified and enlarged that line and constructed another along Third Avenue, making both avenues under the forty-foot-wide railways noisy and dark. As a result, not only did the population density increase but the coastline and Gowanus Canal district became ever more crowded with heavy industry, congested with rail terminals for transferring freight across the Bay, and dotted with towering heaps of salt, coal, and stone.[22]

Repeated large-scale transformations of Brooklyn's physical and demographic landscape never lacked avid boosters, especially among entrepreneurs and speculators. For ordinary families with less control over, interest in, and understanding of these changes, the uprooting effects of development on family and community life often seemed devastating. The less resourceful and most recently arrived usually drew the shortest straw. Living in cities like Brooklyn required acceptance of almost constant adjustment to the impact of change. As former mayor Seth Low lamented in an essay on municipal government published in 1888, in America "the improvement of cities seems everywhere to be made by tearing down and replacing at great cost."[23]

Rapid development produced extravagance and waste because even the foresighted seldom were able to predict the scope and direction of expansion. The vice, graft, and corruption that were inevitable in the confusion of municipal construction projects encouraged the doling out of pork-barrel payoffs by political bosses. Even progressives like Low confessed that universal suffrage had its drawbacks in such a situation, "because the voting population is continually swollen by foreign immigrants whom time alone can educate into an intelligent harmony with the American system." Newcomers strained the structure of all the city's services—housing, schools, transportation, job market, and political system. Popular democracy was nonetheless the wisest course, Low concluded, explaining with an unfortunate comparison: "But because there is scum upon the surface of a boiling liquid, it does not follow that the material, nor the process to which it is subjected, is itself bad."

## Origins of Norwegian Settlement: the Pioneers

The Norwegians who survived and prospered in Brooklyn's "boiling liquid" of rapid change were clearly among the resourceful, resilient, or economically favored. Colony histories and newspaper articles preserved the life stories of such people as proud testimony to the qualities necessary to build a viable ethnic subculture in the city during its pioneer period, which lasted from around 1850 to 1890. A few dozen capsule biographies of exceptional people are hardly representative. On the other hand, the biographies have a surprising number of common elements, especially regarding the immigrants' early experiences in the city, when they had not yet shown exceptional qualities. A careful collation of these elements, linked to the histories of Norwegian seamen's desertion, emigration from Norway, and the city's development, reveals the main outlines of the formative stages in the Brooklyn colony's growth.[24]

The patterns of international migration and settlement the early settlers followed were unusual for Norwegian emigration generally but common in the colony. Instead of inland farmers, most of those who were first attracted to Brooklyn were coastal city-dwellers, who had earlier migrated from agricultural areas to Norway's southern and south-western shipping centers. In a period when most Norwegians arrived in families, the majority settling in Brooklyn came as young single men—sailors who deserted on first arrival or after frequent stops in the city. A few families, however, represented the minority of urbanites who left on emigrant ships during the recurrent waves of America fever that swept the homeland.[25]

It is more than a curiosity that both the earliest settlers in the city's Dutch period and the pioneers of the nineteenth-century colony gravitated to the same geographical areas. Both groups had a sharp eye for the most auspicious combination of access to Manhattan, work in maritime trades, and inexpensive land or housing. Thus, they chose to reside in coastal areas from present-day Greenpoint in the north to Old South Brooklyn, Red Hook, and Gowanus farther south. Through letters, visits home, and contacts with visiting seamen they told of the beachheads they established in coastal Brooklyn and that, along with the city's natural appeal for a seafaring folk, reinforced the special regional and urban bias of the colony's old-world background.[26]

A few brief biographical descriptions vivify the human dimensions of these processes and also introduce some personalities who played important roles in the colony's later development. Aanon Aanonsen, a ship's carpenter from Kristiansand, southern Norway's largest city, arrived in 1849 with his wife, three sons, and small daughter. John Jeppesen, a seafaring friend from the same city, brought his wife and eleven-year-old son on the same ship. This group obviously possessed some capital. Aanonsen and Jeppesen not only could afford to bring their families to America but also had funds to take them along later that year on the families' attempt to strike it rich during the California gold rush. The Aanonsens and the Jeppesens were adventurers and must have had property they could dispose of before leaving Norway, two qualities that were not uncommon among early immigrants from many countries. Aanonsen's financial background and reasons for emigrating are unknown, but Jeppesen's history was a typical success story from that part of Norway. He had advanced from sailor to captain and part owner of his vessel before leaving. Apparently he liquidated his assets and decided to make a new start when he remarried after his first wife's death.[27]

Whether or not the families found wealth out west is unknown, but around 1855 the Aanonsens returned to Brooklyn, where Aanon and his two grown sons, John and Tom, resumed work in maritime trades and changed the family name to Anson. The city's economic opportunities suited their occupational experience and Norwegian maritime career models best. John and Tom were not unlike numbers of other young, ambitious men still in coastal Norway. Tom advanced from ordinary sailor to captain, but in Brooklyn his ship was a Gowanus canal-boat. John Anson rose from sailor to ship's chandler in Red Hook and became an important community leader at the turn of the century.[28]

Jeppesen, now calling himself Jefferson, also returned but—like many area Norwegians—lived in Manhattan for "a short time" before he too settled near Gowanus. Perhaps the family friendships that had given mutual support on the voyages to New York and later to the Pacific coast were as important in drawing his family to that area of Brooklyn as economic opportunity was. Friendship and family networks were among the most common motivations given in newspaper articles and interviews for migrating and relocating. In Brooklyn Jefferson established a more American-style claim to fame as the "first Scandinavian stevedore in New York." The colony remembered Jefferson more for his daughters by his second marriage, who married prominent local Norwegian Americans, than for his occupational path-finding. Stevedoring never became a common trade for Norwegians. Irishmen and later Italians dominated that line of work.[29]

Although Harry S. Christian (Hans S. Christiansen) also emigrated in the forties, his early experiences typify the pattern common to many seamen who arrived in port during the last decades of the century. In time-honored fashion, he left his birthplace in coastal Farsund while still a teenager and went to sea. In Norwegian shipping regions sons usually did that, following their fathers' example and simultaneously reducing the number of mouths to be fed as well as adding to the family's income by mailing or bringing home wages. At eighteen Christian's voyages brought him to New York, and after continuing his itinerant sailor's life and frequenting the harbor for a number of years, he took up work on land in Brooklyn. In the common parlance of colony old-timers, he "went on land." "In the beginning that went as it did with so many others: he worked hard and earned little," according to his obituary in *Nordisk Tidende*.[30]

It seems fair to speculate that Harry Christian worked as a carpenter originally. That was what most Norwegian sailors gone on land did first, both in the nineteenth and the twentieth centuries. Seamen commonly doubled as ship's carpenters and builders, especially in southern Norwegian towns like Farsund, where every cove and inlet bustled with shipbuilding between 1850 and the mid-1880s. Seafaring families not uncommonly had a little coastal farm on which both land and sea were regarded as fields for harvesting. Boys grew up building boats as well as barns. When these people migrated to the period's expanding Norwegian seaports, emigrated, or became seamen stranded in foreign ports, carpentry seemed a natural trade to take up. In Christian's case, the usual pattern seems particularly likely. The combination of his Norwegian work traditions, seafaring, and Brooklyn's frenetic building activity in the years after his arrival suggests that carpentry work would both appeal and be available. The clincher, though, is the fact that he later started a lumberyard and building materials business in Gowanus, where most construction involved ships and boat basins rather than dwellings.[31]

In some senses, even the early careers of the pioneers were exceptional. First, modern Norwegian emigration was only fifteen years old in the 1840s, and hardly the massive movement it would later become. During the last year in the decade, for example, only 4,000 Norwegians came to the United States. Second, just a handful of these settled in Brooklyn, since even in 1865 state census takers found barely 200 living in the city. Third, although the difficulties in counting seamen probably made the enumeration somewhat low, Norwegian shipping with New York did not reach major proportions until the 1870s, and thus desertions remained relatively low until then. Small numbers of Norwegian sailors drifted on land, like Harry Christian. Others helped swell Brooklyn's settled Norwegian population to 372 in the 1870 Federal Census after winning citizenship through serving in the Union Navy. None of seamen's unusual means of settling in could lead to or find support in a sizeable resident population, however, until much larger numbers of Norwegian ships were drawn to Brooklyn.[32]

The fourth essential factor in the transition from scattered pioneer outposts to the founding of a Norwegian colony was the development of world-famous harbor facilities from Old South Brooklyn to the Gowanus Canal. This stretch of shoreline became New York City's main bulk-freight terminal and therefore attracted the largest part of the Norwegian merchant marine. Perhaps more than anything else, this complex of economic factors made the Red Hook-Gowanus section the location of the largest Norwegian settlement in the entire metropolitan area by the 1890s.

When the Aanonsens and the Jeppesens left Brooklyn for California, most of Red Hook and Gowanus that was not under water was salt-water swamp. Shipping activities were still centered in northern Brooklyn, in the Williamsburg and Greenpoint shipyards and the Navy Yard between them. Most commercial docks and warehouses occupied the waterline under Brooklyn Heights. Blunt's map of New York Harbor for 1848 shows that Red Hook was undeveloped marshland except for the newly completed Atlantic Dock Basin on the northwest coast of the peninsula. The city's grid of streets stopped in the middle of Old South Brooklyn where Sackett Street and Hamilton Avenue met the recently established ferry route to Manhattan. Gowanus Canal did not yet exist. That whole area was an extended inlet surrounded by tidewater flats and salt-water ponds. The Atlantic Docks, however, were an impressive beginning to the rapid development of the area. They included a forty-five-acre ship basin where 100 ships could dock, forty acres of warehousing, and grain elevators that received the Midwest's harvest from canal boats that came down the Hudson from the Erie Canal.[33]

When the Norwegian forty-niners returned to Brooklyn in the mid-1850s, the areas that would become the ethnic group's first population center were in a turmoil of transformation. The surge of building arose from both rising immigration and the harbor's growing impor-

Coal-stoking seamen in a steamship engine room. In the latter 1800s, seamen more and more often belonged to the new industrial working class that appeared with the development of steam power. Leah Rousmaniere's *Anchored within the Vail, A Pictorial History of the Seamen's Church Institute*.

tance as the country's primary center for international trade. In Old South Brooklyn and Red Hook cheap tenement housing marched farther south each year, as Irish immigrants flooded into these districts. Docks and factories now crowded the shoreline down to the Atlantic Docks, and more were sprouting up on Red Hook's waterfront. Along the southerly tip of that district dredging had begun for two enormous new docking areas, the Erie and the Brooklyn ship basins. Simultaneously, the inlet and complex of marshes and ponds around Gowanus began to emerge as a canal and network of shipyards and slips.[34]

During the next ten years the Williamsburg-Greenpoint shipyards and the Navy Yard would also expand quickly as a result of the Civil War, but the center of commercial import-export activity shifted increasingly to the newer facilities farther south as the nation moved into the postwar period. Dripps' map of New York Harbor for 1873 reveals a line of shipyards and docking basins, grain elevators, warehouses, and docks stretching from the Atlantic Basin around the Red Hook peninsula and even behind it through the Gowanus Canal. Increasingly, the transshipment of grain and other agricultural products took place on Red Hook's wharves, while the coal mounds, petroleum tanks, and gasworks surrounding Gowanus docks testified to their specialization in fuel handling. Sandwiched between these commercial-industrial districts was relatively new housing that ranged from the most shoddily constructed tenements and shacks near the water to well-built single-family houses on the highest ground.[35]

Between 1850 and 1870 Norwegian shipping interests learned to focus their resources on building fleets designed to carry exactly the kinds of heavy goods that Red Hook and Gowanus dock facilities handled. In southern Norway, wooden cargo ships were cheaper to build than almost anywhere else in the world. Local farmers provided the needed lumber, provisioners supplied food and equipment, captains and other officers signed on, all on the promise of shares in the finished vessel and profits from its voyages as a freighter. Farmers' sons and hired hands often did the actual building for low wages, because ship construction kept them from unemployment during slack periods. Since the seamen got paid when the cargo was delivered, fleets could thus be put in the American freight trade with minimal cash investment beforehand.[36]

With impressive rapidity Norwegian shipping agents and captains learned of and implemented design changes to satisfy international requirements for grain and petroleum freighters. A few years after entering the grain freighting business, the country's ships, because of their exceptionally tight planking and innovations in hold construction that prevented the cargo from shifting during storms, had a wide reputation for delivering grain undamaged by moisture. The Norwegian wooden ship *Lindesnæs*, put in service in 1869, was the world's first specially designed oil tanker. Shipping oil from Brooklyn to the European continent remained important for Norwegian shippers into the 1880s because wooden vessels seemed safer for carrying inflammable petroleum than steamships. Paradoxically, as faster steam-driven ships reduced Norwegian sailing ships' portion of the grain-freighting business in the late seventies, they simultaneously increased the demand for their services to carry the coal required for steam-driven machinery on land and at sea. During the 1870s Norwegian ships carried much of the petroleum leaving Gowanus's docks, and only British freighters carried more of the grain exported from Red Hook than did Norwegian ships.[37]

The fifteen years between 1872 and 1886 were the golden age of Norwegian shipping in Brooklyn. The number of the country's ships docking annually in the Port of New York at both the start and the end of the period was about 300, but during the peak year, 1879, more than 1,100 arrived in the harbor. Because the specialization of Brooklyn's newer docks and Norway's ships coincided, the majority of these incoming vessels touched land in Red Hook or Gowanus. As a Norwegian harbormaster working in the city recalled, "In 1877 we placed in Atlantic Basin alone fifty Norwegian ships at one time. It looked like a forest of Norwegian masts, and you could walk from one of our ships to another all the way across that huge basin."[38]

At last, the decisive development for Norwegian settlement in Red Hook and Gowanus had taken place. Huge numbers of the country's sailors came ashore in the area. By a conservative estimate roughly 40,000 spent shore leaves there during this decade and a half. According to the testimony of Norwegian captains, moreover, crews frequently stayed in port for two or even three months, because Norway's ships often came in ballast and remained until captains could negotiate an agreement to transport an appropriate cargo at a good price. Captain Otto Thoresen described the practical realities of the situation as follows: "We decided the freight and price ourselves. The people at home didn't even know where we were. . . . In 1874–1875 we skippers sat in a bar and thought we were damned fine guys. The 'businessmen' went out and bid for cargo. The captain got ten dollars 'for a new hat' as thanks from the shipping agents."[39]

Meanwhile, the ordinary seamen were free to sit in bars in Brooklyn's sailortown and nurse their grievances over their working conditions compared with those American sailors enjoyed. Topping their list of complaints was pay. From the 1860s into the 1890s American ships in New York paid much better—some said two to three times more—than the common rates in Norway's fleet. And the men on American craft were not required to load and unload cargo or make major repairs to their vessels. On top of that, everyone agreed that American galleys and crewmen's quarters were far better. No wonder Norwegian seamen suffered more often from scurvy and beriberi.[40]

People said only the best ships were put in the "America trade," but these usually carried the most dangerous cargoes. Petroleum, coal, and even grain might explode. Because of the danger of fire, nobody hired on ships carrying oil unless it was the only work available . You could not smoke, and even lighting the paraffin night lamps could be fateful. The danger—and the smell—were awful, which was why the men were known to sleep on deck in hammocks fastened to the rigging. The grain ships often sat very low in the water, and the way Red Hook's four-storey elevators loaded the hold only three-quarters full with loose grain destroyed the advantanges of Norwegian innovations in hold construction. Especially in the fall and winter, these ships and their crews often went to the bottom when tons of cargo shifted during storms on the North Atlantic. It mattered little what the cargo was, Norwegian ships sank more often than any other maritime nation's.[41]

The seamen were the exploited group in Norway's maritime expansion. Fritz Hodne, one of the best-known Norwegian economists today, has no doubt about that, but, as he points out, Norway was an underdeveloped nation in terms of the times. It exported raw materials that more developed nations bought relatively cheaply. The primary means the nation found to accumulate enough capital for industrialization was offering cheaper freight rates than did other nations. The complaints of Norwegian seamen were justified, but few of them or their countrymen at the time thought it possible to change the situation through radical political remedies. Norway was not a fully independent nation, and Swedish authorities as well as the dominant business interests at home rejoiced over the prospects the shipping boom promised for economic development. To many people, including seamen, criticizing Norway's shipping entrepreneurs seemed almost unpatriotic because, as politicians, leading shipowners were among the most effective spokesmen for complete independence from Sweden. From the 1870s onward, moreover, shipowners raised wages in response to seamen's grievances and to compete in the international market for maritime labor that developed in the period. But in New York Norwegian wages lagged behind international pay scales much longer than elsewhere in the Atlantic trade.[42]

Under these circumstances many a Norwegian sailor reached a life-changing decison before docking or during the weeks spent in Brooklyn's sailortown. Instead of assailing captains or patriotic shipowners, many men expressed their opinions with their feet, so to speak, and jumped ship. They deserted in larger numbers in New York than in any other port. Between 1873 and 1886, 6,200 seamen deserted in the city, a desertion rate of 15.5 percent, which was almost four times the rate elsewhere in the world. Of course, deserting in New York most often meant in Red Hook or Gowanus, because that was where most Norwegian ships docked. According to one Norwegian captain, expertise in using a pistol at short range was a necessity if you commanded ships that came to that part of the harbor. Only if you could shoot a man's cap off without risk of killing him could you keep discipline on the return voyage with a crew of assorted foreigners, since all your Norwegian sailors had deserted in port.[43]

Because they lacked the power of shipowners and policy makers, seamen experienced economic exploitation. On the other hand, they were the most numerous human element in Norway's shipping industry. Its prosperity depended not only on fluctuations in international commerce but also on their cooperation. Norwegian sailors were not passive victims of an economic system. They looked out for their own vital interests and actively weighed alternatives for bettering their lives. One significant result of their reaction to exploitation was the rapid development of an unusual ethnic colony in Brooklyn, a community whose social and economic development bore clear marks of their occupational skills and leisure-time tastes.

## The Emerging Colony: The Norwegian Fleet and Population Growth

In the seventies and eighties, both deserters and men who stayed with their ships spurred the growth of a Norwegian population center in the Red Hook-Gowanus area. Not all deserters settled, but the pattern of working on American ships and eventually going on land became commonplace. This year's transient seaman, moreover, was not unlikely to become next year's deserter. In his book on Norway's coastal culture, Svein Moland remarks that sailors often seemed foreign on visits home and "more familiar with New York than with the Norwegian city nearest their hometown." When such men became well acquainted with the local job market and formed personal relationships on shore, boardinghouse masters' arguments for jumping ship became more convincing. Finally, the men who took up residence in the city not only encouraged former shipmates in port to do the same but also bought pre-paid tickets to help relatives and friends join them in the growing settlement.[44]

Transient or resident, seamen and their needs provided an economic foundation for an ethnic community that included other groups as well. The imbalance between settled Norwegians and transient sailors alone is enough to explain why enterprising immigrants saw economic opportunities in the needs of the visiting fleet. In 1870 nearly four transient sailors arrived in the harbor for every Norwegian-born resident counted in the census of Brooklyn. By 1880 the settled population had almost trebled, rising to 874, but by then the visiting Norwegian fleet numbered 4,130 men, almost five seamen for each resident.[45]

Deserters and transient sailors naturally turned to countrymen for room, board, and entertainment. Their captains just as naturally patronized Norwegian-American ship brokers and chandlers, who again turned to other resident countrymen for goods and services the ships required. Such an economic network had already existed in the older Manhattan colony. As the Red Hook-Gowanus shipping center attracted increasing numbers of Norwegian ships, these immigrant businesses moved their operations, if not always their offices, across the East River. In the later 1870s and 1880s, many working-class Norwegians in the maritime trades who had worked and lived on Manhattan's lower east side also relocated, because Brooklyn offered more job opportunities and a better chance of attracting seamen lodgers to augment meager incomes. According to contemporary observers who made their living from sailors entering the port, most transient Norwegian mariners lived as lodgers with countrymen by the late 1880s. As a later seaman's pastor explained, "The majority of ships were now transferred over to Brooklyn and docked in Erie Basin and Atlantic Docks .... And the settled immigrants followed the ships. Not Manhattan, but Brooklyn became the Norwegian colony's capital in New York, and instead of Market Street, Columbia Street was called 'Norwegian Broadway' with Hamilton Avenue as a strong competitor."[46]

Starting about 1880, large numbers of people coming directly from the old country joined the community of seamen and relocated Manhattanites. Norwegian emigration reached its all-time peak early in the decade, and for the first time the seafaring cities of the south and southwest—exactly those that had the strongest connections to New York—experienced departure rates among the country's highest. Since Brooklyn's Norwegian-born population began to increase much more rapidly than Manhattan's at the same time, there can be little doubt that the majority of newcomers preferred to settle in the Red Hook-Gowanus area, where most resided at the next state census.[47]

This new infusion of people was a much more varied group. According to immigrant biographies and interviews, more wives and children as well as a wider range of occupational groups came. Among the newly arrived were seamstresses and maids, skilled craftsmen, white collar workers, and a few professional men. After the Brooklyn Bridge opened in 1883, those who did not immediately find positions related to the settled community or the visiting fleet could live in its cheaper housing and commute to work in Manhattan until a suitable opening nearer the colony appeared. The early careers of a few people who came in the 1880s illustrate this increased variety, the typical patterns of maritime immigration, and the ways newcomers found for coping with local conditions.[48]

On April 18, 1881, as their ship entered the harbor, four steerage passengers—three young Norwegian men and Anna, the young Swedish woman one of them was chaperoning on her way to her Norwegian fiancé—threw their straw mattresses overboard and prepared to meet the immigration officials at Castle Garden. If no unexpected problems developed there, they would proceed to Anna's fiancé in Manhattan and then take the ferry to Brooklyn, where they would celebrate their arrival with Gabriel Ueland, a Norwegian friend who had promised to let the men stay with him until they found work. Ueland had emigrated from the youths' hometown the year before and was doing well, according to his letters home.[49]

As it turned out, the Castle Garden authorities had no objections to their health or papers. Still, it was getting dark by the time the four got through the endless lines of immigrants and took the elevated to meet Anna's fiancé. Finding Gabriel Ueland's house in Red Hook was difficult, and when they finally got there, he was not at home. After waiting as long as they could, two of the men, Anna, and her fiancé returned to New York, leaving the last member of the group, Theodore Kartevold, sitting on the stoop of the tenement in Columbia Steet. Some time later, after having searched for his friends in vain at Castle Garden, Gabriel returned and found Theodore outside, asleep.

The three friends had had much to talk about that day. The men were well acquainted from the voyage and from growing up together in Sandnes in southwestern Norway, where all three had studied watchmaking. Now the dreams of using their training at jobs in New York or Brooklyn would soon become reality. Gabriel could help, since he was already employed as a watch and instrument maker in lower Manhattan. Anna and her fiancé, Ricard Thomsen, could at last make definite plans for beginning married life together. When Gabriel awakened Theodore, the two probably stayed up discussing the events of that first day in America, the voyage, and plans for the future.

Within a month, all three male newcomers had found work in Manhattan. Theodore, who had decided to split the rent on Columbia Street with Gabriel, took the Hamilton Avenue Ferry across the East River each day and then rode north on the elevated to 75th Street, to a watch and jewelry store near the outskirts of town. When he got his second paycheck, Theodore gloated that he had already earned nearly $14 and had not touched the two twenty-dollar bills and 11 *kroner* in gold that he came with, because Gabriel had lent him money. During the following months, he and the others watched each other's careers closely, keeping tabs on how much each earned, how each liked his boss, and what they might all learn from the experiences of old friends like Gabriel and new Norwegian acquaintances.

One man in the original group of four, Johan Johnsen, disliked his job, and even worse, began to drink. Theodore knew what that could lead to from having watched the other apprentice in his father's watchmaker's shop. Gabriel, Johan, and Theodore had attended the Scandinavian Good Templars' meetings in Red Hook together and had pledged total abstinence. Sometime during the months after Johan broke his resolve, he left the city and found work with the Waltham Watch Company in Boston. Theodore remained faithful, both to his pledge and to his job far uptown, even though he disliked commuting so far and did not get as many or as large raises as Gabriel and some other friends.

Finally, in early 1882, Theodore got the opportunity on which he based his career for the rest of the decade. The Swedish manager of a fine jewelry store in downtown Manhattan had to resign because of sickness, and Theodore got the job. Within a few weeks he was earning enough money to pay off his debts, send some money home to Sandnes, and think of saving hundreds of dollars instead of one or five. By May of 1885, he had sent his parents $5,000. In January of the next year, he rented his own apartment, since neither he nor Gabriel needed to save money by sharing rooms. In 1888, he went home for a visit as a successful man. On his return, he opened his own watch and jewelry store at 61 Hamilton Avenue, in the middle of the Norwegian business district, where he shared a lease with Johan G. Normann, a Norwegian tobacconist who was prominent in Red Hook's Scandinavian Good Templars' Lodge.

For three men whose stories illustrate the variety of career paths available for mariners in the 1880s, earlier experiences at sea and in Norway were decisive. Simon Flood's father, a parish minister near a fjord in southeastern Norway, sent him to sea after his confirmation in the mid-1850s to improve his health. Simon prospered and rose from cabin boy to captain by the 1870s, when he went on land in Skien, the nearest seaport to his home parish, and became first a shipbroker and then the city's harbormaster. In 1880, when he was forty-one, Flood came to New York as the general agent for southeastern Norway's maritime insurance companies. With him were his wife, children, and two maiden sisters, all of whom he installed in a single-family house on First Place, one of Red Hook's best inland residential streets. By the late 1880s, he and his sisters served on the executive boards of some of the colony's first institutions and were well known for their charity work among its poor immigrants.[50]

Gabriel Fedde arrived in the same year as Simon Flood, but he was somewhat younger at thirty-seven and not nearly as well connected. On the other hand, his situation was much superior to that of most immigrants because he too had risen to become a ship's captain in Norway. He had also owned shares in vessels that he captained and, before going to sea, had taught school and attended a seminary. After a shipwreck in which he lost much of his capital, he worked for a year and a half as first mate on a ship that regularly sailed to New York but was dissatisfied with his lower status and began to think about seizing better opportunities in America.[51]

Upon learning of Fedde's restless dreams when the ship docked in Brooklyn in 1880, the captain of the vessel suggested they should both immigrate and develop a Norwegian branch of the ship chandlery the captain used there. Fedde had only limited confidence in the plan, because half a dozen Norwegian ship chandlers already competed for that market, but when the ship left for Norway in early 1881, he stayed in Brooklyn. The captain promised to bring his part of the venture capital and Fedde's wife and two sons on his return in the late spring. In the meantime, Fedde asked his wife to liquidate their assets in Norway and have one of Arendal's largest banks send the proceeds to him through a shipbroker in New York. He had saved about $2,000, and his wife added $350 to that after she had paid their debts and sold their home and its contents.

The captain kept his promises but proved to be a poor business partner. When the chandlery was nearly bankrupt in 1882, Fedde sold it to the captain at a loss and started on his own, this time in a storefront in New York, which his wife and sons managed while he went from pier to pier convincing captains to give him their patronage. Gradually, the family built a good reputation for the business, and profits increased. In 1885, the Feddes bought a house and grocery store on 60th Street in Brooklyn. From then on, Mrs. Fedde and the boys kept the store, while Gabriel ran the chandlery. During the rest of the decade, Gabriel helped build the meeting house in Bath Beach Junction and simultaneously became a pillar of the Seamen's Church in Red Hook.

Magnus Andersen's early career was both more typical for most Norwegian seamen and unusually colorful when it deviated from the commonplace. After attending school until his confirmation in 1871 and serving as a domestic servant for about a year—both at his mother's insistence—he satisfied his own inclinations and went to sea as his father had before him. Convinced that neither his teacher nor the chief servant had treated him fairly, he resolved to enjoy the freedom of the seas. During the next eleven years, he followed the developing course of Norwegian shipping and the typical pattern of a seaman gaining deep-sea experience. He sailed first on Norwegian ships between his homeland and European harbors, then on European vessels between Europe and American ports, and finally, as part of the American merchant marine, between American and Asian ports. Like many other sailors, he found that he had to claim a New York address in 1883 and then a birthplace in the United States in 1886 in order to hire on American vessels. At the encouragement of captains who needed experienced officers, he thus became, at least in the harbor records, a resident of Red Hook from Chicago.[52]

Andersen, however, was unusually ambitious, and it frustrated him deeply that he never rose above first mate. For reasons that he could never quite fathom, he irritated some captains as much as he had earlier antagonized his superiors at home in Norway. Many others had no doubt had the same feeling of being held down, but Anderson decided to attempt a daring feat that would guarantee further advancement. He had noticed that the lifeboats on many deep-water vessels were usually quite seaworthy but were just as often used for storing potatoes and fresh vegetables, so that ships might sink before they could be emptied and put to sea. He also reacted against the fact that seamen doubted the dependability of these boats, because often, even on three-year-long voyages, there was not a single lifeboat drill.[53]

With these observations and his hopes of becoming a captain in mind, Andersen decided to sail with a friend from Arendal to New

York in an open lifeboat that he christened the "Ocean." In spite of a collision and two capsizings, Andersen's well-publicized heroism brought him within 375 miles of the coast of Newfoundland. When he returned to New York from Norway in 1887, he found that seamen in Red Hook well remembered his earlier derring-do. That made him popular as a speaker in the colony, but to his disgust, it brought no immediate offer of a captaincy.[54]

When Andersen settled temporarily in Red Hook in 1887 because of an offer to become the first manager of the Scandinavian Sailors' Temperance Home—or Norwegian Seamen's Home, as it was popularly known—he found the job more difficult than he had imagined. The main reason for concern was that a large part of Manhattan's sailortown had moved to Brooklyn during the 1880s. Not only the Norwegian fleet but the majority of all vessels in the bulk cargo trade docked at the ship basins and piers surrounding Red Hook. Many of the boardinghouse owners, saloon and dance hall keepers, brothel madams, crimps, and runners who had fleeced seamen in the South Street Seaport area had therefore begun to do business on Hamilton Avenue and its side streets. Norwegian crewmen could now patronize Scandinavian establishments they remembered from days ashore in lower Manhattan. Stavanger-Larsen's house and runners, Albert Nilsen's saloon and boardinghouse, and Olsen the Swede's crimping operation were now just blocks from the Atlantic and Erie Basins.[55]

Opportunities for profiting from the visiting fleets even attracted Norwegian immigrants with experience from the old country's sailortowns. In 1887, when the Norwegian seamen's pastor wanted to rent the building next to the Seamen's Church, he discovered that a recently arrived couple from Kristiansand were running a clandestine bar and brothel there to profit from their apartment's proximity to the church. Further investigation revealed that they had had the same line of work in Norway and had come to Red Hook after hearing about its sailortown from their clients. At about the same time, New York's Boardingmasters' and Shippingmasters' Union, which coordinated crimping operations for the whole harbor, had its headquarters in Red Hook. If colony residents called Columbia Avenue "Norwegian Broadway," many more people knew Hamilton Avenue as "Sin City."[56]

## Promising Possibilities and Variable Fates

The transfer of the city's main dock area from Manhattan was undoubtedly decisive for the growth of the Red Hook-Gowanus colony, whose economy rested equally as much on maritime activity as the Manhattan colony's had earlier. Most of the new arrivals—whether they came from New York, immigrant vessels, or the visiting Norwegian fleet—crowded into the cheap housing near the ship basins in the Red Hook-Gowanus district. Although it was a low-lying, unhealthy area notorious for its shabby tenement houses and high crime rate, it offered newcomers from Norway the best opportunities for success in the metropolitan area. If living conditions were poor, employment prospects were good. Despite local and national economic fluctuations, work remained plentiful for both skilled and unskilled because of the city's tremendous growth. Even after the turn of the century, the city remained the preeminent Atlantic freight depot, receiving the cargo of nearly four thousand ships annually. Between 1881 and 1885 alone, the housing built was "the equivalent of a city larger than Albany."[57]

Work was available in Brooklyn. However, R. S. N. Sartz, a Norwegian employed at Castle Garden in the 1880s, learned from years of experience that certain categories of his countrymen were among the least likely to find or keep jobs. Greenhorns who had occupational training, some savings, and connections in the colony could expect employment, although their wages would probably be low until they learned the language and American work habits. Worse off were those, such as students, who arrived with no salable trade. Sartz found many unsuccessful immigrants in this group.[58]

Still more pathetic were the Norwegians who came as impoverished steerage passengers. Without money to travel farther inland, many of these people completely lost their sense of purpose. Sartz later commented, "Some of these quickly disappeared, while others reappeared at Castle Garden in the course of the year following to get a free meal or other assistance. Their chief wish was to return to Norway, even if they had to arrive penniless. Returning home, however, proved impossible, and it seems likely that most of them died in poverty and were buried in unmarked graves on potter's field." The thousands of seamen preyed upon in sailortown and the poor or untrained immigrants who arrived in the fleet's wake created the necessary preconditions for the rise of Norwegian institutions in Red Hook and Gowanus. As the following chapter shows, between 1863 and 1889 most organized activity for Norwegians in Brooklyn aimed to offer assistance to transient sailors rather than to immigrants.

# 5

# Saving Seamen in Babylon:
## The First Institutions in Brooklyn's Norwegian Colony

Religious organizations' concern for the spiritual and physical welfare of temporarily resident seamen prompted the beginning of Norwegian and Norwegian-American institutions in the Red Hook section of Brooklyn. The essential fact of the colony's early history was that the number of transient or sojourning mariners greatly exceeded the settled Norwegian population. That reality had far-reaching consequences. Charitable impulses directed toward an exploited and morally wayward occupational group motivated the Methodists and Lutherans who were responsible for starting the first Norwegian institutions. Immigrants were not, initially at least, a part of the organizers' plans. Even when the Swedish–Norwegian consul, his wife, and other affluent members of the Manhattan colony showered largesse on Norwegians in Red Hook for less than purely religious reasons, they chose to work through religious institutions established wholly or partially to serve Norway's merchant fleet. Settlers often felt tolerated only because they assisted in the work of serving the transient merchant marine or because they realized that financial support for meeting their own needs depended on a willingness to take responsibility for seamen's problems as well.

**The Consequences of Putting Sailors First, 1863–1889**

Starting community life with religious institutions for transient seamen also resulted in sectarian rivalry that started early and assumed a special intensity. Methodist efforts to convert Norway's maritime crews seemed particularly galling to Norwegian churchmen because the sailors were not immigrants but countrymen temporarily in Brooklyn because of their occupation. Whether based in Norway or in the Midwest, Norwegian Lutheran clergymen then included exposure to the false teachings of "sects" such as Methodism—along with drinking and loose living—among the evils to which seamen in particular were vulnerable because they frequented the worst districts of the modern Babylon, the world's seaport cities.[1]

In port, men faced the temptation to desert not only their ships but the home country's state church. Because Norway was officially and overwhelmingly a Lutheran nation, seamen who converted seemed to have lost an important part of their cultural heritage. Mariners, moreover, brought the influence of foreign sects home with them. Methodism had established its first congregation in Norway through the efforts of a sailor proselytized in New York.[2] Norwegian Lutherans' linking of religion and national identity cut them off from the assistance some countrymen received from Americans by joining the Methodists. This fusing of patriotism and faith was, however, also a great source of strength. It not only reinforced the will to preserve cultural coherence, but also, by giving their institutions the atmosphere of genuine bits of the old country in the New World, attracted the large majority of the colony's newcomers. The battle against Methodism gave the Lutheran leaders who established and administered organizations in Red Hook a more intense sense of mission.

Having to depend on assistance from outsiders was yet another consequence of the unusual demographic characteristics of the city's Norwegians. Typically, the founders of the colony's first institutions were neither local immigrants nor transient seamen but emissaries from organizations in Norway, Manhattan, or the Midwest who came because Norwegian seamen in the city seemed unable to help themselves. Red Hook settlers were usually not even the people who had called attention to the sailors' plight. Midwestern and Manhattan Norwegians, better established and in possession of more influential contacts, did that and also helped the emissaries mobilize the resources necessary for bringing plans to fruition.

The first conspicuous local leaders were sojourners who arrived in the city with an assignment to complete. They therefore relied on the ready-made institutional models of the mother organizations they represented and established "transplanted" branches of them. The need to adjust these predetermined models to local conditions presented sojourning emissaries with their greatest challenge, especially since they were usually greenhorns in the city themselves. In such a situation, leaders often depended on information from immigrants because of their greater familiarity with the city. On the other hand, as a temporarily resident elite, they reserved the right to interpret this information according to their own goals and were frequently privy to facts or instructions of which immigrants had no knowledge. Misunderstanding and distrust between immigrants and sojourning leaders were probably unavoidable under these circumstances. That danger increased as the settled population grew in size and found its own leaders, because the emissaries rejected the idea of giving immigrants an equal voice in institutions designed according to imported models and meant for transient seamen. Perhaps inevitably, the first stage of the colony's institutional life ended in conflicts that pitted immigrant and sojourning leaders against each other and divided the population into opposing camps.

The founding and early development of Red Hook's Norwegian Seamen's Church amply illustrate the consequences of putting transient seamen's interests before immigrants'. By the late 1880s, the Seamen's Church had been instrumental in founding a second transplanted institution, had aligned itself with the economic groups that depended on a reliable source of marine manpower in the port, and simultaneously had become dependent on the settlers' financial contributions. This was the quandary all contemporary and future sojourning leaders faced, and these were the conditions against which the immigrants eventually rebelled.

The first organized activity among Norwegians in Brooklyn began in 1863 when Ole Helland, a sailor turned teetotalist preacher, inaugurated a five-year series of Methodist revival meetings for Norwegian seamen near the Atlantic docks. Support from American and Scandinavian institutions outside the city made Helland's temperance campaign and Norwegian-language sermons possible. Both the American Seamen's Friends Society and the City Tract Society in Manhattan employed him as their "Norwegian Missionary among Seamen," and the Seamen's Friend Society in addition gave him the use of its Brooklyn mission hall. The floating Bethel Ship Church in Manhattan, a pan-Scandinavian congregation sponsored by New York State's Methodist Conference, supplied Helland with its spiritual and institutional backing by promoting his Brooklyn waterfront work and allowing him to preach to its own seafaring congregation. Thus, the primary force behind the beginning of organized activity among Norwegians was the belief of outside groups that the tenets of Christian evangelism and temperance would more quickly change the hearts of seamen if these were promulgated in their mother tongue.[3]

At the time, Helland could hardly have launched and sustained Brooklyn's first Norwegian institution without outside assistance. Fewer than 200 Norwegians lived in the city, according to the state census of 1865, and since no local associations appeared until a decade later, immigrants who wanted to participate in Norwegian activities traveled to

**The Beginning: Manhattan Methodists and the Norwegian Merchant Marine**

the Manhattan colony. Building on an audience of newcomers temporarily in New York was also unpromising, because more than 90 percent of Norwegian immigrants entered the United States via Quebec until 1870.[4] In short, Helland had to have financial and organizational aid from Americans and Scandinavians in Manhattan because his only large audience in Brooklyn consisted of transient Norwegian seamen.

In the 1860s, Brooklyn's Norwegian maritime population consisted mainly of two groups, those working on American ships and those arriving on Norwegian vessels. According to Knut Gjerset's *Norwegian Sailors in American Waters*, the number of the country's men in the United States merchant marine increased rapidly during the 1850s and the Civil War. These men were transient in a double sense. Not only did they spend most of their time at sea, but they also often left American ships for other nations' vessels when it suited them, especially if they longed for a visit home.[5]

The great change during the early 1860s, however, was the rapid increase in the number of seamen entering the harbor under the Norwegian flag. Norway's shipping industry experienced the first brief surge in its carrying trade with New York between 1860 and 1863, when it joined other maritime nations in supplying both imported goods to the Union and bottoms for exporting grain and petroleum from the city during the Civil War. The visiting Norwegian fleet expanded from twenty-six ships at the war's start to 108 in 1863, and then plummeted back to twenty-two in 1865. In short, Helland and his supporters showed perfect timing when they started revival meetings for Norwegian seamen in the middle of the war. Their choice of location was also auspicious, since most incoming Norwegian crews touched land at the Atlantic Basin at the northern end of Red Hook, only minutes from the Seamen's Friend Society mission hall.[6]

**The First Immigrant Institution: the Bethelship Norwegian Methodist Church**

The number of Norwegian sailors and immigrants arriving in the harbor steadily increased during the early 1870s, but the settlers who established the colony's first immigrant institution also depended on support from American and Scandinavian groups outside the city. The circumstances surrounding the founding of the Bethelship Norwegian Methodist Church illustrate both that fact and the settlers' close connections to seamen's missions. Again, American Methodists' long-standing support bore fruit. By 1874, Manhattan's Bethel Ship congregation contained significant numbers of Norwegian immigrants, and a small group of these had moved to Old South Brooklyn, where they wanted to start their own church.[7]

Lacking funds to rent a hall, they met in a private home and wrote a letter to a Norwegian sailor who had occasionally preached on the older shipboard church. This man, Ole Peter Petersen, seemed likely to be a good advisor because after leaving the Bethel Ship he had organized at least three Norwegian Methodist churches, among them the

Docked until 1876 on the Hudson River side of Manhattan, the floating
Methodist mission church for seamen, the Bethel Ship *John Wesley*, played a
central role as a site of religious conversion for Scandinavian sailors. A. N. Rygg's
*Norwegians in New York, 1825–1925*.

first established in Norway. Petersen now moved to South Brooklyn and
helped the immigrants organize the Bethelship Norwegian Methodist
Church, which was conceived as a land-based daughter congregation to
the original Bethel Ship. For two years, the group's financial need forced
it to hold services in the home where the first planning meeting had
been held. Only during its third year could the congregation scrape together enough money to rent a store-front church near the Hamilton
Avenue ferry.

During the later 1870s, however, the economic situation improved
rapidly. Finally recognizing that Norwegian crews which docked in Red
Hook constituted the majority of transient Scandinavian seamen in
port, the Bethel Ship's leaders offered the young church both the ship
and responsibility for the Methodists' waterfront work. Since most of
the new congregation consisted of settled seamen and their families, it is
not surprising that they accepted the offer and, in 1876, towed the ship
around the tip of Manhattan and anchored it near the northern end of
the Red Hook peninsula.

As might be expected, membership grew more rapidly, since the congregation now operated out of two locations. No one guessed, however, that when even more space was needed, a wealthy American co-religionist would donate a church building—not once but twice by the early 1880s. By 1887 the Norwegian Lutheran seamen's pastor complained bitterly that not more than ten minutes away from his own economically strapped mission were a crowd of Methodists who offered "spiritual sweets and sugar candy" and had the temerity to call themselves the "Norwegian Seamen's Church," even though they had "American gold, . . . agents for the Bible Society and so on" to back them.[8]

## The First Lutheran Institution: The Brooklyn Station of the Norwegian Seamen's Mission

Partly motivated by the fear that Norwegians across the East River were being lost to Methodism, Manhattan colony Lutherans began investigating ways to start religious services in Brooklyn too. By the mid-1860s the first minister at Our Savior's Norwegian Lutheran Church in Manhattan, Ole Juul, felt that the Methodists had already got the upper hand in Brooklyn.[9] Despite the motivation of fighting aggressive Methodist proselytizing, Lutherans experienced more economic difficulties than the Methodists did in getting started. The main obstacle was their self-consciously ethnic view of religion. Norway's state-church Lutheranism seemed to them the only brand of Christianity that was genuinely Norwegian. In Manhattan, as in many other areas of Nordic settlement, even Scandinavian Lutheranism had been acceptable only until Swedish and Norwegian immigrants were sufficiently numerous to form separate congregations. In reaction to the Methodist offensive, Pastor Juul and his successors at Our Savior's reinforced their followers' ethnic exclusiveness, citing the "apostolic admonition" against "deserting your own faith for another" and warning that countrymen who converted to other denominations committed a sin. Under these circumstances, Manhattan Lutherans were very reluctant to accept economic or spiritual support from other denominations—or even from other varieties of Lutheranism—for fear of betraying both their faith and their national heritage.[10]

Since the permanently resident Norwegian-American population on the east coast was relatively small and comparatively poor in the 1860s and 1870s, Lutherans had to look for aid in the Norwegian Midwest and the old country. That required both careful negotiation and considerable time, primarily because the New York area contained only a few hundred Norwegian immigrants but thousands of the homeland's transient sailors. The Midwest's Norwegian Synod, many of whose pastors had been trained by Norway's state church, saw its primary duty as helping to set up congregations for settled immigrants. When Synod officials stopped in New York on their way to conferences in Norway, they responded to calls for Lutheran services in Manhattan by attempting to organize the local congregation that in time became Our Savior's.[11]

The puzzling difficulty was that the congregation more or less dissolved between their visits. For example, when Herman A. Preus, president of the Synod, made efforts to stabilize the congregation during 1865, he came to believe local leaders' estimates that the city contained between ten and thirty thousand Scandinavian residents. Yet the congregation established only a year earlier by another Synod official had become completely inactive. On his lecture tour in Norway two years later, Preus offered several plausible explanations for the decay of the New York church—the lack of a minister to lead the congregation because of the shortage of ministers in the Midwest, his belief that the city's Scandinavians did not live in a cohesive colony, and the common rural view that New York was a sinful Babylon of materialism and false prophets.[12]

Ironically, Preus emphasized the "great number of Norwegian seamen who often resided in the city" but never realized that these men largely accounted for the impression of a considerable settled Scandinavian population there. Perhaps he underestimated the size of the visiting merchant marine because he did not feel primarily responsible for transient sailors. His purpose in drawing attention to their presence in the city was to awaken the conscience of religious organizations in Norway. As he pointed out, the "majority" of these seamen "cannot be considered as Scandinavian immigrants to New York, among whom we [the Synod] usually work. . . . but . . . are resident in and belonging in Norway and only temporary guests in New York."[13] The Synod felt that these Norwegian nationals were more properly ministered to by the Society for the Preaching of the Gospel to Scandinavian Seamen in Foreign Ports (popularly known as the Norwegian Seamen's Mission), which had its headquarters in Bergen, Norway. In 1867 the Synod sent Pastor Juul to the newly rejuvenated congregation in Manhattan with instructions to serve immigrants in the general metropolitan area. At the same time, Preus appealed to the society in Bergen to care for the religious needs of transient seamen.[14]

During the 1860s, President Preus, his predecessor Hans A. Stub, east coast Lutheran ministers, and even ship captains pleaded with the Seamen's Mission to establish a branch "station" in Brooklyn. The mission, however, did not want to be seen as encouraging emigration by giving assistance to Norwegian-American religious organizations, especially when the rising number of departures for the United States was causing anti-emigration feeling in Norway. Established only in 1864, the Seamen's Mission was also wary of draining its limited financial resources by beginning transatlantic operations so early. As a result, it considered the matter for three years before reaching a "temporary" arrangement with the Synod in 1868. From that time on each paid half of Juul's salary, so that he henceforth split his ministry between immigrants in Manhattan and transient crews in the harbor. In 1873 Juul received part-time help in contacting seamen through a similar arrangement. The Mission paid a man as the "seamen's pastor's assistant" to board ships and hand out tracts and announcements of church services, while the Synod gave the same man a salary as its emigrant missionary at Castle Garden.[15]

Near the end of 1876 the second immigrant minister cum seamen's pastor, the Reverend C. S. Everson, elicited the help of the Swedish-Norwegian Consul in New York to start evening services for seamen in South Brooklyn. The consul willingly took responsibility for collecting money from captains and crews to pay for renting a hall and the pastor's increased expenses, but he was dissatisfied with the overall situation. Within days of receiving the pastor's report on the new meeting place in January of 1877, the mission's executive board got a letter from the consul which expressed doubt that Everson could manage work with seamen in Brooklyn as well as his responsibilities to congregations in both Manhattan and Perth Amboy, New Jersey. At the same time, however, the consul begged the mission to give Everson a pay raise so that the important work in Brooklyn could continue. The minister took on so many duties, the consul said, simply because that was the only way he could support his family.[16]

Evidently this situation finally convinced the mission that it could not serve seamen's needs adequately by employing a poorly paid, part-time pastor and assistant. In July of 1878, it officially opened a local branch, the Brooklyn "station," with a full-time seamen's pastor, Ole Asperheim, and Everson henceforth ministered only to his immigrant congregations. Pastor Asperheim, who came to America soon after his ordination in 1872, ministered to a Norwegian Synod congregation in Wisconsin and taught theology at Synod seminaries before answering the call to Brooklyn. Asperheim at once began holding almost daily services a few blocks away from the Methodist Bethelship Church in Red Hook. It was natural that the new pastor should refer repeatedly to the uphill battle he was fighting against the entrenched competition.[17] The Methodists had been preaching to incoming crews in the area for fifteen years. By the time the Brooklyn station got properly under way, Norwegian shipping in the Red Hook-Gowanus area had almost reached its nineteenth-century peak. It had taken over a decade of negotiations involving sea captains, local ministers, the consul, and Synod presidents to transplant the first Norwegian institution to Red Hook.

**The Benefits
and Trials
of the First
Transplanted
Norwegian
Institution**

Once the period of delays and part-time pastors was over, the Seamen's Mission quickly began to master the inter-denominational struggle. There were more than enough Norwegian seamen in town to keep both Methodists and Lutherans busy, but the newer institution had qualities that were especially attractive to practicing Norwegian Christians. The obvious reason for its almost immediate success was that the vast majority of transient seamen had been brought up in Norway's state church. If these men were churchgoers at all, their first reaction would be to attend Lutheran services. The Brooklyn station, moreover, could justifiably claim to be genuinely Norwegian, not Norwegian American. Its pastor was an emissary from an organization in the home country that viewed itself as a branch of the Norwegian state church. As Roald Kverndal, a later seamen's pastor and mission historian, wrote in his lengthy essay on the founding of the Brooklyn station, "The seamen's church was literally an outpost of the Norwegian Church, and for many the most genuine manifestation of Norway in New York."[18]

Local circumstances and the focus on a single occupational group necessarily introduced deviations from practices in Norway, but from the start Brooklyn's Norwegian Seamen's Church self-consciously attempted to make the most of its national character. Pastor Ole Asperheim noticed almost immediately that most seamen cared little for the doctrinal differences between Lutheranism and Methodism, which they felt only led to empty sectarian conflict. The attraction of Methodism lay in its enthusiastic, lively services and its concern for the emotional involvement of the individual, noted Asperheim. Since Norway's state church rejected that kind of low-church evangelism, the Lutheran station's most attractive quality, at least initially, was its genuine old-country style. It was therefore important to reproduce state-church customs and stress the strengthening of ties to home, family, and the parish church. In sermons and individual counseling, for example, Asperheim and his successors made as much as possible of mothers in Norway pining for their absent sons and praying that they would not be led astray. Within months of locating in Red Hook Asperheim also opened a reading room, where sailors could read Norwegian books and newspapers but, more significantly, where they could write and assure families at home of their well-being.[19]

Luckily, the Seamen's Mission was blessed with an eager and impulsive man as its first full-time pastor. During his two years in Red Hook, Asperheim saw needs so pressing that he acted first and explained to the home office in Bergen later. When he began church services in the summer of 1878, he was unfamiliar with the city, had no assistant, and preached in the room rented by the last part-time pastor, which was furnished as a bank and so poorly ventilated that the heat drove away his audience. Asperheim quickly chose his own assistant, deciding the man's pay and duties on his own, and accepted the suggestion of a committee of captains to initiate a building fund for a new church. In his first report, he happily told of these developments, included copies of the fund-raising circulars sent to vessels in the harbor and shipping centers in south and southwestern Norway, and asked for higher wages because of the high cost of living in the city.[20]

The home office's reply was clearly an attempt to put Asperheim in his place. The executive board accepted the hiring of an assistant but informed Asperheim that he would have to abandon the fund-raising campaign as "highly inadvisable . . . for the time being." The chastened pastor apologized abjectly in his next report for causing the board's displeasure, confessing that he had "incompletely understood the relationship between individual missions and the executive board."[21] Within a few months, however, he had found another way to get his church building and a convincing reason to worry less about incurring the anger of the home office. Having noticed that an American Methodist church midway between the Atlantic and Erie Basins would soon be sold at auction, Asperheim checked on the probable price and purchase conditions at the local bank holding a loan on the property. He then enlisted the help of a Norwegian captain to arrange a new fund-raising plan and negotiate low-interest financing through the captain's usual ship broker in Manhattan, who represented shipowners in Norway.[22]

Confident of having met objections to the expenditure of the mission's funds, Asperheim next secured Consul Christian Børs's cooperation. Børs not only agreed to administer the solicitation of money from ships in the harbor but also advised the pastor to buy the building without permission from Bergen if that proved necessary—which it shortly thereafter did. Asperheim's painstaking preparation had the desired effect. By early 1879, he had not only obtained the church but felt sufficiently confident of his position with the board to announce casually that he had also acquired a parsonage and would be grateful for funds to purchase yet another building. At the same time, however, he remarked that one "disadvantage" of working so far from the home office was the necessity of acting independently. Still, if the board would not supply his economic needs, he had other resources.[23]

The Brooklyn Seamen's Church now had its own board of trustees consisting of the consul, a Norwegian ship broker in Manhattan, and an immigrant ship's chandler from Red Hook. With their business contacts these men could arrange fund-raising or additional loans, should that prove necessary. Visiting Norwegian captains and crews now contributed the money needed to pay for the church's daily expenses as well as for the refurbishing of its newly purchased facilities. The station had even managed to get on its feet economically without help from other Scandinavian groups. Asperheim therefore thought the church should be called "Norwegian," even though as the only Nordic seamen's mission in the port it would serve sailors from the other Scandinavian countries as well.

In view of the station's later history, the long-range importance of Asperheim's actions was the precedent he set by turning to nonreligious groups for support. Norwegian shipping interests would follow the example of that first ship broker and feel a proprietary interest in the station they helped sustain—just as their colleagues did when they assisted the home office of the Mission in Norway. The seamen's church was an important ally that helped maintain a reliable work force. Without prompting from the men's employers in Norway, Asperheim and later pastors spoke out against desertion and drinking. The station's emphasis on reinforcing the men's emotional ties to the old country also exerted a powerful if indirect pressure against desertion, emigration, and forms of behavior that were unacceptable by community standards at home.[24]

It would be a mistake, however, to view the Seamen's Church as merely an unconscious tool of employers. From the beginning, the pastors were responsive to the needs seamen expressed. Once captains and crews regularly contributed to the church's upkeep, moreover, they felt they had a right to have a say in the planning of its activities. Within broadly tolerant limits the pastors introduced many programs for the men in the coming years, in part because they genuinely wanted to be of service but also because what pleased seamen also brought them to the church. The station soon functioned as an informal post office, a place to meet prospective employers, and a storeroom for sea chests.[25]

Sailors' requests also led to religious innovations. The seamen's pastors eagerly encouraged the repeated religious awakenings that swept the Norwegian fleet during the last third of the century, even if that meant departing from standard state-church practices. For example, informal evening discussion groups centering on seamen's conversion experiences were among the first innovations of Asperheim's term of service, although he realized that the religious testimonials he heard had probably been originally inspired by Methodist revival meetings. The discussion groups were not his idea, but men asked for them and he thought he could better counter Methodism's false teachings by confronting them than by ignoring them.[26]

Seamen's pastors' views often coincided with those of the owners, especially where seamen's leisure-time behavior was concerned. On the other hand, the pastors' primary goal was always saving souls. If sailors preferred the more personal and emotional atmosphere of other denominations, the pastors were willing to eliminate the outward practices that seemed overly formal or high-church, as long as they felt sure the theology expressed conformed to orthodox state-church Lutheranism. The Norwegian clerics who served the Seamen's Mission were undoubtedly more adventurous and evangelical than the majority of state-church ministers. They had, after all, chosen to accept positions in the unsavory harbor districts of foreign cities instead of comfortable congregations in familiar surroundings. Most made that decision soon after being ordained in Norway, and their youth, combined with the secure feeling that they represented the most recent opinions of the Norwegian church, made them boldly innovative. By the late 1880s, Pastor Everson and congregational leaders at Our Savior's were claiming that the willingness of seamen's pastors to accommodate mariners' wishes had made the Seamen's Church seem more Methodist than Lutheran.[27]

The station's first board of trustees, originally formed to satisfy a New York State law requiring witnesses for the purchase of property and the incorporation of social institutions, represented the business groups that had the strongest vested interest in the prosperity of Norwegian shipping in the harbor. The primary purpose of Swedish-Norwegian consulates in foreign cities was to enhance the home countries' economic interests. In New York, the consul, always a Norwegian after the 1860s, served mainly to aid Norwegian shipping by supplying information on fluctuating freight rates and settling labor problems between captains and crews. The ship broker on the board, the Norwegian partner in the firm of Boyesen and Benham, like the consul, depended for his position on good relations with the homeland's shipping industry. Both these men were emissaries from Norway, the one from the government and the other from shipping interests. As long as their terms of service lasted, they had their residences and offices in New York, where they formed part of the Manhattan colony's socio-economic elite. Only the board's ship's chandler lived in Red Hook and stood for the younger colony's immigrant point of view.[28]

## The Relationship of the Seamen's Church to Settled Immigrants in Red Hook

In the 1870s and 1880s the seamen's pastors were little preoccupied with the long-term ramifications of the means by which the station obtained its buildings. Instead, they were attempting to deal with a problem brought on by being located not only within walking distance of the docks, but also in the middle of the emerging Red Hook immigrant colony. Asperheim's intense campaign to secure attractive buildings with a genuinely Norwegian atmosphere drew large numbers of seamen, as he had hoped. On the other hand, both Asperheim and his successor, Andreas Mortensen, quickly became worried about the problem of the settled Norwegian Americans' relationship to the church. At first writing, for example, Mortensen remarked that the church was rapidly becoming a common "gathering place" that attracted "a lot of Norwegians sailing with the Americans or temporarily resident on land." He also reported performing three weddings, two baptisms, and two confirmations—none of them for seamen.[29]

The dilemma facing the first seamen's pastors resulted from the special character of the Red Hook colony. On the one hand, they had clear instructions from the Seamen's Mission in Bergen. Stations were to serve resident Norwegians only if and when their duties to transient seamen had been fulfilled. On the other hand, the situation in Brooklyn was significantly different from that at other stations. Whereas most other ports had a tiny Norwegian settlement, which usually included at least one or two well-to-do merchants, Red Hook contained large numbers of settlers, none of whom was well-off.

Yet the pastors found it impossible to isolate themselves and the Seamen's Church from the resident population. Refusing needy countrymen aid went against the pastors' charitable orientation and religious scruples. Placidly watching settlers turn to other denominations was intolerable. Worst of all, who was to say where to draw the line between transient seamen and residents in a place where men frequently redefined their status? Some sailors deserted and decided to settle one day and returned to the Norwegian merchant marine the next. Others never left the home country's vessels but shipped out of the harbor for so many years that they established homes and families there while maintaining that they had no intention of immigrating. Because of the unique importance of the Port of New York for Norway's shipping industry and the overwhelming popularity of the United States as a destination for Norwegian emigrants, no other city in the world contained so large a maritime colony with such a wide range of gradations between transient Norwegian seamen and permanently resident immigrants.[30]

The dynamics of the relationship between the Brooklyn station and the settled Norwegians attending the church varied with the personalities involved and changing economic conditions. With his talent for meeting problems head-on, Asperheim used his reports to define the station's special circumstances regarding the immigrants and describe alternative courses of action. During his first months in the city his main concerns were making the station's services well known and avoiding increased competition. In October of 1878 he recommended trying to "reach as many [immigrants] as possible through announcements in newspapers that invite them to services and so on, because in that way it will not be possible to arrange for a congregation of settlers, and so have two Norwegian [Lutheran] churches that rival the station."[31]

By March 1879, the objections of the home office and a better knowledge of his work load had prompted Asperheim to adopt new views. When the executive board reminded him of the rules contained in its statement of purpose and warned of the "riskiness of unnecessarily inviting settlers" to participate in charitable work at the church, he avowed his complete agreement. Now it was "desirable that the station's employees give Scandinavian seamen their complete and undivided attention." The board must have misunderstood his earlier report, he insisted, since the flow of Norwegian ships in and out of the harbor had proved to present rather too much than too little work for the station. Economic conditions were still good for the Norwegian merchant marine at the end of the 1870s, and a man with no previous experience would need time to comprehend the scope of the task he had assumed.[32]

In short, Asperheim appeared to have reversed his position completely. The change was only superficial, however, because he went on to undermine all his statements of agreement with the board in the remainder of his report. By the time one finishes reading it, the implied message seems to be that the board's view is correct for an ideal situation but unworkable and uncharitable in the Brooklyn station's "special circumstances." First, he noted that the Seamen's Church would continue to serve settlers who more properly should attend Our Savior's, since most immigrants resided in Red Hook while it was located in Manhattan. Then he asked how it could be possible to let Red Hook's immigrants attend services but not receive the sacraments at the station—and decided they had to be full members. Partial participation would make them "religious vagabonds" who migrated to Manhattan for the sacraments. Finally, although the seamen's pastor did not mention the fact in so many words, the "damage" was already done. His newspaper announcements and ministerial services had already assured the immigrants that they were welcome to feel at home in the Seamen's Church. Considering these special circumstances, Asperheim concluded by suggesting that the board might want to re-evaluate its decision.[33]

In his typical fashion, Asperheim had told the board what it wanted to hear and had then explained why he followed a different course of action. Until the end of the 1880s, the seamen's pastors who succeeded him used the same tactic to muddle through a situation that offered no easy solutions. Each implemented innovations as he met new conditions and simultaneously promised the home office that the influence of settled immigrants in the station would not get out of hand.

**Easing Social and Financial Ills: The Second Transplanted Institution, Bazaars, and Money from Shipping Circles**

The second seamen's pastor, Andreas Mortensen, also complained of overwork, but instead of limiting the settlers' participation at the station, concentrated on finding other means of reducing his duties. In 1882, he joined the consul's wife, Anna Børs, in initiating plans to found a relief society for transient seamen and immigrants. The society's chief purpose would be to assist countrymen who suffered from medical, social, or economic problems, but it would also relieve the seamen's pastor of handling these people's problems personally. Mrs. Børs persuaded her husband and shipping agents in Manhattan to fund the project by giving her money for its realization. The consular circle and Mortensen thus retained control of planning and financing but, to gain support from the colony, the seamen's pastor also secured cooperation from Pastor Everson at Our Savior's and some immigrant craftsmen-entrepreneurs at the Seamen's Church.[34]

As at the founding of the station itself, an elite of sojourning Norwegian nationals became the prime movers behind the establishment of an important Red Hook colony institution. Given their old-world orientation and experience in getting the Seamen's Church on its feet, it is not surprising that they conceived of the relief society as an extension of another religious charity recently started in Norway, the Deaconess Home and Hospital in Christiania. On this occasion, however, settled immigrants played a more important role. Not only was the proposed institution meant in part for their benefit, but one of them, Gabriel Fedde—the sea captain turned ship's chandler—had the personal contact necessary to bring the project to fruition. Mortensen and Mrs. Børs convinced Fedde to write his sister-in-law, a deaconess from southern Norway, and ask her to undertake relief work in Red Hook.[35]

The local leaders' idea was to offer this deaconess, Sister Elizabeth Fedde, a small monthly salary for helping sick and needy Norwegians in their homes or lodgings. In Christiania, the sisters not only provided such home assistance but also ran a hospital, where they made nursing a

• 

Sister Elizabeth Fedde, a central figure in the development of benevolent institutions among Norwegian immigrants in the United States, came to Brooklyn as a young Lutheran deaconess and, with crucial assistance from the Reverend Carsten Hansteen and Mrs. Anna Børs, founded the first Norwegian Lutheran hospital.

• 

Mrs. Anna Børs drew on her position as the wife of Sweden-Norway's Consul General to lead the work of organizing relief and health services for Norwegian immigrants and transient seamen in Brooklyn. Both photographs from *Brief History of the Deaconesses' Home and Hospital*.

"Christian work of love." In addition, they administered a deaconesses' home, where sisters lived and novices received religious and medical training. The Norwegian diaconate provided both hospital and home aid as well as schooling. Originally, Mortensen and Mrs. Børs planned for a low-cost version of deaconess work. They hoped only to bring one sister to Red Hook and pay her for providing home care. Shortly after her arrival in 1883, however, Sister Elizabeth became convinced that the extremity of the conditions she found among destitute sailors and immigrants called for a full-scale replica of the Christiania institution.[36]

The Red Hook colony presented scenes that wrenched Sister Elizabeth's heart and offended her moral sense. A starving woman from Bergen, who had just given birth to twins, sent the first plea for help. Sister Elizabeth found her living with an Irishman in the damp cellar of a shabby hut, her nakedness barely concealed by rags, her "husband" and infants nowhere to be seen. During the days and weeks that followed, she struggled to assuage the ills that befell poor immigrants and seamen in a congested dockside district. In homes, on board ships, and even in the streets, she nursed the sick or injured and fed the hungry. All the emergencies of life became her province. She consoled the dying and washed the bodies of the dead, delivered babies, and arranged christenings and funerals, comforted unwed mothers and found foster homes for abandoned children, sat with the lonely aged, lectured the drunken or shiftless, searched out employment for newcomers, and secured return tickets for countrymen with no hope of succeeding in the American city. What pride or poverty prevented seamen and immigrants from obtaining, she courageously begged from Consul and Mrs. Børs, the well-off among the Manhattan colony elite, or Norwegians in Brooklyn who had something to spare.[37]

Sister Elizabeth also took over most of the hospital visitations that had strained the seamen's pastors' schedules. Traversing the far-flung harbor, she sought out her countrymen—and Scandinavians generally—at the Emigrants' Hospital on Ward Island, the Mariners' Hospital on Staten Island, the Jersey City Hospital, and in Manhattan at Bellevue, the Maternity Hospital, and Castle Garden. Everywhere, she later wrote, "lay these poor emigrants, sick and in pain, in a foreign land with a foreign language sounding around them." More than anything else, that situation persuaded her to press the Relief Society to convert itself into a deaconesses' home and hospital.[38]

By 1885, Sister Elizabeth had convinced the Relief Society's leaders to rent a house in the Gowanus section as a nine-bed hospital and home, and had started training other deaconesses there after her application for additional sisters from the mother house in Christiania met with refusal. Nevertheless, her first novices came directly from the old country and, at least originally, did not view themselves as immigrants. In only two years, Sister Elizabeth had led the planning group to revise its original goals and establish the Red Hook colony's second transplanted institution, a small hospital and sisters' home modeled as closely as possible on the Christiania institution and staffed by sojourning deaconesses.[39]

Mortensen and Mrs. Børs encouraged the change to a Norwegian deaconesses' home and hospital but kept decisive control of developments in their own hands. The seamen's pastor served as president of the Relief Society, and the consul's wife doled out the money from Manhattan backers to Sister Elizabeth on a monthly basis.[40] Viewed in terms of the pastor's duties, the institution was a great boon. Managing monthly board meetings was much less demanding than personally dealing with the problems of the poor and the sick.

Mortensen also moved to lighten his workload in two other ways. First, he relieved himself and later pastors of the onerous duty of constant fund-raising to ensure the station's continued operation. By the early 1880s, Asperheim's financial arrangements no longer sufficed because other nations' steamships had taken over the lion's share of the grain-carrying trade, with the result that the consulate got contributions for the seaman's church from only half as many vessels. To meet daily expenses, Mortensen started the tradition of relying on immigrant women's auxiliaries that collected money through annual handicraft bazaars and volunteered their time and homemade dishes for seamen's social events. By the mid-1880s, funds raised from the immigrant colony accounted for 40 percent of the station's income, and three quarters of that money came from the women's efforts.[41] Support from the immigrants thus became essential for the church's daily operation even though they remained too poor to solve its larger financial difficulties.

By 1882, meeting loan payments on the station's buildings had become a more serious and increasingly time-consuming problem for Mortensen. By informing Consul Børs and the home office that the station's debt crisis might force it to close its doors, he mobilized the affluent economic groups most interested in the station's survival. At Mortensen's urging, the home office conducted a fund-raising campaign that netted over $1,000 from shipping circles in Norway. As treasurer on the board of trustees, Børs used his personal influence with the ship broker holding the church mortgage to get half the loan canceled and then paid off the rest by donating $500 himself and soliciting larger sums from other ship brokers.[42] The economic importance of the immigrant community paled when compared with such largesse, and therefore its influence on decisions at the station during the financial crisis was limited.

The second way Mortensen lightened his duties was by insisting that the home office enlarge the station's staff. In spite of the falling number of Norwegian ships entering the port, he persuaded the mission to send another pastor to assist him. He and Carsten Hansteen, the new "junior" pastor, split the duties one man had done alone before. Hansteen also became a member of the Relief Society's board and thus strengthened the station's representation there.[43] When Mortensen returned to Norway in 1885, Hansteen took over a station relieved of social work, unencumbered by debt, and assisted by another junior pastor.

Two of the early seamen's pastors, Asperheim and Hansteen, had personalities that emerge clearly from the surviving documents and that left a lasting impress on the relation of the Seamen's Church to the local colony. The self-assured scion of a well-established clerical family, Hansteen dealt with the home office and the consular elite as his equals. No abject apologies for ill-considered decisions appeared in his reports to Bergen. Instead, he presented his independent actions as the only logical course available but, understanding the mission officials' views better, less often disagreed with them.[44]

Hansteen's rapport with Consul and Mrs. Børs was immediate and strong because he shared their upper-class sense of obligation to those in need as well as their instinctive separation of their family and social life from that of the common sailor and immigrant. Asperheim had bought the parsonage adjoining the seamen's church because he believed seamen and settlers would benefit from a personal acquaintance with him and his family, especially its women. Hansteen, like Consul Børs, met such people in his office, and chose to live in a better residential section than the average Norwegian could afford. The Hansteens and Børses socialized freely with their equals but entertained other guests only by written invitation, as Sister Elizabeth and others of a less prominent social background discovered to their discomfort.[45]

**The First Conflict between Immigrant Leaders and the Sojourning Elite**

Hansteen did his best to speed the development of the Deaconess Home and Hospital. Together, he and Mrs. Børs attempted to steer decisions on fund-raising and expansion at the hospital, sending letters back and forth across the East River to plan strategy before meetings were held. From the Relief Society's founding in 1883, however, their plans met resistance from Pastor Everson and a group of immigrant parishioners at Our Savior's.[46] The first ostensible cause of conflict was the problem of finding appropriate means for fund-raising.

Everson agreed that holding bazaars was a good way to bring in money, but he objected to using them as occasions for selling chances on donated merchandise. Lotteries of that sort were popular both in Norway and in the New York settlements and netted relatively large sums at bazaars. Our Savior's alone among the organizations in the colonies shunned lotteries, because Everson maintained that people who bought chances had immoral motives. They were attracted by the idea of winning—and of winning something at much less than its real price—rather than interested in doing good for others. Lotteries, he pointed out, were also contrary to New York State law. At its July 1883 meeting, the board listened to his objections but, because of the Society's poverty, a majority voted to hold lotteries at its annual bazaars.[47]

C. S. Everson
1847 – 1920

• Seamen's Pastor Carsten Hansteen, a man of unusual drive, persistence, and self-confidence, galvanized the Norwegian communities in Brooklyn and Manhattan with his plans for the Seamen's Church and supporting social institutions in the 1880s. *The Norwegian Seamen's Church, Brooklyn 1867–1948.*

• The Reverend Carl Severin Everson served as pastor to Our Savior's Norwegian Lutheran in Manhattan. When that congregation relocated in Red Hook in 1885, Everson became the foremost immigrant opponent of the plans laid by sojourning leaders such as Elizabeth Fedde, Anna Børs, and the Seamen's Church's pastors. The Norwegian-American Historical Association.

A more significant source of disagreement, the different view-points of and competition between immigrant and sojourning leaders, lay beneath the surface of the controversy over lotteries. The stiff-necked morality of Everson's views on games of chance was typical of the differences between his high-church congregation and the more relaxed attitudes and low-church practices of the seamen's pastors and their supporters in Manhattan. From its founding, the Relief Society had strained to balance group interests in a cooperative effort fraught with tension. At the first meeting of the organizers after Sister Elizabeth's arrival, it was necessary to apportion seats on the board of managers carefully to allay fears and avoid future deadlocks. Only Norwegian Lutherans were acceptable, so the group settled on the unusual notion of a board consisting of practicing and nonpracticing Lutherans. The Seamen's Church and Our Savior's received two seats each, and Lutherans who attended neither congregation received four.[48]

Although the representatives for Our Savior's thought Sister Elizabeth's duties ought to include encouraging church attendance, they were afraid that the station might win the religious allegiance of immigrants through her work. Therefore, the minutes expressly stated that she should recommend both Lutheran institutions but send immigrants to Our Savior's when they needed "pastoral care." The Seamen's Church would, whenever possible, confine its spiritual help to the transient mariners that the Sister contacted. Because placing Brooklynites on the board seemed essential for an institution that aimed to serve people in the Red Hook colony, the organizers decided that the four nonpracticing Lutherans had to be Brooklyn residents. Thus, the group excluded meddling Methodists and foreigners, gave the transplanted and immigrant churches an equal footing in the enterprise, and tried to prevent the suspicion that outsiders from the Manhattan colony were foisting charity on Red Hook's Norwegians. At the same time, the total number of board members was nine, which would prevent tie votes.

Anna Børs's influence in the community was more acceptable because she was the consul's wife and represented the active role of upper-class women in charity work in the old country. Norwegian deaconesses, on the other hand, were a relatively new phenomenon. When Elizabeth Fedde came to Red Hook, the Deaconess Home and Hospital in Christiania was only twenty years old, and the notion of women working publicly as religious nurses had not even there gained familiarity or general acceptance. In Red Hook, Sister Elizabeth attended all board meetings to report on her work, but was not a member and had to submit all important decisions about her work to the board's approval. When the male board decided to admit women members in July 1884, she was not among those elected. The chosen few—Mrs. Børs, a nonpracticing Lutheran woman from Brooklyn, and the wives of two deacons at Our Savior's, Mrs. Marie Flood and Mrs. Christine Moller—reflected the men's attempt to maintain a balance between the factions on the board. The women's role, moreover, was supposed to be protecting and guiding Sister Elizabeth, who would have too great an influence over the Society and her own position if she were on the board, according to the men. In other words, the men planned to exercise their influence on her through the new women on the board.[49]

Because Sister Elizabeth was aware that a majority in the colony judged her public work unseemly for a woman, she refused a seat on the board when it was finally offered in 1885. Her real feelings about the situation found expression only in her diary entry for that day, where she wrote, "A terrible day. Board meeting, and I have been left in a powerless position. This is the hardest time I have had in America, . . . I have the whole board against me and everything is wrong and I wish I were dead. God be merciful to me, a sinner!"[50]

Against this background, it does not seem unreasonable to assume that even Mrs. Børs' social and financial power aroused resentment in some male circles. She was, in any event, squarely in the middle of the infighting on the board that occurred in 1886 and 1887. Among the women involved with the work of the Home and Hospital, she alone had the status of a participant whose influence equaled the ministers'. In 1886, after Seamen's Pastor Mortensen had returned to Norway, the board elected Mrs. Børs as its next president. As the organization became embroiled in controversies, she led the sojourner-dominated faction composed of herself, the Lutheran woman from Brooklyn, Hansteen, who served as secretary, and the new junior pastor, Kristen Sårheim. Everson led the opposing immigrant-oriented group, which included his assistant pastor and the two deacons' wives, Mrs. Moller and Mrs. Flood, who voted according to decisions made by their husbands at Everson's church council meetings.[51]

Inevitably, the resolution of the tensions at the Home and Hospital involved choosing either Mrs. Børs' or Pastor Everson's leadership, because they personified different visions of the institution and, indirectly, of the colony. Everson stood for the view that immigrants should control the hospital, colony institutions generally, and the funding of these cooperative community efforts, because settlers better understood local conditions and had committed themselves to life in America. Mrs. Børs represented the social and economic influence of the old country, the contacts of temporarily resident upper-class leaders with Americans on a higher socioeconomic level than that available to most immigrants, and an emphasis on using institutions in the Brooklyn colony to meet the needs of Norwegian transients and seamen.

The training and conduct of new deaconesses was the subject of the first phase of conflict between sojourner and immigrant leaders on the board. When the petition to the mother house for additional deaconesses met refusal, Hansteen, Assistant Pastor Sårheim, and Mrs. Børs supported Sister Elizabeth's hope of training sisters in Brooklyn and, with her assistance, set out a plan by which the seamen's pastors would teach the religion courses. At first, Everson went along with the idea of training deaconesses locally. When Mrs. Børs and Hansteen presented the course plan, however, he denied ever supporting the training and approved it only after he gained an equal role in the teaching.[52]

Everson may have felt that his last-minute opposition had won the board's immigrant faction the most they could hope for under the circumstances. Since steadily more patients came to the hospital, it was difficult to argue against the need for more deaconesses. Because of Everson's initial acquiescence, Sister Elizabeth had already accepted two women as novices, and they had traveled from Norway to take up residence at the Home and Hospital. She cooperated hand-in-glove with Mrs. Børs and the seamen's pastors, who forwarded what were essentially her plans. The novices would very likely see the local situation from her vantage point and support Mrs. Børs and the Seamen's Church. Our Saviors' and immigrants generally were in danger of losing influence in the institution. Their best hope was that Everson's teaching would help the novices see the immigrant point of view.

Then, in 1886, problems developed with the conduct of the first two women accepted for training. The first novice, whom Sister Elizabeth described as having a "soft nature," left to get married before her training was completed, when a widowed sea captain from her hometown docked in Red Hook. The second also fell in love, but before that gave her an excuse for leaving, she had refused to abide by Sister Elizabeth's personal discipline or the board's rules for the conduct of deaconesses. The seamen's pastors, Mrs. Børs, and Sister Elizabeth felt that Everson had worsened the situation by encouraging the second novice's criticism of Sister Elizabeth and by spreading gossip about problems at the Home and Hospital. Everson's faction urged dropping or at least temporarily discontinuing the training of additional sisters because, in their opinion, the course plan had been faulty from the outset.

News of the novices' behavior and the criticism of Sister Elizabeth spread throughout the colony with the result that, during the fall of 1886, the hospital was almost empty. Income from donations and patients reached a low ebb, and a reduction of hospital service was necessary to keep the institution solvent. By the end of the year, the controversy had directly or indirectly reduced the Home and Hospital to the home relief program with which it had begun. Only after a lengthy debate at the board meeting in mid-January of 1887 did the Børs-Hansteen faction end the crisis by winning a majority on the board for continuing the training program.

With that success, the sojourning leaders may have thought they had put struggles on the board behind them. In fact, events at the first board meeting in February proved that the conflict over training deaconesses had been only a prelude. Under new business, Mrs. Børs announced that an anonymous American friend (Alfred Corning Clark) had set aside a fund of $64,000 from which the Home and Hospital was to receive $3,840 in interest annually. On a quarterly basis, the donor's bank would contact Mrs. Børs, so that she would be the channel through which the institution would receive the interest payments. Mrs. Børs again held the key to the institution's financial future. As Sister Elizabeth wrote years later, "Even now, I recall how quiet it became when Mrs. Børs read the letter of donation."[53]

Hansteen immediately set about summarizing the document's main provisions in Norwegian for the secretary's protocol, as expressions of relief and pleasure broke the silence. At that moment, Pastor Everson rose and shattered the celebratory mood of the meeting. He announced his unalterable opposition to the use of lotteries and vociferously expressed his distaste at seeing children drawn into that illegal activity at the most recent bazaar. Further, he was determined that the secretary's protocol should include evidence of his and his supporters' opposition. He wanted to ensure that New York State authorities could not misunderstand his group's position if they should decide to take action against the Home and Hospital. He demanded that Hansteen enter into the protocol a document he had prepared *in English*, which named the specific sections of New York's legal code that lotteries violated and registered his protest against the lottery held at the children's bazaar.

The meeting quickly erupted in controversy. When Hansteen's polite attempt at persuading Everson to permit the recording of his protest in Norwegian failed utterly, Sister Elizabeth lost her temper. In an angry voice, she reminded the minister sharply that she had given him a guided tour of the bazaar and the opportunity of objecting to the lottery before it could take place. "You were our guest," she said bitterly, "and left us in false friendliness." During the debate that followed her outburst, the positions of the board's factions hardened and other tempers flared. Mrs. Børs finally ended the meeting by referring the problem to a committee.

The controversy continued for ten months. Postponing a decision on Everson's demand through the device of a committee only gave both sides time to plan tactics and marshall support. Mrs Børs rejected the committee's suggestions in March and instead presented the board with a letter of resignation. Most important, she also indicated that the hospital would receive no interest payments from Corning Clark's recent donation in her absence, because that income was conditional on her active participation on the board. Leaving the board with the dilemma of choosing whether or not to accept her resignation, she then announced that she had worried herself sick over the controversy and left the city to recuperate.[54]

While she was away, Hansteen and Sårheim argued that the institution could not afford to let Mrs. Børs quit. The funding she controlled was necessary for dealing with the hospital's economic crisis. Apparently, they managed to find a majority for demanding Everson's resignation instead of accepting hers. At the April meeting, following

Sårheim's suggestion, the acting president asked Our Savior's minister to give up his place on the board before answering Mrs. Børs's letter. He flatly refused, however, and when a lengthy heated discussion presented no other alternatives, the board had to accept Mrs. Børs's resignation as official.

Between April and August, the board failed to find a way out of its quandary, and the details of the controversy became public in the colony. Among the participants, only Sister Elizabeth attempted to keep the proceedings of the board secret. A series of highly partisan articles in *Nordiske Blade*, which remained loyal to Manhattan colony interests, defined the positions of the individual board members in the public mind and, therefore, made shifting one's allegiance more difficult.

By August, Hansteen concluded that he would have to manage the annual board elections successfully if the controversy were to end as he wished. The public debate had aggravated personal antagonisms and hardened the opposition between immigrant and sojourning leaders to the point that they could no longer cooperate on the board. Therefore, the only solution was to remove the most adamant immigrants from Our Savior's, so that the sojourning faction could achieve a clear voting majority. In other words, Mrs. Børs could not return to the board unless Everson and his group failed to get reelected. Having ascertained which members would be absent from the election meeting, Hansteen then worked out a mathematical table of how his faction had to vote to exclude the three "conspirators" and circulated it among his supporters.[55]

The complete success of Hansteen's scheme testified not only to the accuracy of his detailed planning, but also to the inflexibility of board members' positions. On August 18, three pledged adherents of the sojourner group replaced Everson and the deacons' wives on the board. The newly constituted group promptly appointed Mrs. Børs as a member and soon after elected her president. With the annual interest from Corning Clark's donation and an additional $3,000 that Mrs. Børs persuaded her husband, Charles Vanderbilt, John D. Rockefeller, and other Manhattan businessmen to give, Hansteen and Mrs. Børs then set about realizing Sister Elizabeth's fondest dreams. By 1889, the building campaign that they spearheaded had resulted in the opening of a separate home for deaconesses and a thirty-bed hospital at Fourth Avenue and 46th Street, near the end of the built-up part of the city. Because of their comfortable majority on the board, all opposition to her leadership and, by proxy, Hansteen's disappeared. Only in the 1890s after the Børses and Hansteens had returned to Norway did immigrant leaders take decisive control over further developments at the Home and Hospital. In the intervening years, lotteries were a standard feature of the Hospital's annual bazaars, some of which were even held in the basement of Everson's church.[56]

The conflict at the Home and Hospital resulted from a constellation of factors arising from New York harbor's importance to Norway's merchant marine. The idea of establishing a relief society and the resources to convert it into a deaconesses' home and hospital came from seamen's pastors and the consul's wife, sojourning leaders who were in Manhattan and Brooklyn because of Norwegian shipping in the port. Naturally, therefore, they included seamen in the institution's plans from the outset. Being temporary residents, moreover, undoubtedly contributed to their belief that bringing a Norwegian deaconess to Brooklyn was the most effective way to ease the social problems of both immigrants and sailors, even though the old country's deaconesses had no special training to deal with that occupational group. The economic significance of the harbor for Norway set in motion the forces that placed two representatives of the country's upper class, Carsten Hansteen and Anna Børs, in the cities and on the Relief Society board. When disagreement arose about whether or not to approve Sister Elizabeth's plans and actions, these leaders' class background gave them the confidence to believe that they knew best, and their status as sojourners inclined them to trust her opinion more than the opposing views of immigrant leaders. Although Sister Elizabeth was not of the same class, she at least shared their perspective, that of Norwegian nationals who naturally turned to old-country models instead of solutions suggested by Norwegian Americans.

In several other ways, however, the Home and Hospital represented a turning point. It evolved from sojourning leaders' first attempt to take responsibility for the well-being of settlers as well as transient seamen. Both Mrs. Børs and the seamen's pastors acted on the realization that the permanently resident colony had grown too large to be ministered to by the Seamen's Church alone. A whole spectrum of settlers' problems demanded training and time that the station's staff lacked. From the start, therefore, sick and needy immigrants had an equal right to receive assistance from Sister Elizabeth and never had to feel they were less preferred as objects of her concern than were seamen.

Equally important, immigrant leaders had had a voice in the Home and Hospital's organization and administration from the first planning meeting. The Home and Hospital was a transplanted institution in two senses. Its sojourning staff came from the old country, and its goals, organizational structure, and daily routines made it a near replica of the mother institution in Christiania. Still, as a transplanted institution, it was significantly different from the Seamen's Church. Neither Sister Elizabeth nor her mentors in Norway could overrule decisions made by its board, and board members concerned themselves with all aspects of the institution. Seamen's pastors, on the other hand, usually made their plans without consulting the station's board and spent enormous amounts of time and energy dealing with the Mission Society's home office in Bergen. In its structure and decision-making process, the

Home and Hospital was only partially a transplanted institution. Mrs. Børs's power over the purse strings alone kept it from becoming wholly immigrant-controlled.

The strife at the Home and Hospital also exemplified a later phase in the colony's early history because it was an internal quarrel among Lutherans. Sectarian competition with Methodists played no role in the disagreement even though events at the board meetings became an important public issue in the colony. Fear of Methodists had been clear in the early decision to exclude them from the Relief Society board, but after that they became no more than spectators. Lutherans managed to develop home relief and a hospital with no further concern for rival denominations. As a result, differing Lutheran views on the propriety of lotteries and the deeper cleavage between sojourner and immigrant leaders became the focus of debate.

In this sense, too, the conflict presaged the effects of the long-term trend away from a little settlement attached to institutions for transient mariners. From the mid-1880s onward, a sizable settled colony demanded ever more attention as it became aware of its own needs and its importance for the visiting merchant marine. The Home and Hospital and the strife that threatened it were transitional phenomena, the first clear evidences of the larger transformations that were taking place.

# 6

# In the Foundry of Change:
## Coping with the Transformations of the 1880s

The molding influence of transient Norwegian seamen on the Red Hook colony entered a new phase during the 1880s. During previous decades, the rapid expansion of Norway's involvement in the bulk-cargo carrying trade had flooded the Red Hook peninsula with transient and deserting Norwegian mariners. That, in turn, had prompted the rise of the colony and the establishment of its first institutions. In the 1880s the need to convert to steamship technology caused a crisis in Norwegian shipping that had far-ranging effects on the settlement's further development. Contemporary responses to this crisis polarized the community, as leaders struggled to comprehend rapid change, represented the clashing interests of immigrants and transient sailors, and enlisted support for specific plans of action.

This turning point in the history of Norway's carrying trade put enormous pressure on the transplanted institutions, the Seamen's Church and the Deaconess Home and Hospital. The mission station especially felt the brunt of the change. The Hospital's sojourning leaders had already weathered immigrant leaders' attempt to assume control of its operation. During the middle and late 1880s, seamen's pastor Carsten

**Who Led Local Responses to the Crisis in Norwegian Shipping?**

Hansteen sponsored an array of new organizations to cope with the strains of change and simultaneously struggled with other leaders over the station's influence in these same institutions. The station even had to stave off an attempt to deprive the seamen's pastors and the Mission Society in Bergen of control over the Seamen's Church itself.

Several groups produced opponents to the station, and their leaders' tactics drew other elements of the population into the institutional conflicts. One kind of opponent represented the interests of immigrants who moved to the colony from Manhattan or those of newcomers coming directly to Red Hook. Another sort stood forth as secular champions of transient and settled seamen's interests. Yet a third had its constituency among the Norwegians, other ethnic groups, and Americans who made their living in or through Brooklyn's sailortown. Spokesmen of these groups involved seamen and settlers by airing their views publicly in order to arouse and exploit reactions in the colony. They also held confidential meetings and conferences to recruit supporters and form coalitions. Not satisfied with verbal allegiance, they expressed alternative conceptions of institutional purposes as well as contrasting ideas of what was best for transients and immigrants and then asked followers to change their habits and attitudes.

Pressure for change did not just filter down from leaders at the top of colony society, however. Mostly through group action, but also in the opinions they caused leaders to remember, ordinary immigrants and sailors found a voice. Independent action by the users of institutions forced leaders to change or give up plans. Leaders depended on their support in the final analysis, because the sum of their small financial contributions was decisive in spite of their individual poverty. In the composite picture of the decade that emerges, the leaders occupy the foreground, largely because they committed their views to paper in reports and memoirs. In the background, one can glimpse other ethnic groups and Americans, whose economic interests and ideas also had a vital influence on events in the colony. Immigrants and seamen appear as a mass in the middle distance, their individual opinions and experiences seldom known except through the leaders' writings, but the weight of their presence felt as the determining element in the composition.

**The Mission
Station's
Changing
Relationship
to
Immigrants**

During Pastor Hansteen's years at Red Hook's Seamen's Church, the tension involved in serving both immigrants and the visiting merchant marine rose to a climax. Between 1883 and 1889 the number of Norwegian ships arriving in New York fell precipitously, and economic depression threw thousands out of work in southern and southwestern Norway. As a result, the station's relationship to settled immigrants became more complicated and uncomfortable than ever before. The settled colony grew at an unprecedented rate, and, judging from contemporary Norwegian government statistics, a larger proportion of the newcomers were seamen and their families—people who instinctively headed for the Seamen's Church if they needed help after arriving in Brooklyn. The seamen's pastors were besieged with pleas for help from newcomers, and at Sunday services the 400 or more immigrants attending left little room for mariners.[1]

At the same time, Hansteen emphasized in reports to the mission's home office, the number of Norwegian seamen arriving increased rather than decreased. Instead of coming mostly on the home country's ships, the majority now worked on American vessels, found long-term employment on Norwegian steamships chartered by American companies, or arrived in other nations' merchant marines after having deserted in foreign ports. Between 1885 and 1888 Hansteen's experience was that 20,000 Scandinavian sailors, mostly Norwegians, entered the harbor each year. Of these an average of only 3,000 came under a Scandinavian flag. In 1889 he predicted that the total number would rise to between 23,000 and 25,000 while the proportion on Scandinavian ships would continue to sink.[2]

The cumulative effect of these trends for the seamen's pastors was greater difficulty in making contact with the Norwegian sailors in port. Boarding all incoming ships seemed an impossibility, but helping the men in other nations' fleets was now deemed imperative. In the pastors' experience, these men were more likely to fall into the hands of predatory runners and boarding masters, who hurried them down the road to drunkenness and immorality. Red Hook's Hamilton Avenue and Van Brunt Street, moreover, housed the harbor's main sailortown by the latter 1880s. The group the pastors wished to contact was nearly on the church doorstep but was separated from them by the hostility of boarding masters and others who profited from mariners' nights on the town.[3] Searching for and trying out methods appropriate for the new situation preoccupied Hansteen from the time he took over leadership of the station in 1885.

Before confronting the challenge of sailortown, Hansteen first attempted to reduce the pressure on the Seamen's Church from the constantly growing number of immigrants asking for its assistance. Hansteen shared the home-office view that the settlers ought to form their own congregation. The problem was that the station had become financially dependent on their contributions. Meeting the station's expenses through collections from sailors had become increasingly difficult because of the continuing decline in the number of Norwegian ships arriving and the unsolved puzzle of how to contact Norwegian seamen on foreign ships. As Hansteen announced to the executive board in 1887, "No matter where I look, there is nothing else left than this, 'Thank God, because you have the settled immigrants to get money from, until it pleases God to open new sources so we do not need them.'"[4]

Until the station could find another source of income, he thought

•

The first Norwegian Seamen's Church in Brooklyn. After its founding in 1878, the Seamen's Church became the center for those transient sailors and immigrants who were practicing Lutherans and wanted a genuinely Norwegian, rather than immigrant American, religious and social experience. The Norwegian-American Historical Association.

it best to continue with the annual bazaars and collection boxes for seamen, through which immigrants now contributed $860 to the yearly budget. Those methods seemed preferable to starting a general fund drive among the settlers because making a direct appeal would make the station's dependence obvious. Although he knew it was morally duplicitous, Hansteen worked to make the immigrants believe they contributed from a "feeling of gratitude" to the station for the benefits it gave them. As he put it, "In short, the money must be brought in, but nothing shall be said directly, so that all will have the feeling that we are those giving and the public those receiving."[5]

The necessity of keeping the immigrants from breaking away until an alternate source of income could be found was especially painful to Hansteen because he sincerely believed the immigrants' spiritual welfare would be better served in a separate congregation. In 1889 he told the home office, "in the Seamen's Church everything is arranged in set forms, [while] they are only guests without any rights or duties, beyond what pleases the personalities of the pastors to demand." They thus became in his view a "religious proletariat" who worked for the station but held no firm Lutheran convictions arising from a full personal commitment to the church's welfare. For that very reason they were especially susceptible to the first evangelist who came along and disappeared from the Seamen's Church each summer when tent meetings were held in Brooklyn.[6]

The chief way Hansteen found to maintain the settlers' loyalty while reducing their demands on the station's pastors was to encourage the formation of a laymen's group within the resident congregation. The most religious immigrants attending the Seamen's Church had already begun prayer meetings in private homes. In early 1885 Hansteen held a series of sermons for this group and urged them to become lay preachers to the Norwegian immigrants in the metropolitan area. The surest way to a richly religious personal life, he told them, was to take responsibility for a definite Christian project that would bring others to the Lutheran faith. Inspired by this suggestion, the group organized a few months later as the "Free Lutheran Mission Society in Brooklyn" with Gabriel Fedde, who had cooperated so well in bringing a deaconess to Brooklyn, as its leader. By 1889 the Mission Society ran a Sunday school for immigrant children in Red Hook and sent lay ministers not only to several locations in Brooklyn but also to all boroughs of present-day New York City as well as to several communities in New Jersey.[7]

Hansteen was justly pleased with these results. No longer merely a passive proletariat at the station, the immigrants were being prepared to lead independent religious lives. When the Seamen's Church filled to overflowing, the pastor could remind immigrants of the layman-led meetings they could attend. Having done his Christian duty by the immigrants, Hansteen could concentrate more on sailors' needs and still feel confident that the settlers would support the station financially until the time was ripe for them to establish separate congregations.

During the mid-1880s Hansteen needed the assurance of the immigrants' continued loyalty for yet another reason. In 1885, when Our Savior's Norwegian Lutheran Church moved from Manhattan to Brooklyn, the latent conflict between the station and the immigrant congregation became an open struggle. Until that year, only the Mission Society's home office had put pressure on the seamen's pastors to limit the station's work with settlers. Our Savior's minister, C. S. Everson, had been satisfied to let the Seamen's Church relieve him of pastoral responsibilities across the East River. Now, however, economic difficulties stemming from the move to Red Hook apparently prompted him and other leaders in the congregation to claim immigrant Lutherans as their exclusive province.[8]

Our Savior's had had but little choice about moving because the old Manhattan colony on the southeastern side of the island was dissolving. Many of the congregation's members had already moved to Brooklyn, and while that drain on finances continued, others left to establish a new Norwegian community in Harlem. The faster growth of the Red Hook colony made moving there the logical choice, but difficulties in selling the old church and unexpected expenses in erecting a new building on Henry Street near the station saddled the congregation with debts.[9] Fifteen months after opening its doors, the Henry Street church claimed to have doubled its membership to 600 but reported meeting only slightly more than half of its expenses. Faced with this desperate situation, the Reverend C. S. Everson and the president of his church council, Simon W. Flood, grasped at the most obvious solution, getting another large influx of new members from the Seamen's Church. In 1886 and 1887, they put mounting pressure on the seamen's pastors to release their immigrant parishioners.[10]

Early in the conflict, Pastor Hansteen identified Simon Flood as the most dangerous of his opponents. During 1886, he referred to Flood as the station's "enemy" in personal letters and saw his influence behind every setback he or the Seamen's Church experienced. In April, his dislike for the church councilman was so intense that he secluded himself in his study rather than receive Flood's visits. In October, when he returned from his wedding in Norway, he suspected that the Flood family had convinced his assistant pastor, Kristen Sårheim, to move out of lodgings at the pastor's home in order to reduce his income and increase the chances of persuading Sårheim to argue against working with immigrants at the station. Guessing the cause and motives involved at once, Hansteen prepared to join battle. "Floods are, of course, behind this," he wrote home in his first letter after returning to Brooklyn, "They stick their noses into so many things, but they always lose in the long run, of that I am certain." In a later report to Bergen, Sårheim confirmed Hansteen's suspicions by detailing Flood's and Everson's frequent attempts to show him that the station had no right to serve anyone but transient seamen. In March of 1887, Hansteen decided that Our Savior's minister was merely the church councilor's tool, describing the two men's working relationship succinctly as follows, "Floods and Everson form a company, where the first-named even run the religious services in the second's church."[11]

By the time Hansteen reached that conclusion, the leaders at Our Savior's had taken much more definite steps to win their objective. In March Everson and Flood issued a circular to all Norwegian Lutherans in the colony. This flier first informed readers that the only correct religious home for resident Norwegians was Our Savior's, because it alone of the two immigrant congregations in Red Hook followed the fatherland's state-church theology and used its liturgy and hymnal. Having established that it was the station's equal in Norwegianness, the authors' last paragraph closed by explaining pointedly that the original agreement between the station and the church had limited the station's work to a ministry among transient Scandinavian mariners. Around the same time, Hansteen reported in his correspondence that the editor of *Nordiske Blade* published a series of attacks on his "official conduct, authority, high-handedness, and fanaticism" that lasted until mid-August, when the editor and the pastor discovered that Simon Flood had engineered their disagreement.[12]

In the meantime, tempers in the colony "seethed and simmered like a stew," according to Hansteen. Because the editor seemed to be systematically destroying his reputation, the pastor met calumny with vituperation and, as he later admitted, aggravated the feud with the vehemence of his replies. As the public strife continued, the leaders of each party rallied support among the rank and file of its constituency. The atmosphere was rife with "confidential" conversations between minister and parishioner, deaconess and patient, journalist and informant. Gabriel Fedde reported hearing Hansteen say that every time the ministers of the two churches met "the fur flew." Everson called the seamen's pastors Methodists and they answered by berating Our Savior's coldly "objective" Christianity. Sensing an opportunity to feather his own nest, the minister at the Norwegian Methodist Bethel Ship Church exploited the infighting among Lutherans by delivering a series of sermons on the differences between the two denominations and the advantages of being a Methodist.[13]

The strife culminated in early fall for several reasons. For one, the *Blade*'s editor and Hansteen reached an understanding after realizing that Flood had provoked them both. More important, Everson and Flood concluded that the station's immigrant congregation would not leave voluntarily because they had become accustomed to its low-church, layman-oriented organization and accepted the seamen's pastor's view of Our Savior's stiff orthodoxy. Therefore, the leaders at the Henry Street church played their last card. A "well-meaning soul" ensured that some of the *Blade's* articles arrived at the Mission Society headquarters in Bergen, where the cause of the newspaper feud was not known. Flood secretly acquired copies of the station's accounts and convinced Everson to write an appeal to the mission's director, which accused Hansteen of misusing the station's funds by diverting them from seamen to immigrants and, further, asked the director to confirm the rule that the Seamen's Church was not to involve itself with settlers.[14]

Having received several defenses for ministering to immigrants at the station earlier, the executive board in Bergen responded cautiously. The director did not accept Everson's view but nonetheless asked both Hansteen and Sårheim to consider whether or not current circumstances suggested the "necessity and possibility" of running the Seamen's Church without the settlers' support.[15] For the seamen's pastors, support from the home office was indispensable. Their next reports, therefore, expressed their total agreement with the general policy of strictly limiting immigrant participation at mission stations and then detailed in dollars and cents why the Seamen's Church in Brooklyn had to be an exception to the rule. Knowing that the home office was strapped for funds, Hansteen declared his willingness to exclude the settlers immediately on the condition that headquarters supply over $800 annually to replace immigrant contributions.[16]

Sårheim took another tack. Armed with census figures, he demonstrated that during its twelve to fifteen years in New York, Our Savior's had attracted only about three percent of the urban complex's Norwegian residents. One of the most important reasons for its small size, he concluded, was best suggested by Everson's claim, concerning his sermons, that "there are few people who are so objective as I." That Norwegian Brooklynites stayed away from Everson's church showed that they wanted a more feeling, "subjective" faith. In any case, Sårheim concluded, when population statistics proved that the metropolitan area held at least 5,000 Norwegians who attended no church, there was little reason for the station and Our Savior's to quarrel over immigrant support.[17]

None of these arguments, however, was so convincing as another matter that Hansteen's report took up first. At Flood's instigation, members of the station's board of trustees had examined the incorporation papers of the Seamen's Church and concluded that the trustees, not the Mission Society in Bergen, owned the station. According to New York State law, the seamen's pastors could not be members of the board and, moreover, the trustees alone were empowered to determine the allocation of funds. In short, the immigrant-dominated board claimed legal control of the station and excluded the mission's emissaries from having a voice in its affairs.[18]

Flood had overplayed his hand. Nothing could have guaranteed firmer support for the seamen's pastor's views from the mission's home office. Therefore, Hansteen merely reassured the director that he had taken appropriate steps to secure ownership of station property for the mission. Five months later, all Flood's supporters had been ejected from the station's board of trustees. With the full support of the home office, the Seamen's Church continued to maintain its immigrant congregation while it discreetly searched for other sources of financial support.[19] For the time being, the atmosphere of inner conflict that had permeated the colony dispersed. How well Flood accepted defeat is not known, but Our Savior's situation improved significantly during 1887 and 1888 because of the large numbers of newcomers entering the colony and the city's improving employment conditions.[20] At last, Hansteen felt he could concentrate his energies on improving the lot of Scandinavian seamen in the port.

**Pastor Hansteen's Campaign against Sailortown**

In mounting his offensive against the district that effectively segregated seamen from his church, Hansteen first moved to increase the number of his fighting troops. He convinced the home office to pay for a second assistant and thus raised the station's staff to four—two pastors and two assistants—which freed time for both pastors to use combatting the related problems of sailortown and contacting men on foreign ships.[21] Hansteen's next initiatives mobilized members of the immigrant community in a direct attack on sailortown's bosses, the people who earned their living from seamen's wages. At the end of 1887 he organized a "'vigilance committee' of 50 Scandinavian family men" in the Red Hook colony who were to act as a kind of neighborhood watch. They reported the "moral outrages" of Van Brunt Street's dance halls, brothels, and saloons to him, and he notified not the precinct officers, who he said often conspired with the perpetrators, but Brooklyn's main police station.[22]

Hansteen also decided to strike at the root of sailortown's economy by depriving its boarding masters of Scandinavian seamen's business. The boarding masters and their runners used the entertainments of the district to lure men to the boardinghouses and keep them in debt. To pay off these debts, they encouraged sailors to desert Scandinavian vessels for the higher wages on American ships. This the boarding masters offered to arrange, but only if the men allowed them to take control of hiring for future voyages. Thus, they brought mariners to sailortown and kept them returning. Attacking the power of the boarding masters, therefore, was the key to effective action against the whole range of evils the Seamen's Church opposed.[23]

What was needed, reasoned Hansteen, was alternative lodgings for seamen that would expose them to moral instead of immoral influences. To achieve that end he planned a seamen's home with a clear set of goals. Lutherans would have to organize and run the home, to provide the men with daily opportunities to strengthen their faith. But the new institution had to be entirely independent of the Seamen's Church, and its manager would be a devout layman with maritime experience rather than a pastor. In that way the men would not feel they were "cloistered" in a religious institution. On the other hand, the home and the church would advertise for each other, and seamen's pastors would both visit the home and sit on its executive board. The manager and organizers of the home had to be Norwegian, so it would bind the men closer to the old country and weaken the temptation to desert. Like the Seamen's Church, it would have to emphasize a family atmosphere and aim to be a home away from home.[24]

To exemplify living according to the principles of temperance, the institution would have to be alcohol-free and discourage men from returning drunk at night. The home ought also to offer men a framework in which they could practice a responsible personal economy. By providing comfortable lodgings at the lowest possible price it would help sailors save money and by arranging for them to send their savings home to relatives in Norway it would remove the temptation to squander wages on illicit pleasures. Further, the home would admit not only sailors on Scandinavian ships but all Scandinavian seamen, regardless of the flag they sailed under. In that way it would make contact with the rapidly rising number of Norwegian mariners working in the American merchant marine. Since the home would cooperate with the Seamen's Church, it would give pastors a much easier way of reaching these men. Of course, with such goals the home would simultaneously undermine the boarding masters' hold on seamen.

Well meant and idealistic, Hansteen's plan revealed notions about Christian charity and seamen that were common among seamen's pastors and their backers in the Manhattan elite. Charity had to be based on a sound faith, but it also needed to be appealing and practical. Thus the weight given to home, family, Norwegianness, and thrift as well as to Lutheranism. The Norwegian leaders who supported Hansteen's plan for the home took it for granted that all these qualities would attract seamen and do them good. In the leaders' view, most sailors were easily led and needed their lives organized for them. They succumbed to the blandishments of runners and boarding masters merely because no better alternative was immediately apparent. All one had to do was show them the right way and they would naturally take it.[25]

The men were not by nature evil, but they were more thoughtless and immature than most people their age. Those negative qualities resulted in large part from their occupation. By going to sea at an early age, they left parents and community before their upbringing and socialization was complete. On their first deep-sea voyage they were deprived of relaxation and social outlets for a long period. Then, green and unsophisticated, they arrived in a foreign port where the denizens of sailortown exposed them to more immoral temptations than most people experienced in a lifetime. Given a knowledge of this situation, any good Christian could see that sailors were often overgrown boys who needed parental guidance if they were to survive the moral hazards they faced. That, in any case, was the common conclusion in reports from the seamen's pastors, the shipping agents, and the consul who supported the founding of a seamen's home in Red Hook.

Some years earlier Seamen's Pastor Mortensen had launched the idea of establishing a boardinghouse for Scandinavian sailors. Although his goals were not as well thought out as Hansteen's, he had succeeded in convincing Norway's famous whaling ship builder, Svend Foyn, to give $2,000 for renting a building. Mortensen's hopes, however, came to nothing because he could not find a man willing to manage the boardinghouse. In late 1886 he hired an assistant to run a seamen's home, but sailortown's "boardinghouse-master ring" threatened the assistant so viciously that he soon resigned and left town.[26]

Hansteen looked for a man brave or clever enough to stand up to the ring that now called itself "The Boardingmasters' and Shippingmasters' Union." Without the knowledge of the seamen's pastor, Magnus Andersen had begun investigating the possibility of starting a Norwegian seamen's home in the summer of 1887. Andersen's motivations for establishing the institution were, however, rather different from Hansteen's. Having completed three years as second mate on an American deep-water sailing ship, Andersen had recently married. His closest friend in Brooklyn claimed that he therefore ought to stay on shore with his wife and further argued that Andersen was bound to succeed with a boardinghouse because his attempt to cross the Atlantic in a lifeboat had made him admired and well known among Norwegian crews. This appeal to marital responsibility and the flattering view of his prospects—combined with the idea that running such a home might provide a way to save money for starting another career later—convinced Andersen.[27]

Andersen decided that the home was a promising opportunity, but only if Consul Børs and Seamen's Pastor Hansteen would recommend it to seamen. Accordingly, he arranged interviews and secured their approval. Neither official found fault with Andersen's qualifications to run a sailor's home, but both made it clear that they would supply start capital and help with further fund-raising only if he accepted their advice on how the home was to be run. Andersen quickly decided he would rather administer a home under others' guidance than put his own savings into an independent boardinghouse. The only problem that remained was getting the approval of the boarding masters' ring and, as it happened, Andersen had contacts with sailortown which made that difficulty seem manageable. He went immediately to his brother-in-law, Anton Andersen, who had been one of Red Hook's most famous runners in the 1870s and who now wielded considerable influence with the boarding masters' ring. Soon Anton reported that the ring's council had agreed to a deal. The ring claimed that a Seamen's Church-supported home had become acceptable because most Scandinavian sailors no

•

Magnus Andersen from 1893. A man with a reputation for boldness and charismatic leadership, Magnus Andersen was chosen to direct the first Norwegian Seamen's Home. *70-aars tilbakeblik paa mitt virke paa sjø og land.*

•

The Norwegian Seamen's Home on Hamilton Avenue with a horse and carriage outside; the sign on the Home says "Scandinavian Seamen's Temperance Home." The Norwegian–American Historical Association.

longer patronized boardinghouses but instead lodged with private families. The boarding masters thus foresaw little loss of business from a
sailors' home, especially one that might fail because the mariners for
whom it was planned had found other quarters.

Just as Norwegian shipowners had been caught unprepared by the
men's massive desertion in the 1870s, the ring had not expected the
mariners' rejection of sailortown's boardinghouses a decade later. Both
had tried to maximize their economic advantages at seamen's expense
and had had to adjust when the men circumvented their plans. Now
Hansteen and the consular elite in Manhattan were intending to manage the sailors' living conditions for the men's own good. Nothing in
these leaders' reports indicates their awareness that the settled immigrants had already offered seamen an alternative that both satisfied the
men and constituted important extra income for the immigrants. Because of their insufficient respect for mariners' capacity to act independently, these local leaders would also have to accept a reality that differed
significantly from their expectations.

As soon as Andersen learned of the ring's acquiescence, he began
negotiations with Hansteen about the manager's position. Since he
brought the seamen's pastor an agreement that had seemed impossible
earlier, Andersen felt he could conduct talks with Hansteen on equal
terms. Andersen's strengthened bargaining position, his divergent concept of the home's main purpose, and the seamen's independent action
in finding other lodgings resulted in a home different from the one
Hansteen had envisioned.

The seamen's pastor discovered he had to make several concessions
if the home was to open its doors. The ring's council had set strict conditions on its approval, even though it believed the home was doomed
to fail. There was to be no direct connection between the home and the
Seamen's Church, which had to agree not to advertise the home or advise seamen against sailortown's boardinghouses. The home was to recruit its lodgers only from Scandinavian ships or American vessels in the
coastal trade.[28] Hansteen found these limits hard to accept, since he had
hoped the home would bring men to the church and be a new way to
reach the Scandinavian seamen employed on other nations' ships. He
agreed because Andersen refused to work without the ring's approval
and because he hoped to realize his goals by other means.

Hansteen had never thought the relationship between the home
and the church should be obvious. His plan was that the seamen's pastors would work behind the scenes by sitting on the home's board.
Hansteen had, moreover, decided on a location for the home that would
make going from it to the church almost unavoidable. Since the pastor
held the money donated for establishing the home, Andersen had to accept the site, which was the building next to the Seamen's Church.[29]

The pastors themselves had best stay outside the home, Hansteen agreed, to give the appearance of meeting the ring's demand for a separation of the institutions. In their absence, the manager would have to maintain the feeling of a Lutheran family home. Andersen balked, however, when Hansteen asked him to play the role of a Lutheran father for the men by sitting at the head of the table during meals and leading the boarders in prayer. Andersen based his model for daily operations at the home on shipboard practices. Like a captain, he planned to eat separately from the men who, he insisted, were used to taking their meals without a superior "constantly sitting over them." Religious observances on board ship were a matter of personal choice. Andersen flatly refused to lead group prayer. Hansteen's concept of a family home that exerted a gentle but clear moral influence had finally collided with Andersen's idea of a boardinghouse that met the needs of a specific occupational group and netted its manager a neat profit.[30]

At that point negotiations broke down. In his memoirs, Andersen claims he no longer felt "especially" interested in the project. Hansteen remained inflexible for over a month, perhaps believing Andersen's lack of futher interest in the home was merely pretended. When he learned that Andersen was seriously thinking of going to sea again, he dropped his demand for prayers at meals, promised Andersen a "completely free and independent situation—without rules or interference," and offered him complete control over the funds the pastor had for establishing the home.[31] Feeling he had won the conditions necessary for the type of boardinghouse he had in mind, Andersen accepted. In practice, however, freeing himself from the pastor's unwanted assistance proved impossible. Not daring to alienate Hansteen for fear of losing recommendations from the Seamen's Church and its main supporter, Consul General Børs, Andersen tolerated the pastor's involvement in the home's affairs.[32]

When the Norwegian Sailors' Temperance Home officially opened in June 1887, Hansteen was one of the speakers. Not only the location of the home and Hansteen's presence at the ceremonies, but its very name announced a connection with the Seamen's Church. Hansteen insisted on that exact name, because the Norwegian seamen's pastor in London had used it when he started a similar institution. In other words, Hansteen relied on mariners making an association between the two homes and hoped the implied connection to the Mission Society's international operations would be clear. During the home's first two years of operation its informal executive board consisted of Andersen, Hansteen, and the junior seamen's pastor, Kristen Sårheim. Thus the manager was a voting minority, even though he supposedly had control over the home's daily operation. Andersen spent long hours recruiting boarders for the home and not infrequently had to persuade them to leave private lodgings in the colony. The seamen's pastors continued fund-raising efforts and arranged publicity. In practice, this division of labor meant that Andersen told everyone he met that the home was independent of the Seamen's Church, while the pastors' work reinforced the connection between the institutions in people's minds.[33]

**The Conflict Between Alternate Notions of Sailors' Welfare**

From late 1887 until the summer of 1889, Andersen and Hansteen worked at cross-purposes and the submerged current of irritation between them grew. In Andersen's view, the most effective means of filling the home with men was to demonstrate that the sailors who patronized it got suitable employment faster and cheaper than those who stayed at sailortown's boardinghouses. He therefore used his and his brother-in-law's contacts in local shipping circles to set himself up as an employment agent and organized a hiring office in the home. Unlike other agents, he charged no fee for his services and more often emphasized securing work at or above the men's last shipboard positions. Like the boarding masters, he extended credit to sailors short of funds, but in contrast to those leeches, he did not encourage indebtedness, allowed men to pay their bills on easy terms, and even helped some ship out before their debts were entirely liquidated. At the same time, he set up an informal bank and postal service for seamen and mailed money home to relatives in Norway when the men requested assistance with that.[34]

The men's response was overwhelming. During the home's first year, Andersen had to fill the halls and his own office with cots to accommodate forty men in a building planned to house only fifteen. By the end of 1887, the home was running at a profit even though it had to turn away men Andersen could have placed on outgoing ships. Consequently, the manager could successfully argue for a new location in a larger building. In March of the next year, the home's office and main building moved to Hamilton Avenue near the ferry to Manhattan, and the building next to the church served only as an overflow dormitory. Andersen had at last put some physical distance between himself and the seamen's pastors, whom he gave no credit for making the move financially possible. In July of 1889, the home's first published report showed that in two years over 4,000 mariners, 3,340 of them Norwegians, had stayed at the home. These men, moreover, had sent almost $30,000 to their families in Norway.[35]

At the same time, Andersen enjoyed mostly peaceful relations with the boardinghouse ring, even though the new home often held over a hundred men during peak periods. Andersen later claimed that the key to his success was keeping strictly to the deal his brother-in-law Anton had cut with the ring. In his memoirs he does, however, admit that on two or three occasions conflicts arose, and then only Anton's experience as a former runner for the ring prevented open attacks on the home. The Seamen's Church, Anton reported, was the chief cause of problems with the boarding masters "because they believed that it agitated for the home among both sailors and captains in spite of all assurances to the

contrary." Moreover, Andersen recalled, many experienced seamen refused to stay in the home because they wanted no part of Pastor
Hansteen's war on sailortown, which could only be to their disadvantage if they later needed assistance from boarding masters.[36]

Pastor Hansteen attributed the home's prosperity to quite different
causes in his reports to the Mission Society's home office. While appre-
ciating the importance of Andersen's maritime contacts, he emphasized
that contributions he had solicited from Consul Børs, Manhattan shipping agents, and Norwegian shipowners had made moving to a new
building possible. Hansteen continued to see the home as a nonprofit,
charitable institution rather than as a business proposition. Moreover, he
maintained that its ultimate value was in undermining the boarding
master ring's power.[37] Hansteen had no illusions that the ring had resigned itself to the home's continued existence and had no intention of
keeping a deal with it that would benefit the ring. He claimed that Andersen had escaped the boarding masters' criticism primarily because of
a prior agreement by which the staffs of both the home and the church
conspired to name Hansteen as the source of all actions that called
down the "boarding masters' outbreaks of wrath and threats." Hansteen's person was to serve as a kind of lightning rod for the ring's continuing opposition until the home had become so well established that
the ring could not crush it.[38]

In the pastor's opinion, Andersen himself was expendable. "Magnus Andersen," he wrote to the mission board in Bergen, "is in many
ways an unusually equipped man for this position—yes, so excellent that
it would be dangerous if he should resign." Andersen's capability gave
him power, and Hansteen already knew that the manager was willing to
use the threat of dropping work with the home to win concessions. In
preparation for Andersen's next attempt to force his will on the home,
Hansteen quietly began organizing a board of trustees that would not
only take out New York State incorporation papers and set up the "detailed organization" of the home, but also hire a first mate to be Andersen's assistant—and replacement should the manager unexpectedly
quit.[39]

**Building
Coalitions and
Constituencies
to Resolve an
Impasse**

Inevitably, as both men aired their differing views and aims, the facade
of cooperation began to crumble and blocks of opinion began to form
behind each man. In this way, the various conflicts in the colony during
the 1880s found a focus and rose to a climax at the end of the decade.
The outcome of the leaders' struggle for influence, however, revealed
the limits of their control over events as much as it testified to their ability to marshal public support. Most seamen continued to consult their
own perceptions of their best interests. While availing themselves of the
home's and the station's services, they generally preferred lodgings with
relatives or at least in Norwegian-American family homes. Many attended the Seamen's Church but, taken together, more visited other de-

*Nordiske Blade*, published in Red Hook Brooklyn from 1878 until 1910 and the
first purely Norwegian-language newspaper on the East Coast, was the established
press that *Nordisk Tidende* represented as the voice of upper-class conservatism in
the 1890s. Norwegian-American Collection, University of Oslo Library.

nominations and sailortown missions or attended no church in port, depending on their individual religious convictions and practical needs.
Few wanted to antagonize sailortown's boarding masters and runners as
long as their employment might depend on their assistance.

Through his vigilance committee, Pastor Hansteen had directly involved at least fifty devout family heads in the colony in his fight against
sailortown. Consul Børs and the Manhattan elite were also ready to de-
fend the pastor's views, having cooperated with him to fund and establish both the Deaconess Hospital and the Seamen's Home. Hansteen's
initiatives, however, lacked other important kinds of support. First and
foremost, he needed increased long-term funding that would give him

effective control over the home and the possibility of ending the station's dependence on contributions from immigrants. Second, he required the official blessing of higher authorities than the consul, which would make securing stable financial support easier and discourage local opposition. And all this had to be accomplished while continuing to offer seamen competitive religious and housing alternatives in circumstances that made the specifically ethnic qualities of the mission church its greatest drawing card.

Starting in late 1887, Hansteen negotiated with Brooklyn municipal authorities and the American Seamen's Friends Society for public recognition and financial assistance. Recognition came easily when he presented letters from the mission's home office in Bergen, but after a year's discussions budgetary help was still beyond reach. The available records do not include the city's reasons for withholding funding, but in his reports to Bergen Hansteen bitterly suggested that municipal officials taking bribes from the boarding masters' ring undermined his efforts. Neither the home nor the mission station received city moneys at that time, and while Andersen succeeded in running the home at a profit, the station sorely needed increased funding, especially if it hoped to operate without immigrant support.[40]

The Seamen's Friends Society offered the hope of assistance but, apparently, only if the Norwegian Seamen's Church economized by adopting their style of operations. By the summer of 1888 Hansteen was willing to make that change and planned to save money as the American seamen's church did by employing only one seamen's pastor with a staff of five assistants. One key to the success of the American system was a steam-powered launch that could quickly reach any point in New York's huge harbor. With it, the assistants met incoming vessels while they waited for customs clearance off Staten Island and distributed tracts and announcements of their church's activities. As these assistants needed no professional training and could be hired locally, their combined salaries represented a significant savings over the mission station's current outlays for the pay and travel expenses of a second ordained seamen's pastor from Norway and two assistants. Because of its speed and operational range, moreover, the steam launch offered the advantage of at last being able to contact the many thousands of Norwegian seamen in other nations' merchant marines—and of doing so as quickly as or even sooner than the boarding masters' runners could.[41] If that were possible, Hansteen could rather painlessly give up the idea of using the home as a means of reaching these men, which in turn would eliminate the necessity of his ongoing struggle with Magnus Andersen.

Of course, the American system would work for the station only if it no longer had to minister to an immigrant congregation. For several reasons, the time seemed ripe for urging the immigrants to form their own church. Not only did ministering to immigrants make the services of a second pastor necessary, but it was also the source of continuing conflict with Our Savior's. The laymen's organization established in 1885 at the station had reached a kind of maturity, moreover, and could help the immigrants call their own minister if they found joining Our Savior's unappealing. That eventuality was not unlikely and could not have displeased the seamen's pastor, who in that way could both get even with Everson and end the station's responsibility for ministering to immigrants.

Many pieces of the situation's complex puzzle would begin to fall into place if only Hansteen could get the money to put his new plans in motion. In October of 1888, during a tour of the Scandinavian capitals, he not only won the official patronage of the countries' monarchs for the home but also raised enough money in shipping circles to pay for the improvements needed at its new building on Hamilton Avenue. With these funds, he could demonstrate the dependence of the home on the station's ability to tap charitable sources of income and thus ensure that the home would not remain Andersen's private business enterprise. More important, he convinced the whaling ship magnate Svend Foyn to donate the price of a steam launch. Now he could use it to forward his plans for changing the station's staffing, eliminating the necessity of serving immigrants, and contacting more seamen.[42]

On his side, Andersen had already aligned himself with the less religious transient seamen and, through his brother-in-law, with the ring. In 1888 he became increasingly interested in the situation of immigrant seamen, who had always been important for him, because during periods of high shipping activity the home had to recruit crews among the semi-settled mariners living in private family lodgings. Hansteen and Consul Børs had not intended that the home should provide room and board or hiring services for immigrants. Early in 1888, Andersen departed from this general understanding of home policy when he noticed the local effects of the depression in Norwegian shipping. The home experienced a business boom when he decided it should serve as employment office and equipment store for hundreds of seamen arriving "directly from Norway as emigrants."[43]

While Hansteen was in Scandinavia in October, Andersen took an initiative that established his own base of organized support among immigrant sailors in Brooklyn. Calling together four colony leaders with maritime backgrounds, he proposed founding a secular self-help society for local immigrant seamen. Such an organization, he thought, ought to satisfy the men who resented being excluded from residence at the home and getting jobs through its hiring office only when all transient mariners had berths. Before the end of the year, these leaders invited men to join the Norwegian-American Seamen's Association, which they advertised as a nonreligious organization combining the aims of a social club, mutual benefit society, and political association. Since it viewed Andersen as its disinterested founder, the new organization made him its first honorary member and unfailingly supported his views during local disputes.[44]

**Unexpected Circumstances and the Final Crisis**

By early 1889 both Hansteen and Andersen found the situation in the Brooklyn colony untenable and therefore worked for radical change. Hearing of Hansteen's plans to visit all parts of the harbor with a steam launch, Andersen quickly concluded that the home's future was bleak, since the boarding masters' ring would certainly view the boat as final proof that the Seamen's Church functioned as a recruiter for the home. Preparing for the worst, he sent his brother-in-law Anton to gauge the strength of the ring's reaction to Hansteen's plans and simultaneously interested a yacht builder in erecting a "bigger and completely modern, more international home" on a lot adjoining the present Seamen's Home. Anton reported that the ring would indeed treat the launch as the home's "runner-boat." He also warned that the ring might resort to violence if the launch visited ships outside those docked in the East and North rivers or other vessels than the Scandinavian and American ships defined as the home's recruiting base by the original agreement with the ring.[45]

Andersen advised Hansteen of the limits imposed by the ring but could not dissuade him from using the launch or make him believe he would expose himself to bodily harm if he ventured as far as Staten Island. Judging from insinuations in Hansteen's later reports to Norway, Andersen's frustration with the pastor's stubbornness made him desperate. In any case, both men recalled that the *New York Herald* published a very inflammatory article about Hansteen's plans for the launch in late winter, based on an unauthorized translation of the pastor's report to the Mission's news magazine. The *Herald* reveled in Hansteen's lack of discretion when writing for a Norwegian audience. In an attempt to impress the difficulties facing the home on his readers' minds, the pastor had not only catalogued the immoralities of sailortown and the means by which the boarding masters' ring fleeced sailors, but also named the British consul general and a New York police captain as examples of the general willingness of officials to take bribes. Perhaps even worse, in view of Hansteen's plans, the *Herald* concluded that the Seamen's Church was the power behind the home and meant to use the launch to recruit men for the home before the ring's runners could contact them.[46]

Even though his recent experience made him use deliberately ambiguous language, Hansteen left no doubt in a later letter to the home office that Andersen's brother-in-law Anton was the culprit who had informed the ring about the launch and "obtained in quietness an excerpt" of the now infamous report to the mission magazine. The pastor resisted blaming Andersen himself in writing, but noted that Anton was "in very intimate contact with an official at the Seamen's Home." (In his memoirs, Andersen admitted only having a personal connection with someone employed at the newspaper.) Hansteen made no mention of his conclusions, however, until months after the affair of the *Herald* article.[47] In late winter, he was preoccupied with other problems which he quite naturally wished to conceal from Andersen and other Norwegians in Brooklyn as long as possible.

Hansteen's March report to Bergen pivoted on the changes his wife's and his own health problems had made in his plans. Mrs. Hansteen had not returned to Brooklyn in November of 1888 because Red Hook's climate had broken her health. Her most recent letter had informed the pastor that she could return only for a short period without the risk of permanently impaired health. In February the pastor had contracted malaria, and a month later he was experiencing fits of shaking so violent that he had to dictate his report to Assistant Pastor Sårheim. Hansteen claimed that the cause of his illness was the unhealthy air of the station's location. The home office must never demand that staff members live in the parsonage by the Seamen's Church, he asserted, because "'Red Hook Point,' the section of the city where the church lies, is so infested with malaria that even the doctors are moving out, which, according to American folk wisdom, is decisive proof."[48]

Because of his wife's illness, in January Hansteen had reluctantly begun investigating the possibility of returning to Norway permanently. In a confidential letter that he asked the Mission Society's director to burn as soon as it was read, he explained his personal problems and asked for a discreet assessment of his chances of being employed by the society at home in Norway. At the same time, he emphasized that this was the worst possible time for him to leave the Brookyn station. All that he had striven for during the last six years seemed at its "most critical point." He awaited the delivery of the steam launch and the realization of its possibilities. The Sailors' Home would be incorporated with a hand-picked board of trustees within a short time. The campaign to secure American sources of financial support for the Seamen's Church was at a turning point, he felt, and Assistant Pastor Sårheim could not continue it because his command of English was limited.[49]

Finally, the situation among the church's immigrant parishioners necessitated their formation into an independent congregation under a full-time Lutheran minister as quickly as possible. For this he felt a personal responsibility, because the independence his laymen's movement had fostered seemed at least partly the cause of an extreme pietism that was developing among the membership. Without the close supervision of an ordained minister, a splinter group had formed. Calling themselves "electric Christians" after the new street lighting that had begun appearing, these renegades claimed that they alone were entirely saved and that Lutheranism, like gas lighting, was an outmoded relic of the past. Worst of all, their views had not only sown strife in the Seamen's

Church but had also attracted followers among the hospital's deaconesses, transient seamen, and members of Our Savior's congregation.[50] More than ever before, the Reverend Everson and his supporters
seemed to have reason for identifying the Seamen's Church as the
source of low-church evangelism.

When Hansteen's malaria attacks persisted into late March, he felt
forced to leave Red Hook but, under the circumstances, decided to
delay departure until he had surmounted the present crises. His March
report included an official application for employment as the society's
traveling emissary to congregations in the home country "as soon as
conditions in New York make that possible." He also gave a formal pre-
sentation of his arguments for reorganizing the station along the lines of
the American Seamen's Church, but admitted that he faced an unexpected new difficulty. Now that Assistant Pastor Sårheim knew of
Hansteen's decision to leave within a half-year, he realized he would
soon assume the duties of senior pastor and could be saddled with the
responsibility for carrying out his predecessor's ambitious plans if he was
not careful. He therefore openly questioned all Hansteen's ideas and actively opposed some aspects of the reorganization plan, such as employing only one ordained pastor and relying completely on the steam
launch for contacting seamen.[51]

Sårheim's new assertiveness forced Hansteen to put his proposals
to the test while he still held the reins of power at the Brooklyn station.
The maneuvering of his opponents in the colony, moreover, continued
to show that he had to act before their plans undermined his own. For
example, Magnus Andersen and his four supporters called a mass meeting to organize the Norwegian-American Seaman's Association with
pomp and ceremony in early April. Andersen himself and the well-
known Norwegian-American author and professor at Columbia University, Hjalmar Hjorth Boyesen, used the occasion to emphasize the
new organization's secular character and ability to meet all the seamen's
needs. Therefore, in spite of the public commotion over the *Herald's* article, which had hardened the ring's opposition to the use of the
launch—and his own fragile health—Hansteen decided to ignore Andersen's warnings. When the motorboat arrived on May 17, Norway's
Constitution Day, he immediately consecrated it for the church's use
with an impressive ceremony that reached a climax when the launch
steamed into the harbor flying the Norwegian and Seamen's Church
flags.[52]

Anton Andersen soon reported the ring's agitation at seeing the
launch with flags brazenly waving, and Magnus hurried to Hansteen to
repeat his warnings. The seamen's pastor cavalierly stated his disbelief
that the runners would physically attack a minister peacefully distributing information about his church and turned a deaf ear to further debate.[53] Much more depended on the launch than Andersen knew. If
Hansteen could not succeed with the launch, his whole complex of in-

terrelated plans would collapse, and little would remain as evidence of his efforts in Red Hook. On June 5, a beautiful sunny day, Hansteen invited his wife and one of the station's two unordained assistants to join him for his first trip on the launch to Staten Island. Finally, he would demonstrate that the boat's speed enabled the station to contact *all* newly-arrived ships while they lay clustered for customs clearance and before the ring's runners could poison the crews' minds against the Seamen's Church.[54]

Hansteen enclosed a minute description of the day's events in his July report. The trip from Bay Ridge was short. Soon the line of waiting vessels loomed ahead and he decided to take them in order. The first in the queue, the *Abbie S. Hart*, had the added advantage of being a Nova Scotia ship, since meeting its crew would inaugurate the important business of reaching the growing number of Norwegian seamen on foreign ships. The assistant and Mrs. Hansteen stayed in the launch when it had tied on to the ship's ladder, and the pastor climbed to the deck. With religious tracts and brochures about the station's activities in hand, Hansteen greeted the Norwegian-Canadian mate and won immediate permission to distribute his materials and talk to the men, many of whom proved to be exactly the Norwegian nationals he wished most to persuade.[55]

In a friendly atmosphere Hansteen conversed with every crew member and prepared to leave. Just then a man he had not seen earlier stopped him by aggressively asserting, "I guess you won't let anyone else in the world live now, will you?" When Hansteen asked why he thought that, the man only made sure he was talking to the Scandinavian seamen's priest and claimed that gave him every right to accuse. Hansteen ascertained that he was talking to a Staten Island runner and started to explain that he was not recruiting for the home, when six to nine men rushed out of a gangway, jumped him, pulled him inside, and began beating his face and head. The first blow bloodied him, but he determined to hold his ground and remain conscious so he could explain their mistake after they had vented their anger.

As the blows continued unabated and spread to his groin, he screamed for help from the crew. Receiving none, he managed to run out on the deck before the runners overtook him and threw him down. There he lay doubled up to protect his head and vital organs while they kicked him, until someone yelled, "Get off the ship quick!" and he heard the mate repeat that desperate advice. The realization that no one would help him even if he was beaten senseless gave Hansteen the strength to spring to the ladder leading to the launch. As he hurriedly stumbled down it, the runners kicked at him and shook the ladder to shake him off. Falling into the motorboat with clothes "as bloody as a butcher's" and his face a "single cake of blood," Hansteen noticed five boats full of runners and ordered the assistant to escape at top speed.

In his July report, Hansteen showed that being beaten and landing humiliated in front of his wife had not discouraged him. Instead, both his sense of having a religious call and his proud upper-class conviction that he could handle any situation fueled his outrage and eagerness for action. Sårheim claimed that Mrs. Hansteen and the assistant feared he might die en route to a doctor. Hansteen, on the other hand, limited his description of the medical examination to the doctors' statement that his wounds resulted from "assault with the intention to kill."[56]

That was the legal complaint he demanded that Consul Børs lodge with the police and announce to the press and municipal authorities. According to the pastor's version of the story's denouement, the Consul's quick action resulted in police raids in Manhattan's and Brooklyn's sailortowns as well as newspaper articles that raised a wave of public opinion against the ring and the runners who served it. Meeting possible opposition head on, the pastor contacted Andersen's instrument, the Norwegian-American Seamen's Association, to give his version of events and gather information about the ring's reactions to the public alarm over the case. Although it never openly took the pastor's side, the Association held several meetings to debate its course of action and through its contacts answered many of the pastor's questions.[57]

The runners who had attacked Hansteen, it seemed, had not acted on orders from the ring. They were members of Staten Island's Irish-American Runners' Society, one of two ethnic organizations that divided between them the profitable business of supplying sailors to boarding masters at between one and five dollars a head. The earlier story in the *Herald* had convinced the Irish runners and their colleagues in the "Dutch" Runners' Society that the Seamen's Church would use the launch to recruit for the home. Independently of the ring, the societies had agreed that if a seamen's pastor approached the island on the launch and boarded an American, English, or Nova Scotia ship, the Irishmen would attack. Since all other vessels were the Dutchmen's market, they would take action if a pastor contacted one of these.

Having several boats in the area on normal business, the Irishmen had noticed the launch at a distance and sent a few runners on board the *Abbie S. Hart* to surprise the pastor and scare him off once and for all. The same men threatened the crew with exclusion from boardinghouses and violence from reinforcements alongside if they interfered. According to the stories association members heard, the ring had become furious with the Irish Society when the story appeared in city newspapers and had hustled the men involved out of town. After three extraordinary meetings, the ring's council decided the attack had been a great mistake, since public opinion had already been against them.

In view of this information, Hansteen thought the Seamen's Church should strike while the "sword of righteousness" and the threat of imprisonment hung over the runners' heads. Their brutal assault had created an opportunity to negotiate directly with the runner societies from a position of strength. While public reaction was still strong, Hansteen should offer to have Consul Børs drop the charges if the runners pledged never again to interfere with the pastors when they contacted ships at Staten Island. He could also promise as part of the deal never to mention the Sailors' Home, since the pastors could contact many more newly-arrived seamen with the launch than they ever could through the home's limited number of boarders. If the station acted quickly, it could actually use the ring's anger over the unfavorable publicity to put added pressure on the runner societies. If it waited, the runner societies would find out that the predominantly Irish police force "could not or would not do anything" about the assault on Hansteen.

The pastor's bitterness must have been great when Sårheim and "several others with him" opposed his plan of action. Asserting that Hansteen presented the greatest obstacle to a solution of the conflict, they refused to make any direct contact with the runner societies until September, when he had left Brooklyn. Sårheim, not Hansteen, should negotiate with the runners since he would soon inherit responsibility for the station. Further, the home's incorporation with a board of trustees had to be delayed until then. Because the main purpose of that change would be to demonstrate that all direct connection with the station had ended, no seamen's pastor would serve on the board. Instead, Sårheim's group would propose Magnus Andersen and the other leaders of the Norwegian-American Seamen's Association! Perhaps later, when sailortown's anger had cooled, a seamen's pastor could quietly assume a place on the board. In the meantime, the pastor was to keep a low profile because "so much hate was concentrated" against his person.[58]

Hansteen vented his frustration to his superiors in Bergen. After nearly four months' delay, he wrote, making a deal with the runners would be much more difficult. Sårheim still said he wanted to meet the ships at Staten Island, but now a long-term, extensive campaign would be necessary to reach agreement. The station would have to mobilize support among the leaders of the American Seamen's Church, the charitable harbor agencies, and the mission societies. All these reform-minded groups would have to put pressure on politicians through meetings and by making their case in the press, both of which would be more difficult now because the story of the assault was no longer news. For twenty years New York State had had a good law that would have protected seamen against boarding masters and runners, if only the commission in charge of it had demanded the enforcement of its provisions. Sårheim and a reformer coalition could also try to "breathe life" into that old law, but that would be difficult because the commissioners who had not done their duty were the same reform leaders whose cooperation Sårheim needed.[59]

Unfortunately, not even the Mission's executive board seemed to support Hansteen's ideas by the summer of 1889. Because of the pastor's lame-duck status, the board instead accepted Sårheim's assessment of the situation and, furthermore, took a more direct hand in setting the course of the station's future activities. Rather than reorganize its staffing along American lines, to Hansteen's disbelief, the board advised dropping the campaign for American aid and restricting the station's work to contacting seamen on Scandinavian ships. In a special report to Bergen, Sårheim had mentioned that he could manage with a smaller staff in the future if one gave up the idea of visiting foreign ships, and perhaps the board had grasped that as a hint of his real hopes. Whatever the board's motivations might have been, such a policy change would clearly avoid further conflict with the runner societies. Where was the need for a steam launch if pastors were not to contact seamen serving in foreign merchant marines by going out to Staten Island?[60]

The mission's board also ordered the station to stop administering the sacraments to immigrants by the summer's end, so that they would have to join another congregation or form their own. The Bergen office had recently received a number of letters from sea captains complaining that Brooklyn's Seamen's Church no longer had room for sailors because so many settlers attended. Moreover, when *Nordiske Blade* had published similar complaints from seamen during the spring and voiced its agreement, an anonymous person had sent the articles to the executive board.[61]

These latest proofs of conflicts arising from serving immigrants seem to have put an end to the board's patience with economic arguments for waiting with the break. The home office announced that Brooklyn's Seamen's Church would have to raise funds through the same Norwegian channels other mission stations used and restrict its activities to a level that those funds could support. Since the church still depended on the immigrants for $1,500 in annual operating expenses, the board's action precipitated an immediate crisis. Despite their falling out over other matters, Hansteen and Sårheim had to cooperate in a scramble to get funds through the consul and shipping agents. Simultaneously, they pondered how to break the news to the immigrants in their congregation.

In the event, few of Hansteen's initiatives turned out as he had imagined. He had left an indelible impression on local institutions, but a combination of his own limitations and forces beyond his control altered most of his carefully laid plans. A week after Hansteen left, Sårheim announced the home office's decision to the immigrant congregation, and the settlers founded a separate church, Trinity Lutheran, within a year. To a degree, that development satisfied Hansteen's idea of what was best for the immigrants. They became fully participating congregational members under a minister whose only duty was attending to their religious needs, and as Hansteen had hoped, they rejected the idea of joining Everson's stiffly orthodox congregation.[62]

On the other hand, under the influence of the Free Lutheran Mission Society he had encouraged, Trinity became so low-church and lay-

oriented that it suffered schisms and criticized the Seamen's Church.
The more conservative members fled to Our Savior's, and the sect of
electric Christians first caused intense infighting within the new congregation and then left to form a store-front church. While they were
still attending services at the station, the younger immigrants had
claimed that the seamen's pastors were becoming "more and more
high-church." Even Gabriel Fedde and the other responsible lay leaders
in the group had evolved views that diverged from the theology of
Norway's state church. The minister they chose came from what they
saw as the least orthodox Lutheran organization in the Midwest, which
they referred to as the Minneapolis Conference.[63]

Worse, these leaders and most Trinity members grew bitter toward
the station when they saw it admit other immigrants in their place even
before the new church was founded. As Gabriel Fedde remarked sarcas-
tically in his memoirs, "When most of the Seamen's Church's best
friends had been thrown out, it continued to give full service to settlers
and seamen without preference. Yes, there were even announcements
and invitations in the narthex to settlers promising them all the service
they could wish."[64]

Within a few months Sårheim felt forced to accept immigrants because he failed to find funding to replace their financial contributions.
Even if he had solved the station's economic crisis, however, he could
not maintain a strict policy of excluding immigrants. The great wave of
Norwegian immigration that began in 1880 lasted until 1893 and continued to bring more immigrants to Brooklyn than previous waves. Because Norwegian shipping remained depressed, these bona fide immigrants included unprecedented numbers of seamen and maritime
workers. At the same time, sailors still jumped ship in port. The number
of deserters from Norwegian ships dropped to around 200 a year by
1890, but by then the American merchant marine and other nations'
ships frequenting the harbor had accumulated large numbers of Norwegian seamen, most of whom did not consider themselves immigrants. In
the early 1890s, the United States Commissioner of Navigation estimated that four-fifths of the sailors in the American coastal trade were
Scandinavians, and *Nordisk Tidende*, the Red Hook colony's new newspaper, claimed that Norwegians constituted the largest nationality group
among all seamen entering the harbor.[65]

Regardless of occupation or legal status, newcomers tended to seek
out the Seamen's Church when they needed assistance and often attended services there during their first months in the city. While the
seamen's pastor could now advise those arriving on immigrant ships to
join Trinity or Our Savior's, it remained practically impossible to exclude the many sailors who drifted into settled residence. These men
and the families they established viewed the station as their home
church. Their maritime background enabled them to understand transient seamen's needs and to provide the familial, genuinely Norwegian

atmosphere that was one of the station's chief attractions for transients. Under these circumstances, the decision of the mission's home office had not only been premature but inimical to the station's effectiveness.[66] Gabriel Fedde was right. Of necessity, the station merely exchanged one group of immigrant friends and supporters for another.

The Sailors' Home also evolved differently than Hansteen had imagined. It was much better than no alternative to sailortown's boardinghouses but it did not serve many of his original goals. Ironically, the secular aspects of the pastor's plan were almost the only ones that remained fixtures in its organization. By providing room and board at low prices and running a postal service for sending savings home to Norway, the home helped men practice a more responsible personal economy. Strictly enforcing the total ban on alcoholic beverages, Andersen and later managers excluded any man who appeared intoxicated.[67]

Each of these achievements, however, reflected different notions than those Hansteen had had in mind. Having a Norwegian atmosphere at the home only brought it on a par with the colony lodgings that large numbers of sailors had already begun choosing in preference to sailortown's boardinghouses. Financially more mature than Hansteen had thought, the men stayed in the home only when its prices were lower than the rooms immigrant families offered or, more important, when residence at the home enabled them to find work more rapidly. Seamen had mailed money to Norway though the consulate in Manhattan before the home opened. The new institution had, therefore, not brought sailors up to a willingness to send their savings home. It had only made doing so more convenient for those who chose to reside there. The home's rule against alcohol remained in force because the manager found it essential for maintaining order.[68]

In short, the somewhat patronizing notion of the men's immaturity that Hansteen shared with leaders in the Manhattan elite had had little to do with the success of these policies. Practical considerations, the seamen's enlightened self-interest, and competition from private lodgings in the colony had ensured the achievement of Hansteen's secular goals. Hansteen's overtly religious hopes for the home failed completely. Instead, Magnus Andersen's concept triumphed, even though he had resigned in May and left Red Hook only a few months after Hansteen. The home had become a secular ethnic lodging house and hiring office instead of an institution dedicated to familial Norwegian Lutheranism. The basis for its operational style was the shipboard relationship between captain and crew. Seamen voluntarily accepted Andersen's rules of order, granting him the honorary title of captain on that basis, but his authority stopped at the door to the home and did not include their spiritual welfare.[69]

A more damaging development, in Hansteen's view, was that the home prospered through willing, although mostly tacit, cooperation with the boardinghouse masters' ring. Because of the ring's opposition, the home did not try to contact the increasing numbers of Norwegian seamen on foreign vessels. Instead, it placated the ring, found Norwegian sailors berths on American ships, and looked for support in the only local organization dedicated exclusively to seamen's interests. During his last days in the city the seamen's pastor had the bitter experience of seeing the group that had founded the Norwegian-American Seamen's Association take seats on the home's first executive board while, according to Sårheim's wishes, the Seamen's Church was unrepresented. The formation of the board and the home's incorporation went down in colony history as the end of all direct connection between the mission station and the home.

On the other hand, as Sårheim had earlier suggested, seamen's pastors became "honorary" members of the board when the current crisis had passed. Sårheim had, moreover, a voice in the selection of the next manager of the home, Captain Ullenæss, who was a pious man with strong connections to the Seamen's Church and the Deaconess Home and Hospital. Essentially, the difference in the station's influence on the home resulted from Sårheim's decision to work patiently behind the scenes. Hansteen's unhappy experience had taught his successor to emphasize the avoidance of open conflict.

**The Larger Trends and Issues**

For over a decade, pastors at the Seamen's Church served as matchmakers and midwives who arranged the establishment of other institutions in the Red Hook colony. They urged unions of differing interests, scavanged for funds and managed compromises to nurture plans through their gestation stage, and then presided over the practical difficulties when new institutions saw the light of day. In this fashion, fund-raising bazaars, the Deaconess Home and Hospital, Brooklyn's Free Lutheran Mission Society, the colony vigilance committee, and the Sailors' Home came into being. Since the pastors administered the new organizations or served on their executive boards, they could use the new institutions to ease their work load and also ensure that the aims of the station were furthered.

The pastors had only a partial realization that basic conditions for the colony's existence were steadily eroding the station's status in the community even as they gave their energies to enlarging its influence. Circumstances had prevented the founding of the Seamen's Church until the golden age of Norwegian shipping in the city was almost over. By the start of the 1880s, the industry was already falling into an economic depression because of its difficulties in adjusting to the rise of steam technology. That change in turn meant that the majority of Norwegian sailors arriving in New York came either on other nations' vessels or as immigrants. At the same time, the importance of shipping for Norway's economy as a whole contributed to the hard times that pushed Norwegian emigration to unprecedented levels. Together, these two factors changed the course of the colony's development.

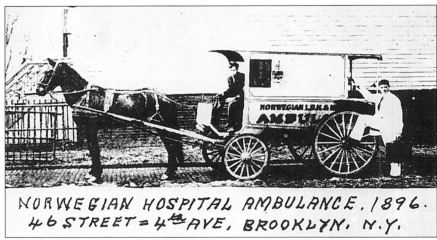

•

The Norwegian Lutheran Hospital at its first location at 109 William Street. The
Norwegian-American Historical Association.

•

By 1896, when this picture was taken, a year has passed since Sister Elizabeth had
returned to Norway, and the Hospital, Deaconess Home, and school of nursing
were prospering near the outskirts of the built-up Brooklyn at 46th Street and 4th
Avenue. Courtesy Sigurd Daasvand.

The pastors were among the first to notice the rising tide of immigrants and the swelling numbers of Norwegian mariners on foreign ships. They stressed the movement of settlers from the Manhattan colony to the Red Hook area as a major factor in the conflict with Our Savior's. On the other hand, they did not remark that the population balance in the colony was shifting toward a predominance of settlers over transient seamen or that the newcomers were more often men and women whose livelihoods were not dependent on the harbor. Nor did they comment on the accelerating process of seamen going on land to find work in new occupations. Finally, only when it was too late did the station's primary leader during the decade, Carsten Hansteen, realize the importance of Norwegian seamen for groups outside the colony and understand the strength of a secular world view among seamen.

The combination of trends that the pastors did not fully comprehend played an important role in the conflicts of the decade. As the settled immigrant community grew in size, its desire for more control over local institutions increased, and its leaders found the decisive voice of emissary leaders in colony affairs steadily more irritating. These two factors informed the immigrants' attempts to seize control of the executive boards of the hospital and the Seamen's Church. The socioeconomic background of the sojourning leaders, the seamen's pastors, and the consular elite in Manhattan aggravated the situation. The station's conflict with Our Savior's, the disagreements between Andersen and Hansteen over the Sailors' Home, and the exclusion of immigrants from sacraments at the Seamen's Church were all more bitter because, to some immigrants, the sojourning leaders seemed to extend the power of Norway's arrogant official class to the New World.

On the one hand, the sojourning leaders controlled the purse strings. They not only had access to funding in Norway but also competed with immigrant groups for the limited financial support available in the Red Hook colony. On the other, they ruled on what was proper conduct for Norwegians in the city by attempting to set moral guidelines. In fact, their status as the guardians of unadulterated Norwegianness resulted largely from their situation as temporary residents who did not have to make a long-term adjustment to American conditions. Like the members of their class in Norway, then, they had a large degree of financial and cultural influence over services for other groups without having to share the living conditions of those groups.

In Brooklyn, the sojourning leaders' authority had a positive side because they operated as a reliable lifeline to the old country that was renewed each time a new emissary arrived. Their influence also had negative effects, however, because sojourners were less committed to local problems and knew less about local conditions. Had Pastor Hansteen known as much about the area's runner organizations and other ethnic groups as Anton Andersen and members of the Norwegian-American Seamen's Association did, for example, he might have been more wary of meeting incoming ships at Staten Island. With that added caution, he could have avoided a brutal beating, the defeat of his plans for the Sailors' Home, and the reaction of the Mission Society's home office that led to the ejection of immigrants from the Seamen's Church.

The influence of American conditions permeated the struggles of the decade. The issue of preserving Norwegianness arose because both sojourning and immigrant leaders hoped that institutions as nearly like those in the homeland as possible would better attract immigrants or transient sailors. The main problem at the Seamen's Church was that its supposedly pure Norwegian character attracted both, while at Our Savior's the effort to replicate Norwegian forms produced an orthodoxy that was unappealing to many immigrants.

Perhaps because they felt an absolute security in their national identity, sojourning leaders were more willing to attempt institutional experimentation. Ready to imitate the organizational structure of the American Seamen's Church to gain American funding, Hansteen expressed no fear of sacrificing the station's ethnic identity in the process. Nor did he worry about diluting Norwegian Lutheranism by introducing layman-led services among the immigrants at the station. Only when young people at the Seamen's Church formed a radical sect and leaders at Our Savior's labeled him a Methodist did he see the disadvantages of his actions. In similar fashion, Magnus Andersen gave no thought to the notion that the Sailors' Home and the Norwegian-American Seamen's Association might encourage a drain on the homeland's maritime manpower until visiting Norwegian captains asserted that view. Inadvertently, both these sojourning leaders added to the differences between the colony's institutions and those in Norway and thus contributed to the trends working toward the evolution of a distinctive Norwegian-American ethnic community.

By 1890, the institutional configuration of the colony reflected the increased size and diversity of its population. Four churches, three for immigrants and one intended for maritime transients, showed a range of religious views from Methodist to high-church Lutheran. The Sailors' Home and the Norwegian-American Seamen's Association evidenced both the importance of maritime occupations and the trend toward more secular institutions. The home and the Seamen's Church flourished because large numbers of transient sailors continued to arrive. The Deaconess Home and Hospital occupied the middle ground in the sense that its purpose was to serve immigrants as well as transients. The Seamen's Association and the immigrant churches best revealed the trend of future developments by documenting the increased importance of the settled colony.

# 7

# Living and Working Together in the 1890s

People who knew Emil Nielsen said he came off the boat in a silk hat and white vest, carrying a caged parrot. He was like the north wind that swept everything before it and was totally indifferent to other people's opinions and beliefs unless he could arouse them into activity by challenging their assumptions. When he started *Nordisk Tidende* in Red Hook in 1891, its confrontational approach may therefore not have surprised his acquaintances. In his first editorial, he declared that the New York area had needed a second Norwegian newspaper for over a decade. Relying on *Nordiske Blade* ensured neither objectivity nor the "proper polemics" his countrymen ought to expect from their local press. Nielsen said his newspaper ought to be a "big step forward" for the Norwegians who called the Red Hook section "Little Norway." It ought to succeed, since he was an experienced, well-qualified printer and the newspaper was a community service that should draw the immigrants together.[1]

The only question, in Nielsen's view, was whether or not area Norwegians really composed a colony in the sense of a cohesive ethnic community. Even though a large group made homes in Red Hook,

**In Search of Little Norway**

many others lived in widely scattered districts, and all shared "their" territory with many other nationality groups. Instead of "rowing in one boat," each Norwegian rowed his own and rejoiced most when his boat sank a countryman's. In short, Nielsen claimed that Norwegians were perhaps too limited in their group awareness and sense of community territory to warrant their own newspaper. He dared local readers to prove him wrong. Even when Nielsen died in 1907, there were reasonable doubts about whether common goals could unite the diverse elements among Brooklyn Norwegians and make them pull in the same direction.[2]

Was Norwegians' group awareness strong enough in the 1890s to create ways of living and working together that formed the basis of an ethnic community in Brooklyn? Did the area the immigrants called *Lille Norge* have recognizable residential and occupational characteristics? The treasury of information in the manuscript schedules of New York State's 1892 census brings the main outlines of an answer into focus. Views and commentary from a variety of other rich depositories—from federal censuses, community histories, period maps and drawings of the area, *Nordisk Tidende*'s columns, contemporary narratives written by residents, and the collective memories of over sixty immigrants—fill out those outlines with a wealth of vivid, telling details that confirm the existence of a vibrant Norwegian colony in Brooklyn.

## Which Settlement was Destined to Become the Metropolitan Area's Primary Norwegian Center?

When Nielsen spoke about area Norwegians, he was thinking about his potential audience and therefore included those spread throughout metropolitan New York. After the migration of the 1880s, Manhattan Norwegians no longer lived in a compact section but in neighborhoods near both ends of the island. Those in New Jersey congregated in coastal towns from Hoboken to Perth Amboy. Still others lived and worked in Staten Island's northern dock and shipyard districts. In Brooklyn, Norwegians were scattered over the whole length of the city's shoreline, from today's Bay Ridge in the south to Greenpoint in the north. A large part of *Nordisk Tidende*'s potential readership, the transient merchant marine and the people living on harbor craft, had no permanent address but looked for news about their homeland and local Norwegians wherever they docked.

Norwegian enclaves ringed New York Bay and dotted the harbor. In 1892, however, only Brooklyn's Red Hook settlement seemed to show promise of becoming a stable center, a nucleus around which the others could revolve. The old Manhattan colony, Nielsen realized, was the nearest competitor. It still held the most important elements in the bay area elite—the consulate and major old-country shipping agencies, as well as the loyalty of *Nordiske Blade*. On the other hand, the migration to Harlem and Red Hook had reduced its immigrant population. The development of docks across the East River had made the Red Hook-Gowanus section of Brooklyn the most attractive settlement area.

Most Norwegian sailors went ashore at the piers and ship basins surrounding the peninsula. The same commercial facilities created employment opportunities for Norwegian immigrants. Consequently, the Red Hook colony's working-class population grew, while the Manhattan colony began to resemble a ship with several captains but too little crew. Precisely because of that fact, the public-spirited among the Manhattan elite had been directing their charitable impulses toward Red Hook-Gowanus Norwegians since the late 1870s.

The more northerly concentrations of Norwegians in Brooklyn held little promise of becoming the focal point for which Nielsen was searching. By 1892 the Greenpoint group in Ward 17 numbered no more than 104 adults, divided among nineteen different lines of work. The people there had the cohesion to want their own church but could only muster the resources to arrange for a Norwegian minister from Red Hook to hold services in rented quarters. Within two years, Greenpoint's Norwegian population had declined by a third. The next appreciable concentration of Norwegians fell into three distinct groups appropriate to the disparate sections of Ward 1 that they inhabited. Unmarried female domestics who worked in the fine homes on Brooklyn Heights formed by far the largest occupational category, but in only one instance did two work at the same residence. Single seamen, the next largest group, lived among a welter of different nationalities in the dockside tenements along the narrow strip of land below the Heights. In the lower-lying district at the southern end of the ward, the third group, composed mostly of laborers and craftsmen, had gathered in tenements behind Atlantic Avenue.[3]

Neither the struggling Greenpoint settlement nor the small Norwegian population in and around Brooklyn Heights constituted an ethnic community. Only when a visitor went farther south into Ward 6 did the fringes of what could be called a Norwegian colony appear. Somewhere between Atlantic and Hamilton avenues began the territory in which Emil Nielsen thought his countrymen should establish a Norwegian community center for the whole metropolitan area. The contiguous parts of two wards, 6 and 12, in the Red Hook-Gowanus section housed a bustling Little Norway composed of 1,834 adult immigrants and an undetermined number of children in 676 families. In addition, the area contained most of the itinerant maritime population. Many of the nearly 1,700 transient seamen on Norwegian ships entering the harbor during the year were at least guests and perhaps even temporary residents in the colony. Very likely, a much larger number of Norwegian mariners frequented the colony during shore leaves from other nations' vessels. In 1889, the seamen's pastors had predicted that most of the more than 20,000 Norwegian sailors coming to New York would arrive in "foreign" fleets. An unknown number of these men may have become more stable colony residents after jumping ship in the harbor. Although the area's Norwegian population fluctuated greatly because of seamen's transiency, around 23,000 people probably had, at the least, a temporary residence in Little Norway during 1892.[4]

Little Norway's northwestern corner appeared where Baltic Street met New York Bay in the northern part of Ward 6. The waterfront boundary that ran south around Red Hook and up the Gowanus Canal to Fourth Place defined three sides of Ward 12. The rest of the colony's perimeter went up Court Street from Fourth Place to a northeastern corner at its intersection with Baltic Street. Norwegians with homes in the narrow strip along Third and Fourth avenues in Wards 22 and 8 lived in the colony's sparsely populated southern and western marches. The southwestern corner of dense Norwegian settlement appeared farther north where Hamilton Avenue crossed the Gowanus Canal.[5]

This colony contained not only four-fifths of Brooklyn's settled Northmen but also manifold evidences of the socioeconomic interdependence that made it more than a collection of Norwegian individualists rowing in different directions. The proofs of cohesive neighborhoods and cooperative endeavor to reach common goals were clearest in the colony's demographic and socioeconomic center, which covered the streets on both sides of Red Hook's Hamilton Avenue between the Bay and the Gowanus Canal.[6]

**The Physical and Socio-economic Geography of the Red Hook Colony**

Enormous changes had occurred in Red Hook and Gowanus since the Norwegian 49'ers came through. Even the more numerous Norwegian settlers and seamen who came to Old South Brooklyn in the 1860s would have found the area hard to recognize. Overlay after overlay of urban development had obscured the original shape of the land and obliterated most of the oldest structures on it. In 1873, Dripps' Map of Brooklyn and Vicinity showed the original shoreline as well as the Dutch and English surnames of colonists whose American descendants still owned the land that once had bordered New York Bay. Although *Nordisk Tidende* made no mention of the fact in 1892, the surnames of two Norwegian pioneers from America's colonial period, Bergen and Bensen, were among the original owners marked on Dripps' map.[7]

Even in 1873, the mountains of dirt and stone on which the Atlantic Drydocks and Erie Ship Basin stood covered much of the red earth that had given the peninsula its name. Red Hook Point, which harbor pilots had once carefully sighted to avoid the shoals near Remsen Island, was by that time not the highest elevation on the island but a part of a landmass more than twice its original size. Most of Hamilton Avenue and all the streets near the piers of the 1870s had once been under water. The Gowanus section was also largely made land produced by draining swamps and ponds during the rechanneling of the streams that eventually produced the Canal and its several boat basins.

State census maps from the 1890s showed drastic changes in the Erie Basin district. What had been two basins was now one with several parallel piers on one side. Ship channels ("slips") or piers had replaced the southern ends of Columbia, Hicks, and Henry streets, and in the process, several blocks on nearby east-west streets had disappeared.

By the turn of the century, all this work had transformed Red Hook and Gowanus into adjacent parts of a congested urban district that housed not only harbor facilities but a large resident population. Because most of the district was on land reclaimed from New York Bay, however, it was rather unhealthful for those who lived and worked in its dockside neighborhoods, as Seamen's Pastor Hansteen had discovered in the late 1880s.

In 1892, the pulse of Norwegian community life was strongest along Hamilton Avenue and its side streets. Starting with the ferry from Manhattan, the Avenue crossed sailortown on Commercial Wharf, Imlay, and Van Brunt streets, where large numbers of Norwegian immigrants lived among warehouses, small businesses, and lodging places for transient mariners. Beyond the immediate vicinity of the Atlantic Docks, several dozen Norwegian shops and businesses occupied storefront locations on both sides of the Avenue and the next side streets, Columbia, Hicks, and Henry. Above the shops and in the blocks behind them were the tenement neighborhoods that held the largest Norwegian populations.

Between Henry Street and the Gowanus Canal, four blocks to the east, the districts behind the Avenue changed character rapidly. Within easy walking distance of the Avenue on the north, a purely residential neighborhood of single-family homes with gardens started on Fourth Place and increased in exclusivity as it rose to the high ground around First Place. Few Norwegians other than female domestics lived on "The Places," but somewhat larger numbers benefited from better housing and health conditions nearby. The higher-class residential area was only two to three blocks wide, and north of First Place it was rapidly assuming a working-class character. The ground began to slope downward toward the Gowanus Canal at Court Street, where wage-earners and their families crowded into tenements on both sides of Hamilton Avenue. Norwegians were particularly numerous below Fourth Place and on Smith Street, where the back windows of apartments gave views of barge traffic on the Canal.

The Avenue itself housed a great many Norwegians. It throbbed with life, primarily because it ended in the Hamilton Avenue Ferry. Even nine years after the opening of the Brooklyn Bridge, the ferry remained the most direct way of traveling between Manhattan and the rapidly-expanding southern part of Brooklyn. During that time, the Avenue had rung with the clatter of the horse cars, but by the 1890s the animals were shying at the noise of electric trolleys. For over a decade, developers had been converting Carrol Gardens, Park Slope, Gowanus, and Sunset Park from thinly-settled farmland to miles of terraced housing adapted to fit the needs of all classes. Finally, the city responded to the increasing traffic in 1892 by opening two electrified trolley lines

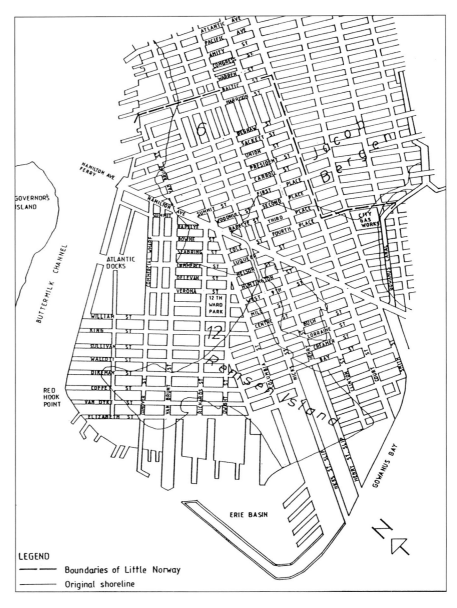

Red Hook's Little Norway in 1892.

meeting in Red Hook. One ran from the Brooklyn Academy of Music down Smith Street to the Avenue. The other, coming in from the Prospect Park area, met it where Hamilton Avenue crossed the Gowanus Canal.[8]

Although only wide enough for two-lane traffic, the Avenue allowed room for crowds to gather at several points along its length. Not only was there a large ferry landing, but several paved triangles formed from abbreviated blocks made room both for pedestrians and, near the ferry, for thirsty horses. A jumble of two-to-four-story brick buildings topped with elaborate cornices lined the Avenue's Red Hook segment. Businesses of various kinds occupied the first and occasionally the upper floors all the way to the Canal. The Hamilton bank with its impressive archways and the massive India Wharf that covered much of the first block by the ferry landing were probably the most noticeable. Most buildings had one or more small shops on the first floor and apartments or boardinghouses above them. Family groceries, bakeries, barbershops, notions and stationery stores, watchmakers and tobacconists were wall to wall with saloons, dance halls, and liquor stores. Norwegian merchants joined other ethnic and American entrepreneurs in making sure customers could find just about all the wares and services they wanted without leaving the Avenue.

These businesses had a large and varied clientele. Morning and evening crowds of commuters rushed through, stopping perhaps to do a few necessary errands before or after work. Many who resided in the Red Hook-Gowanus district, Norwegians among them, joined the river of humanity that was dependent on New York's larger job market. They and the thousands who packed the area's tenements provided the local merchants with most of their regular customers. At various times of the day, groups of immigrants arrived by the ferry if their destination was southern Brooklyn. The surviving accounts of Norwegian newcomers seldom neglect to mention the boat trip and their first impressions of meeting fellow countrymen in Red Hook.[9]

Sailors and dock workers of various kinds swarmed into the area as other commuters flowed out. The Atlantic Docks, Erie Ship Basin, and Gowanus Canal were, after all, the area's main businesses. Their construction had necessitated first the ferry connection and then warehouse facilities, a grid of streets, and housing for workers. Some managers and workmen very likely still commuted from New York. Mariners whose ships docked at Manhattan or New Jersey piers often arrived by the ferry to take berths on ships leaving from Old South Brooklyn, Red Hook, or the recently completed wharves in Sunset Park.[10]

Norwegian seamen disembarked from piers or the ferry at any time of day, but especially after working hours. According to records of the time, most captains and crews left their ships at night. One seaman or, more often, a night watchman guarded the vessels in their absence. During the evening, seafarers came ashore to stay with relatives, shop, or have a night on the town. The possibilities for involvement in the life of Red Hook ranged from temperance and revival meetings to the entertainments and pleasures of sailortown. Pastors at the Norwegian Seamen's Church handed out flyers all over the bay area inviting Scandinavian men to their services, social affairs, and reading room. Because Hamilton Avenue was the hub of a sailortown that included Commercial Wharf, Imlay, and Van Brunt streets, however, the pastors' directions to the ferry crossing may have led as many Norwegian sailors to temptation as to church.[11]

Eight or nine blocks away from the Avenue, Norwegians gathered in two districts, one on the north side and one on the south. Between Hicks and Henry streets on the north, the working-class families of carpenters and laborers made up the majority of Norwegians in a neighborhood almost equally Scandinavian and Irish. On the south, Norwegian immigrants working on the wharves or in the harbor shared the quarter surrounding the Erie Basin with seafaring countrymen and mariners of many nations.[12]

Only the streets around the Atlantic Docks, just three blocks away, contained larger numbers of Norwegians than the area close to the Erie Basin. Together, the harbor-related neighborhoods housed the second largest immigrant population in the colony, including 694 adults and the children in 182 families. The largest neighborhood filled the first six blocks on and immediately north of Hamilton Avenue on Court Street. It included most of the Norwegian business people and professionals, and numbered a total of 736 adults and the children in 188 families. These two populous centers in addition probably hosted the majority of transient seamen, since they included the dock areas and sailortown. Construction workers and their families dominated the third largest population center, which appeared on both sides of the Avenue along the Gowanus Canal. It contained 174 adults and children in 68 families.[13] All three centers were overwhelmingly working-class.

Notable groups of Norwegians with a higher socioeconomic status lived elsewhere. The majority of working women, whatever their occupations, had difficulty finding work on the peninsula. Almost all the members of the female professional elite, for example, lived outside the Red Hook colony. The deaconesses, who composed the only cohesive group of highly trained women, were located far to the south in Sunset Park. On the peninsula, running or assisting in the management of small businesses such as boardinghouses or stores represented the pinnacle of women's work outside the home. Two-thirds of all employed Norwegian women lived in other areas of Brooklyn, where they worked as domestics.[14]

Although the pay was low, being in service had its advantages. When visiting Little Norway on their days off, domestics could impress friends and relatives by telling about the fine accommodations and food they shared and the opportunities they found to acquire upper-class American manners and speech. Women living in the colony most often worked in less appealing surroundings as seamstresses, dressmakers, and shop assistants. Former domestics interviewed in the 1980s said they always envied these women the chance to contribute to the family economy while living near or at home. Looking back, elderly women said being a maid was never anything but a way of earning money and learning American customs until one could find a good man.[15]

Most men residing in the colony centers did unskilled labor or worked in the construction and maritime trades. Day laborers, who often shifted from one poorly paid short-term job to another, formed the largest single occupational group, comprising 21 percent of the Norwegian workmen in the two wards. Brooklyn's construction boom provided reasonably steady employment and relative prosperity for many by employing another 20 percent of the colony men. About an eighth of Little Norway's male work force consisted of those who had made the transition from general sailor to skilled or semi-skilled harbor worker. Sailors on deep-sea ships or vessels in the American coastal trade made up a larger seafaring group. The general category of maritime work, a low-status sector in both social and economic terms, paid the bills for 35 percent of male wage-earners. A clear majority of all Norwegians fell into this category, if one counted transient seamen as well. Most members of the male occupational elite lived and worked in Red Hook, but their choice residential areas on the peninsula, in and near the Places, separated them from the mass of local Norwegians.[16]

Like many domestics who helped immigrant families make ends meet, a large majority of Norwegian men spent considerable time outside the colony. Construction workers followed contractors to the less built-up parts of the city and metropolitan area. Boatmen and lightermen spent their days, and not infrequently most of their lives, out in the Bay. Deep-sea sailors were away on voyages for months, even years. On the other hand, sizeable numbers of harbor workers and laborers had good chances of finding employment on the peninsula and going home for both lunch and dinner.[17]

All three Norwegian population centers were also commercial-industrial areas. Stores, businesses, small workshops, warehouses, and piers competed with tenements for primacy of place. In some ways, the character of these areas was particularly well-suited for the location of the colony's business district. Low property values gave first-generation immigrants the possibility of scraping together sufficient capital to rent or buy space for small businesses. The commercial-industrial establishments and the city's transportation network brought a steady flow of customers and large numbers of countrymen who were sure to patronize Norwegian shops and boardinghouses. Considering these facts and the areas' high concentration of settled Norwegians, it was natural that all but nine of the fifty-eight Norwegian businesses in the wards analyzed were clustered together in the population centers in the Red Hook colony.[18]

Nearly half a hundred ethnic enterprises in such a small geographic district gave Little Norway, for shopping at least, exactly the kind of magnetism for metropolitan area Norwegians that *Nordisk Tidende*'s editor desired. Because Nielsen's livelihood depended primarily on the patronage of these business people, it is not surprising that his newspaper contained advertisements for several more businesses than the census enumerators recorded. In an effort to promote both his loyal supporters and his own undertaking, Nielsen published a series of articles that documented how a handful of colony businessmen made their stores popular gathering places by filling multiple needs for their fellow Norwegians and taking responsibility for leading ethnic organizations.[19]

There were also great disadvantages to the three Norwegian population centers in the Red Hook colony. They were simultaneously the most densely populated, lowest-lying, and, therefore, least healthy parts of the peninsula. Commercial-industrial development made them noisy and squalid. Their working-class populations often lacked the time or money to keep their buildings in repair. Two of the quarters that housed large numbers of Norwegians were also inhabited by Italians, a nationality group that Norwegians found it difficult to accept as close neighbors. The blocks of most concentrated Italian settlement, moreover, adjoined the largest Norwegian population center. In short, the vast majority of Norwegians coped with the same living conditions other working-class immigrants experienced. In 1892, the description of the area that the first seamen's pastor had given thirteen years earlier still fitted local realities. To justify having bought instead of renting a church and parsonage there in 1879, the Reverend Ole Asperheim explained to the Mission Society's home office in Bergen, "The area is poverty-stricken and wretched, so it is highly unlikely that suitable facilities can be rented. . . . [By purchasing property,] the station got its own building, which can be put in decent shape."[20]

On the other hand, a few traits made the areas of heaviest Norwegian settlement unlike most of Brooklyn's and Manhattan's immigrant quarters. One salient difference showed in the maritime character of many commercial-industrial establishments on the Red Hook peninsula. Red Hook's small size and the unusual possibilities its coastline presented for efficient communications between bulk cargo piers had encouraged the development of massive harbor facilities. That, in turn, created employment opportunities that attracted Norwegians more than many other ethnic groups. The result was an unusual concentration in a relatively limited geographic area. Compared to the rest of the metropolitan area, seven state electoral districts in Red Hook offered Norwegians a unique experience, the distinction of belonging to the largest single foreign-born group. The experience did not include much local political power, since the combined population of Irishmen, Germans, Americans, Britons, or Italians was larger in every case. Still, the psychological and economic advantages of the situation were considerable.[21]

In all the "Norse" districts (and even in the two additional election districts where Scandinavians comprised the largest ethnic group), Norwegians easily outnumbered Swedes. Immigrants from Norway, used to calling Sweden "big brother" in terms of both politics and population, found the local situation gratifying indeed. Even in America, widely published federal statistics showed that Swedes were much the larger group. In Red Hook, Norwegians could call the tune for Scandinavians for once, instead of deferring to immigrants from their more powerful old-world neighbor. The virulence of *Nordisk Tidende*'s frequent attacks on Swedish royalty, Sweden, and Swedes in general during 1892 showed Emil Nielsen's instinctive awareness of local realities as much as it resulted from the rising independence movement in Norway.[22]

**Family Life, Hallboys, and Tableboards: Common Residence and Informal Community in Little Norway**

Nielsen's doubts about the viability of a Norwegian colony were not merely the challenges of a commercial provocateur. Even on the Red Hook peninsula, establishing community cohesion was usually difficult in some ways. Norwegians were a small group even in the area of their greatest concentration. Although they or Scandinavians comprised a majority in nine election districts, Nordics were a minority in the peninsula's other 39 districts. The Irish dominated politics in Wards 6 and 12, because they were the largest single ethnic group in thirty districts. The Norwegian population was, moreover, far more mobile than that of most other foreign-born groups.[23] Little Norway's economy depended on seafaring, and that kept many of its men away from home for lengthy periods of time. The number of Norwegian maritime transients who came and went far exceeded the immigrant population, and the settled community's largest occupational groupings consisted of people whose work often kept them in other parts of the harbor or at other ports along the East Coast.

Members of the colony counteracted the centrifugal forces of small size and transiency through a wide range of cooperative techniques. They cemented their community together through means that varied from the casually informal to the formally institutional. Binding individuals together informally was often a private, practical matter. When they remembered how the previous generation "managed," most elderly Norwegians interviewed said it was just common sense to ease the strain of life's crises by helping each other. Many also claimed that first-generation immigrants benefited from thrifty habits learned during hard times in the old country. A few remarked that helping each other also meant knowing how to enjoy oneself without spending much money.[24]

In the early 1890s, *Nordisk Tidende* and the state census testified to Norwegians' ingenuity in finding informal ways to satisfy their housing needs economically. Each issue of the newspaper had a short list of announcements about reasonable rooms available or sought. Frequently, it also printed articles and advertisements for boardinghouses offering inexpensive room and board. Local census-takers, however, could have told Nielsen that he had touched only the tip of the iceberg. Judging by the much larger number of family rooming arrangements and boardinghouses the census recorded, immigrants advertised in the colony newspaper only as a last resort.[25]

Among the Norwegian households of Red Hook, discussing housing with relatives and workmates usually provided the best solution. Over half the single people in the colony lived with families in private homes or apartments. Slightly more than three-tenths took their room and board with relative strangers in a boardinghouse, but these almost always lived with fellow Norwegians and usually with people in the same line of work. Judging by the sample taken from the census manuscripts, only about one in eight lived on their own with no evident relationship to other Norwegians.[26]

There were many means of binding unattached individuals to the community and saving money at the same time. Adult relatives found a welcome place with the family member who had a wife and children. Aunts, uncles, and grown children made up a large group, just under a third, of the single people staying in private homes. Colony old-timers confirmed the census evidence that men were the great majority of those lodging with close family, but live-in relatives also included cousins, nieces, and nephews, who were impossible to identify in the official count. Extended families were the rule in Red Hook, old-timers claimed, who smiled as they told anecdotes passed down to their generation about the men who "lived in" with this or that side of the family until they could find a bride or bring wives and children over from the old country. Many of these people, they said, were not really single, because they had families in Norway.[27]

The census materials and America letters reveal another side of the story. What did one do if parents did not emigrate and there was no related couple to stay with in Red Hook? About 15 percent of the individuals in the colony gave tacit answers to the question by living with their single siblings. The watchmaker Theodore Kartevold convinced three sisters and one brother to join him for varying periods of time.[28] Until Kartevold managed to bring relatives over, he had avoided living alone by moving in with his best friend, Gabriel Ueland. In 1892, another ninth of the Norwegian singles on the peninsula did the same, making surrogate siblings of friends who were willing to split the rent. Extended or truncated families were part and parcel of the process by which Norwegians migrated to the colony. Economizing on housing was essential, elderly residents emphasized, especially if you wanted to send pre-paid tickets and financial contributions to relatives at home. The shared concern for blood ties, adjusting to the city, and getting by

• Theodore Kartevold with case of pocket watches. Private Collection of Bertha and Gudrun Kartevold. His early career exemplifies the combined importance of family, occupation, and friends for international migration. In this picture, taken three years before he departed for Brooklyn in 1881, he is a proud teenage apprentice watchmaker who worked in his father's watch and jewelry shop with an older apprentice, Gabriel Ueland, in Sandnes, Norway. Ueland preceeded Theodore in Brooklyn by one year and shared lodgings with him during his first year in America.

• Theodore Kartevold, his brother, and an apprentice in front of Theodore's store at 61 Hamilton Avenue. By 1889 he was a prospering small businessman with a store located squarely in the middle of Red Hook's Little Norway.

on limited incomes thus made living together seem both natural and satisfying.[29]

Kartevold's story also exemplifies the combination of residential and occupational cooperation in the migration process. After voyaging to Brooklyn with two friends who were watchmakers, he shared lodgings with a third, Gabriel Ueland. Shortly after helping his brother Otto to settle in the colony, he not only shared rooms with him but funded a partnership so they could run a watch and jewelry store together. Meanwhile, both sent money home to their father, who had launched their careers and who still operated the family watch business near Stavanger. The partnership was doomed to failure because the brothers disagreed on business practices, but it gave Otto time to find his own way in the city. For years after the joint venture dissolved, he was the proprietor of one of several watch and jewelry businesses in the colony that comprised Theodore's primary competition.

Census enumerators who thought a bit about the information they collected could have found similarities between the Kartevolds' experience and that of many other colony residents. The specific trade was unusual, as was the ambition to become self-employed entrepreneurs, but the process of migration, the way of finding housing, and assistance in entering the local job market were not. In 1892, the colony contained many relatives and friends with the same residence and occupation. Perhaps one could expect to find family and friendship groupings of common occupations, such as dressmaker, laborer, carpenter, and seaman, but the census also revealed that people in less usual lines of work saw the advantages of uniting in a common cause. Little Norway also had its residential family clusters of boat people and lightermen, tugboat sailors, smiths, machinists, tailors, bakers, and even "stovemen."[30]

In late October of 1892, Theodore Kartevold's friend, Gabriel Ueland, advertised in *Nordisk Tidende* for roomers. During the time since he and Theodore had stopped being roommates, he had become an optician, married, and been recently widowed, and he now paid a German woman to mind the house and his three young children. The advertisement gave his address as 161 President Street, several blocks from Hamilton Avenue and quite close to First Place, simultaneously the peninsula's most attractive residential area and highest elevation. He lived on the edge of the district containing the greatest concentration of Norwegians in Red Hook but also in the heart of the neighborhood where the colony's socioeconomic elite resided.[31]

Having come far in only a few years, Ueland now experienced changed marital circumstances and additional expenses that very likely prompted his announcement describing the availability of a "furnished room with access to hot and cold water bath for a gentleman." His intimate friends no doubt read the advertisement and were moved by all that it signified. For Ueland had made public the fact that he hoped to find a "hallboy," a nonrelative lodger to supplement his family economy.

If he had had family in Red Hook, he would probably have preferred to take the course so many others did and have reserved his home for a blood relative, but apparently that option was not open.[32]

Ueland's action signaled a critical turning point in his family fortunes but it was not at all singular. Taking in hallboys, and occasionally even hallgirls, was a way of life in Little Norway. The term itself was a coinage of the colony, as was "tableboard," a Norwegian-Americanism used to describe the common practice among families of offering not only rooms but board in return for an average of about 5 dollars a week. According to old-timers, the word "hallboy" resulted from the circumstance that so many Brooklyn row houses had "dead-end" hall space on the second floor directly over the first-floor entrance. By hanging a curtain or mounting a temporary wall across the hall it was relatively simple to create a semi-private room. And of course, as Ueland announced, that room was but a few feet from the bathroom.

Around four-tenths of all lodgers in private homes were hallboys, and an undetermined number of these 160 individuals also enjoyed the good Norwegian fare of colony tableboards.[33] Couples in early middle age who had children to feed and rent or a mortgage to pay made up the majority of people who had hallboys and tableboards. Their clients were mostly young men in their early twenties with no families, at least in Brooklyn. These arrangements thus represented common economic techniques practiced during specific stages of the families' and hallboys' lives. In that sense, they were patterns of adjustment connected and similar to two other processes elderly residents often talked about. Boys commonly went to sea after confirmation in Norway and went on land during their twenties or thirties in Red Hook.

According to old-timers, many a hallboy was a seaman gone on land, because that was what men did when they wanted to save money before marrying and settling down. "Go on land now" was the usual advice young men like Magnus Andersen received if they married but dreamed of continuing to sail the seven seas. Magnus was not the only one who hesitated before giving up ambitions of running his own ship. And sometimes, as in Gabriel Ueland's case, families found it necessary to take in hallboys when they thought they had avoided or were through with that stage in life.[34]

Those were only two of the reasons why the families and men involved with tableboards and rooming belonged to a variety of age groups. Another important fact of life in the colony also had a bearing on the situation. Male immigrants often came to Red Hook alone and lived as hallboys until they could save enough to bring their families to America. Finally, as Red Hook's boarding masters' ring discovered in the late 1880s, the majority of transient Norwegian seamen—whatever their age—chose to be hallboys rather than boardinghouse residents.

The census showed many more hallboys in one year than the number of rooms advertised in the colony newspaper over three years.

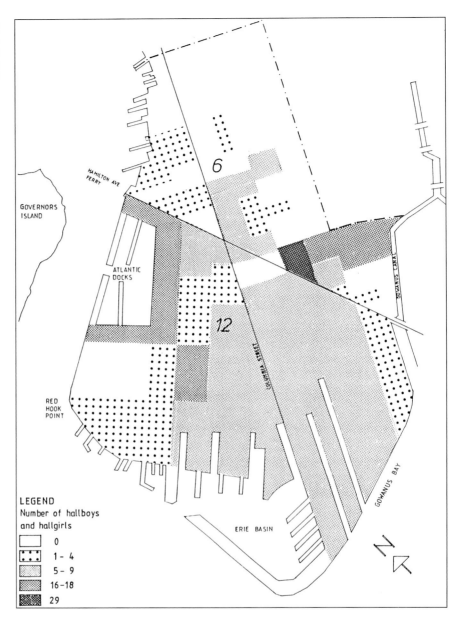

Distribution of Hallboys and Hallgirls, Wards 6 and 12 in 1892 (based on 10% sample).

Yet these young men not only found lodgings but frequently secured rooms with household heads or other family members who had the same occupation as they did. Now and then, enumerators recorded examples of households where father, sons, and hallboys all did the same kind of work. While roomers normally earned a living at a different trade than the family they lived with, hallboys often worked at the same trade.[35]

Obviously, immigrants looking for hallboys used a number of other methods than newspaper advertisements to find them. Very likely they discussed the housing situation with family members and then kept their ears open for hints about men at work who needed a place to stay. If they advertised, perhaps they turned away those who had a different occupation. When asked how people found hallboys, the elderly people interviewed usually said Norwegians talked to family and friends and asked them to spread the word about the available space and the price. One man explained the requirements for hallboys simply, asserting, "You wanted people you could trust. . . . They had to be people who understood what you did too."[36]

The result of such thinking and the tendency of relatives to help each other enter the local job market was that the colony's residential streets contained occupational clusters which, in general, reflected the distribution of trades in its work force. Hallboys lived in sub-communities of laborers, seamen, harbor workers, and carpenters. Less frequently, members of less common occupational groups shared quarters. For example, near Hamilton Avenue a young porter roomed with the family of an older man with the same job. At Red Hook Point a father, two sons, and one roomer all made livings as machinists.[37]

Two variations on the theme of utilizing the connections between vocation and housing are thought-provoking. In four cases, small-time ethnic entrepreneurs seemed to have recreated an almost preindustrial living pattern by providing room and board for men who may well have worked for them. A boat captain's only nonfamily roomers were three sailors. Were they crew, perhaps? One contractor shared his home with four brothers who were framers and an older carpenter. A bookkeeper with an address in one of the better neighborhoods of Ward 6 took in no fewer than six hallboys, but they were all clerks. The hallboy with a Hamilton Avenue grocer worked as a delivery man. It did not take much imagination to see advantages to this kind of arrangement, and maybe the idea was not recent but a carry-over from habits acquired in the old country.[38]

The housing arrangements of a twenty-eight-year-old harbor boatman and his wife who lived in sailortown may be taken as an example of how colony rooming practices assisted mariners in the process of going on land. Three hallboys lived with the boatman: a dockbuilder his own age and two younger sailors. The two older men had found employment not at sea but in the harbor. The dockbuilder worked primarily on land. These two presented the younger men with illustrations of career paths available in Red Hook for Norwegians who decided to leave seafaring behind them. The colony itself had grown up not least because of the many sailors who had patterned career changes on examples like these.[39]

## Sailortown, Boarding-houses, and Homeless Birds

The family household was Little Norway's primary instrument for integrating "unattached" men (single men and men whose families resided elsewhere) into the community. Over two-thirds of the unattached Norwegian men with an apparent connection to the Norwegians listed with them in the census resided with families, either as relatives or as hallboys. Being taken into colony homes helped these men avoid depressing loneliness and the lack of stable routines that too often led to a disorganized life, drinking, and ending one's days on the streets. During the 1890s, *Nordisk Tidende* warned repeatedly of the dangers that awaited the immigrant who tried to make it on his own in Brooklyn. Usually its advice appeared in sensational horror stories about seamen and greenhorns who had succumbed because they tried to resist temptation alone and were exploited by city con men before they had learned how to do so.[40]

In 1897, the newspaper's front-page headlines shouted, "In Potters' Field. A Young Norwegian's Last Days in the Tuberculosis Hospital. Is He Buried or Have They Sent his Corpse to Wander?" Two entire columns filled with sentimental details hammered home the underlying message that colony professionals and ordinary settlers were eager to help young people establish a well-regulated life if only they would not persist in letting "life in America" draw them into wild paths. The deceased was the perfect object lesson. "But he remained a loner. . . .Once he was used to a life of carousing, he had problems pulling himself together again and on and on it went, until one day he contracted a deadly sickness."[41]

Despite the lecturing tone, the concern the newspaper expressed was real and was shared by many in the colony. The 1892 census showed that not just mariners but large numbers of immigrant families lived in sailortown. It was no accident that the highest concentration of surrogate and extended families and hallboy combinations appeared along Hamilton Avenue and the waterfront. Red Hook's sailortown, which was infamous throughout the city for its clever sharpers and its vices, was the colony's untidy backyard. *Nordisk Tidende*'s public utterances also represented other aspects of this very real social problem that Little Norway struggled with daily. Most important, other lives were too often ruined by transient sailors and undisciplined immigrant men. They led settlers' sons and daughters astray, leaving young women with fatherless children in their wakes. Using face-to-face personal contacts to find and screen hallboys allowed parents to select the company to which their

•

The Kiland family in front of Kiland's Tableboard, their home-business. Provided by Nere Kiland and Erik Aalvik Evensen in Grimstad, Norway.

A typical sailortown boardinghouse. *Harper's New Monthly Magazine*, July 1873.

children were exposed. Live-in relatives and hallboys often became role models for the very young.[42]

Seamen's Pastor Hansteen had enlisted the help of colony family men years before to limit the deleterious effects of sailortown, but the most memorable result of his efforts was his replacement by his assistant not long after runners had thrown the pastor into the Bay. By 1892, stories of what went on in Red Hook's sailortown had circulated so widely that they attracted the attention of the Reverend Charles Henry Parkhurst, a well-known American reformer in Manhattan. Using the public visibility his chairmanship of the Society for the Prevention of Crime gave him, Parkhurst attacked not only New York's but also Brooklyn's police department and municipal government for corruption and inaction in connection with sailortown. The waterfront in both cities fell naturally under his purview since New York City owned and collected revenues from Brooklyn's shoreline.[43]

Parkhurst's activities soon emboldened critics of machine politics on both sides of the river. New York City authorities responded to continued calls for a political cleansing by appointing an investigatory group, the Lexow Committee. In the municipal elections of 1893, Brooklyn's Republican Party succeeded in ending Boss McLaughlin's domination of city politics and replaced Mayor David Boody's scandal-ridden administration with that of the German-American reformer, Charles A. Schieren. In 1894, the Lexow Committee's published findings revealed "many ill-smelling facts" about dockside dives in both cities' sailortowns. Finally, when Theodore Roosevelt became New York's Police Commissioner in 1896, he extended cleanup efforts to the cities' waterfront areas and forced many of the most infamous dockside dives to close or move.[44]

The cities' sailortowns were only one of the cesspools of corruption that Parkhurst spotlit in his campaign against police and political profiteering. For Little Norway's leaders, however, that aspect of his exposé was the most unsettling. The damaging publicity devoted to a district commonly known to host much of the visiting Norwegian fleet gave the colony's social problem an aspect that especially concerned Little Norway's newspaper editor, shopkeepers, organizational leadership, and the Manhattan colony elite. Between 1890 and 1910, problems related to sailortown informed much of the formal cooperation—and conflict—among these prominent local Norwegians.

The better-off residents of Little Norway had both vested interests in and charitable impulses on behalf of the residents of sailortown. In part, local leaders' ambiguous relationship to the maritime district had prompted the major conflicts of the 1880s, when immigrant groups in Red Hook attempted to assume control of the welfare institutions established earlier by the Manhattan elite and old-country organizations. By the 1890s, Emil Nielsen and several other prominent colony businessmen were convinced that Little Norway should manage its own problems—and economic opportunities—rather than be managed by outsiders.

When Nielsen was struggling to get *Nordisk Tidende* on its feet financially in early 1891, he began the practice of taking advertisements for sailortown's saloons and boardinghouses. At some point, probably when the newspaper's income was stable, he allowed its bar and saloon owners to pay him personally in kind, in other words by giving him free liquor. That cozy arrangement continued until the winter of 1907, when he died suddenly of pneumonia after being placed in an intoxicated condition on the stoop of the building where he lived. During 1892, the newspaper advertised six sailortown boardinghouses owned or operated by Norwegians. Most of these were probably among the ones whose owners could not be identified from the census schedules. In August, Nielsen reported the brutal treatment one Georg Hansen, a Norwegian boarding master from 17 Hamilton Avenue, had received at the hands of New York police when he was arrested at Charlie Hansen's saloon on the lower East Side. That news must have made some readers speculate whether the Hansens were brothers operating parallel operations on each side of the river. When two of the elderly sailors interviewed were told about this incident, they said it illustrated the close connections among boardinghouse masters and sailortown proprietors all around New York Bay.[45]

Many other colony entrepreneurs had slightly concealed channels like Nielsen's or an open connection to sailortown. Ship chandlers, such as John Anson and Gabriel Fedde, supplied Norwegian vessels and sailors who docked there. A third Mr. Hansen, this one living near the Erie Basin, made his living by supplying the incoming fleet with fresh water. In March, Edwin O. Lee's steamship and train ticket office opened a "Scandinavian Savings Bank," which promised reliable service to both immigrants and seamen who wanted to open savings accounts or send funds to Norway. In August, the newspaper noted that Johan G. Normann, the temperance advocate with whom Theodore Kartevold shared store space at 61 Hamilton Avenue, used the premises to house not only a tobacco shop but an informal hiring agency for sailors who wanted to sign on as crew on the yachts of wealthy Americans such as the Vanderbilt family. Normann must have been able to pick and choose among many applicants from sailortown, since men looking for a way to 'go on land' could not earn higher wages than those paid on the yachts.[46]

As a group, however, the many immigrant families who supplemented their incomes by helping mariners escape waterfront boardinghouses probably constituted the colony's most important connection to sailortown. By becoming roomers with Norwegian families, many seamen signaled more than their preference for immigrant compatriots and the homelike surroundings they could offer. As the foregoing analysis of hallboy lodgers illustrated, moving out of sailortown often represented a crucial step in mariners' progress toward permanent residence.

Most Norwegians in the Red Hook colony lived within the comforting and restraining bounds of families. In 1892, however, nearly a third of the men and a few women in the sample of unattached people lived in boardinghouses, most of which were in sailortown. According to anecdotes told about him much later, Helge Amundsen was a sea captain who spent part of his shipboard leisure time writing stories based on his experiences in the colony's boardinghouses. These he eventually published, first in Norway, later as a serial for *Nordisk Tidende*, and finally, as a book released by one of the colony's first publishers in 1910.[47]

In its final form, *Hjemløse fugle* (homeless birds)was a collection of closely related stories with a central set of characters, the Norwegian lodgers at a sailortown boardinghouse in Red Hook. Amundsen clearly selected a title to emphasize the theme that he had woven through the stories, the crucial importance of home and family life for immigrants. The words he used to introduce this theme, Victorian in their sentimentality, were another way of stressing the same advice *Nordisk Tidende* gave loners in 1897: "One can struggle hard and be miserable in many ways in life,and still not think there is any special reason to complain, if only one has a home or at least a place that resembles one to fall back on when the workday is over. Perhaps the only secret in life worth mentioning is contained in the meaning of the word 'home.' In any case, there are enough people who cannot and will not accept any other view of the matter. For such people, home is—with slippers and little kisses and profound comments about baby's teeth—life itself, the harbor where one's anchor holds fast, no matter what forces are used against it. For those who have not managed to come any further than dreaming about all these virtues, there is an unfortunately often undeserved halo around the word itself. The workings of the unachievable are so singular."[48]

Nearly two-fifths of the Norwegian immigrants who could only dream of having their own homes were seamen. Laborers comprised the next largest group (26 percent) living in boardinghouses, and construction workers (13 percent) made up the only other sizeable contingent. Men in menial white-collar jobs, harbor sailors, and a variety of skilled craftsmen—none of them amounting to 5 percent of the over 200 boardinghouse residents—rounded out the lists drawn up by census enumerators. The small size of the last three categories revealed much about the connection between a better standard of living and the transition to a more settled lifestyle. For example, only eight mariners who had made their residence in Red Hook relatively permanent by taking work on harbor craft lived in a boardinghouse. The eighty-three seamen very likely still sailed up and down the coast or shipped out on deep-sea vessels. In other words, most of the seamen were probably transients.[49]

Boardinghouses were sure to contain some of the freshest greenhorns without the personal contacts or financial reserves to live elsewhere. A large contingent of day laborers might be expected, since unskilled labor demanded less knowledge of English and local work routines. Sons entering the job market on their own often started their careers as general laborers when no better opportunities appeared. Amundsen commented that "heavy work, loading and unloading on the docks" was usually available for newcomers but structured his book on the conviction that the general category of "laborer" concealed a much more diverse group. He made excuses for putting Palle Pallesen, one of his main characters and a former sea captain like himself, in a boardinghouse.[50]

Palle had saved up considerable capital and bought shares in his ship but then made the mistake of investing it all in Oslo real estate during a building boom. Only months later, he lost everything and had creditors pounding on his door. Seeing no other solution, he returned to Red Hook, where he was sure one of his many maritime friends could get him another ship. That last hope, unfortunately, also turned out to be an illusion. He could have signed on as an ordinary seaman, but found the idea of taking orders from a captain several years his junior difficult to swallow. Besides, men who had reached the age of thirty-five did not receive many offers of a berth as an able-bodied sailor.[51]

When Palle hit bottom, he took a cheap boardinghouse room and applied for whatever temporary, unskilled work the city had to offer. "Laborer" was the occupation of men who had fallen on hard times. It was also the public label for many who had learned skills or completed advanced education in the old country that could not be put to use in the United States. As his other important male character, Amundsen chose a lawyer who had become a laborer after discovering that his knowledge of Norwegian law was worthless in America. The Swedish-Norwegian consul and the country's representative at Castle Garden joined Amundsen in warning such people, as well as family black sheep and office workers, to stay at home in Norway.[52]

Considering the large number of construction workers in the colony, it was likely that at least a part of the colony's second largest occupational group would live in boardinghouses. Sojourning carpenters from the Lista peninsula on Norway's southern tip often found the cheapest possible accommodations in boardinghouses so they could send every penny saved to family at home. In May of 1986, a Bay Ridge Norwegian told a riddle about the "Lista-folk." "What is a Lista sandwich?" he asked and, having stumped his listener, chuckled as he explained, "Two slices of bread with a crust in the middle! Those people sat in an empty room on an orange crate and ate Lista sandwiches while

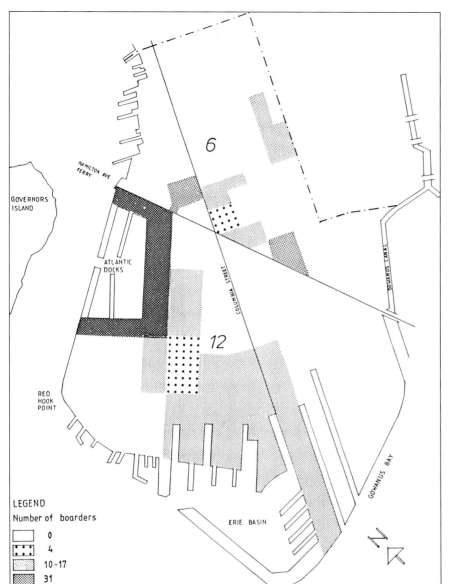

LEGEND

Number of boarders

| | |
|---|---|
| | 0 |
| | 4 |
| | 10-17 |
| | 31 |
| | 61 |

Distribution of Boarders, Wards 6 and 12 in 1892 (based on 10% sample).

they dropped every cent they earned into the crate. Then they went back home and bought a boat or a barn or a house."[53]

In July of 1892, *Nordisk Tidende* reported that a "series" of sojourners from the Lista region had complained repeatedly about local authorities in their home districts who laid a "very significant income tax" on money earned abroad. The newspaper supported the sojourners' point of view valiantly and made the issue's importance for the colony clear. "It is obvious that this [problem] concerns only that large flock of our coastal people who do not make their permanent home in America but instead seek employment here, and otherwise, each in his own way, maintain the connection with the old country."[54]

Undoubtedly, isolation and transiency were more prevalent in the districts of Little Norway with the most boardinghouses. Lodgers came and went, not only because of the temporary or itinerant nature of their work but because of their poverty. The landlord at Palle Pallesen's boardinghouse had developed a hard-nosed attitude because tenants too often fled in the night without paying their rent. "The only rule that was strictly followed in the house was the one of paying the rent every Saturday. Otherwise, Sunday was spent under open skies."[55]

All but one of the twenty-eight boardinghouses containing Norwegians in the sample from the 1892 census were located in sailortown's crowded slum districts, where transiency and rules to deal with it were necessities. In sailortown, even a Norwegian woman with two young sons gave her occupation as "boarding," although she had only four lodgers, three sailors and one shoemaker. The one exception was on the territorial fringes of sailortown in a less populous neighborhood a considerable distance to the north, and the Norwegian working-class family who operated it offered a more homelike atmosphere. Their ten male roomers included groups common in sailortown, however, four laborers and three unemployed men, but it also housed four clerks.[56]

The majority of unattached Norwegian lodgers—the big groups of seamen, laborers, and carpenters—probably experienced living conditions similar to those Amundsen described as typical for the "cheap sort." Rooms there were not for the squeamish or the coddled. "Four walls, a bed with sheets of doubtful cleanness and a towel of undoubted dirtiness, together with a chair whose rheumatic legs complained loudly whenever anyone was thoughtless enough to sit on it—that was the complete equipment." For the roomers there neighborhood and community shrank to a small group of men who stayed longer than most and shared perhaps both national origin and employment prospects. Pallesen and his boardinghouse associates called themselves the "Norwegian clique," the "gang," and most poignantly, the people on the "second floor, where the Colony had its shelter."[57]

Of course, equally to the point, these men in a lodging house operated by an Irishwoman and tenanted by several nationalities *had* united and described themselves as a distinct sub-group. The informal cooperation that they found desperately important was not unusual, judging from information in the census. Only four of the boarding-houses in the sample of Norwegian residences housed lodgers of other nationalities. At only two of those did "foreigners" far outnumber Norwegians. Near Hamilton Avenue, a Scottish woman ran a house where the seventy-nine tenants included large contingents of Americans and Irishmen, a few Germans and Englishmen, and five Norwegians.[58]

Four of the five Norwegians had the same occupation, laborer, which was also the kind of work over 80 percent of the other lodgers had. In that sense, their situation was the common one. The boarding-houses Norwegians patronized were often dominated by one occupational group, usually mariners but in a few cases laborers or construction workers. Four-tenths of the houses where Norwegians lived, however, contained a mix of workmen in different trade groupings. In short, many of the men without families who inhabited boardinghouses stuck together in two of the same ways Norwegian families and hallboys did. Their shared Norwegian identity and vocational experience created the common ground for informal cooperation.[59]

A lodging house's downstairs parlor sometimes gave residents the chance to discuss their daily experiences. According to Amundsen's fictional account, "Lodgers were not, however, just shown to their rooms. They had at their disposition a large parlor with a carpet which in some worn places resembled a burlap bag and in others reminded one of spilt clots of paint. The furnishings consisted only of excuses, except for a piano, which the landlady recommended as an attraction to prospective tenants. The piano and the landlady had a certain similarity—they both produced false notes."[60]

When Amundsen published his book in Brooklyn in 1910, there was a strong probability that Norwegians in comparable surroundings might read it. His scathingly ironic commentary was therefore not only an outlet for his own feelings but a gesture to any contemporary sufferer who shared them. The Norwegians in *Hjemløse fugle* meet in the shabby parlor after work and discuss their recurrent problems—paying the rent, finding work, and, if they find a job, scraping together enough money to join the union so they can keep it. Time and again in Amundsen's fictional Brooklyn, someone in the boardinghouse's Norwegian colony would finally get a job only to lose it because he could not afford to pay union dues. Caught in this cycle of unemployment, these characters practice a mutual assistance that has none of their landlady's only seeming generosity.[61]

Pallesen pays the others' rent when he has work and they have none. Later, when he needs help most because he has run away from a private hospital without paying his bill, they are solidly in his corner. Finally, when Pallesen's fortunes improve, he proposes to a Norwegian domestic from the colony in that same run-down parlor, and they decide to return to Norway. As their ship, the *Hellig Olav*, pulls away from the pier, the four lodgers left behind think regretfully, "Now we can fly home to our empty rooms, we homeless birds." They may lack a home in the usual sense, but they are not without dependable friends. When the former lawyer leaves the boardinghouse and goes west, in the hope of earning enough to send more money home to his family in Norway, he only barely escapes being convicted of a murder he did not commit. Amundsen's conclusion seems to be that such a travesty of justice is all too possible in America for a Norwegian without fellow countrymen to assist him.

**Ethnic
Mutual
Assistance,
Migration,
and the
Americaniza-
tion of Crafts
in the City**

Sharing the same ethnic background and general place of residence, as editor Emil Nielsen knew, did not guarantee a cohesive community. Even in the Red Hook colony center, Norwegian immigrant neighborhoods were not monolithic. Equally important, at least for the development of a feeling of community cohesion, the very location of the colony was not static but shifting. The northern fringes of the colony near Atlantic Avenue did not threaten to draw Norwegians away from the compact center on the peninsula, but entrepreneurs and settlers in the rapidly expanding Sunset Park housing developments did. The everyday contacts among newcomers and colony residents that caused migration to the south were the same kind of informal cooperative mechanisms that held the Red Hook neighborhoods together.

Urban development in many coastal parts of Sunset Park (the east side of Wards 22 and 8) was so far along by the 1880s that building contractors were erecting homes and apartments at full speed. Ward 22 started on the east bank of the Gowanus Canal and continued in that direction to Grand Army Plaza, where it ran down the whole west side of Prospect Park. Most of the northern part had been built up earlier, and the northeastern quarter was by 1890 one of the most populous districts in Brooklyn. The canal-area tenements there and the fine homes closest to the Park showed recent but contrasting results of the ongoing Brooklyn building boom. Parts of the almost rural southern stretches were currently submitting to the plans of contractors.[62]

Norwegian settlement in Ward 22 was diverse in 1892. To the east in Park Slope, forty single Norwegian women worked as domestics and had to leave the area if they wanted to enjoy the company of countrymen not in service. Farther west, working-class Norwegian families formed an extension of the Red Hook colony. In the northern part of this area, Harry S. Christian, the seaman who progressed from carpenter to building materials supplier, still operated his business. The difference between occupational patterns here and those in the main colony showed the importance of the building boom for secondary Norwegian settlements. In 1892, just three families supported by marine workers lived in the ward, but there were six times as many men in the construction trades, over half of them with their nearest relatives.[63] The causes for such a marked divergence from the employment pattern on the Red Hook peninsula were best explained by old-timers who had heard about developments farther south in Sunset Park, most of which was in Ward 8.

Ward 8 was the center of building activity in the 1880s. A long, narrow arm of coastal land extending from the canal inlet to the city line, it was a contractor's dream. Not only was the street grid in place but docks, piers, and shipyards were growing up all along the Bay. Maritime workers were commuting out to the area or landing at its wharves daily. In short, it was high time contractors put up tracts of working-class housing there.[64]

Among the builders who took advantage of this situation was Ola Nilsen from Red Hook. Like many others, he hoped to profit from piece-work contracts that gave bonuses for the number of completed units within a limited time. Carpenters made up the largest group of land-based craftsmen in the colony, and Nilsen and others like him hired countrymen in the local area to work for them. Only one Norwegian contractor and a handful of "builders" showed up in the state census of 1892, but the oldest men interviewed in Bay Ridge in the 1980s insisted that there were many such men. Their relatives and people they knew had been "contractors for the short term." That meant they were ordinary carpenters whom a builder tempted with higher pay if they could complete the construction of a row or block of houses quickly. The old-timers said some carpenters went into the contracting business full-time after a while, but most went back to working for others. Two men remembered their fathers telling bitterly how "jacked-up" Norwegian carpenters would sometimes "give away" all the jobs on a project to congregation members after church on a Sunday. The next day, when nonchurchgoing carpenters showed up at the building site, no jobs were left.[65]

Word of mouth in the colony brought both groups of carpenters to Sunset Park. It also kept them informed about the most reasonable prices the market there offered. According to the men interviewed, contractors sometimes allowed men to work on the building they had arranged to buy—at a reduced price because of their relationship with the boss. As the census schedules show, many of the row houses recently built in Sunset Park could house three or four families, in a pinch. If these family men worked on a building together, splitting a reduced purchase price three or four ways could put home ownership within the reach of ordinary workmen. According to the elderly men interviewed, precisely that kind of cooperative effort had helped relatives and acquaintances buy their first apartments around the turn of the century.[66]

Similar processes may have assisted construction workers in other ethnic groups to settle in Sunset Park. By 1892, the bayside streets from 17th to 42nd Street were densely populated, and the more westerly and southerly parts of Ward 8 had more residents than many sections of the city. Carpentry was a common trade among the working-class Scandinavians, Irishmen, Germans, Britons, and smaller numbers of Italians and Poles who lived in these areas. Whatever else Norwegians may have accomplished by moving south, they had not, at least not for any long period of time, escaped having to share neighborhoods with groups whose culture and habits they found distasteful.[67]

At the time of the state census, men in the building trades were a very prominent occupational group among the Norwegians in Ward 8. No fewer than sixty-four carpenters, fifty-one of them living with their families, had taken up residence in Sunset Park's bayside districts. As in Red Hook, however, maritime workers outnumbered people in the construction trades. Census enumerators counted seventy-one men in maritime work in the ward. Forty-one families gained their living from the harbor economy. Mariners had moved south by a process similar to that which guided the migration of carpenters. As previously mentioned, wharves and piers began to appear along the coast before housing developments went up. Norwegian immigrants' long-term involvement in dockside work and waterfront construction farther north along the coast made it natural for them to follow when employment opportunities opened in Sunset Park. The intimate connection between seafaring and marine construction in their old-world background meant that only limited adjustment to American conditions was necessary.[68]

The shipyards in Sunset Park built mostly wooden harbor craft at the time, so Norwegian craftsmen did not have to learn to build metal deep-sea ships. Multitudes of wooden barges and scows were used to ferry goods and garbage to and from places around the bay and rivers. Fleets of lighters took cargo off large, oceangoing steamers at the mouth of the bay, which then sat high enough in the water to enter its shallower docking areas. Just under two-fifths of the maritime workers in Ward 8 supported themselves by building, repairing, or manning these harbor vessels. The whole ward contained only two marine boardinghouses, where four-fifths of the twenty-six single, seagoing sailors lived. The more than forty remaining maritime workers were, in order of group size, ship's carpenters, settled coastal seamen, lightermen, boatmen, riggers, sailmakers, sparmakers, dockbuilders, and longshoremen.[69]

The developing coastline also offered opportunities for small-scale Norwegian entrepreneurship. Unlike the Red Hook peninsula, Ward 8's long coast in 1892 was not a solid line of dock facilities operated by large concerns. Instead, it was developed in patches and contained mostly small and medium-sized piers and shipyards. Bush Terminal did not consolidate and systematize marine enterprise in the area until a decade later. Here then was a natural niche for men who had grown up in a region of Norway where ordinary workers and even their wives had owned shares in vessels built during the golden age of the white sails. In July of 1892, *Nordisk Tidende* announced that shipbuilder

Thomas Olsen, a Sunset Park resident, had recently launched the 117-foot dumping scow he had built for an American contractor at the foot of 24th Street. When Gabriel Fedde's ship chandlery in Manhattan fell on hard times in 1895, he formed a partnership with a carpenter from Trinity Church and began building and repairing barges in Sunset Park. Fedde was already in late middle age, but the opportunities for men like him on Sunset Park's coast proved to be a good gamble. In the next twelve years, he and his partner built fifty barges and repaired another half a hundred. Olsen and later Fedde provided employment for countrymen. Like some churchgoing house builders, Fedde reserved many of the jobs he had to offer for members of the church he attended.[70]

There were strong similarities between the occupational concentrations in the Sunset Park settlement and the Red Hook colony. Most notably, marine and construction workers composed by far the largest trade groupings, for many of the reasons presented earlier. In a sense, though, the likenesses were superficial, because the circumstances that permitted skilled workers to relocate in the new settlement also transformed them. Norwegian contractors, like employers of other immigrant groups, offered a number of advantages to the developers of Sunset Park. Because they understood compatriots' native tongues and work habits, they were best suited to teach immigrants how to work under American conditions.

Old-timers said it was a time-honored tradition among Norwegian contractors to hire some countrymen with only related skills and no union membership for reduced wages. The plentiful ship's carpenters from Agder and Rogaland counties made the transition rather easily. So did the many men from the same region who had learned to build barns on coastal subsistence farms before migrating to its coastal cities. Many a Norwegian seaman turned carpenter in the 1880s and 1890s, as Harry Christian had done earlier. Hiring such men benefited everyone involved except local unions, who at first complained of cheap foreign labor. Developers saved in labor costs, Norwegian contractors got a competitive edge in bidding for building projects, and greenhorns broke into the skilled-labor market.

According to old-timers, Brooklyn unions were soon satisfied too. Wages and experience on their first jobs made it possible for greenhorns to meet construction unions' membership criteria and to save money for paying their union dues. The men interviewed insisted that very few Norwegians had ever been anti-union. After all, joining the labor organizations made it easier to get in on new projects and gave Norwegians a better relationship with the men who protected their rights. In this way, many Norwegian newcomers with contacts in one of the colony's two largest skilled trade groups avoided the constant conflict with unions described in Amundsen's *Hjemløse fugle*.[71]

Norwegian contractors were men who had adjusted more quickly and successfully to American expectations and techniques. As such, they became a bridge that allowed both skilled and unskilled countrymen to cross into the city's work force. In the process, many a Norwegian carpenter lost his preindustrial view of carpentry as a folk art or fine craft. Helping to put up Sunset Park's vast tracts of mass-produced row houses encouraged new work habits and values. The section's Norwegian settlement contained, therefore, a more Americanized brand of construction worker.

The maritime workers in the newer southern settlements were also easily distinguishable from the seafarers who dominated the Red Hook colony. On the peninsula, deep-sea sailors set the tone for the maritime community because of the enormous number of transient Norwegian seamen and the smaller group of immigrant mariners employed in the international freight trade. Together, these men composed a population larger than the whole settled colony. The economic character of Red Hook came from the waterfront business it did with the fleets of many nations. Maritime workers in Sunset Park did not have so overwhelming a presence compared to construction workers. In 1892, the district was as much a bedroom suburb of downtown Brooklyn as an emerging shipping center. Norwegian maritime workers there, moreover, depended on the harbor economy rather than on international trade. The craftsmen employed in building ships were as important as the men sailing on them. Among the seamen, harbor and coastal sailors outnumbered seafarers.[72]

The maritime workers in Sunset Park were quite naturally more oriented toward American conditions and more bound to the local economy. In the shipbuilding centers that dotted the coasts of southern and southwestern Norway, men had learned to feel a special loyalty to the ship they sailed. Its officers and owners were often neighbors and kinsmen, and its craftsmanship was the proud face that their hometown presented to the world. In Sunset Park, lightermen and boatmen had to learn new attitudes. According to the testimony of latter-day bay seamen, many harbor vessels around the turn of the century were "just floating boxes," rapidly built containers that soon became battered and grimy in the business of ferrying heavy cargoes across the harbor. Unless a man could stay with a boat he had built or renovated himself, it was hard to take pride in harbor craft. The oldest surviving mariners also said Norwegian crewmen had to unlearn their traditional loyalty to the ship, which seemed at best misplaced to members of American coastal seamen's unions. Walkouts were an important weapon for boatmen during labor disputes in the Bay, and Brooklyn locals blacklisted scabs who stayed on board.[73]

The process of everyday cooperation that had brought maritime and construction workers to Sunset Park thus led to significant differences in the character of the two settlements. Not only did the men in the largest occupational groups farther south learn different techniques and work habits, but they also absorbed new attitudes toward their vocations. Their more complete dependence on Brooklyn's economy and closer contacts with local unions produced ties that distanced them from some aspects of their old-world heritage. Inevitably perhaps, they encouraged not only increased migration to Sunset Park and later Bay Ridge, but also general acceptance of their new views.

**Businesses and Institutions in the New Settlements: Leaders and Followers**

As might be expected, a few Norwegian shopkeepers had joined their compatriots in Gowanus (Ward 22) and Sunset Park (Ward 8). At the 1892 state census, the two more southerly wards both contained a handful of Norwegian family stores. Each had its grocer, tailor, and watchmaker. The working-class settlers in Gowanus could also patronize their local hatter, furrier, fish dealer, and woman music teacher. In Sunset Park the pioneering business people included a shoemaker, a real estate agent, a seamstress, and a dressmaker. Most of these small-time entrepreneurs had probably come with or after other settlers.[74]

Like their colleagues in the main colony, some tradesmen farther south filled multiple functions to make ends meet. The tailor in Ward 8, for example, advertised that his tailor shop was being expanded into a store offering reasonable new and cheap used clothes. Gabriel Fedde's wife and boys operated a corner grocery in Sunset Park, but it was really supplementary to the family's main businesses, ship supplies and then barge building. The Feddes proved that business people sometimes migrated south before rather than after most settlers. When they opened their store, too few Norwegians lived in southern Sunset Park to base sales on ethnic foods. Ironically, Fedde recalled that they had to close the grocery later, because "the Brooklyn grocers' clerks and delivery vans swamped the neighborhood at the same time as it was built up."[75]

The Feddes were not the only ones who drew people south after them instead of following other pioneers to new settlement areas. After being refused status as full parishioners at the Seamen's Church in 1889, the Free Lutheran Mission Society left Red Hook. They established their own congregation, Trinity Lutheran, in rooms at Sunset Park's Fallesen Hall and rented a house for their first minister nearby. In early April of 1892, Isak Petersen announced the founding of the Norwegian Workmen's Association in northern Sunset Park. Claiming that the first meeting had drawn forty skilled workers to the area, he predicted that the association had a bright future because "Ward 8 contains so many Norwegians." In fact, there were few nearby, compared to the dense working-class neighborhoods on the peninsula. Petersen was advertising not only a new organization but a new settlement.[76]

The leaders of the Deaconess Home and Hospital were the most notable groundbreakers. They moved their institution from a building adjoining the Seamen's Church in Red Hook farther south to Ward 22 in 1885. By the start of the next decade, they had moved south again, this time to the hospital's permanent location at 46th Street and Fourth Avenue near the Brooklyn city line. Sister Elizabeth Fedde and the board members commented that real estate was cheaper in less developed areas and that more rural surroundings were more healthful for patients. In 1892, the institution's doctor, three maids, five deaconesses, and sixteen patients were almost the only Norwegians in the immediate vicinity. By the next state census, however, many members of Trinity Lutheran's congregation had settled nearby. By 1911, they had built a new church across the street from the Home and Hospital.[77]

Thus, a variety of motives prompted the migration to the south. Those who had made the move were wont to point out the benefits they had reaped. They also wanted company and so encouraged countrymen in the Red Hook colony to follow them. If a family found that payments on a home became a burden, a common solution was to check if countrymen farther north wanted to "escape the city" by becoming their boarders. Since the Norwegians workmen knew best were often others in the same trade, the first construction and marine workers in Sunset Park brought others to the new settlement areas as their boarders. If they had attended the same church in Red Hook, they were soon agitating for a daughter congregation closer to home. In just such a fashion, settled seafaring Norwegians in the colony had encouraged countrymen in Manhattan and Norway to join them in the Red Hook section. In Sunset Park, however, local boosters could make the most of the district's remaining rural areas. During the hot summer months of 1893, *Nordisk Tidende* carried announcements for "John A. Holm's Summer Retreat" at 39th Street and 7th Avenue and a "Real Norwegian Country Hike in Brooklyn" with the Norse Women's Club on an excursion to the "woods around 43rd Street and 8th Avenue."[78]

**A Real Colony: Intimate Community Achieved**

In 1892, the Red Hook peninsula's compact neighborhoods had a more important advantage than a suburban setting. Most Norwegian immigrants still lived and most of Norway's fleet still docked there. Only the peninsula's greater numbers of countrymen in a smaller geographic area could give rise to a full and varied spectrum of institutions. Sunset Park would not become the home of Little Norway until a decade or more later when its Norwegian population had grown so large that many more community organizations on the peninsula felt forced to relocate there.

Most but by no means all Norwegians on the Red Hook peninsula experienced the kind of social relationships Ferdinand Tönnes called typical of *Gemeinschaft*, an intimate community based primarily on face-to-face contacts and familial relationships.[79] Informal cooperation through families to manage occupational and residential adjustments and on-the-job contacts between workmen ensured that kind of community for most. Parents helped sons and daughters to enter their own or a related trade. A few married craftsmen-entrepreneurs seem to have created a latter-day version of the preindustrial master-apprentice relationship by renting rooms in their homes to subordinates. Wives not only had responsibility for home and children but almost certainly managed the lion's share of work with hallboy lodgers and tableboard boarders. When the family had a small business, they usually assisted there as well. Single working women clustered in small groups of seamstresses and dressmakers, which in at least two cases were composed of sisters or other relatives. Female domestics lived outside the colony but visited when they could and contributed to the family economy.

Sailortown's mariners, laborers, and construction workers counteracted isolation and transiency by patronizing Norwegian tableboards and rooming as hallboys when they could. Those who lived in boardinghouses usually chose ones run by countrymen. They often gathered in lodging houses where the majority of men had the same line of work. Carpenters from Norway's southern Lista peninsula banded together to protest taxes in their home communes that threatened to reduce the profits of sojourning in Red Hook. Amundsen's homeless birds may well have been just one of a larger number of boardinghouse groups that welded themselves into tiny sub-colonies by discussing their lives in shabby parlors and rendering each other vital assistance. Even the mostly self-interested arrangements of some Little Norway businessmen, like Nielsen and Johan Normann, were based on face-to-face dealings with the inhabitants of sailortown, and Normann's hiring office helped some men to the best maritime positions available.

All this and more the colony's inhabitants managed through informal cooperation in one of Brooklyn's poorer industrial sections. With its waterfront commercial slums and extensive harbor facilities, Red Hook might have seemed better fitted to Tönnes' diametrically opposite concept, *Gesellschaft*, a society characterized by anonymity, institutionalized contacts, and egotistic self-interest. In the Little Norway of 1892, that kind of community and *Gemeinschaft* coexisted, but the latter was predominant.

Through *Nordisk Tidende*, Emil Nielsen, his assistants, and supporters urged a more ambitious definition of community than that won through working and living together in a compact geographical area. Between 1891 and 1910 the newspaper became a means of proposing and propagandizing for a range of large-scale institutional cooperation. In other words, Nielsen and company were ambitious on the colony's behalf for varieties of *formal* cooperation. They wanted to see their fellow countrymen working together through structured institutions. With mixed motives of self-interest and social concern, they spearheaded a drive to unite Norwegians across the whole metropolitan area for social welfare and political projects. Inevitably, as the next chapter in Little Norway's story shows, such a concept of community brought not only larger-scale, more formal cooperation, but also conflict.

# 8

# Our Own Little World:
## Community Life in
## Little Norway, 1890–1910

**Our Own
Little World**
Around the turn of the century, Norwegian immigrants created a complete social milieu on the Red Hook peninsula. After nearly three decades of serving as a haven for maritime transients, Little Norway emerged as a self-sustaining entity. The settlers not only won greater influence at the institutions for visiting seamen but also established a wide spectrum of voluntary associations to supplement their residential, occupational, and family networks. The colony's more formally structured social organizations frequently reflected the influence of its largest working-class population, maritime workers and their families, and its largest regional grouping, those from the southern coast of Norway. Like many other ethnic communities, Little Norway allowed many of its inhabitants to satisfy their social needs without turning to outsiders. First-generation Norwegian adults frequently spent their leisure time wearing "ethnic spectacles" that filtered out other dimensions of life in Red Hook. As long as they saw life through the lens of Norwegian language and culture, the colony constituted "our own little world," a separate and more vivid reality.[1]

Immigrant domination of Little Norway's community affairs represented a momentous change in the colony's history. From the 1860s until the end of the 1880s, settled residents in the colony were little more than tolerated guests at institutions for transient mariners. Religious charities and economic interests involved with Norway's merchant marine, not immigrants, were the prime movers in the creation of Norwegian organizations in the city during these decades. By 1890, however, a series of related events transformed the situation. Among these, the most important for the development of settler-led institutions were the departure of the sojourning elite that had managed colony affairs in the 1880s and the rapid growth of the immigrant population.

The first immigrant-run institution in Red Hook, the Bethelship Norwegian Methodist Church, appeared as early as 1874. It survived, however, largely because its members were willing to take over the New York Methodist Conference's work with transient Norwegian seamen in the port. Not until Our Savior's Norwegian Lutheran Church moved from Manhattan to Red Hook in 1885 did the younger colony gain its second immigrant organization. During the intervening years, sojourning leaders at "transplanted" institutions directed community affairs in Little Norway. The Seamen's Church, the Deaconess Home and Hospital, and the Scandinavian Seamen's Home were all "transplanted" in the sense that their organizational structures, staffs, and funding were imported from the old country with the assistance of the Manhattan colony elite.

Our Savior's relocation coincided with the start of the period of conflict between sojourning and immigrant leaders that ushered in immigrant control over community life by the end of the 1880s. That tension built to a climax primarily because the size of the settled population reached an awkward stage. The colony grew so large that it strained the energies of sojourning leaders and the resources of the transplanted institutions. In fact, Little Norway became sufficently large and well established to support its own associations and produced local leaders who could argue for the immigrants' right to a larger share in community affairs. Yet the settlers were so accustomed to relying on the transplanted institutions that their first generation of spokesmen attempted to wrest these institutions from the control of sojourning leaders before they directed their energies to the founding of indigenous immigrant organizations. The immigrants had to be denied essential services at the Seamen's Church and the Sailors' Home, for example, before they founded Trinity Lutheran Church and the Norwegian-American Seamen's Association near the end of the decade.

By that time, the crisis in the colony's development had passed, and the scales of influence had shifted in the immigrants' favor. One major cause of the change was the near-simultaneous departure of the entire sojourning leadership elite that had resisted the settlers' attempts to gain control over the transplanted institutions. When Seamen's Pastor

Hansteen, Superintendent Andersen at the Sailors' Home, Consul and Mrs. Børs, and Head Deaconess Elizabeth Fedde returned to Norway in 1889, only two sojourning assistants remained. Having seen their former superiors' exhaustion from years of struggling with the immigrants, these two, Assistant Seamen's Pastor Kristen Sårheim and Vice Consul Christopher Ravn, trod carefully as they tried at the same time to avoid antagonizing the colony further and to satisfy the expectations of organizations and interest groups in Norway.[2]

Immigrant leaders eagerly moved to fill the leadership vacuum created by the sojourning elite's mass exit. After Consul Børs left, for example, the Seamen's Association boldly attempted to influence the choice of his replacement by sending the Swedish-Norwegian government a petition signed by over 1,100 local residents in favor of its hand-picked candidate, Vice Consul Ravn. When authorities in Stockholm selected another man instead, local leaders adopted a critically watchful attitude toward the new consul and, finding his performance wanting, excoriated him publicly and gave Ravn the positions the consul traditionally held on the boards of the transplanted institutions.[3]

Only months after Seamen's Pastor Hansteen returned to Norway, Pastor Sårheim tacitly admitted the vital role immigrants played at the Seamen's Church. Urging them to return to the station, he announced that he had gained permission from the Mission's home office to reverse the decision that had excluded them from the sacraments. Abandoning Hansteen's aggressive campaign against Red Hook's sailortown, he also took the advice of local leaders and abstained from running for a position on the boards of the Sailors' Home and the Deaconess Home and Hospital, where the station was not officially represented until the mid-1890s.[4]

No longer inhibited by the close cooperation of Pastor Hansteen, Mrs. Børs, and Sister Elizabeth, immigrant board members at the Deaconess Home and Hospital immediately took a firmer hand in institutional policy. Although they chose another sister from the mother house in Christiania to manage the hospital, the settlers interfered so much in its daily operation that the new head sister suggested when she tendered her resignation after two years that they hire a woman more familiar with American language and customs.[5] The settler majority elected to the board of the Sailors' Home in 1889 retained control throughout the next two decades but soon became a source of disagreement. On the one hand, some colony spokesmen thought the institution's growing financial dependence on shipping circles in Manhattan and Norway meant the home would have to give priority to shipowners' rather than sailors' interests. On the other, the board's new leaders so quickly stamped the institution with their conservatively pious views that *Nordisk Tidende* reported seamen's complaints in 1892 under the headline, "A Depressing View of Life or 'Throw Him Out!' A Christian Place: The Sailors' Home and its Boys."[6]

Thus, although the most experienced leaders in Red Hook after 1889 were immigrant spokesmen, the transition to local control did not always produce harmonious relationships in the colony. Some elements in the settled community harbored bitter memories of sojourning leaders' arrogant disregard for their wishes during the previous decade. Most of those who had earlier attended the Seamen's Church did not return at Pastor Sårheim's urging, claiming that the station had become too high-church for their tastes. Pastor Sårheim had not forgotten either, as his acute sensitivity and sharp reaction to criticism from *Nordisk Tidende* showed in the early 1890s.[7] Both he and the majority of greenhorn sojourner leaders who arrived later found adjusting their policies to suit the immigrants a practical necessity. Still, old resentments and the growing diversity of the colony's associational life sometimes made disputes unavoidable.

The second and decisive factor in the transition to an immigrant-dominated community was the rapid increase in the size of the settled population. The massive wave of Norwegian emigration between 1880 and 1893 transformed Red Hook's Norwegian settlement. Until sometime in the early 1880s, the Norwegian population of all Brooklyn numbered less than a thousand people. Yet by 1890 the city had 4,500 Norwegian inhabitants and, two years later, the Red Hook peninsula alone housed over 2,800.[8]

As the conversion to steam-driven vessels caused a prolonged depression in coastal southern Norway, emigration rates from those regions rose dramatically in relation to the rest of the country during the mid-1880s and remained exceptionally high until after 1910. According to the seamen's pastors, the number of transient Norwegian seamen in port on foreign ships, most of them from the same region, mushroomed from around 4,000 to 20,000 about the same time. Apparently, Red Hook's decades-long familiarity for these people encouraged large numbers of later immigrants and mariners to settle in the colony rather than travel farther west. The influx must have been especially great during the latter part of the 1880s, because the colony's growth rate during the decade (416 percent) was the highest it would ever experience.[9]

*Nordisk Tidende* claimed that the colony continued growing rapidly until late 1893, when the economic downturn in the United States led to a sharp decline in immigration. The newspaper reported remigration to Norway from the colony because of the depression as late as the summer of 1897. Still, the Norwegian-born population of Brooklyn rose to almost 8,000 by the end of the decade. During the next ten years, when the local economy improved and Norwegian emigration reached its twentieth-century peak, the number of Norwegian inhabitants in the city shot up to over 15,000. The study of destinations in Norway's emigrant protocols suggests that in the early twentieth century the colony's appeal was weakest in middle and northern areas of the country, moderately strong in the nation's capital, and greatest in southern coastal areas.

In short, immigrants from the Agder and Rogaland counties very likely remained Little Norway's dominant regional group through 1910 and beyond.[10]

By the 1890s, circumstances were ripe for the appearance of the colony's first sizeable group of immigrant-run associations. By 1910, additional cohorts of newcomers and a widening range of interests and views among the settlers had led to a diversification of the enclave's associational life.

## The First Flowering of Immigrant Associations in Red Hook

As A. N. Rygg remarks in *Norwegians in New York*, the wave of Norwegian immigration to Brooklyn in the 1880s created a "demand for more associations." The lack of Norwegian initiatives was so apparent by the end of the decade, he reports, that an Irish society with "eyes open for the main chance" arranged Norwegian Constitution Day festivities in Red Hook. Rygg very likely preserves a just sense of his countrymen's dismay at this Irish intrusion, but in fact Little Norway already had some organizations that marked the old country's national day—the institutions for transient mariners, two immigrant churches, the Norwegian Seamen's Association, a mutual benefit society, and a social club.[11]

Rygg's main point, however, is well taken. By 1889, the colony's few immigrant organizations no longer satisfied the needs of its rapidly growing population. During the next twenty years, Norwegian immigrants founded dozens of organizations on the peninsula. In the 1890s alone, the spectrum of new associations included six singing societies, four theater groups, three churches, two mutual benefit societies, two temperance lodges, an organization for people from the city of Bergen, and a range of political, sports, and women's clubs. Two Norwegian-language newspapers competed for the settlers' loyalty during the decade, *Nordiske Blade*, which began publishing in Red Hook in 1878 but traditionally associated itself with Manhattan colony interests, and *Nordisk Tidende*, which was founded in 1891 and championed the views of immigrant groups in the younger colony.[12]

As the colony nearly doubled its population again in the next ten years, the number and diversity of its voluntary associations expanded rapidly. Churches and International Order of Good Templar (IOGT) temperance lodges comprised the largest categories among the more than thirty new organizations established between 1900 and 1910. The almost yearly appearance of new IOGT lodges during these years gave a clear indication of mounting concern about alcoholism among local Norwegians. By 1910 Little Norway contained ten IOGT chapters organized under a district lodge that claimed almost 750 members. Two organizations independent of the American IOGT, a total abstinence society for seamen and a branch of the old country's Good Templar organization, rounded out the colony's anti-liquor groups.[13]

There can be little doubt that the colony's temperance movement had its roots in southern and southwestern coastal Norway. The area

Group photograph of IOGT Lodge "Lindesnæs" taken in 1921. Many joiners preferred an organized ethnic social life and involvement in a larger social cause, which led to other forms of adjustment to American life. Founded in 1904, this temperance lodge ardently supported the total prohibition of alcoholic beverages. Norwegian Emigrant Museum.

that provided Little Norway with its largest group of newcomers also gave old-country movements for restriction or prohibition their staunchest supporters throughout the nineteenth century. Colony veterans were unanimous in their assertion that most Red Hook teetotalers had come from Agder and Rogaland counties, and two Brooklyn lodges chose names that explicitly identified the same regional origins. Articles in *Nordisk Tidende* and local Norwegian-language IOGT publications announced that prominent leaders based their campaigns on experience gained in Norway's southern and southwestern port cities.[14]

Little Norway's temperance spokesmen adapted their old-country methods to suit the new situation. To appeal to an urban immigrant population, they attempted to attract members by offering most of the entertainments and services available from other kinds of ethnic associations. Eager to convert the hard-drinking inhabitants of the colony's sailortown, they developed special programs for mariners. A local immigrant barber with experience from Bergen, for example, spearheaded the founding of the Seamen's Total Abstinence Society in 1892 and convinced the Seamen's Church to provide space for the group's meetings. IOGT lodge Lindesnæs, many of whose members were sailors, held a regular "Brothers' Evening," when the "brig" Lindesnæs symbolically passed the equator and Neptune arrived to shave maritime neophytes, initiating them into the lodge.[15]

The half-dozen new congregations founded between 1900 and 1910 also exhibited tendencies suggesting the growing size of the regional group from southern Norway. Only one of the new churches was orthodox Lutheran. The others—Baptist, Methodist, Seventh Day Adventist, and two varieties of "free church" evangelical Lutheran—all represented forms of the layman-oriented pietism for which the coastal areas of the Agder counties were known. According to colony veterans, these groups' regional origins also showed in their habit of mixing revivalist awakenings with anti-drinking campaigns—a tendency the Norwegian historian Per Fuglum also found along the old country's southern coast.[16]

By 1910 Little Norway's churches provided one indication that the colony had grown large enough to create niches for a variety of socioeconomic and regional groupings. The oldest immigrant congregation, Our Savior's Lutheran, occupied one end of the spectrum because it offered the closest approximation to the old country's state-church liturgy and had a membership originating in many parts of Norway but sharing a preference for old-world standards of propriety in language, dress, and entertainment. The "free" churches represented the other end of the spectrum because of their layman-oriented pietism and predominantly working-class southern and southwestern Norwegian origins. These congregations had the least sympathy for Our Savior's socioreligious atmosphere. Many of their members had rejected upper-class control of Norway's state church before emigrating and as many opposed high-church Lutheranism's conservative refusal to support total abstinence from alcoholic beverages on the Biblical ground that Christ had enjoyed wine.[17]

The Bethelship Methodist and Trinity Lutheran congregations occupied the middle of the religious spectrum. Their close connection to the colony's maritime beginnings had, at least originally, given them a working-class membership and aspects of the Seamen's Mission's low-church adaptation to local circumstances. By the early 1900s, however, they were also known as bastions of the colony's growing entrepreneurial class, which in many cases consisted of sailors and ships' officers who had left the sea to become shopkeepers. That the membership of Bethelship Methodist and Trinity shared to a degree the free churches' regional background in Agder and Rogaland, according to colony veterans, explained their low-church style and gave additional evidence of those regional groups' dominant size in an enclave that developed largely because of Norwegian shipping in the port of New York.

The colony's growing diversity was also evident by 1910 in the development of associations for different socioeconomic groups. The working-class majority organized primarily through mutual benefit societies, labor organizations, temperance lodges, and a variety of clubs that developed treasuries for sickness, unemployment, and funeral payments as well as for social activities. The officers of these working-class organizations, however, were often men who had risen to the status of small-scale entrepreneurs.[18]

The colony's first benevolent institution for the poor and needy appeared in 1891, when leading Norwegians attempted to mobilize the resources of Nordic business and religious leaders on behalf of the large wave of newcomers. Unfortunately, the Scandinavian Assistance Association for Unemployed Emigrants became a source of bickering when coalitions formed behind different plans for placing a Scandinavian representative at Castle Garden's, and later Ellis Island's, employment bureaus. During the depression of the mid-1890s, temporary relief organizations resulted from the efforts of various groups to help the less fortunate. The Norwegian-dominated Seamen's Corps of the Salvation Army as well as immigrant churches set up soup kitchens. Forming the Willing Workers' Relief Society, colony women joined forces to sew clothes and raise money for the poor through charity bazaars. The Seamen's Association mounted successful campaigns to establish a hospice cum workhouse for the homeless and a hiring office for unemployed mariners.[19]

During the century's first decade, the full range of Little Norway's socioeconomic scale became clearer as the colony's elite defined its own social arena and role. The first institution with by-laws that limited membership to an elite, the Norwegian Club, originated in 1902 as an association for architects and engineers. As the Norwegian-American historians Kenneth Bjork and Odd Lovoll have commented about similar societies, the Club at first represented an "imported elite" of highly trained technocrats, a small segment of the larger drain of the well-educated from Europe to American industry. Because the Brooklyn group in 1900 was too small and geographically mobile to maintain a stable organization, it soon reorganized as a social club for academically trained professionals and businessmen. By 1910, the Club's first president, Doctor of Philosophy Peter Groth, had established a round of private lectures, concerts, and gala balls meant to mark it as the pinnacle of colony high culture. Through receptions for high-ranking Norwegian visitors, such as the Arctic explorer Roald Amundsen, and notable American guests, the Club claimed the role as the colony's proper link to the outside world.[20]

Judging from its lists of members and guests, the Norwegian Club did not include many of Little Norway's shopkeepers in its social sphere. The petty proprietors whose careers we have followed (Theodore Kartevold and Gabriel Ueland, for instance) do not appear in the Club's early records. Starting in 1909, the Norsemen Lodge of the Masonic Order helped satisfy the desire of such middle-class businessmen for an association that would both forward their own social, commercial, and charitable interests and establish contacts with American and other ethnic groups' business circles. Prominent men in the Norsemen Lodge and the Norwegian Club did, however, cooperate at the end of the decade, when they joined forces on committees for erecting a monument to Edvard Grieg and founding a children's home.[21]

Thus, both the development of the colony's religious life and the expansion of its secular organizations revealed a trend toward greater diversity. In one sense, that variety was positive because it indicated the enclave's growing ability to provide niches that satisfied the needs of widely different elements of the population. In another sense, however, the appearance of voluntary associations patronized by or limited to distinct socioeconomic, regional, and religious groups had a negative effect: it institutionalized divisions in the community that made cooperation across these now visible boundaries more difficult.

Almost annually, starting with the joint effort to help newcomers in 1891, representative central committees came together to solve common problems, arrange receptions for visiting celebrities, or plan Constitution Day celebrations. Time and again, these umbrella organizations dissolved in dispute over claims that a self-interested clique had usurped authority or mismanaged funds and plans. Of these, the Norwegian National League (Det Norske Nationalforbundet) finally survived, perhaps because it seemed a monument to the burst of national patrotism during which it was created on Norway's achievement of full independence in 1905. Still, by 1909 the League's ongoing recruitment campaign had convinced less than half of the colony's associations to send delegates, and six of those stalked out to form the "United Norwegian Societies" after a tumultous debate over plans for the Constitution Day parade.

Clearly, even the appearance of unity became difficult for Little Norway's diverse groups to maintain once the glow of the old country's fight for independence had faded.[22]

No portrait of Little Norway's social life would be complete without an examination of the role the colony's maritime background played in determining its organizational configuration. Here, continuity rather than increasing diversity is most apparent. As A. N. Rygg remarked, nothing characterized the community more than the "strong whiff of the briny sea" that permeated all its activities. Norway's shipping traditions produced maritime sub-communities in Boston, Philadelphia, Baltimore, the Great Lakes cities, Mobile, Alabama, and San Francisco, as well as in the port cities of other continents, but in no other large Norwegian community in the United States was the most common link between individuals and differing socioeconomic groups a current or previous personal or family experience with seafaring.[23] Only Seattle's Norwegian settlement—which depended greatly on deep-sea fishing—supplies a possible parallel.

The New York State Census of 1892 showed that one third of the colony's immigrant workmen had maritime occupations. At the same time, a group of transient seamen several times the size of the total settled population frequented the enclave. When the state conducted its 1905 enumeration, maritime workers accounted for only 29 percent of the male work force, and the volume of visiting sailors, while still large, was smaller compared to the settled colony. Was the 'whiff of the sea' getting weaker? Rygg and colony veterans answered with a definite negative. As one old-timer expressed their common view, "Don't forget. Most of those carpenters you hear about in Brooklyn were really old sailors. They didn't forget the sea just because they became landlubbers." Successive state censuses supported one aspect of this man's assertion. Between 1892 and 1925, the percentage of seamen in the colony fell by 12.8 points and the percentage of carpenters rose 12.5. The patterns of maritime influence on community life at the turn of the century confirm the other point the old-timer was making. Residents with a seafaring *background* gave Little Norway its distinctive character.[24]

For decades, individual seamen had "gone on land" in the Red Hook-Gowanus section of Brooklyn. Giving up the wandering life of deep-sea sailors, they had adjusted to the more settled routines of harbor or land-based occupations. By the turn of the century, the great number of such individual decisions had skewed the colony's leadership group of small-time entrepreneurs so that it contained many men whose interests and attitudes were influenced by their experiences at sea. Since a large part of the immigrant organizations' rank and file membership had very likely made similar transitions, many leaders and followers shared a sympathetic understanding of each other's life experiences.[25]

Not surprisingly, therefore, as the colony as a whole went on land,

**Maritime
Influences on
the Colony's
Associational
Life**

many of the voluntary organizations it harbored reflected a combination of old maritime loyalties and newer concerns related to long-term residence in the city. Around the turn of the century, seamen's living and working conditions never ceased to be topics of intense interest to immigrant clubs and institutions in the enclave. As the end of the first decade in the new century approached, however, the colony's associations became increasingly preoccupied with the needs of their land-based members. By 1900, for example, the leadership of the two immigrant congregations that had grown out of missions for itinerant sailors, Our Savior's Lutheran and Bethelship Methodist, included many shopkeeper-entrepreneurs who had once worked on ships. During the next ten years, these men supported the founding of daughter congregations in the newer Sunset Park settlements, and thus assisted the migration to the south that resulted in communities that were less dependent on seafaring.[26]

In the early stages of Little Norway's organizational life, many important immigrant institutions functioned as improvised supplements, replacements, or duplicates of the older transplanted institutions for transient mariners. The Norwegian-American Seamen's Association, which provided mariners and seamen-gone-on-land with a number of the services originally offered by the Sailors' Home, represented the most important example of a secular organization of this kind. In the 1890s, the Association had the largest membership of any nonreligious organization in the colony. During the following decade, only the temperance movement could claim more adherents, and then only if one counted all ten separate groups in the IOGT district lodge together. The Association addressed the concerns of immigrant and transient seamen, played a crucial role in the establishment of other immigrant institutions, and served as a focal point for conflicts in the colony and between it and the Manhattan shipping elite.[27]

The origins and early history of the Seamen's Association illustrate the mixture of interests that motivated sailors who had settled down on land. The community leaders who started the Association in 1888 had all started their careers as transient sailors and later become managers, businessmen, or professionals. Like Trinity Lutheran Church, moreover, the Association was a product of the tension between settled immigrants and sojourning leaders at institutions for itinerant mariners. Magnus Andersen, the freethinking first manager of the Sailors' Home, originated the idea of an organization for immigrant seamen in the hope that it would simultaneously relieve the home of the burden of assisting maritime settlers and win him local support in his struggle with the Seamen's Church over control of the home. He therefore promoted the organization as one which would help mariners achieve the goal he cherished for the home itself: independence from sojourning upper-class representatives whose charity was tainted by their need to serve shipowners and their belief that most sailors were irresponsible seafaring boys.[28]

As a result, the Association was from its inception secular, free of the seamen's pastors' paternalistic attempts to reform the men's behavior, and oriented toward mobilizing maritime workers in opposition to the long arm of shipowners' influence that reached the colony through the consulate and shipping agents in Manhattan. Because the Sailors' Home grew increasingly pious and teetotalist after Andersen's departure in 1889, the Association frequently also found itself opposed to the institution that had occasioned its founding. The programs initiated during the organization's first year gave expression to all these aspects of the group's outlook and aims.[29]

The overall purpose of several initiatives was to end sailors' dependence on aid and advice from the consulate or transplanted institutions. Organizing as a benevolent society, the Seamen's Association collected dues and held bazaars to establish a treasury for unemployment, sickness, and funeral benefits available to transient as well as settled members. By hiring their own local Norwegian doctor, the men not only had a reliable health service but also avoided the moralizing commentary that sometimes accompanied treatment for alcoholism or venereal diseases at the Deaconess Home and Hospital. To represent the interests of mariners who complained of difficulties with American authorities, mistreatment from boardinghouse masters, brutality from officers, and insupportable working conditions onboard ship, the Association retained its own lawyer. One of its founders, August Reymert, met the men's requirements perfectly because his personal experience as a seaman gave him a sympathetic understanding of sailors' needs and a dedication to protecting the rights of exploited immigrants. Thus, the men found an advocate who was prejudiced in their favor and so ended their traditional reliance on the old country's consul, who was usually inclined to agree with hiring agents and captains because the consulate's primary purpose was serving owners' economic interests.

All these initiatives demonstrated a practical, down-to-earth resourcefulness in finding substitutes that in fact improved on the services mariners had previously received from sojourning leaders at institutions for transients. Certainly, these actions should have belied the notion of the men's immature irresponsibility. At its twentieth anniversary celebration in 1909, the Association claimed that it had spent 95 percent of its income on the various welfare services outlined above. Unfortunately, during the organization's first year of existence, its social events rather than its mutual benefit programs captured the public's attention.[30]

Many Association members did not relinquish their nostalgic desire to recapture the free-wheeling abandon of transient seamen on shore leave when they took on the sober work of assisting colleagues and winning independence from the groups that patronized or exploited them. The men's old life called powerfully, and one of the organization's first orders of business was establishing a tradition of parties in sailortown bars following each weekly meeting and monthly parties at which crewmen on newly arrived vessels mixed with their more settled friends. Before long, the Association had a reputation for rowdy, boisterous affairs that started with the hearty camaraderie of drinks all around and not infrequently ended in brawling fistfights.[31]

Critical reactions in and outside the organization soon brought both reform and counterattack. Temperance-minded members like Gabriel Ueland and Helmin Johnsen deplored the "debilitating" excesses. At first, outside criticism seemed limited to disparaging remarks made in colony stores, meetings, or sermons. When *Nordiske Blade* converted such gossip into a public issue in 1890 through its scathing editorial comments, however, Association leaders began searching for ways to restore the organization's good name. After all, these men were ambitious to gain approval from the most respected levels of Norwegian-American society from the start. In 1889, they secured Norwegian-born Columbia professor Hjalmar Hjorth Boyesen as the main speaker at the Association's founding ceremonies, and Boyesen gratified their wish for recognition by calling sailors the "class of Norwegians in which the nation's most excellent strength showed itself and made itself known."[32]

During the next two years, the need to repair the organization's local reputation intensified the group's original desire for public recognition and led to the founding of the first of many colony institutions that owed their existence to the Association. Ueland converted the infamous monthly parties into a series of lectures and concerts at which the presence of female guests dampened the tendency toward wild intoxication. Johnsen founded the Seamen's Total Abstinence Society to provide nondrinking members of the Association with a separate social program. When the Association agreed to supply him with start-up capital, Emil Nielsen, an early member, began publishing *Nordisk Tidende* in 1891. From the outset, he used it to cudgel not only *Nordiske Blade* but the whole array of reactionary upper-class groups he felt it represented: Our Savior's Lutheran Church, the sojourning leaders, and all the economic groups with vested interests in Norwegian shipping that exploited seamen. That fall the Association capped off its public relations efforts by arranging the colony's first Leif Erikson Day parade and bringing in Rasmus B. Anderson, "the very 'hub'" of Norwegian-American cultural life and author of *America Not Discovered by Columbus*, to speak at the affair.[33]

*Nordisk Tidende* and the Seamen's Association cultivated a symbiotic relationship. Despite occasional differences of opinion, each supported the other's projects. The newspaper gave the Association front-page credit for initiatives such as those mentioned earlier and the Leif Erikson Day Parade, the relief program for unemployed newcomers, and the local campaign for Norway's full independence from Sweden. For example, when the Association campaigned for the "pure flag"— Norway's flag with the rectangular symbol of the union with Sweden removed, cut the offensive patch out, and sent it to the Norwegian parliament with a lengthy call for freedom and self-determination, *Nordisk Tidende* reported the event in three successive issues. When the *Blade* suggested that the Association's action showed a lack of deference to duly constituted authority, Nielsen commented that its competitor's "antediluvian" views made it similar to a "decrepit dog that toothlessly casts slime on people."[34]

In return for such unflinching support, the Association willingly championed Nielsen's goals, defended the newspaper's reputation, and helped increase its circulation. When Seamen's Pastor Sårheim called the newspaper a "scandalous rag" and refused to have it in the station's reading room, the Association rallied to Nielsen's defense and claimed that *Nordisk Tidende* was a necessity at the Seamen's Church because it was the only newspaper sailors read. When Nielsen urged the purchase of a community center that would house all the colony's voluntary organizations, the Association donated the proceeds of several bazaars toward the realization of that dream. In response to the owner-editor's call for a central committee that would arrange Constitution Day celebrations for the whole metropolitan area in Red Hook, the Association discontinued its tradition of marking the day in Manhattan and recruited representatives for the committee.[35]

In general, the Seamen's Association's cooperation with *Nordisk Tidende* contributed to the organization's increasing preoccupation with the concerns of immigrants working on land. The newspaper was genuinely concerned about the problems of transient seamen, but Nielsen's projects for centralized institutions focused the Association's attention on helping settled immigrants use their limited resources to create stable community traditions in an urban environment. In the 1890s, *Nordisk Tidende* praised the Association most highly when it planned relief efforts to help greenhorns find work in Red Hook or organized patriotic parades that assisted the immigrants in locating their ethnic identity in a polyglot city.[36]

By 1910, three years after Nielsen's death, the Association had socially "gone on land." That is, it had developed goals, responsibilities, and social activities typical of a permanently resident group. Gone were the days when its parties revealed a nostalgic wish to be transients reveling in sailortown. Its members were now instrumental in founding sports clubs and choirs. Its annual affairs had become tux-and-tie banquets and balls, and its monthly parties had changed to combined evenings with other colony societies. It now contributed to fund-raisers for the Norwegian Children's Home Association and the Grieg Monument Committee as a founding member of the Norwegian National

League.[37] In the process of making this transition to settled propriety, the Association had also illustrated Little Norway's distinctive history as a haven for itinerant mariners that evolved into an immigrant-dominated community.

## "A Great Social Life in Red Hook— Under the Circumstances": Obstacles to Participation

Having traced the flowering of Little Norway's associational life and the maritime influences on its development, it is important to consider whether a small minority or a large part of the immigrants participated in this multifarious activity. Otherwise, the concerns of a few people could wrongly appear to be those of the majority. The common view among historians is that only a small part of the Norwegian-American population (between 4 and 15 percent) were active participants in or "directly touched" by ethnic associations, even at the turn of the century when the number of the immigrants who joined these groups increased rapidly. Olaf M. Norlie, for example, estimated that only one in nine Norwegians living in American cities was a member of a Norwegian church.[38]

Many of the colony veterans interviewed took a similar view. After telling impressive stories about the large ethnic gatherings they or their parents had experienced in Brooklyn, old-timers asserted that the tiny group of joiners who ran the colony's organizations drummed up crowds only with great difficulty. The obstacles were considerable and the leaders few but the participants and beneficiaries many. As one elderly Norwegian commented, "My mom and dad said Norwegians had a wonderful social life in Red Hook—under the circumstances."[39]

The obstacles that limited engagement in the colony's voluntary associations were many, but the time and strength devoted to earning a living probably reduced the ranks of leaders and ordinary members more than any other factor. Many in the huge waves of newcomers that arrived at the turn of the century had to give first priority to the problem of finding jobs that would provide at least subsistence incomes. Only with stable employment was there the opportunity to learn the occupational and language skills needed to improve their economic prospects. Yet because well over half of the period's Norwegian greenhorns were single, between the ages of 15 and 30, and semi-skilled or unskilled, such stability was not easily achieved. The search for suitable work not infrequently forced many of these immigrants to become unwilling birds of passage who wandered from one American city to another.[40]

One anonymous Norwegian youth's diary from 1901, for example, describes how he and two others with some training in drafting began an itinerant life after they had earned their passage to Red Hook as seamen. Although they had acquaintances on the peninsula and had been told they could easily find jobs on the docks, weeks of effort resulted in no more than an occasional day's work. Becoming desperate as their savings dwindled to nothing, they borrowed from Norwegians in

A family picnic in Prospect Park in the 1890s. Norwegian Emigrant Museum.

the colony to finance a move to Bayonne, New Jersey, where it was rumored that work was available. By the end of the year, a fruitless quest for steady employment had forced the friends to go separate ways and taken the author as far west as Pittsburgh. On repeated return trips to Brooklyn, the writer borrowed more money and participated in the colony's associational life by patronizing its benevolent institutions.[41]

The more settled working-class majority—maritime tradesmen, construction workers, unskilled laborers, and domestics—worked long hours under trying conditions for relatively low pay. *Nordisk Tidende*'s steady stream of articles about accidents in the bay, on the docks, or at building sites only confirmed the stories old-timers told about families whose scramble to survive economically was complicated by occupational injuries or disablements. Moreover, most of Little Norway's workers spent six days a week outside the colony and so had less leisure time to devote to organizational work because of commuting. According to the elderly men interviewed, the two largest groups of workmen, carpenters and seamen, were often away from home or unemployed for months during the depression of the 1890s and in the winter when both shipping and building regularly entered a slack period.[42]

The strain of everyday work routines is sometimes clearest in letters home. For example, on June 6, 1892, a young pharmacist's assistant who had worked in Brooklyn for six weeks apologized to his parents in Norway. "It's already late," he wrote, "so this won't be a long letter. I have long working hours, from 7 in the morning until 10 at night. When I know the language, even till 11." On June 15 he described the effects of a local heat wave. "It's terribly hot here now. . . . in the drugstore it was 92 degrees Fahrenheit in the middle of the day and that was at least a little cooler than outside. People who have to work outside fall dead of sunstroke. . . .Here in the store it's worst in the evening when the the gas lamps are lit. Last night it was 102 degrees when we closed." For a newcomer from a cooler Scandinavian climate such weather must have been especially trying.[43]

But the effects of exhausting work were not merely a greenhorn's problem. Five years later the young letter writer was working at the same drugstore and had, he felt, mastered English. Yet on January 22, 1897, he protested perhaps too vehemently, "I have now got used to my long working hours, so I am not as a rule sleepy or exhausted, and the work in itself isn't really so strenuous, only that the long day over longer periods of time blunts one's energy, and most likely because of that it's such an effort for me, for example, to write letters in the evening." Other immigrants striving to get established probably shared the fatigue he reluctantly admitted. Young and unattached, he came not as an unskilled worker but rather after some years' apprenticeship to a druggist in Norway. With such training he found employment within a week of his arrival. The physical demands of his job were minimal compared to factory or construction work. Yet, if one accepts his own account of the situation, he had neither time nor energy for social activities.

Even when working-class families had an enduring interest in particular clubs or societies, their support often flagged. A woman who told *Nordisk Tidende* about her family's situation regarding social activities in the 1890s probably spoke for many in similar circumstances. Soon after arriving in 1895, she was "disappointed over the long hard working day for small pay" but nevertheless joined a Norwegian women's club and attended ethnic choir concerts. Still, she indicated a basic limitation on the support these organizations could expect from her family when she stressed that she and her husband "did not have money for concerts and dances if we wanted to save something each month."[44]

Many of the colony's veteran activists reported that eliciting the support of exceptionally successful fellow countrymen was often an uphill battle. Such people, they said, were frequently more interested in making a name for themselves in the American community than in Little Norway. The latter career of Harry S. Christian, the sailor who went on land in the late 1840s and became a building materials supplier, illustrates this point. Although Christian achieved material success, the years of deprivation through which he suffered marked him as a tight-fisted miser in some people's eyes. The obituary *Nordisk Tidende* published about him in 1895, based on "other sources" in the colony, is a virulent broadside on his stinginess and lack of sympathy for needy countrymen.[45]

Possibly piqued because Christian's widow and son offered him so little information, the newspaper's reporter went to people who "knew him better" and patched together the local grievances held against the dead man. After forty years with a prosperous business in Gowanus and a current annual income estimated at $12,000, gossips noted that he lived in a tenement but two blocks from Red Hook's wharves and sailortown dives. "Even the full-grown son," who would now assume control of the business, still lived there. Few in the colony knew Christian, claimed the writer, because "oddly enough he has never given a thought to countrymen here in need, or even once offered one cent to fund drives or Scandinavian charitable institutions."[46]

What especially galled the journalist and his informants was that Christian refused support to Norwegian organizations but was generous to his American Methodist church. When friends of the Norwegian Deaconess Home and Hospital observed that it needed building materials, he earned their resentment by denying aid with the claim that the "times were so difficult." Christian had earlier belonged to the colony's Norwegian Methodist congregation and even served on its council for several years, but he never donated any money to that church. On the other hand, after he shifted his membership to a nearby American Methodist church, he served not only as president of its council but also as Sunday school superintendent, and gave financial support.

The evident spite in *Nordisk Tidende*'s obituary reveals as much about colony expectations toward the economic elite as it does about the deceased's career. His neglect of countrymen, according to old-timers, was not unusual. Most, like Christian, preferred to court the approval of their American contacts, to assure future economic benefits and as the ultimate proof of "making it" in America. Inadvertently, *Nordisk Tidende*'s journalist revealed that Christian won exactly that kind of native approval when his American church's council rewarded him with a "very costly present" one month before his death.[47]

Little Norway's pool of leadership potential was unusually circumscribed because of the colony's special relationship to Norway's shipping industry and its representatives in the Manhattan settlement. Being a major freight depot on Norwegian shipping routes brought well-trained sojourning leaders to Red Hook, but this elite's first obligations were to serve maritime transients, follow directives from old-country organizations, and avoid alienating major contributors in Norway's shipping centers or in Manhattan. Most of the oldest and best established Norwegian immigrant families lived there rather than in Red Hook and devoted their energies to the older settlement's few remaining organizations rather than to upstart projects suggested by newcomers across the East River. The largest groups in the Manhattan elite—ship brokers, maritime lawyers, and insurance agents who served the home country's shipowners—gladly reached into their own pockets or forwarded their employers' donations to support Red Hook's institutions for nationals working in the homeland's merchant marine. Few of them, on the other hand, were interested in aiding Little Norway's associations for settled immigrants, since these contained many seamen who had left Norway's fleet, legally or illegally, and gone on land.[48]

There were, of course, exceptions to the pattern followed by most Manhattan colony leaders. August Reymert may stand as the most prominent representative for the minority of Norwegian Manhattanites who became deeply involved in Little Norway's associational life. The money-making side of Reymert's law practice consisted largely of negotiating contracts for export firms and shippers in the old country. Another side of his career developed early, however, when he began offering advice to newly arrived Scandinavian immigrants and the older colony's businessmen.[49]

As ethnic organizations proliferated across the East River, Reymert apparently extended that part of his work without any second thoughts. Thus, he recalled having been "godfather" to *Nordiske Blade*, and later "both midwife and doctor at the birth" of *Nordisk Tidende*. Around the turn of the century, he functioned as chief attorney for not only *Nordisk Tidende* and the Seamen's Association but also the Norwegian Singing Society, the Seamen's Church, the Sailors' Home, and the Deaconess Home and Hospital.[50]

Reymert's Norwegian and Norwegian-American antecedents and early life experiences would seem to offer the best explanation for his lasting commitment to the fortunes of Little Norway. Although he was born in an inland valley, his father came from Farsund, one of the southern shipping towns that had lost a sizeable number of residents to Red Hook. Like many men in the Brooklyn colony, Reymert went to sea at fifteen and jumped ship after crossing the Atlantic. The ship he best remembered working on had transported Norwegian emigrants to America, and his memories of the shabby treatment those people received, he claimed, had resulted in a resolve to help immigrants whenever he was able.

The only significant difference between Reymert's life experience and that of the majority of Norwegians in Red Hook consisted in his upper-class birth, which provided both private schooling before he left home and an uncle in Manhattan with whom he could begin his law practice. Unfortunately, most prominent leaders from the Manhattan colony either preferred to forget the beginnings of their American careers or had begun their lives in New York as established representatives of Norway's shipping interests. Red Hook's Little Norway, therefore, had to develop a home-grown organizational leadership.[51]

Lack of funds caused the most serious problems Norwegians faced in establishing and maintaining ethnic organizations. As the foregoing discussion of obstacles documents, Little Norway's exceptionally large contingent of maritime workers (and many of its carpenters) were away from their home community far too often and earned too little to contribute much time or money to fund-raising efforts. Thus, their efforts on behalf of ethnic organizations were often limited to canvassing for donations during weekends and evenings. Few housewives and daughters in Little Norway, on the other hand, worked outside their homes. The New York State Census manuscripts of 1892 and 1905 showed that only about a fifth of colony women had jobs. Many of those without jobs—over 1,000 in 1892 and many times more in 1905—provided a solution to organizations' financial difficulties, according to the reports of the old-timers interviewed as well as evidence from the period.[52]

Somehow many women managed not only to care for their homes and children but also to raise money for Little Norway's associational life. The bazaars that nearly all of Little Norway's institutions used to create or supplement a treasury for their activities depended on women's organizational skills and handicrafts. Working at home in between other chores or meeting informally in "ladies circles," women produced the baked goods, household articles, and clothing that provided salable wares at bazaars. At the event itself, the most successful or appealing of these products supplied the prizes for lotteries, and raffling off the women's box lunches or dinners provided yet another source of income. For a community with few financial resources, these affairs had several advantages. The women donated their work and, according to several experienced female organizers, used materials that the men "never missed" from the family budget. At the same time, the people who attended fund-raising bazaars could feel that they had acquired

**Our Own Little World: Overcoming the Obstacles to Participation**

useful items at bargain prices rather than given away their hard-earned money. Several of the patrons interviewed recalled getting "things that cost almost nothing." Colony old-timers unanimously claimed that these activities represented the transplantation of an old-country tradition: "Women's groups always supported secular and religious organizations back in Norway," said one, expressing the common view.[53]

Once a group had organized a bazaar, moreover, it usually became an annual event. Women looked forward to the social activity of working together and planned how to make the coming affair more successful than previous efforts. The elected officers of associations, who were almost always male, were loath to lose a source of income once a bazaar had been held. Thus, each new bazaar became a permanent fixture on the colony's social calendar. In 1883, Seamen's Pastor Andreas Mortensen and Sister Elizabeth Fedde introduced this old-country means of fund-raising to Red Hook to help finance the colony's first transplanted institutions. Within a decade, the rapidly growing immigrant colony had spread the practice to many kinds of organizations. Immigrant churches, temperance lodges, mutual benefit societies for workmen, women's clubs, and campaigns to aid the victims of disasters in Norway held bazaars between 1890 and 1910. As early as 1897, *Nordisk Tidende* complained that the endless round of bazaars had become a trying duty and a drain on one's purse.[54]

As promoters of widespread participation in community activities, these fund-raising events were as important as the organizations they supported. The more than sixty organizations in the colony by 1910 held dozens of bazaars each year. Producing articles for sale involved hundreds of immigrants. Bazaars drew crowds because they were informal, grass-roots affairs that provided opportunities to satisfy a variety of social needs. Families came together and chatted with friends and acquaintances as they moved from table to table admiring the women's handiwork. As parents became involved in shopping or adult topics, children found chances to play. Single men came to be introduced to marriageable women in the company of relatives, older women, and ministers. Admiring and buying the women's handiwork as well as their lottery tickets and lunch boxes gave ample opportunities for getting acquainted in an approved setting. *Nordisk Tidende* regularly reported that several hundred attended just a single bazaar, and even spoke of thousands when the fund-raiser extended over several days or weekends, as it usually did for the Seamen's Church, the Deaconess Home and Hospital, the Seamen's Association, and campaigns to assist the victims of disasters in Norway.[55]

The extent of participation in the colony's social life becomes more impressive when one remembers that bazaars were just the means used to support other activities. Little Norway's calendar of more purely social occasions included concerts, dances, balls, theatrical performances, sports competitions, social evenings, excursions to the countryside or up the Hudson, public debates, patriotic parades, and religious celebrations. The largest musical group, the Norwegian Singing Society, held autumn and spring concerts each year and always drew a crowd of hundreds that included not only friends and relatives but all Norwegians who enjoyed hearing the music that celebrated the old country's scenic beauty and folk culture. Comic revues that parodied or pilloried local celebrities such as *Nordiske Tidende*'s Emil Nielsen and movements such as pietistic awakenings and temperance campaigns were also a sure-fire success.[56]

In a community as wholeheartedly religious and patriotic as Little Norway, however, Christmas, Easter, Leif Erikson, and 17th of May celebrations commanded the broadest-based planning and the largest audiences. In both 1891 and 1909, Christmas festivities at the Seamen's Church alone reportedly drew crowds of between seven and eight hundred people. Few were so destitute that they lacked a coin or two to drop in the offering plate. Anybody could participate in the public part of patriotic celebrations on the 17th of May or Leif Erikson Day without spending money. As early as 1892, *Nordisk Tidende* reported that "at least 2,500" people marched in the Leif Erikson Day parade. The federal census recorded only 4,500 Norwegian-born residents in the city two years earlier. Even if one makes allowances for the exaggeration that might be expected from a colony newspaper, active participation in the parade was impressively widespread. After all, the journalist claimed to estimate only the number of marchers and did not add Norwegian spectators who must have been in the crowds lining the parade route. In 1909, the newspaper perhaps more realistically claimed that 300 marched, and then described "thousands" of spectators and 1,500 at the program in Prospect Hall after the parade.[57]

Most veterans agreed that fund-raising and publicity for the sponsoring group were the main motivations for social events. During the peak seasons of Little Norway's social calendar, organizations frequently combined several different types of events to ensure a level of participation that would cover costs and maximize profits. "You had to make the most of your big event of the season," remarked one veteran, "or you'd lose out to other clubs that had had better attractions, and then what would you do for money the rest of the year." Even affairs that were sure to draw a large crowd, such as the Norwegian-American Seamen's Association's annual masked ball, included a program of other entertainments calculated to make the evening memorable. In 1891, for example, the Association's ball featured a comic revue, a lottery, competitions of strength, and classical music.[58]

If women's lack of outside employment made them the economic backbone of Little Norway's associational life, a combination of other local circumstances relegated leadership responsibilites to the small-time businessmen, professionals, and ministers who lived and worked on the peninsula. As we have seen, there was a dearth of other volunteers. The sojourners and the Manhattan elite had other priorities. Working-class men were frequently absent because of the all-important business of making economic ends meet for their families. Local entrepreneurs and churchmen, on the other hand, could make involvement in ethnic organizations a part of their everyday routines, because their stores, offices, and churches were natural centers of social contact in the colony.[59]

Equally important, ministers and shopkeepers were positively disposed toward the development of an active immigrant community because that would strengthen their own positions. Intercourse with the public gave them daily opportunities to found new associations or recruit members for old ones as they passed the time of day with parishioners or customers. People who shared an interest in the social causes and activities that concerned them most and joined them in voluntary organizations, moreover, had an additional reason to patronize their churches or businesses. In America, not only shopkeepers but ministers, even high-church conservatives like the pastor at Our Savior's Lutheran, depended on the local population's willingness to provide a financial platform for their activities.[60]

Around the turn of the century, *Nordisk Tidende* repeatedly complained that clubs and businessmen profaned the sanctity of Leif Erikson Day and the 17th of May because they exploited these patriotic festivities to line their own pockets. Yet the newspaper's owner was among the businessmen who willingly "made a spectacle of themselves" on well-publicized social occasions to keep their enterprises in the public eye. One Seamen's Ball late in the 1890s, for example, included a costume competition between the editors of Red Hook's two Norwegian-language newspapers. A half century after the event, an elderly woman recalled that the two men "were both attempting to make *Nordisk Tidende* and *Nordiske Blade* popular. Martin Nielsen [the *Blade*'s editor] appeared in sackcloth and ashes. Emil Nielsen came riding in triumphantly on an elephant and won, of course. *He* paid $4 for my basket dinner, even though it was only canapes and cakes. 'Tasted excellent,' said Nielsen, as he poured me a cup of coffee."[61]

It is difficult to exaggerate the instrumental role Little Norway's business district played in the expansion of the colony's associational life. Centered on Hamilton Avenue and Columbia Street, the colony's downtown area was composed mostly of stores that opened in the middle or late 1880s, when few organizations for Norwegian immigrants existed. The area's compactness brought the immigrants together when they shopped and made the district seem the natural place for taking a stroll and discussing local affairs with fellow countrymen. Old-timers frequently described how their parents' generation discussed colony issues and ideas for new societies in the business district. Families and couples often stood and talked in the open triangles at intersections along Hamilton Avenue. Norwegians called one of these spacious crossings "Grimstad Corners" because countrymen from the region surrounding that seaport in southern Norway used it as their particular gathering place. In the collective memory of colony veterans, the combination of sailortown bars and revival meetings in the buildings at Grimstad Corners was sure to attract the two main groups from the region: carousing sailors and religious pietists.[62]

In general, men congregated in tobacco shops, bars, and the newspaper offices, where the talk centered on issues that interested the proprietors. Discussions in Hammerstad's bar, for instance, led to the establishment in 1895 of both a Democratic Club and the Bergen Regional Society. Because of his strong anti-liquor stance and large premises, Helmin Johnsen's furniture store on the Avenue became the colony's temperance nerve center. Three of Little Norway's IOGT lodges were founded in Johnsen's store and yet others held meetings there. In the early 1890s, ideas for theatricals were often hatched on *Nordisk Tidende*'s premises because some of its staff members were amateur actors or writers. As previously mentioned, Emil Nielsen's flamboyant personality and the competition between the enclave's two newspapers made natural topics for comic colony revues.[63]

Women usually gathered informally in groceries and the homes of laundresses, dressmakers, seamstresses, and midwives. They also met during 17th of May or Leif Erikson Day parades through the colony's commercial area. When wives of men in the Norwegian Singing Society saw the choir march through the business district in 1891, they noticed that it lacked a banner to announce its approach. Later conversations between women "downtown" resulted in organized evenings of entertainment to raise money for buying one. In the process, however, the women formed a female octet that toured Norwegian colonies in Connecticut and apparently became the main focus of their activities.[64]

Some entrepreneurs on Columbia Street and Hamilton Avenue converted their businesses into replicas of Norwegian-style country stores by offering a broad range of merchandise and services to attract a variety of customers. "That was just good business," commented the daughter of one turn-of-the-century shopkeeper as she told about Johan G. Normann's tobacco store, "but a lot of organizations got born in that place. He was a famous man, you know."[65]

There were at least three such general stores at the turn of the century, but Normann's tobacconist shop provides perhaps the clearest example of their importance for the evolution of community life. Normann's shop also functioned as a post office, money exchange, travel bureau, hiring office for yacht crews, and bookstore. For many years, moreover, he split his storefront with Theodore Kartevold, whose watch and jewelry business brought in yet other groups of customers. Normann's tobacco store became a center for voluntary associations because he was a joiner himself. Actively engaged in politics, the temperance movement, the Norwegian Singing Society, and the Norwegian-American Seamen's Association, Normann promoted both his business and local debate by opening a "smoking saloon and reading

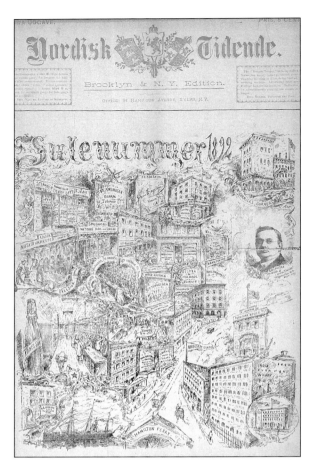

*Nordisk Tidende*'s front page, Christmas issue 1892, showing Little Norway's business district. Norwegian-American collection, University of Oslo Library.

room" on Columbia Street, where at least one Norwegian temperance lodge and the colony's first Democratic Club were founded.

These examples illustrate how businessmen encouraged the development of local organizations from a mixture of personal conviction and the desire for economic gain. But Little Norway's entrepreneurial and professional elite was vital to the colony's voluntary associations in a number of other ways as well. Lists of donors in *Nordisk Tidende* and pages of advertising in anniversary booklets show that shopkeepers, lawyers, doctors, and ministers could be counted on to give more money to a greater number of local organizations than any other socioeconomic group. Notices of colony events indicate that the same men were reliable as spectators, guest speakers, circulators of petitions, and sellers of lottery tickets. Most important, they were willing to serve again and again as officers, board members, and committee chairmen.[66]

Citing these facts, many colony veterans waved aside questions about leaders' motives. What mattered, they said, was that having dependable leaders made it possible to establish and maintain a wide range of social activities. Most people interviewed claimed they had contributed little and urged the author to talk with other "famous" residents who had done the "important" work. The modest majority had only given their support by helping at bazaars and attending other colony functions. Yet the most convincing proofs that the immigrants had overcome the obstacles to widespread participation in voluntary associations came through interviews with old-timers, for almost all veterans who could trace their families' residence back to the early 1900s unintentionally revealed that they had spent their lives in the colony's separate little world.[67] Their social contacts, or their parents' contacts, had been almost exclusively other Norwegians in Red Hook. Many who had immigrated as adults neglected to say that their social activities were limited to their countrymen because they took that for granted. When asked if they were speaking Norwegian when events took place or if an occasion was sponsored by a colony organization, they blinked in surprise because they assumed these things were true. The few adults who had voluntarily associated with other nationality groups in their leisure time were highly educated professionals, exceptionally successful businessmen, people with non-Norwegian family connections, or committed advocates of social causes such as temperance, which united many ethnic groups in efforts toward a common goal. The large majority did not recall having participated in any social world but Little Norway's.[68]

The American-born and those who came as small children commonly showed a self-conscious awareness of moving between a Norwegian and a wider milieu. For example, the daughter of one former domestic laughed as she remembered her first day at school. She had been surprised that her teacher could speak English perfectly, "like a kid," instead of mixing Norwegian words with her English and talking with a Norwegian accent, "like my mother and all the other adults I knew." First-generation adults frequently used a blend of English and Norwegian that both identified insiders and excluded the uninitiated. In 1904, *Nordisk Tidende* commented on the colony's patois through a long anonymous poem in which a greenhorn is baffled by the local mixture of languages that neither Americans nor Norwegian newcomers understand.[69]

A man who arrived as a five-year-old during the same year told about "acting Norwegian" at home and whenever he "went out" with his parents but "going American" when he played and "mixed together with Italians, Germans, and Irish." One elderly man summed up the common view of Norwegian-born adults: "Oh yes, we had contact with Americans and others, of course. But we didn't know them the same way. Socially we kept to ourselves mostly. So did they, now that I think about it." Both generations, even the people who moved in wider social circles, took Little Norway's clannish cooperation as a given and claimed that concentrating limited resources by keeping to their own sphere had helped a small ethnic group in a big city overcome the difficulties of maintaining voluntary associations.[70]

# 9

# A Den of Pirates with Many Tales to Tell

In 1943–1944, *Nordisk Tidende* presumed to conduct a national survey of Norwegian-American cultural preferences and published a series of articles evaluating what the results suggested about the entire ethnic group. In one of the milder responses that came from other Norwegian settlements, Bertram Jensenius, a Norwegian-American journalist in Chicago, wrote to *Nordisk Tidende* to report that "something hair-raising" had happened: The Brooklyn colony seemed to think it was Norwegian America's "center of gravity." That "fatally wounded midwestern Norwegians' vanity," explained Jensenius, because "respectable Norwegians had put their noses in the air to avoid that den of pirates and marched in a straight line" to the Midwest since the "noble Sloopers" had passed through in 1825.[1]

Although phrased in exaggerated language meant to tease both Brooklynites and Chicagoans, these remarks not only captured the essence of the Brooklyn colony's reputation in midwestern Norwegian-American enclaves but also suggested the historical processes behind its distinctive development. The city attracted only a tiny group of Norwegian immigrants while their countrymen were streaming to the Great

Plains, but Red Hook's Little Norway began to grow rapidly in the 1880s. By 1930, Brooklyn *had* become a sort of Norwegian center of gravity in the United States because it then contained the largest urban concentration of Norwegian-born people outside the old country and was jokingly called a "suburb" of Oslo and Bergen.[2] More important, transient seamen jumping ship or drifting into permanent residence after shore leaves in Red Hook's sailortown ("that den of pirates") rather than peasants from inland valleys searching for land ("respectable Norwegians") had formed the basis for the growth of Brooklyn's Little Norway.

The roots of the colony's twentieth-century characteristics are to be found in long-term processes of change that occurred during the previous century in Norway, international shipping, and the port of New York. The old-country sources of Norwegian emigration to Brooklyn lie in the differential development of Norway's regional economies. As rapid population growth in inland agricultural communities threatened to reduce the socioeconomic status of coming generations, increasing numbers of Norwegian peasants resorted to internal or international migration. Farming in the Arctic North provided an answer for some. Moving to the city seemed better to many others, although that alternative was often peasants' last choice because the cities' administrative class culture made them seem almost foreign to people from the countryside. Largely because the country's expanding shipping industry offered plentiful opportunities for combining farming with seafaring or shipbuilding, Norway's southern coast became one of the country's most popular "internal Americas" between 1845 and 1875.

Peasants who thought international migration promised better opportunities provided the foundation for most of the United States' midwestern Norwegian colonies around the same time. Immigrant vessels carrying large numbers of Norwegians who intended to settle in Red Hook, on the other hand, did not start arriving until the old country's shipping centers were thrown into a protracted depression in the late 1880s. The vast majority in a sample study of Norwegians who gave their destination as New York or Brooklyn in 1904 departed from these areas, most of them from southern shipping districts in Norway's Agder counties. The disproportionately large number of maritime workers in this group reflected the region's long familiarity with the port of New York as much as it did the poor employment prospects caused by the depression at home.

Norwegian sailors had a long tradition of leaving other nations' ships in the port of New York to join the American merchant marine or take up work on shore. This mostly undocumented immigration produced only small Norwegian settlements in Manhattan and Old South Brooklyn until the 1870s. During that decade, however, the expansion of Norway's shipping brought nearly 33,000 Norwegian sailors a year to New York Bay, and for ten years wages on American vessels or opportunities in the cities led over five thousand of these to jump ship annually. By the beginning of the 1870s, moreover, the port's terminals for bulk freight were concentrated in Brooklyn. Because the cargoes in which Norwegian shipowners specialized were handled at piers along Red Hook peninsula, most of the old country's ships and transient or deserting mariners touched land there, and that in turn led many dock and harbor workers, sailors, and sailortown proprietors from the Manhattan colony to migrate across the East River.

Through the combination of these factors, the Red Hook colony grew to three times the size of its sister settlement by 1880 and became a natural destination for immigrants fleeing the depression in southern and southwestern Norway by the mid-1880s. Even near the end of the decade, when Little Norway's burgeoning settled population approached 4,000, however, five times as many Norwegians arrived as itinerant mariners because they had chosen to continue their vocation in other nations' fleets rather than become immigrants. But distinguishing mariners temporarily ashore in sailortown from sojourning seamen or settled seafaring residents was almost impossible. These three stages in the process of going on land were reversible and represent convenient labels for sections of a sliding scale. The only certainties are that census officials regularly undercounted all three groups, that the colony's size was therefore larger than authorities assumed, and that its population was unusually volatile because so many men literally floated in and out of the community.

These processes of maritime migration resulted in Norwegian settlements in American harbor cities as disparate as Pensacola, Boston, and San Francisco, and in world ports as different as Durban, South Africa, Singapore, and Sydney, Australia. Records of emigration from Canadian crews and immigration through entering the United States merchant marine, moreover, leave no doubt that sailors from all the maritime nations were migrating in a similar fashion. That is why in New York the Norwegian Seamen's Mission Society designed its institutions to aid men from all the Scandinavian countries, and why it cooperated with American and German Seamen's Aid Societies, to name just two of the many such organizations commonly operating in the world's major sailortowns.[3] The contribution of maritime migration to population movements during the last century and a half has been too little studied, and its effects on the development of ethnic enclaves in port cities around the globe have been even less investigated.

Domestic and international migration to Brooklyn promoted a galloping urban expansion that supported a nearly constant building boom after the 1830s. New England Yankees, Irish, Germans, and Britons had settled in large numbers before Scandinavians and the so-called 'new' immigrants from southern and eastern Europe made their presence noted. Irishmen and Germans had crowded into Red Hook before Norwegians began to congregate there. Offering a classic example of residential succession in an urban neighborhood, Italians from Genoa moved in and went to work on the peninsula's wharves as Norwegians relocated to newer housing farther south.[4] Like other working-class immigrant groups, Norwegian Americans clustered in a compact community bordering on the commercial-industrial district that provided most of the jobs for the group.[5]

Governmental, shipping, and religious groups in Norway began to express agitated concern about Norwegian maritime transients and deserters in the port as early as the 1860s and 1870s. The Norwegian Bureau of Statistics reported that the country's deep-water fleet was suffering a rising manpower loss primarily because of desertions in New York Bay. The Swedish-Norwegian consul in Manhattan traced increases in ship-jumping on an annual basis and lamented the exploitation of transient mariners in Red Hook's sailortown. Officers from the Midwest's Norwegian Synod visited state-church officials in the old country, complained of difficulties in establishing an immigrant congregation for the metropolitan area because most Norwegians there were temporarily resident sailors, and insisted that, as these men were not immigrants, religious authorities in Norway should take responsibility for their spiritual welfare.

These outside pressures moulded the configuration of the Red Hook colony's organizational life and shaped its social history for the rest of the century and beyond. Because of the concern of powerful external groups for transient sailors, Little Norway remained a haven for itinerants for nearly three decades before developing an immigrant-dominated community life. Major social and religious institutions in the Brooklyn enclave were "transplanted" Norwegian rather than Norwegian American in their origins. That is, organizations in Norway had established, staffed, and determined their institutional structures in the 1870s or 1880s and continued to fund them primarily for the use of seamen temporarily in port.

The Seamen's Church, the Scandinavian Seamen's Temperance Home, and the Deaconess Home and Hospital all fell into this category, although old-country control at the last named came through the consulate, the Seamen's Church, and an individual deaconess rather than from the mother organization. The consular circle in the Manhattan colony, the Seamen's Mission Society in Bergen, and the institutions' leaders in Red Hook frequently petitioned shipowners in Norway or their agents in New York for financial aid. And shipowners contributed readily. The transplanted institutions served their economic interests well by discouraging sailors from deserting or emigrating, mounting campaigns against their drinking and carousing in sailortown, and helping them establish well-regulated Christian lives.

The staffs at these institutions were not immigrants but sojourners, Norwegian nationals imported for limited tours of duty. Relegating immigrants to the status of second-class clients or reserving specific pro-

•

Three young women by a car in the 1950s. Norwegian Emigrant Museum.

grams for incoming crews was part of their duty. In such a situation, colony residents developed ambiguous feelings about both the transplanted institutions and sojourning leaders. Immigrants cherished the genuine small pieces of un-Americanized Norway that had been planted in the middle of Red Hook, but they also resented the low valuation of their needs and financial contributions. The implied assertion that they were no longer as genuinely Norwegian or at least not as deserving of assistance from the old country became particularly galling by the late 1880s.

Because of the economic crisis in Norway's shipping industry, sojourning leaders became dependent on immigrants' financial aid at the same time as increasing immigration swelled the size of the settled colony and gave its spokesmen the courage to demand more influence. As a result, two of the transplanted institutions had to weather settlers' attempts to assume control of their executive boards by the end of the

Norway Ski Club's Lodge at Lake Telemark, New Jersey. Even before 1900 some members of Little Norway moved out of the colony to surburban or rural areas on the fringes of Brooklyn. Norwegian Emigrant Museum.

decade, and the Sailors' Home developed into a secular boardinghouse structured around seamen's habitual routines rather than plans for moral improvement.

According to the federal census, in 1890 Brooklyn and surrounding Kings county contained just over 5,000 Norwegian-born residents and so ranked as the sixth largest county-wide concentration of Norwegians in the United States. If one counted transient mariners and remembered that even settled seamen were usually undercounted—as the seamen's pastors fortunately did—it was clear that the number of Norwegians in and around the port probably rivaled that in the country's most heavily Norwegian county, Cook county (Chicago), Illinois.[6] Manuscript schedules from the New York State Census of 1892, contemporary narrative sources, and insights gained from interviews with dozens of colony old-timers provide the basis for an examination of the residential and occupational patterns of that now large and clearly more self-aware population.

Over three-fourths of the ethnic group lived in neighborhoods near the Red Hook peninsula docks on side streets adjoining its sailor-town, which also housed the colony's business district. Immigrants with the same or a similar line of work frequently lived together, confirming veterans' claims that their parents' generation had often found employment and housing through friends and relatives. The schedules also provide hard evidence of living arrangements that the people interviewed emphasized as common ways of supplementing the family economy while placing the colony's many unattached young people, mostly male, within the stabilizing atmosphere of immigrant homes.

Over six-tenths of these people lived with relatives or as "hall-boys" lodging with Norwegian-American families. The rest of Little Norway's unattached people lived in boardinghouses, but most often in Norwegian boardinghouses with members of their own ethnic group. A collection of short stories set in one of these establishments, more-over, strongly suggests—as did many interviews—that this overwhelmingly male and often seafaring group also gave "taking care of our own," as one man put it, a high priority.[7] A tabulation of the size of all foreign-born groups on the peninsula shows that Norwegians comprised a majority in only a few of its districts. Their residential and occupational patterns indicate that through effective cooperation they nonetheless managed to create a distinctly Norwegian milieu in the midst of other, larger groups.

The processes involved in the founding of many voluntary associations at the turn of the century show how Little Norway changed from a way station for maritime transients to a settled community with a rich and varied social life. The transition began at the transplanted institutions, where conflicts led first to the founding of important immigrant organizations and then to settler-dominated executive boards and more conciliatory attitudes on the part of sojourning leaders. As the resident population continued to grow, the colony supported the whole range of associations common to ethnic enclaves. Its increasing diversity found expression through a spectrum of religious denominations, temperance lodges, benevolent institutions, and class-related social clubs. During 1905, the nationalistic fervor produced by Norway's struggle for independence helped the immigrants unite a considerable number of the colony's often antagonistic sub-groups in the Norwegian National League, but continuing divisiveness threatened its existence only four years later.

Little Norway evolved its own little social world by overcoming obstacles more serious than the bickering caused by inner divisions. Problems in holding the League together could only become a preoccupation for a colony that had already found the resources to provide associations for a variety of interest groups. Both the money and the manpower needed to establish the community's panoply of organizations were in short supply. In addition to the problems usually faced by working-class immigrants, Norwegian Americans had to deal with an unusual degree of demographic instability because of the huge number of itinerant sailors who frequented their community. Ship-jumping was on the rise again by 1903, moreover, and in the last half of the decade hundreds of men left the Norwegian for the American fleet or went on land.

Over half of the settled men in the colony were construction or maritime workers, who suffered from the seasonal underemployment common in their trades and were seldom available for community activity because they spent long working hours in the harbor or at building sites on the edge of the city. Finally, Norwegian Americans' fund of leadership potential was unusually restricted because most sojourning and Manhattan leaders—and many of the colony's most successful entrepreneurs—were unwilling to give immigrants' interests first priority.

Three factors played major roles in helping the settlers surmount these hindrances: women's bazaars, the shopkeepers and professionals in the colony's business district, and the maritime background that a majority of the immigrants shared. Women's bazaars provided a practical way of financing colony activities, because nearly all Norwegian women were housewives who had handicrafts to sell and the organizational ability to turn fund-raisers into family-style social events with negligible overhead costs. Although motivated by a mixture of altruism, personal advocacy of specific social views, and economic self-interest, the enclave's businessmen and professionals, like the women, stole time from daily tasks to perform vital services for the group. Taking advantage of their central location, several of these men converted their places of work into informal community centers. A larger number served repeatedly as officers and spokesmen for various organizations and supplemented bazaar profits by becoming a reliable source of small donations.

Little Norway's maritime background, however, was perhaps the *sine qua non* of community life. Nothing else created so much understanding between leaders and followers as their own or their families' common career experiences with seafaring. From experience in Norway if not in Brooklyn, wives and daughters were accustomed to taking charge while their men were at sea. Most men, whatever their socioeconomic status, were personally familiar with the economic conditions and social pressures that had given rise to the colony by encouraging so many mariners to leave the sea in Red Hook. The proofs of the community's roots were all around the immigrants: a dockside location, ship chandleries and sailortown dives, transplanted institutions with sojourning leaders, and finally, associations and churches that had grown out of those services to maritime transients, or that typified the pietistic religion and temperance crusades characteristic of the old country's southern and southwestern shipping districts.

By 1910, the Norwegian community in Red Hook was "going on land." It had many more carpenters than sailors. Its residential, occupational, and organizational networks were binding many footloose seafaring elements in its population to a more stable life involving greater civic responsibility. Its Seamen's Association sponsored a children's home and a monument to Grieg and entertained members with tux-and-tie balls instead of brawling parties in sailortown. On the other hand, the very fact of the Association's prominent role in community affairs reminded inhabitants of their seafaring origins.

In the years that followed, few could doubt the continuing vitality of the migratory traditions established during the colony's long history as a way station for maritime transients. The irregular or concealed forms of immigration that had given birth to Little Norway gained renewed strength between 1910 and 1920. As the approach of World War I revived Norway's shipping industry, the number of maritime transients and deserters in the port of New York rose to levels similar to those of the 1870s. As America's immigration restriction laws took effect during the 1920s, the Norwegian consulate in Manhattan and Little Norway's newspapers were deluged with pleas for assistance from sailors who had settled in Brooklyn without applying for immigration papers and who now feared they would be deported as illegal aliens. In the 1940s, New York became the economic nucleus of Norway's government-in-exile as the country's merchant fleet ferried supplies to America's embattled allies. Thus, the Brooklyn colony yet again became a temporary home for the old country's maritime manpower. Considering this series of events spanning the decades from 1910 to 1940, it was no wonder that Little Norway's reputation as a den of pirates had become a permanent fixture in the minds of many Norwegian-American midwesterners.[8] These later chapters in its history should also prompt further research into the processes of maritime migration and its effects on community building, of which Brooklyn's "colony that rose from the sea" is a prime example.

# Appendix

# APPENDIX I

## A. ANALYSIS OF EMIGRANT PROTOCOLS[1]
## EMIGRATION FROM BERGEN IN 1904

| CATEGORY | NUMBER | % OF TOTAL EMIGRATION (2,857) |
|---|---|---|
| NORWEGIANS | | |
| first-time emigrants to the U. S. | 1,832 | 64.12% |
| (first-time to New York/Brooklyn) | (179) | (6.26) |
| (included in emigrants to the U. S.) | | |
| repeat emigrants to the U. S. | 303 | 10.60 |
| repeat emigrants to New York/Brooklyn | 93 | 3.25 |
| transients to the U. S. | 312 | 10.92 |
| transients to New York/Brooklyn | 213 | 7.45 |
| emigrants to other countries | 84 | 2.94 |
| no destination given | 8 | .28 |
| OTHER NATIONALITIES | 12 | .44 |
| | 2,857 | 100.00 |
| TOTAL NORWEGIANS TO THE U. S. | 2,753 | 96.34 |

**Percentage of these leaving for NY/Brooklyn**   485 (17.62% of 2,753)

## NORWEGIANS LEAVING FOR N.Y./BROOKLYN FROM BERGEN:

| | N | % of 2,753 | of 2,857 |
|---|---|---|---|
| first-time emigrants to New York | 137 | 4.98% | 4.80% |
| first-time emigrants to Brooklyn | 42 | 1.53 | 1.46 |
| repeat emigrants to New York | 22 | .80 | .76 |
| repeat emigrants to Brooklyn | 71 | 2.58 | 2.49 |
| transients to New York | 213 | 7.73 | 7.45 |
| transients to Brooklyn | 0 | 0 | 0 |
| **Total Norwegians to NY/Brooklyn** | 485 | 17.62% | 16.96% |

| CATEGORY | NUMBER | % OF TOTAL EMIGRATION (3,827) |
|---|---|---|
| NORWEGIANS | | |
| first-time emigrants to the U. S. | 2,952 | 77.14% |
| (first-time to New York/Brooklyn) | (1,913) | (49.99) |
| (included in emigrants to the U. S.) | | |
| repeat emigrants to the U. S. | 87 | 2.27 |
| repeat immigrants to New York/Brooklyn | 445 | 11.62 |
| transients to the U. S. A. | 66 | 1.72 |
| transients to New York/Brooklyn | 55 | 1.44 |
| emigrants to other countries | 82 | 2.14 |
| no destination given | 0 | 0 |
| OTHER NATIONALITIES | 140 | 3.66 |
| | 3,827 | 100.00% |
| TOTAL NORWEGIANS TO THE U. S. | 3,605 | 94.20% |

**Percentage of these leaving for NY/Brooklyn**   2,413 (66.93% of 3,605)

## NORWEGIANS LEAVING FOR N.Y./BROOKLYN FROM KRISTIANSAND:

| | N | % of 3,605 | of 3,827 |
|---|---|---|---|
| first-time emigrants to New York | 1,907 | 52.90% | 49.83% |
| first-time emigrants to Brooklyn | 6 | .17 | .16 |
| repeat emigrants to New York | 441 | 12.23 | 11.53 |
| repeat emigrants to Brooklyn | 4 | .11 | .10 |
| transients to New York | 55 | 1.52 | 1.44 |
| transients to Brooklyn | 0 | 0 | 0 |
| **Total Norwegians to NY/Brooklyn:** | 2,413 | 66.93% | 63.06% |

# C. ANALYSIS OF EMIGRATION FROM TRONDHEIM IN 1904

| CATEGORY | NUMBER | % OF TOTAL EMIGRATION (5,697) |
|---|---|---|
| NORWEGIANS | | |
| first-time emigrants to the U. S. | 2,885 | 50.64% |
| (first-time to New York/Brooklyn) | (214) | (3.76) |
| (included in emigrants to the U. S.) | | |
| repeat emigrants to the U. S. | 341 | 5.99 |
| repeat emigrants to New York/Brooklyn | 84 | 1.47 |
| transients to the U. S. | 0 | 0 |
| transients to New York/Brooklyn | 0 | 0 |
| emigrants to other countries | 434 | 7.62 |
| OTHER NATIONALITIES | 1,953 | 34.28 |
| (includes 1,905 Swedes and 36 Finns) | 5,697 | 100.00% |
| TOTAL NORWEGIANS TO THE U. S. | 3,310 | 58.09% |

**Percentage of these leaving for NY/Brooklyn**   298 (9.00% of 3,310)

## NORWEGIANS LEAVING FOR N.Y./BROOKLYN FROM TRONDHEIM:

| | N | % of 3,310 | of 5,697 |
|---|---|---|---|
| first-time emigrants to New York | 212 | 6.40% | 3.72% |
| first-time emigrants to Brooklyn | 2 | .06 | .04 |
| repeat emigrants to New York | 84 | 2.54 | 1.47 |
| repeat emigrants to Brooklyn | 0 | 0 | 0 |
| transients to New York/Brooklyn | 0 | 0 | 0 |
| **Total Norwegians to NY/Brooklyn** | 298 | 9.00% | 5.23% |

# OCCUPATIONAL GROUPINGS OF EMIGRANTS

| PORTS: | Kristiansand | | Bergen | | Trondheim | |
|---|---|---|---|---|---|---|
| **MALE**: | | | | | | |
| Maritime | 445 | 48.2% | 320★ | 94.9% | 40 | 31.2% |
| Agricultural work | 175 | 19.0% | 3 | .9% | 20 | 15.6% |
| Construction work | 108 | 11.7% | 2 | .6% | 1 | .8% |
| Professional | 1 | .1% | 0 | | 2 | 1.6% |
| White collar | 6 | .6% | 0 | | 0 | |
| Low white collar | 31 | 3.4% | 3 | .9% | 11 | 8.6% |
| Skilled | 72 | 7.8% | 3 | .9% | 19 | 14.8% |
| Semi-skilled | 44 | 4.8% | 2 | .6% | 7 | 5.5% |
| Unskilled | 26 | 2.8% | 4 | 1.2% | 22 | 17.2% |
| Miscellaneous | 15 | 1.6% | 0 | | 6 | 4.7% |
| Total | 923 | 100.0% | 337 | 100.0% | 128 | 100.0% |

★297 were hired in Bergen, Norway to work on Norwegian ships in New York

| | Kristiansand | | Bergen | | Trondheim | |
|---|---|---|---|---|---|---|
| **FEMALE:** | | | | | | |
| Professional | 2 | .3% | 0 | | 0 | |
| White collar/business | 8 | 1.0% | 1 | 2.3% | 1 | 1.6% |
| Low white collar | 27 | 3.5% | 8 | 18.6% | 3 | 5.0% |
| Skilled | 69 | 9.0% | 6 | 14.0% | 2 | 3.3% |
| Domestic occupation | 378 | 49.2% | 9 | 20.9% | 41 | 67.2% |
| Semi-skilled | 6 | .8% | 0 | | 1 | 1.6% |
| Unskilled | 5 | .6% | 1 | 2.3% | 0 | |
| Miscellaneous/wife | 273 | 35.6% | 18 | 41.9% | 13 | 21.3% |
| Total | 768 | 100.0% | 43 | 100.0% | 61 | 100.0% |

## FAMILY RELATIONSHIPS OF EMIGRANTS

| PORTS: | Kristiansand | Bergen | Trondheim | Total | Percent |
|---|---|---|---|---|---|
| Children | 277 | 12 | 25 | 314 | 12.2% |
| Relatives | 148 | 29 | 14 | 191 | 7.4% |
| Alone | 1,543 | 351 | 175 | 2,069 | 80.4% |
| Total | 1,968 | 392 | 214 | 2,574 | 100.0% |

The 148 adults traveling with relatives from Kristiansand included 5 married couples with no children, 6 sets of parents with children, 7 family units consisting of adult relatives, 5 fathers with children, and 106 mothers with children.

# APPENDIX II

## Past and Present Residents of Little Norway
## Who Contributed to this Book through
## Interviews or Written Responses[2]
(names, interview dates, and occupations)

Johannes Aardahl, November 18, 1986; seamen's pastor

Gyda Andersen, November 9, 1986; domestic

Inge Berge, November 15, 1986; seaman and carpenter

Hans Berggren, December 30, 1985; seaman, carpenter, salesman

Myrtle Smith Berntsen, housewife

Ralph and Geta Berntsen, November 12, 1986; pilot and housewife

Einar Bredland, farmworker, sailor, fisherman, bridge painter, office worker, salesman, lawyer, university professor

Rolf Broun, November 15, 1986; seaman, dockworker

Norman Brouwer, January 16, 1986; maritime historian

Alfred Otto Carlsen, fisherman, truckdriver, worker for the maritime department
of the Pennsylvania Railroad, U. S. Coast Guard Marine Officer, maritime
workers' union official

John E. Carlson, aircraft mechanic, attorney

Per Christiansen, November 2, 1985; seaman

Sigurd and Synnøve Daasvand, February 2, 1985; September 3, 1986; newspaper
editor and housewife

Joy Edwardsen and Steve Kotrch, May 24, 1986; soprano and choir director

Cecilia Tessdal Felt, September 7, 1986; housewife

Alice and Daniel Fjelldal, October 25, 1985; February 5, 1986; housewife; sailor,
fisherman, dockbuilder

Former domestic 2, January 23, 1986

Former domestic 3, January 23, 1986

Freddie Fredricksen, March 1, 1986; sailor, carpenter

Erik Friis, August 16, 1985; editor

Finn Gjertsen, March 1, 1986; dockbuilder

Annemor Grimsland, February 9, 1986; secretary

Hans Hagen, November 21, 1995; tugboat fleet manager

Carsten Hansen, February 13, 1986; laborer, dockworker, waterboat sailor

Astrid Heggeland, November 12, 1986; saleswoman, secretary

Mr. and Mrs. Kristoffer Henricksen, February 27, 1986; sailor and fisherman, carpenter; housewife

Kari Alice Hesthagg, May 31, 1986; November 17, 1995; administrative assistant

Paul Igeland, February 19, 1986; former seaman

Bjørn and Kitty Jakobsen, May 24, 1986, November 18, 1995; seaman, marine
cook, ship steward, smørgåsbord chef, salesman, restaurant manager, owner
of furnace cleaning business; secretary, teletype operator, administrative
assistant

Harold E. Jansen, draftsman, church youth worker, pastor, school administrator,
school dean, Lutheran bishop

Sophie Jarnes, May 16, 1986; newspaper office worker, secretary for the Norwegian Shipping and Trade Mission, the Norwegian Purchasing office, the

Norwegian Industries Commission, and the Norwegian-American Chamber of Commerce

Ole Jensen, June 3, 1986; carpenter

George Joa, September 7, 1986; gardener

Eileen Johansen, March 13, 1986; secretary, administrative assistant

Bertha and Gudrun Kartevold, December 28, 1985; April 29, May 8, May 14, and May 25, 1986; housewife; parochial school principal, proprietor of watch and jewelry store

Karl K. Kjendal, seaman

Erling and Vera Lande, May 8, 1986; engineer; housewife

Arne D. Larsen, steamboat engine room assistant, sailor, elevator operator, hotel night manager, chief engineer on steamship, partner in paint and varnish company

Einar Larssen, cartoonist, journalist

Lulu (Jonassen Hansen) Lawrence, February 9, 1986; former domestic

Walter Lee, June 2, 1986; dockbuilder, dockbuilders' union official

Helen Livingstone, December 9, 1985; May 18, 1986; hospital nurse, private nurse

Lina Logan, July 26, 1985; March 21, 1986; former domestic, antiques store proprietor

Fred Løken, September 6, 1986; July 8, 1988; farmworker, bookbinder, carpenter

John and Hjørdis Mortensen, May 10, 1986; seaman, carpenter; daughter of seamen's church choir director, saleswoman, journalist

John Nersten, January 28, 1986; November 27, 1995; dockbuilder, New York City and State Ethnic Advisory Councils

Helen and George Nielsen, May 6, 1986; owners of machine shop

Paul Nord, January 20, 1986; sailor, carpenter

Ed Nordberg, January 16, 1986; former ship's captain

John and Liva Nordskog, December 19, 1985; fisherman; housewife

Kåre Nygaard, medical doctor

Kristoffer Oftedal, May 27, 1986; Lutheran minister

Paul and Ruth Qualben, May 5 and 13, 1986, November 18, 1995; Lutheran minister, medical doctor, and psychologist; medical doctor

Birgit Rasmussen, November 16, 1986; former domestic

Bernie Reinertsen, June 2, 1986; dockbuilder, dockbuilders' union official

Reinert and Jennifer Reinertsen, November 30, 1985; dockbuilder; housewife

Karsten Roedder, September 3, 1986; sailor, journalist, newspaper editor, historian, novelist

John Rønnevik, June 2, 1986; carpenter, inventor

Erling Rosand, December 5, 1985; seaman, carpenter

Sigurd Rosseland, November 16, 1986; seaman

Elsie Thorsen Rosvold, May 24, 1986; member of family moving company

Solveig Salvesen, February 20, 1986; secretary

Hannah Simonsen, September 10, 1986; shopkeeper

Stanley Solaas, May 27, 1986; carpenter, carpenters' union official

Serene Sortland, September 6, 1985; former domestic

Sivert Strøm, April 18, 1986, November 27, 1995; ship's steward, chef

Tom Svennevik, November 27, 1985; seaman, carpenter, metal ceiling worker, owner of metal ceiling business

Gus Tallaksen, November 13, 1985; former seaman

Charles Turgesen, June 2, 1986; dockbuilder, dockbuilders' union official

John E. Widness, engineer

# APPENDIX III

## THE NEW YORK STATE CENSUSES

### Methodology[3]

The New York State manuscript census of 1892 provided a huge mass of raw data about the Red Hook-Gowanus colony. Because the 1890 federal manuscript census for Brooklyn was destroyed by fire, the state's canvass of the local population is one of the few sources available for facts about the great majority of the colony's population in the early 1890s. The state's tally opened avenues for interpreting the experience of people on all socioeconomic levels of Little Norway by giving additional information about prominent Norwegians and a nucleus of basic facts about less renowned individuals.

The census manuscripts assumed a special importance because they offered chances to check the reliability of the explanations and opinions offered by elderly Norwegians during interviews in 1985–1986 and 1995. The analysis of the state census supported the old-timers' assertions in most cases. Answers to interview questions about the migration of the colony to the south, for example, suggested a reasonable interpretation of the significance of the newer settlements' occupational structure. The interviews also revealed the connection between the process of stepwise immigration called "going on land" and Little Norway's common residential patterns. As a result, Chapter 7 emphasizes the role of "tableboards" and "hallboys" in helping men make the transition from an itinerant maritime trade to a harbor-related or land-based occupation.

Like all census materials, this state-wide enumeration has definite limitations. Enumerators made mistakes and had difficulties communicating with immigrants. The information collected reflects the facts on a particular day and does not take into account processes of change. The range of questions asked narrows the possiblilties for interpretation. The 1892 census gives the resident's name, age, country of birth, citizenship, and occupation. On the other hand, it does not *state* the individual's sex or family relationship, include *explicit* labeling of boarders, always make clear divisions of household units, or always give the street number of residents' addresses. In Wards 6 and 12, where the overwhelming majority of Norwegians lived, most enumerators noted only the name of each street as they began interviewing people there. The manuscript schedules for Ward 22 and parts of Ward 8, on the other hand, usually include exact street addresses, but less often for the districts where Norwegians clustered.

The information based on census data comes from that given by all Norwegian-born adults (people 15 years old or older) living in the Brooklyn election wards close to New York Bay where the colony lay. In Wards 1, 6, 8, 12, 17, and 22 there were 3,632 people in this category. The manuscript schedules explicitly noted Norwegian birth. Since the published summaries for the federal census two years earlier showed a *total* Norwegian-born population of 4,508 (including people under 15) for *all* of Brooklyn, this study takes into account the overwhelming majority of residents in the colony.

The table below shows the absolute number and percentage of adults (relative to the total Norwegian-born population counted) in each of those wards.

| Ward | Number of Norwegian-born | Percentage |
|---|---|---|
| 1 | 141 | 3.9 |
| 6 | 1,381 | 38.0 |
| 8 | 430 | 11.8 |
| 12 | 1,453 | 40.0 |
| 17 | 104 | 2.9 |
| 22 | 123 | 3.4 |
| Total: | 3,632 | 100.0 |

The state census manuscripts proved invaluable for understanding Norwegian immigration and settlement at the turn of the century. The census represented an unparalleled data-base, but the *meaning* of its information lay elsewhere. Its significance became apparent only in conjunction with a wide range of qualitative sources. Colony histories and newspapers, accounts of Brooklyn's history, diaries, letters, organizational archives, Norwegian state statistics, and interviews supplied the necessary guides for locating significant facts in the near-inexhaustible storehouse of the census.

# APPENDIX IV

## INSTITUTIONS AND ASSOCIATIONS
## IN LITTLE NORWAY, 1890–1910*
(listed in order of founding date)

**1874**
The Bethelship Norwegian Methodist Church
**1878**
The Norwegian Seamen's Church
*Nordiske Blade* (newspaper; only scattered issues survive)
**1880**
Bethany Norwegian Lutheran Church
**1883**
The Norwegian-Lutheran Deaconess Home and Hospital
**1885**
Our Saviour's Norwegian Lutheran Church (1866 in Manhattan)
**1887**
The "Brooklyn Six" Seamen's Corps of the Salvation Army
The Norwegian Brotherhood Society (a shopkeepers' self-improvement club with
     a library)
**1888**
The Salvation Army Scandinavian Temple
The Norwegian-American Seamen's Association
South Brooklyn's Norwegian Mutual Benefit Society (for skilled workers)
**1890**
Norwegian Lutheran Trinity Church
The Norwegian Singing Society (a men's choir)
Court Leif Erickson of the Order Foresters of America (a small businessmen's
     mutual benefit society)
**1891**
*Nordisk Tidende* (newspaper)
The first Leif Ericson Day Parade in Brooklyn
Scandinavian Assistance Association for Unemployed Immigrants
Nordic Mutual Benefit Society (skilled workers)
"Three Crowns" No. 1 of Brooklyn, Scandinavian Society (a mutual aid society
     for skilled workers)
Good Templar Mutual Benefit Society, International Order of Good Templars
     (IOGT, temperance and self-help club)
Norwegian Republican Club
Scandinavian Socialist Society
The Amateur Club (theater and singing club)
**1892**
The Norwegian Turner Society (gymnastics club)
The Seamen's Association's Singing Society
Youth Club of the Norwegian Seamen's Church
Harpen (a singing society for mixed voices)
The Norwegian Labor Union
Kings County Scandinavian Democratic Club
**1893**
Brooklyn and New York Seamen's Total Abstinence Society

Bergen Association
Hjørdis (a women's mutual benefit society)
**1894**
The first 17th of May Norwegian Constitution Day Parade in Brooklyn
The Free Scandinavian Hostel for the Homeless
Norge (a women's club and mutual benefit society)
The Norwegian Women's Association (club and mutual benefit)
**1895**
N.A.S.A. Gjøa Sporting Club (a division of the Norwegian-American Seamen's
    Association)
Viking Norwegian Boatclub
The Willing Workers Relief Society (a women's group)
South Brooklyn Scandinavian Democratic Club
Scandinavian Republican Club
The Norwegian Glee-Club
The Nordic Friendship Circle (a Scandinavian social club)
**1896**
Norsemen Cycle Club
Harmoni (a mixed choir)
Fjeldljom (a women's choir)
Scandia IOGT Lodge
**1897**
The Norwegian Evangelical Free Church, later called the 66th Street Free
    Church
Norwegian-Danish Republican Club of Eastern District
**1899**
Bethesda Mission (inner-city mission sponsored by the midwestern Norwegian
    Synod of the Lutheran Church)
Norumbega (a social club)
**1900**
IOGT Lodge Dovre
**1901**
The Bond of Peace, later called 59th Street Norwegian Lutheran Brethren
    Church
**1902**
The Norwegian Club (an elite organization primarily for professionals and
    academics)
IOGT Lodge Norge
**1903**
The Norwegian Seventh Day Adventist Church
The Hansons' Scandinavian Home for Old Ladies (In 1911 the name was
    changed to The Norwegian Christian Home for the Aged, and elderly men
    were also admitted)
IOGT Lodge Vort Land
IOGT Children's Lodge Hope
**1904**
IOGT Lodge Lindesnæs
IOGT Lodge Breidablik
**1905**
The Norwegian Methodist Episcopal Church
Norwegian National League (the representative assembly of Brooklyn colony or-
    ganizations)

IOGT Norwegian District Lodge Eidsvold

IOGT Norwegian-language newspaper Norge

**1907**

IOGT Lodge Oslo

IOGT Lodge Solvang

IOGT Lodge Asbjørn Kloster

**1908**

The First Norwegian–Danish Baptist Congregation Mission

Zion Norwegian Lutheran Church

Ebenezer Tabernacle

IOGT Lodge Stadt

Norwegian IOGT Lodge Luren (IOGT based in Norway)

**1909**

The Tabernacle of Truth Mission Church

The Norwegian Children's Home Association. They built The Norwegian Children's Home within five years.

Tysnes Association

Scandinavian Benevolent Association in Greater New York

The Norwegian-American Political Association of Greater New York

The Christian Male Chorus

The Norwegian Drama Society

The Norsemen Lodge of the Masonic Order

Edvard Grieg Monument Fund

*Appendix 3 in Mauk, "The Colony that Rose from the Sea," 559–574, provides documentation of and information about the institutions and associations listed here.

# Notes

[1]Jon Gjerde, *From Peasants to Farmers: The Migration from Balestrand, Norway, to the Upper Middle West* (Cambridge, Massachusetts, 1985), xiii–xiv, 1–5, 9–11. On the relation of Gjerde's work to studies of immigrants in urban industrial settings see James P. Shenton, "Ethnicity and Immigration," in *The New American History*, Eric Foner, ed. (Philadelphia, 1990), 255–256, and John R. Jenswold's review in the *Journal of American Ethnic History*, 6: 2 (Spring 1987), 74–76. Some standard surveys of Norwegian immigration that concentrate on rural-to-rural migration are Theodore Blegen, *Norwegian Migration to America* (Northfield, Minnesota, 1931, 1940); Carlton C. Qualey, *Norwegian Settlement in the United States* (Northfield, 1938); and to a lesser degree, Ingrid Semmingsen, *Veien mot Vest* (Oslo, 1941, 1950). Odd S. Lovoll's *The Promise of America: A History of the Norwegian-American People* (Minneapolis, 1984) and *A Century of Urban Life: The Norwegians in Chicago before 1930* (Northfield, 1988) have made significant changes in the traditional emphasis on rural settlements.

[2]Knut Mykland, ed., *Norges historie* (Oslo, 1978, 1979), 11:78–86, 119–121, 185–194, 202–203, 212; 12:305–307; 13:177–180. See also Gjerde, *From Peasants to Farmers*, 13–19; Arnold R. Alanen, "Companies as Caretakers: Paternalism, Welfare Capitalism, and Immigrants in the Lake Superior Mining Region," in Rudolph J. Vecoli and Suzanne M. Sinke, eds., *A Century of European Migrations, 1830–1930* (Chicago, 1991), 371–373; Einar Niemi *et al., Trekk fra Nord Norges historie* (Oslo, 1976), 60–61, 97–101, 104–110; and Niemi, "Emigration from North Norway: A Frontier Phenomenon? Some Perspectives and Hypotheses," in *Norwegian-American Essays, 1996* (Oslo, 1996), 127–156.

[3]See, for example, Maldwyn A. Jones, *American Immigration* (Chicago, 1960), 103–106; Philip A. M. Taylor, *The Distant Magnet: European Migration to the U. S. A.* (New

**Chapter 1**

York, 1971), 6,8, 80–81, 92, 145–164; and Leonard Dinnerstein and David M. Reimers, *Ethnic Americans*, (3rd ed., New York, 1988), 24–26, on shipping's influence on immigration. Knut Gjerset, *Norwegian Sailors in American Waters: A Study in the History of Maritime Activity on the Eastern Seaboard* (Northfield, 1933); Jacob S. Worm-Müller, *Den norske sjøfarts historie. Fra de ældste tider til vore dage,* 2, Parts 1–3 (Oslo, 1935, 1950, 1951); a few articles in the Norwegian-American Historical Association's series, *Norwegian-American Studies* (32 volumes) deal with transient Norwegian sailors in American ports, but no published study, to this writer's knowledge, focuses on the effects these men (or seamen of other nationalities) had on the evolution of urban immigrant colonies.

[4]Johan Nicolay Tønnesen, "Rømning 1850–1914 fra norske ship i fremmede havner," in Worm-Müller, *Den norske sjøfarts historie,* 2:3, 150.

[5]Norwegian Bureau of Statistics (hereafter NOS; Oslo, 1873–1918), *Norges skipsfart* and *Konsulatberetninger.* "Fra Amerikas nordmænd," "Medelelser fra Nordmanns-Forbundet," and "Nordmenn jorden rundt" in *Nordmands-Forbundets Tidsskrift* (Oslo, 1908–1931); United States Commissioner of Navigation, *Reports* (Washington, D. C., 1870–1919); interviews with Norwegian immigrants, July 26, 1985–November 18, 1986. See also Gjerset, *Norwegian Sailors in American Waters,* 74–75, 249; and Worm-Müller, *Den norske sjøfarts historie,* 2: 2, 209–210.

[6]Stan Hugill, *Sailortown* (New York, 1967), surveys the world's dockside maritime districts and the reasons for their development. See especially 72–95 and 157–166.

[7]Worm-Müller, *Den norske sjøfarts historie,* 2:3, 151, 155, 162–164. Fritz Hodne, *Norges økonomiske historie, 1815–1970* (Oslo, 1981), 142–143. Gjerset, *Norwegian Sailors in American Waters,* 181–183.

[8]Konsulatberetninger (Oslo, 1922–1926). Worm-Müller, *Den norske sjøfarts historie,* 2: 3, 164–165.

[9]Worm-Müller, *Den norske sjøfarts historie,* 2:1, 579–581; 2:2, 209–210; 2:3, 152, 164–165. In 1921 for the first time a time limit for alien seamen's temporary residence went into effect; after July 3 of that year foreign sailors had sixty days in which to hire on a foreign ship before they could be deported. In 1929 the Norwegian Bureau of the Foreign Language Information Service still found it necessary to repeat that, although irregular immigration was "not considered such a serious matter" before the 1920s, it now resulted in deportation. "Foreign Language Information Service, Norwegian Bureau, Reports, 1925–1931," in Norwegian-American Historical Association (hereafter NAHA) Archives. On the prohibition of contract labor on land, see Taylor, *The Distant Magnet,* 241, and Charlotte Erikson, *American Industry and the European Immigrant* (Cambridge, Massachusetts, 1957), 3, 82–87, 168–169.

[10]Silas Blake Axtell, *Merchant Seamen's Law* (New York, 1945), 114–117; Worm-Müller, *Den norske sjøfarts historie,* 2:3, 159–162.

[11]Worm-Müller, *Den norske sjøfarts historie,* 2:1, 579–583; 2:3, 148, 150–155, 162–165. See also Hyman Weintraub, *Andrew Furuseth, Emancipator of the Seamen* (Berkeley, 1959), 4–7, 55–56.

[12]*Konsulatberetninger* (Oslo, 1882–1887); Magnus Andersen, *70 års tilbakeblikk på mitt virke på sjø og i land* (Oslo, 1932), 37, 40; interviews with Carsten Hansen (February 13, 1986), Paul Nord (January 20, 1986), and Hans Berggren (December 30, 1985); Gjerset, *Norwegian Sailors in American Waters,* 72–76. The percentages were calculated from the table in Gjerset, 75.

[13]Ralph T. Paine, *A Chronicle of Ships and Sailors* (London, 1921), 137, 173. United States Commissioner of Navigation, *Reports* (Washington, D. C., 1886), 24–26. Worm-Müller, *Den norske sjøfarts historie,* 2:3, 151–156. Carsten Hansteen, "Brooklyn, New York," manuscript version of the seamen's pastor's report, March 19, 1889, in Seamen's Mission archives (Bergen).

[14]Worm-Müller, *Den norske sjøfarts historie,* 2:3, 150.

[15]"Sjømannsmisjonen og de utflyttede nordmenn" in *Den norske sjømannsmisjon i 75 år, 1864–1939* (Bergen, 1939), 242–246; "Fra Amerikas nordmænd," "Meddelelser fra Nordmanns-Forbundet," and "Nordmenn jorden rundt," in *Nordmanns-Forbundets Tidsskrift* (Oslo, 1908–1914); Gjerset, *Norwegian Sailors in American Waters,* 219–247.

[16]NOS, *Utvandringsstatistikk* (Oslo, 1921), 14–17, 100–103. Semmingsen, *Veien mot vest, utvandringen fra Norge til Amerika, 1825–1865* (Oslo, 1941), 196–198; Andres Svalestuen, "Om den regionale spreiinga av Norsk utvandring før 1865," in *Utvandringa—det store oppbrotet,* Arnfinn Engen, ed.(Oslo, 1978), 78–79.

[17]Hodne, *Norges økonomiske historie*, 136–137, 141–145: Gjerset, *Norwegian Sailors in American Waters*, 94–96; "Generalkonsulatet i New York", papers of the consulate in New York, Norwegian National Archives, Oslo.

[18]Semmingsen, *Veien mot vest, utvandringen fra Norge til Amerika, 1865–1915* (Oslo, 1950), 222–225, 367–368; Hodne, *Norges økonomiske historie*, 134–135, 141, 145–148, 167–169; Svein Moland, *Vår gamle kystkultur*, 2(Oslo, 1986),160; Knut Mykland, ed., *Norges historie*, 11:122–123, 12:238, 245; Worm-Müller, *Den norske sjøfarts historie*, 2:2, 357–359.

[19]Mykland, ed., *Norges historie*, 11:121, 134. Hodne, *Norges økonomiske historie*, 142. Blegen, *Norwegian Migration to America: The American Transition* (Northfield, 1940), 334–337, gives an overview of Norwegian government reports about desertions in American ports from the mid-1840s. Worm-Müller, *Den norske sjøfarts historie*, 2:2, 214–215; 2:3, 162–164.

[20]Hodne, *Norges økonomiske historie*, 141–142, 150–151, 154; Mykland, *Norges historie*, 12:238–239, 243, 247.

[21]Hodne, *Norges økonomiske historie*, 142.

[22]Gjerset, *Norwegian Sailors in American Waters*, 67, 74–75.

[23]A. N. Rygg, *Norwegians in New York, 1825–1925* (Brooklyn, 1941), 28, 269. Interviews or questionnaire responses: Einar Bredland (May 15, 1986), Hans Berggren (December 30, 1985), Daniel Fjelldal (October 25, 1985), Erik Friis (August 16, 1985), Carsten Hansen (February 13, 1986), Bjørn Jacobsen (May 24, 1986), Ole Jensen (June 3, 1986), Paul Nord (January 20, 1986), and Erling Rosand (December 5, 1985).

[24]Louise Lamphere, *From Working Daughters to Working Mothers: Immigrant Women in a New England Industrial Community* (Ithaca, New York, 1987), 70–74, 95–102, 134–13; Ronald Takaki, *Strangers from a Different Shore: a History of Asian Americans* (New York, 1990), 57, 61–62, 321–337; Dinnerstein and Reimers, *Ethnic Americans*, 78–79, 109–117; Gary R. Mormino and George E. Pozzetta, *The Immigrant World of Ybor City: Italians and their Latin Neighbors in Tampa, 1885–1985* (Chicago, 1990), 76–81, 184–188.

[25]Moland, *Vår gamle kystkultur*, 43, 158–160; Cæcilie Stang, "Arbeidsvandring og utvandring fra kystbygda Feda i Vest-Agder ca. 1750–1950" (unpublished master's thesis, University of Oslo, 1983), 104–108, 143–145, 148. See also interviews in note 23.

[26]Worm-Müller, *Den norske sjøfarts historie*, 2:3, 148.

[27]Thorvald Moe, "Demographic Developments and Economic Growth in Norway, 1740–1940" (Ph. D. dissertation, Stanford University, 1970), Table IV–3, 131–134; Hansteen, "Brooklyn, New York"; *Konsulatberetninger* (Oslo, 1910, 1911), 72 and 55, respectively. Dirk Hoerder, "International Labor Markets and Community Building by Migrant Workers in the Atlantic Economies," in *A Century of European Migrations*, 78–107, places seamen among the people who facilitated demographic movements because of their "market connections and travel experience" in a general conceptualization of Atlantic migration that emphasizes the role of transience and sojourning in chain migration.

[28]Moe, "Demographic Developments and Economic Growth in Norway," Table IV-3, 131–134. Interviews listed in previous notes. Norwegian Emigrant Protocols for Kristiansand, Bergen, and Trondheim in 1904 at the Regional Archives (Statsarkiv) in those cities.

**Chapter 2**

[1]Svalestuen, "Nordisk emigrasjon—en komparativ oversikt," in *Emigrationen fra Norden indtil 1. Verdenskrig, Rapporter til det Nordiske Historikermøde i København* (Copenhagen, 1971), 12–13, 39.

[2]Peter A. Munch, "Norwegians," in the *Harvard Encyclopedia of American Ethnic Groups*, Stephan Thernstrom, ed. (Cambridge, Mass., 1980), 751–752. Semmingsen, "Amerikaferd," in *Utvandringa—det store oppbrotet*, 12–13, and *Veien mot Vest*, 2:291–295. NOS VII 25, *Utvandringsstatistikk* (Kristiania, 1921), 74, 100–103. The percentage of Norwegian emigrants who left between 1880 and 1914 was calculated from Table 1, 100–103. The percentage of emigrants traveling to the United States was calculated from the table of major destinations on page 74.

[3]Moe, "Demographic Developments and Economic Growth in Norway, 1740–1940," 131–134, Table IV-3. Brooklyn's Norwegian-born population increased by 10,642 people (236 percent) between 1890 and 1910. U. S. Census, Population, 1890, 1:675–676, and 1910, 1:948.

[4]Svalestuen, "Nordisk Emigrasjon," 9–10, 18–19. *Folkemængdens Bevægelse, 1866–1885* (Kristiania, 1890), NOS, third series, No. 106, 17.

[5]Hans Try, *To kulturer, en stat: 1851–1884*, vol. 11 of *Norges historie,* ed. by Knut Mykland (Oslo, 1979), 9–10, 13. Gjerde, *From Peasants to Farmers*,18.

[6]*Jordbrukstellingen i Norge*, NOS XI. 87, June 20, 1949, Part 3 (Oslo, 1952), 9–19, gives the essential climatic and topographic facts that divide Norway into many distinct agricultural regions.

[7]Try, *To kulturer*, 241–244, 247, and Francis Sejersted, *Den vanskelige frihet, 1814–1851*, vol. 10 of *Norges historie*, 123–124, 137–140, 260–261. Jan Oldervoll, "Kva hadde befolkningsveksten å seie for utvandringa?" in *Utvandringa—Det store oppbrotet*, 27–28.

[8]Sejersted, *Den vanskelige frihet*, 142–145. Try, *To kulturer,* 238–241. Gjerde, *From Peasants to Farmers*, 25–26.

[9]Sejersted, *Den vanskelige frihet*, 149–152, 158–163, 261–262. Try, *To kulturer*, 154–155, 162–167, 241, 341–344.

[10]Sejersted, *Den vanskelige frihet*, 192–195. Try, *To kulturer*, 119–124, 139–142. Worm-Müller, *Den norske sjøfarts historie*, 2, Part 2, 347–348, 391, 398.

[11]Ståle Dyrvik *et al.*, *Norsk økonomisk historie, 1500–1970* (Oslo, 1979), 146–149. Sejersted, *Den vanskelige frihet*, 113, 120–125. Oldervoll, "Kva hadde befolkningsveksten," 23.

[12]Sejersted, *Den vanskelige frihet*, 113, 120–125. Oldervoll, "Kva hadde befolkningsveksten," 23–24, 27–29. Try, *To kulturer*, 86–93.

[13]Semmingsen, *Veien mot vest, 1865–1915*, 62–68.

[14]Try, *To kulturer*, 98. NOS, *Folkemængdens bevægelse, 1866–1885*, 24–27.

[15]Gjerde, *From Peasants to Farmers*, 18–19. Sejersted, *Den vanskelige frihet*, 191–194. Try, *To kulturer*, 87, 93–95, 102–103, 106, 120–121.

[16]NOS, *Folkemængdens bevægelse, 1866–1885*, 29, 32. Dyrvik *et al.*, *Norsk økonomisk historie*, 129–131.

[17]NOS, *Folkemængdens bevægelse, 1866–1885*, 17. NOS, *Folkemengdens bevægelse, 1886–1900* (Kristiania, 1906), 8.

[18]Try, *To kulturer*, 95–96.

[19]Sejersted, *Den vanskelige frihet*, 171–172, 183, 274, 276, 284–286. Dyrvik, *et al.*, *Norsk økonomisk historie*, 56–59, 208–210.

[20]Sejersted, *Den vanskelige frihet*, 16–19, 274–275, 278–280.

[21]Sejersted, *Den vanskelige frihet*, 119, 275.

[22]Sejersted, *Den vanskelige frihet*, 282–283. Try, *To kulturer,* 10–12, 21.

[23]Sejersted, *Den vanskelige frihet*, 276–277.

[24]Try, *To kulturer*, 16–17. The quotation is on page 16.

[25]Try, *To kulturer*, 100, 103. Svalestuen, "Nordisk Emigrasjon," 18–19. Sejersted, *Den vanskelige frihet*, 119.

[26]Sejersted, *Den vanskelige frihet*, 114–115.

[27]NOS, *Folkemængdens bevægelsen, 1866–1885*, 23n, 23–24. Sejersted, *Den vanskelige frihet*, 102–103. Try, *To kulturer*, 103. Hodne, *Norsk økonomisk historie*, 96.

[28]*Folkemængdens bevægelse, 1866–1885*, 21–23. Try, *To kulturer,* 99–100.

[29]Sejersted, *Den vanskelige frihet*, 117–119. Try, *To kulturer,* 96–97.

[30]Sejersted, *Den vanskelige frihet*, 117–119.

[31]Try, *To kulturer*, 139–145, 198–201.

[32]Try, *To kulturer*, 156, 188. Hodne, *Norsk økonomisk historie*, 89–90, 92–93.

[33]Semmingsen, *Veien mot vest, 1865–1915*, 194–195, 227–228, 235–236. Try, *To kulturer*, 76, 96. Karen Løvland, "Utvandringen fra Arendal/Barbu, 1875–1900: En studie i Sørlands utvandring" (Master's thesis, University of Oslo, 1979), 155–172. NOS, *Folkemængdens bevægelse, 1866–1885*, 21, 24. NOS VII 25, *Utvandringsstatistikk* (Kristiania, 1921), 25–29, 34–39. In "Family Emigration from Bergen, 1874–1892: Some Preliminary Results of a Statistical Study," in *Americana Norvegica*, 3 (Oslo, 1971), 3:38–63, Semmingsen notes that the intensity of emigration among the non-city-born was greater than among native city-dwellers, and concludes that for many rural migrants, movement to the city was a stage in a journey that began with the break from a rural neighborhood and continued with the departure for America. Further, she postulates that country people's rural background hindered their advancement in the city and so, along with urban conditions, contributed to the decision to emigrate.

[34]The percentage was calculated from NOS VII 25, *Utvandrings- statistikk*, Table I,

100–103. Gjerde, *From Peasants to Farmers*, 21–24, 166–167. Try, *To kulturer*, 78–79, 82. Svalestuen, "Nordisk emigrasjon," 17, 28–31; and "Om den regionale spreiinga av norsk utvandring før 1865," in *Utvandringa—Det store oppbrotet*, 62–77, 81–82. Semmingsen, "Amerikaferd" in *Utvandringa*, 15–17. Kjell Haarstad, "Utvandrerne fra bygdene—Presset eller lokket," in *Utvandringa*, 50–51. Blegen, *Norwegian Migration to America, 1825–1860*, 147, 191–192, 350–351.

[35]See Rygg, *Norwegians in New York*, 9, 13–16, 23, 27–33, 38–40, 50–53, 59–60, for the urban coastal origins of most prominent early settlers in New York and Brooklyn.

[36]Helge Ove Tveiten, "En utvandring blusser opp—og slokner: sørlansk emigrasjon på 1800-tallet" (Master's thesis, University of Oslo, 1974), 96–97, 99, 104–107, 111–112, 116, 120.

[37]Blegen, *Norwegian Migration to America, 1825–1860*, 19, 79–80, 331. Gjerset, *Norwegian Sailors in American Waters*, 63–63, 66–71, 217. Rygg, *Norwegians in New York*, 17–18. Robert Ernst, *Immigrant Life in New York City, 1825–1863* (New York, 1949), 195, 206–212, 214–217.

[38]Semmingsen, *Veien mot vest, 1865–1915*, 54–58, 70–72, 74–75, 84–85, 196.

[39]NOS, *Folkemængdens bevægelse, 1886–1900*, 67–68. Svalestuen, "Nordisk Emigrasjon," 41–47. Semmingsen, *Veien mot vest, 1865–1916*, 192–195, 204–209.

[40]Semmingsen, *Veien mot vest, 1825–1865*, 186–187. Haarstad, "Utvandrerne fra bygdene," 50–52.

[41]Semmingsen, *Veien mot vest, 1825–1865*, 196–198. Svalestuen, "Om den regionale spreiinga," 78–79.

[42]Rygg, *Norwegians*, 16–17. "Received Money from Emigrants" (an interview with the Norwegian-American attorney August Reymert), *The Mail and Express* (New York), December 12, 1893. Ernst, *Immigrant Life in New York City*, 214–217. Worm-Müller, *Den norske sjøfarts historie*, 2, 1: 569–574, 626–628.

[43]Semmingsen, *Veien mot vest, 1865–1915*, 222–225, 367–368. Løvland, "Utvandringen fra Arendal/Barbu 1875–1900," 36–37, 69–71, 127–139. Moland, *Vår gamle kystkultur*, 2:160.

[44]Semmingsen, *Veien mot vest, 1865–1915*, 225–230, 361–366. Svalestuen, "Om den regionale spreiinga," 39, 44–50.

[45]Brooklyn Norwegians include people from Rogaland county in their definition of Southerners even though in Norway that county's residents usually call their home *Sør Vestlandet*, "the southern west country." For the colony's perception that Southerners were and are its largest regional group, see Roald Kverndal, "Sørlendinger og sjøfart i den nye verden," in *Land, land, land hør herrens ord, årbok for Agder Bispedømme*, 25 (Kristiansand, 1975), 48–51; Sigurd Folkestad, "Norske i Brooklyn—New York," in *Symra* (Decorah, Iowa, 1908), 89–91; and Carl Søyland (editor of *Nordisk Tidende*), an internal summary report of the survey results, in Carl Søyland Papers, in NAHA Archives.

[46]See Svalestuen, "Om statisktisk grunnmateriale til utvandringshistorien," in *Heimen*, 15 (Oslo, 1970–1972), 16–17, for a brief general discussion of the emigrant protocols' usefulness for historical research. The protocols include each emigrant's name, age, sex, marital status, last residence in Norway, occupation, family relationship to other emigrants leaving on the same ship, destination, and a "comments" column with a wide variety of information, such as citizenship, the reason for being in Norway or for leaving, permission to emigrate from various Norwegian authorities, and work desired abroad. Unfortunately, analyzing departures from the emigrant depot nearest the southern coast, Stavanger, was impossible because its emigrant protocols were lost in a fire. The computer print-out of Bergen's emigrant protocol for 1904 prepared by Jan Oldervoll of the Bergen University History Department provided the basis for data from that city.

[47]Semmingsen, *Veien mot vest, 1865–1915*, 361. The size of Norwegian emigration in 1904 in relation to earlier years was calculated from "Tabell I, Ut- og Innvandring . . . i Norges Folkemengde, 1821–1914," in NOS VII 25, *Utvandringsstatistikk*, 100–103.

[48]NOS V 34, *Folkemængdens bevægelse, 1903–1904* (Kristiania, 1906), "Tabell 15, Udvandring til lande udenfor Europa, De udvandrede fordelt efter hjemsteder," 17. NOS VII 25, *Utvandringsstatistikk* (Kristiania, 1921), 31–33. Semmingsen, *Veien mot vest, 1865–1915*, 361–362, 366–367.

[49]Rolf Kåre Ostrem and Peter Rinnan, "Utvandringen fra Kristiania, 1880–1907" (cand. philol. thesis, University of Oslo, 1979), 229–233. See also the overview analyses of emigration from the three port cities in the appendix. Of course, residents from Agder

and Rogaland emigrated from other ports than Kristiansand. According to the Norwegian Bureau of Statistics (NOS V 34, *Folkemængdens bevægelse, 1903–1904*, 71), there were, for example, 1593 emigrants from Aust Agder in 1904. Of these, 884 (55%) left from Kristiansand. Of 1648 emigrants from Vest Agder, 937 (59%) left from the same port. Presumably, most of the remaining emigrants from the Agder counties departed from conveniently located ports in the region, such as Arendal and Stavanger, but since not all of these cities' protocols exist, a complete search of Agder emigrants' destinations is not possible. There is, moreover, no apparent reason to believe that people from Agder and Rogaland who left from other ports chose New York–Brooklyn less frequently as a destination.

[50]This and the following paragraphs on conditions in Norway at the turn of the century build on Semmingsen, *Veien mot vest, 1865–1915*, 356–370, and Hodne, *Norges økonomiske historie*, Chapters 5, 6, and 10. Statistical data on Norwegian emigration in 1904 is based on calculations derived from NOS V 34, *Folkemængdens bevægelse 1903 og 1904* (Kristiania, 1905), 71–75. For the data on the characteristics of emigrants leaving from Kristiansand, Bergen, and Trondheim, see the Appendix.

[51]Løvland, "Utvandringen fra Arendal/Barbu," 66–67, states that this practice inflated official statistics for the skilled worker category of emigrants leaving Arendal between 1875 and 1900, and such an interpretation seems to fit Kristiansand equally well.

[52]Løvland, "Utvandringen," 168. Try, *To kulturer*, 120–121. Moland, *Vår gamle kystkultur*, 158–160.

[53]See Mauk, "The Colony," Appendix, for the table of female occupations based on the New York State Census for 1892. Interviews with Former Domestics 2 and 3 are the source of the comparisions between service in Norway and in America. Almost all the women interviewed, however, shared these views and claimed that even in the 1920s most Norwegian women who worked were domestics.

[54]Letter from Tore L. Nilsen at Bergen's Sjøfartsmuseum, dated September 29, 1987.

[55]See Mauk, "The Colony," Appendix, and NOS V 34, *Folkemængdens bevægelse, 1903 og 1904* (Kristiania, 1906), 71–75.

[56]During interviews, Gyda Andersen, Hans Berggren, Cecilia Tessdal Felt, Former Domestics 2 and 3, Carsten Hansen, Sophie Jarnes, George Joa, Hjørdis and John Mortensen, Paul and Ruth Qualben, and Serene Sortland particularly emphasized how women were accustomed to managing alone because of their seafaring men. Many others mentioned the same traditions, however.

[57]The Kartevold Collection of letters and diaries, in the possession of Bertha and Gudrun Kartevold. "Diary, 1901," NAHA Archives, an unpublished record of that year by a now anonymous maritime immigrant to Brooklyn, tells of emigration encouraged by information given by sailors in Red Hook. Autobiographies and fiction written by Norwegian immigrants in Brooklyn which emphasize the colony's maritime origins include the following: Helge Amundsen, *Hjemløse fugle* (Brooklyn, 1910); Edward M. Andersen, *From Ship to Pulpit* (Minneapolis, 1910); Magnus Andersen, *70 års tilbakeblikk på mitt virke på sjø og i land* (Oslo, 1932); and Karsten Roedder, *Knus ikke en elendig i porten* (Aurdal, Norway, 1982).

[58]The quoted phrase comes from the interview with Lina Logan. Other interviews which clearly indicated internal migration to southern or southwestern coastal districts and towns include those with Ralph and Geta Berntsen, Inge Berge, Alice and Daniel Fjelldal, Mr. and Mrs. Kristoffer Henricksen, Gudrun and Bertha Kartevold, Lulu Lawrence, Birgit Rasmussen, Karsten Roedder, Hannah Simonsen, and Tom Svennevik.

[59]The quoted phrases come from the interview with Carsten Hansen. The Kartevold Collection provided evidence of the strongest reactions against representatives of Norway's official class in Brooklyn, but interviews with numbers of colony veterans also indicated irritation with university-educated sojourning leaders because of their Norwegian class background.

**Chapter 3**

[1] For full-length studies of this earliest immigration, see Oddleif Hodne, "Fra Agder til Amsterdam. En studie av norsk emigrasjon til Nederland i tiden ca. 1675–1800" (Master's thesis, University of Oslo, 1975) and John O. Evjen, *Scandinavian Immigrants in New York, 1630–1647* (Minneapolis, 1916).

[2]Gjerset, *Norwegian Sailors in American Waters*, 54–57.

[3]Oddleif Hodne's work in progress in 1996 documents the development of commercial connections between West Agder, Germany, and northern Holland. New York City's harbor and property records from the colonial period include a small but unending mention of identifiably Norwegian names. See also Rygg, *Norwegians in New York, 1825–1925*, 70, and Gjerset, *Norwegian Sailors in American Waters*, 56–57. For further comment on this colonial settlement, consult Munch, "Norwegians," 750; Henry Isham Hazelton, *The Boroughs of Brooklyn and Queens, Counties of Nassau and Suffolk, Long Island, New York, 1609–1924* (New York, 1925), 3:1102–1104, 1150; Torstein Jahr, "Nordmænd i Ny Nederland, Anneke Jans fra Marstrand, hendes farm og hendes slegt," in *Symra* 9 (Decorah, Iowa), 9–34; and Halvdan Koht, "First Scandinavian Settlers in America," in *American-Scandinavian Review*, 32 (June 1944), 136–142.

[4]Fritz Hodne, *An Economic History of Norway, 1815–1970* (Trondheim, Norway, 1975), 102–104, and *Norges økonomiske historie, 1815–1970*, 142–143. Sverre Ordahl, "Emigration from Agder to America, 1890–1915," in *Norwegian-American Studies*, 29 (Northfield, Minn., 1983), 313–338, especially 316–317.

[5]David Ment, *The Shaping of a City: A Brief History of Brooklyn* (Brooklyn, 1979), 38, 40–41. *Brooklyn Daily Eagle*, April 17, 1910.

[6]See Lewis R. Fischer, ed., *The Market for Seamen in the Age of Sail* (St. Johns, Newfoundland, 1994), for a collection of articles that represent current views on the effects of the trade expansion on marine manpower in the 1800s. Hodne, *An Economic History*, 101–106, 114–123, and *Norges økonomiske historie*, 152–158. Ordahl, "Emigration from Agder," 317–318, 321–323. Løvland, "Utvandringen fra Arendal/Barbu," 125–131, 139–147, 163–167. Rygg, *Norwegians*, 23–25.

[7]Johannes Nordboe to Hans Larsen Rudi, April 30, 1837, in "Johannes Nordboe and Norwegian Immigration, An 'America Letter' of 1837," Arne Odd Johnsen, ed., C. A. Clausen, trans., in *Norwegian-American Studies and Records*, 8 (Northfield, Minn., 1934), 23–38. The quoted phrase is my translation of "Svedisker Norveisk Mand," which remains untranslated in the above article. Gjerset, *Norwegian Sailors in American Waters*, 62–71. Blegen, *Norwegian Migration to America, 1825–1860*, 80n, and *Norwegian Migration to America: The American Transition* (Northfield, Minn., 1940), 336. *Uddrag af aarsberetninger fra de forenede rigers konsuler for aaret 1880* (Christiania, 1881), 141.

[8]Blegen, *The American Transition*, 333–339. Rygg, *Norwegians*, 22–23, 31–34. Interviews with Inge Berge, Hans Berggren, Rolf Broun, Per Christiansen, Sigurd and Synnøve Daasvand, Erik Friis, Carsten Hansen, George Joa, Paul Nord, Sigurd Rosseland, and Charles Turgesen.

[9]For the example from the 1905 New York State Census, see the Third Assembly District, Election District 2, block M, 71. The number of Norwegian ships arriving in the city appears in "New York, Aarsberetning for 1905 fra Generalkonsul Chr. Ravn," in *Konsulatberetninger, Uddrag af aarsberetninger fra de norske konsuler, 1906* (Kristiania, 1906), 71.

[10]Norman Brouwer, "The Port of New York, 1860–1985: The Coming of the Railroads," in *Seaport, New York's History Magazine*, 20 (Summer, 1986), 42–47. Benjamin M. Squires, "New York Harbor Employees," in *Monthly Labor Review*, 7:1 (July, 1918), 1–21.

[11]Interviews with tugboat fleet manager Hans Hagen in 1995; and with retired seamen Hans Berggren, Paul Nord, and Karsten Hansen and former domestics 2 and 3 (names withheld) in 1985–1986. See Rygg, *Norwegians*, 14, 17, 24, and 33. The 1905 New York State Census, Seventh Assembly District, Election District 10, block W, 39.

[12]*Nordisk Tidende*, August 7, 1891. Interview with Norman Brouwer and Captain Ed Nordberg. Squires, "New York Harbor Employees," 13–14, and "Lighterage—Its Function," in *Pilot Tales and Historical Sketches*, ed. Edward L. Allen (New York, 1922), 277–278.

[13]Gjerset, *Norwegian Sailors on the Great Lakes* (Northfield, Minn., 1928), 1–12, 61–77, and *Norwegian Sailors in American Waters*, 61–78, 81–85, 217–252.

[14]The work of Lewis R. Fischer and Helge W. Nordvik represents an important exception to the judgment in the text, but as economic and maritime historians they have not been primarily concerned with the development of immigrant/ethnic communities resulting from maritime migration. In addition to Fisher's 1994 book, see their articles in *The Emergence of a World Economy, 1500–1914: Papers of the IXth International Congress of Economic History*, eds. Wolfram Fischer, R. Marvin McInnis, and Jörgen Schneider

(Stuttgart, 1986); *Maritime Aspects of Migration*, ed. Klaus Friedland (Cologne, 1989); and *The North Sea: Twelve Essays on the Social History of Maritime Labor*, eds., Lewis R. Fischer *et al.* (Stavanger, Norway, 1992).

Blegen, *The American Transition*, 331–356. Semmingsen, *Veien mot vest: 1825– 1865*, 419–420, and *Veien mot vest, 1865–1915* (Oslo, 1950), 277–286, 367–370, 372–374, 545 (notes 45–46). Tønnessen, "Rømning 1850–1914 fra norske skip i fremmede havner," 148–166, provided the statistical base for Semmingsen's comments on ship-jumping immigrants. See also Christen T. Jonassen, "The Norwegians in Bay Ridge: A Sociological Study of an Ethnic Group" (Ph. D. dissertation, New York University, 1947), 242–245, 380–387, 393; Knight Hoover, "Norwegians in New York," in *Norwegian-American Studies*, 24 (Northfield, Minn., 1970), 221–234; and Jenswold, "'I Live Well, But . . .': Letters from Norwegians in Industrial America," in *Norwegian-American Studies*, 31 (1986), 113–129.

American historians outside the field of Norwegian-American studies have seldom been more critical of census materials regarding seamen. For example, when Ernst, *Immigrant Life in New York City*, 195, 206–212, 214–217, surveyed the 1855 state census schedules to determine the size of Manhattan's ethnic groups—and found only 227 Norwegians—his occupational statistics included river boatmen, but no coastal or deep-water seamen, and he did not explain this omission.

[15]Norwegian consuls prepared annual reports after 1905, when the union between the two Scandinavian countries was dissolved, but in New York most of the consuls appointed before that time were also Norwegians. See David C. Mauk, "The Colony that Rose From the Sea: The Norwegians in the Red Hook Section of Brooklyn, 1850–1910" (Ph.D. dissertation, New York University, 1991), 89–112, for a detailed criticism of sources, statistical tables, and discussion of the methodology employed here.

[16]Jørgen Gjerdrum, "Fra Amerika: Brev til *Dagbladet* fra Jørgen Gjerdrum, II," November 19, 1874 (printed in *Dagbladet* December 10, 1874), typescript in Norwegian, NAHA Archives; Carlton C. Qualey, "Jørgen Gjerdrum's Letters from America, 1874–75," in *Norwegian-American Studies and Records*, 11 (Northfield, Minn., 1940), 82–97; Ole Juul, *Erindringer* (Decorah, Iowa, 1902), 44; Hodne, *Norges økonomiske historie*, 144–145; Moland, *Vor gamle kystkultur*, 159; D. Koren, *Omkring Lindesnes* (Kristiania, 1914), 16–19, and Rygg, *Norwegians*, 22–23, 28, 103.

[17]Fischer and Nordvik, "The Price of Labor: Seamen's Wages in the British, Canadian and Norwegian Merchant Marines, 1861–1900," paper delivered at the Ninth International Congress of Economic History, Berne, Switzerland, August 26, 1986, 31–35.

[18]Tønnesen, "Rømning fra norske skip," 148, 150. Worm-Müller, *Den norske sjøfarts historie*, 2:1 (Oslo, 1935), 579–580.

[19]Gjerset, *Norwegian Sailors in American Waters*, 333–337. Tønnesen, "Rømning fra norske skip," 150. "Vor sømandsstand og dens kaar i fremmede havne," in *Annonce Tidende* (*Nordisk Tidende*), February 7, 1893. Since Rygg, *Norwegians*, 239, estimated that "the average crew on board the small Norwegian barks of 1880 numbered 12 men," the newspaper's suggestion of 10 men per ship does not seem too high. Tønnessen, "Rømning fra norske skip," 149, describes the growing number of foreigners in Norway's merchant marine.

[20]Worm-Müller, "Emigrant- og Kanada-farten," in *Den norske sjøfarts historie*, 2:1, 580–581, includes many of the totals for Norwegian ships arriving in New York in his brief discussion of desertions. See the introductions and tables in *Norges skipsfart 1871–1878* (Christiania, 1873–1880), NOS, C. No. 3. c., and *Norges skipsfart, 1879–1882* (Kristiania, 1881–1884), NOS, C. No. 3. b., for confirmation of Worm-Müller's figures and totals for other years cited in the text through 1880.

Totals reported by Swedish-Norwegian consuls in specific foreign ports were the basis for the NOS statistics. The description of ship arrivals from 1885 to 1900 comes from the annual reports of New York's consul for that period. See "New York" in the following series: *Uddrag af aarsberetninger fra de forenede rigers konsuler* (Kristiania, 1886–1890), NOS, third series No. 17, for 1885–1889; *Beretninger om handel og skibsfart: Uddrag af aarsberetninger* (Kristiania, 1891–1900), for 1890–1899; and *Konsulatberetninger* (Kristiania, 1901–1918), for 1900–1917.

[21]Worm-Müller, "Emigrant- og Kanada-farten," 580–582; Tønnessen, "Rømning fra norske skip," 154, 160–161.

[22]For A. N. Kiær's remark, see *Norges skipsfart i aaret 1871*, in NOS, C. No. 3 c,

(Christiania, 1873), xiii. Tønnessen, "Rømning fra norske skip," 148. Fischer and Nordvik explain the formidable difficulties in tracing individual deserters in New York during the second half of the nineteenth century, difficulties which prompted this study's strategy of using consular reports to uncover the outlines of how deserters contributed to the origins and growth of the New York area's Norwegian communities. See Fischer and Nordvik, "The Sea as Highway: Maritime Service as a Means of International Migration, 1863–1913," in *Maritime Aspects of Migration*, 294–295.

[23]Fischer and Nordvik, "The Sea As Highway," 293–307.

[24]See Tables 1 and 3. Only the scattered annual consular figures published in *Den norske sjøfarts historie* are accessible for the period from 1850 to 1870, but for the rest of the century the consul's reports allow the tabulation of near complete five-year desertion totals. To exclude foreign deserters and set comparatively low rather than exaggerated figures, the analysis cuts the local consul's figures in half and ignores unreported Norwegian deserters. See also Semmingsen, *Veien mot vest, 1865–1915*, 279–284. Rygg, *Norwegians*, 22–25. Tønnessen, "Rømning fra norske skip," 148.

[25]Worm-Müller, "Navigationsaktens ophævelse og frihandelens seier," 2:1, 254–255, and "Krimkrigen og den første verdenskrise," 2:1, 528 in *Den norske sjøfarts historie*; Nils A. Ytreberg, "Pionertiden i fraktfart med damp," 2:3, 244. William L. Standard, *Merchant Seamen, A Short History of Their Struggles* (Stanfordville, New York, 1979), 20–21. Gjerset, *Norwegian Sailors in American Waters*, 79–81.

[26]Fischer and Nordvik, "The Price of Labor," 31–35.

[27]The 1873 figure is probably high because the consul claimed that well over half the year's offenders were non-Norwegians. See Worm-Müller, "Emigrant- og Kanadafarten," 581–582. David H. Donald, "Uniting the Republic, 1865–77," in *The Great Republic, A History of the American People*, 2 (2nd ed., Lexington, Mass., 1981), 580, describes the high unemployment rates in New York through the mid-1870s.

[28]On the recovery of the American economy, see Donald, "Uniting the Republic," 598. "New York," *Uddrag af aarsberetninger for aaret 1880* (Christiania, 1881), 141–142, includes the translated and quoted remarks of New York's consul and the statistics for 1879–1880.

[29]John L. Thomas, "Stabilizing the American Economy," in *The Great Republic*, 2:596–598.

[30]Tønnessen, "Jern- og stålseilskuter: siste treseilskutetid," in *Norges sjøfarts historie*, 2:3, 86–88. Per Fuglum, *Norge i støpeskjeen* (Oslo, 1978), 243.

[31]Tønnessen, "Rømning fra norske skip," 150–151, 164–165.

[32]Tønnessen, "Rømning fra norske skip," 150.

[33]Magnus Andersen, *70 års tilbakeblikk på mitt virke*, 82. Carsten Hansteen, "Brooklyn, New York," March 19, 1889, Journal Nr. 234/89, Seamen's Mission Archives (Bergen), 3. In the same archives are many circulars about this matter. The Swedish-Norwegian consul reported the same trends, but limited his remarks to the migration of Scandinavian seamen to the American merchant marine. In 1887 Consul Børs estimated that at least 25 percent of America's deep-water sailors and a "much higher portion" of her coastal seamen and yacht crews were Scandinavians. Given the fact that Norway's fleet was very much larger than Sweden's or Denmark's, it is fair to assume that most of these men were Norwegians. *Uddrag av aarsberetninger fra de forenede rigers consuler for aaret 1887* (Kristiania, 1888), 525.

[34]The translated quotation comes from "New York," *Konsulatberetninger, 1909* (Kristiania, 1909), 64. "New York," *Konsulatberetninger, 1903* (Kristiania, 1904), 252, contains the consul's remarks on the few desertions in 1902.

[35]"New York," *Konsulatberetninger, 1910* (Kristiania, 1910), 72. "New York," *Konsulatberetninger, 1911* (Kristiania, 1911), 55.

[36]The quoted phrase comes from the interview with Hans Berggren. Men who supported his views during interviews included Inge Berge, Rolf Broun, Per Christiansen, Paul Nord, and Sigurd Rosseland. "New York," *Konsulatberetninger* (Kristiania, 1914), 37–38. "New York," *Aarsberetninger fra norske legationer og konsulater, 1918* (Kristiania, 1918), 87, 89. See also Roedder, *Av en utvandrer-avis' saga*, 1 (Brooklyn, 1966), 55, 74; and Rygg, *Norwegians*, 177–182.

[37]In addition to the immigrants cited in the previous note, the following colony veterans spoke of Norwegian seamen joining the United States Navy and merchant marine or taking work on land: Alice and Daniel Fjelldal, Carsten Hansen, Mr. and Mrs.

Kristoffer Henricksen, Bertha and Gudrun Kartevold, John and Hjørdis Mortensen, Elsie Thorsen Rosvold, and Charles Turgesen.

[38]Interviews with Hans Berggren, Inge Berge, Rolf Broun, Per Christiansen, Alice and Daniel Fjelldal, Paul Nord, and Sigurd Rosseland.

[39]Ernst, *Immigrant Life*, 37–38, 45, 195, 236n. Rygg, *Norwegians*, 22–23, 31, 66. Hugill, *Sailortown*, 157–158.

[40]Ernst, *Immigrant Life*, 39–44, 193–195. Thomas Kessner, *The Golden Door: Italian and Jewish Immigrant Mobility in New York City, 1880–1915* (New York, 1977), 130–133.

[41]Ernst, *Immigrant Life*, 37–40. Hugill, *Sailortown*, 157–158. Rygg, *Norwegians*, 22–23.

[42]Rygg, *Norwegians*, 22–23. Hugill, *Sailortown*, 157–166; for the quotation, see page 158. Gjerdrum, "Fra Amerika: Brev til *Dagbladet*, II," 16–19, is the source for his observations.

[43]Rygg, *Norwegians*, 22–23. Ernst, *Immigrant Life*, 57. Gjerset, *Norwegian Sailors in American Waters*, 164–170.

[44]Ernst, *Immigrant Life*, 71–72, 75, 81–83, 215, 253n. Rygg, *Norwegians*, 22–23, 26–28, 32, 34. Juul, *Erindringer*, 69–70.

[45]Rygg, *Norwegians*, 6–7, 26–27, 30–32, 38, 40–42, 75. Juul, *Erindringer*, 69–70. Ernst, *Immigrant Life*, 214–217. Gunnar J. Malmin, trans. and ed., *America in the Forties: The Letters of Ole Munch Ræder* (Minneapolis, 1929), 106. "Johannes Nordboe and Norwegian Immigration," 32–33.

[46]Rygg, *Norwegians*, 9, 49, 133. Martin L. Reymert, "James Denoon Reymert and the Norwegian Press," in *Norwegian-American Studies and Records*, 12 (Northfield, Minn., 1941), 79–90, especially 81–87.

[47]Rygg, *Norwegians*, 40, 60–61, 75, 88.

[48]Rygg, *Norwegians*, 9, 17–18, 40–42, 75–76, 62–63, 114. Gjerset, *Norwegian Sailors in American Waters*, 145–148, 154–55. August Reymert Papers. Correspondence, in NAHA Archives. "Received Money from Emigrants," *The Mail and Express* (New York), December 12, 1893.

[49]Rygg, *Norwegians*, 40–42, 88–89, 92, 103. Juul, *Erindringer*, 5–9, 69–73. Magnus Colbjørn Ihlseng, "Nordmænd i New York," *Nordisk Tidende*, December 8, 1921, in NAHA Archives.

[50]Rygg, *Norwegians*, 56–57, 59–60, 63.

[51]Rygg *Norwegians*, 6–13, 22–23, 36–38, 59–63, 75–76, 117, 133–134. Carl Søyland, *Skrift i sand* (Oslo, 1954), 15–16. Roedder, *Av en utvandrer-avis' saga*, 1: 9–13. For evidence of continuing pan-Scandinavian activities and organizations, see Jenswold, "The Rise and Fall of Pan-Scandinavianism in Urban America," in *Scandinavians and Other Immigrants in Urban America: the Proceedings of a Research Conference October 26–27, 1984*, Odd S. Lovoll, ed., (Northfield, Minn., 1985), 159–170, and the announcements of pan-Scandinavian organization in *Nordisk Tidende*, August 11, 1898, 7.

[52]Rygg, *Norwegians*, 75–76; Gjerdrum, "Fra America, Brev til *Dagbladet*, II," 12–15.

[53]*Vor Frelsers norsk evangelisk lutherske menighet, 60-aars jubilæum, 1866–1926* (Brooklyn, 1926), 4–5. See also the historical sketch in *Our Savior's Ev. Lutheran Church, 1866–1956* (Brooklyn, 1956), n. p. "A Short History of Our Church," in *Our Savior's Lutheran Church, 237 East 123rd Street, New York* (New York, 1933), 5.

[54]Rygg, *Norwegians*, 66. *Festskrift i anledning sjømannskirkens 75 års jubileum* (Brooklyn, 1953), 9. Margaret Latimer, *Two Cities: New York and Brooklyn the Year The Great Bridge Opened* (Brooklyn, 1983), 23–24, 26. Ment, *The Shaping of a City*, 40–41.

[55]Beulah Folkedahl, ed. and trans., "Elizabeth Fedde's Diary, 1883–88," in *Norwegian-American Studies and Records*, 20 (Northfield, Minn., 1959), 170–196. Rygg, *Norwegians*, 88–90, 103–107. Gjerdrum, "Fra Amerika: Brev til *Dagbladet*, II," 16–19.

[56]Rygg, *Norwegians*, 36, 66–67, 117. The description of the flag-raising over New York's City Hall is on page 76. "Gjennem Hamilton Ave og Columbia St," *Nordisk Tidende*, November 13, 1891.

**Chapter 4**   [1]Ron Miller, Rita Seiden Miller, and Stephen Karp, "The Fourth Largest City in America—A Sociological History of Brooklyn," in *Brooklyn USA, The Fourth Largest City in America* (Brooklyn, 1979), 6, 17–18. Harold Coffin Syrett, *The City of Brooklyn, 1865–1898: A Political History* (New York, 1944), 12–13. Ment, *The Shaping of a City*, 38–39. *Brooklyn Almanac*, Latimer, ed. (Brooklyn, 1984), 24. Hazelton, *The Boroughs of Brooklyn and Queens,* 3:1597.

[2]*Brooklyn USA*, 18–19. Ralph Foster Weld, *Brooklyn is America* (New York, 1950), 36–37, 40, 62–75, 79, 95–97, 122–127.

[3]*Brooklyn Almanac*, 22. Ment, *The Shaping of a City*, 39, 55. *Brooklyn USA*, 18–19.

[4]Jacob Judd, "Brooklyn's Changing Population in the Pre-Civil War Era," in *Journal of Long Island History*, 3 (Spring, 1964), 10–13. Weld, *Brooklyn is America*, 55–59, 87–88, 92–95, 98–99. Syrett, *City of Brooklyn*, 236, quotes the *New York Tribune* article at length.

[5]Ment, *The Shaping of a City*, 63–64. Weld, *Brooklyn is America*, 95–95, 104–105, 124–125. Syrett, *The City of Brooklyn*, 66–69, 88–89, 71–83, 218–232.

[6]Syrett, *The City of Brooklyn*, 13–19. Ment, *The Shaping of a City*, 42–43. Weld, *Brooklyn is America*, 51, 54, 88, 91–92, 127. Judd, "Brooklyn's Changing Population," 14–15.

[7]Syrett, *The City of Brooklyn*, 18–19; *Brooklyn USA*, 19; and Weld, *Brooklyn is America*, 87, 90, 117–118. Ment, *The Shaping of a City*, 55. Latimer, *Brooklyn Almanac*, 22. Syrett, *The City of Brooklyn*, 236.

[8]John S. Billings, *Vital Statistics of New York City and Brooklyn* (Washington, D. C., 1894), Map 7 and 173–228, 242–244. See Latimer, *Almanac*, 68, for neighborhood names.

[9]Joshua Brown and David Ment, *Factories, Foundries, and Refineries: A History of Five Brooklyn Industries* (Brooklyn, 1980), 22–26. Rowland Tappan Berthoff, *British Immigrants in Industrial America* (Cambridge, Mass., 1953), 43, 149, 193.

[10]Ment, *The Shaping of a City*, 40–44, 56–58. David McCullough, *The Great Bridge* (New York, 1972), 480–484, 514–515, 519, 545. Syrett, *City of Brooklyn*, 14–15. Hazelton, *The Boroughs of Brooklyn and Queens*, 3: 1586–1587, 1598–1600. Brown and Ment, *Factories, Foundries, and Refineries*, 5–7.

[11]Ment, *The Shaping of a City*, 40–41, 55–56. Brown and Ment, *Factories, Foundries, and Refineries*, 6–7. Syrett, *The City of Brooklyn*, 13–14, 16, 19. Latimer, *Two Cities*, 21–26. *Brooklyn Almanac*, 14.

[12]Billings, *Vital Statistics*, 165. Ment, *The Shaping of a City*, 59–60, 68, 73. Syrett, *The City of Brooklyn*, 233–239. *Brooklyn USA*, 20.

[13]*The Brooklyn Daily Eagle*, September 30, 1891, May 18, 1892, and July 12, 1892. The ranking of Scandinavians among Brooklyn's ethnic groups comes from an addition of the figures for Sweden, Norway, and Denmark for 1880 and 1890 in Latimer, *Almanac*, 22.

[14]For urban emigration from Denmark, see Svalestuen, "Nordisk emigrasjon," 18–19, 22, 38. Briant Lindsay Lowell, "Scandinavian Exodus: A Multivariate Analysis of 19th Century Rural Communities" (Ph. D. dissertation, Brown University, 1985), 130–136, includes an interpretation of the importance of cities in Swedish emigration.

[15]Latimer, *Almanac*, 22. Billings, *Vital Statistics*, Map 7 and 168–169, 171–173, 175, 181–183, 185–187, 210–212, 215–220, 224–228. Eleventh U. S. Census, 1890, Manuscript Schedules for Wards 1, 3, 7, 8, 20, 23, 25. "Maritime Acquisition of Scandinavian Line, Brooklyn, with Great Norse and Swedish Population, its Natural Environment," *Brooklyn Daily Eagle*, August 16, 1903, in *Brooklyn Daily Eagle* Clipping Morgue of the Brooklyn Central Library's Brooklyn Collection.

[16]Billings, *Vital Statistics*, 166, 176–177, 197–201. Manuscript Census Schedules, New York State Census for Brooklyn, 1892, Wards 1, 6, 8, 12, 17, 22. Wards 6 (Old South Brooklyn) and 12 (Red Hook–Gowanus) contained 78 percent of the city's Norwegians. Brown and Ment, *Factories, Foundries, and Refineries*, 57–62. *Nordisk Tidende*, June 29, 1894. Ingolf Olsen, *Trinity Through the Years, Trinity Lutheran Church 1890–1965* (Brooklyn, 1965), 8. Gabriel Fedde, "Pennestrøg – Oplevelser," unpublished autobiography, in NAHA Archives. Rygg, *Norwegians in New York*, 95–96. Hoover, "Norwegians in New York," 225–227, gives evidence that Bay Ridge contained Brooklyn's Norwegian colony after World War II.

[17]See, for example, Rygg, *Norwegians*, 24, 28; *Fifty Years of Service: The Norwegian Sailors' Home, Brooklyn, New York* (Brooklyn 1939), 11–17; and Olsen, *Trinity through the Years*, 8, 13. U. S. Census, *Population*, 1890, 1:675–676; 1900, 1:773; 1910, 1:948; 1930, 2:248.

[18]John Higham, *Strangers in the Land: Patterns of American Nativism 1860–1925* (2nd ed., New York, 1973), 140–142, 146–157. Howard B. Grose, *Aliens or Americans? A Forward Mission Study Course* (New York, 1906), 19–27, 126–127. Edward A. Steiner, *On the Trail of the Immigrant* (New York, 1906), 112–125. Syrett, *The City of Brooklyn*, 237, gives the main gist of the *Tribune* article's attitudes. Frederick Boyd Stevenson, "Scandinavians

in Brooklyn," in *The Brooklyn Daily Eagle*, March 5, 1916. Weld, *Brooklyn is America*, 196–197.

[19]Stevenson, "Scandinavians in Brooklyn." Fuglum, *Norge i Støpeskjeen,* 75–124, especially 75–86. For a range of comments on the involvement of Brooklyn and Manhattan Norwegians in the conflict between Sweden and Norway as well as their feeling that Norway showed a more democratic spirit, see Rygg, *Norwegians,* 79, 143–145; numerous articles in *Nordisk Tidende,* 1892–1905; and Mauk, "Mobilizaton and Conflict: The Background and Social History of the Norwegian Colony in Brooklyn to 1910," in *Immigration to New York* (New York, 1991).

[20]Kessner, *The Golden Door,* 145–146. Latimer, *Almanac,* 22. *Nordisk Tidende,* May 28, 1897. Roedder, *Av en utvandrer–avis' saga,* 1:31–33.

[21]Ment, *The Shaping of a City,* 41–42, 46–48, 56, 58. Latimer, *Two Cities,* 40–41, 46. Syrett, *The City of Brooklyn,* 18–19.

[22]Ment, *The Shaping of a City,* 60–61, 73, 76. *Annual Reports, City of New York Department of Docks and Ferries, 1900,* 48, 174–176, 222–225; *1910,* 358, 387–394, 427–428. Robert A. Caro, *The Power Broker, Robert Moses and the Fall of New York* (New York, 1975), 329, 522–523.

[23]This and the following paragraph build on Seth Low, "An American View of Municipal Government in the United States," in *The American Commonwealth* (London, 1889), 1:620–635. The quoted material is on 634–635. See also Syrett, *The City of Brooklyn,* 70–86, 107–119, 121–126. Ment, *The Shaping of a City,* 62–65. Latimer, *Two Cities,* 58–61.

[24]The most concentrated source of colony biographies is Rygg, *Norwegians in New York.* See also the two major colony newspapers, *Nordisk Tidende* (1891– ) and *Norgesposten* (1924–1933), as well as organizations' and churches' anniversary histories and archives.

[25]Rygg, *Norwegians,* 9, 13–16, 23, 38–40, 50–53, 59–60. Try, *To kulturer en stat,* 74–76, 78–79, 82–83, 89–90, 95–96, 100; and Svalestuen, "Nordisk Emigrasjon," 17, 41, 44–47.

[26]Rygg, *Norwegians,* 64–65, 69–70. Jonassen, "The Norwegians in Bay Ridge," 226. Hazelton, *Brooklyn and Queens,* 3:1102–1104.

[27]Rygg, *Norwegians,* 14–15. *Nordisk Tidende,* June 3, 1892. Thomas J. Archdeacon, *Becoming American, An Ethnic History* (New York, 1983), 43–44, 132–135. John Christianson, "Scandinavian Immigrants on a Pluralistic Frontier," paper given at Norwegian–American Seminar III in Hamar, Norway, 1989. See also Try, *To kulturer en stat,* 74–76; Semmingsen, "Amerikaferd," in *Utvandringa – det store oppbrotet,* 6–17; and Blegen's chapter on "Emigrant Goldseekers" in *Norwegian Migration,* 1:267–271.

[28]Rygg, *Norwegians,* and *Nordisk Tidende,* June 3, 1892. See also Johan H. Kloster, "Sjømann – Fisker – Bonde, En Sjøbruksstudie fra Hidra i Vest–Agder" (Master's Thesis, University of Oslo, 1975), 200–202, 208–210.

[29]Rygg, *Norwegians,* 15. Charles B. Barnes, *The Longshoremen* (New York, 1915), 2–12.

[30]Rygg, *Norwegians,* 15–16. *Nordisk Tidende,* January 5, 1895, and January 11, 1900. Kloster, "Sjømann – Fisker – Bonde," 28–31, 122–135, 168–169, 191, 223–227, 316–317. Cæcilie Stang, "Arbeidsvandring og utvandring fra kystbygda Feda i Vest–Agder, ca. 1750–1950" (Master's thesis, University of Oslo, 1983), 129–132. Moland, *Vår gamle kystkultur,* 2:158–159. Koren, *Omkring Lindesnes,* 16–19.

[31]Kloster, "Sjømann – Fisker – Bonde." Try, *Gardskipnad og bondenæring: sørlandsk jordbruk på 1800–tallet* (Oslo,1969), 194–195. Løvland, "Utvandringen fra Arendal/ Barbu," 66–67. Rygg, *Norwegians,* 114–116. Sejersted, *Den vanskelige frihet,* 188–193; and Try, *To kulturer en stat,* 139–151. Worm–Müller, "Seilskibsrederiet," in *Norsk sjøfarts historie,* 2:2, 391–417.

[32]Latimer, *Brooklyn Almanac,* 22. Arlow W. Andersen, *The Norwegian–Americans* (Boston, 1975), 38. Rygg, *Norwegians,* 46, 49–53.

[33]E. and G. W. Blunt's 1848 map of New York harbor, Map Collection, Long Island Historical Society, Brooklyn. Billings, *Vital Statistics,* 165, 171–174, 176–179, 181–182, 185–187, 218–219. Ment, *The Shaping of a City,* 40–41, 46.

[34]Ment, *The Shaping of a City,* 40–41, 48, 58. Syrett, *City of Brooklyn,* 13, 18.

[35]M. Dripps' "Map of Brooklyn and Vicinity, 1873," in "New York Stasjon, 1879," Seamen's Mission Archives. Ment, *The Shaping of a City,* 32–33, 43–44, 56. Jonassen,

"The Norwegians in Bay Ridge," 253. Billings, *Vital Statistics*, 165, 171–174, 176–179, 181–182, 185–187, 218–219.

[36]Hodne, *Norges økonomiske historie 1815–1970*, 142–143. Worm–Müller, *Den norske sjøfarts historie*, 2:2, 212–214, 218.

[37]Hodne, *Norges økonomiske historie*, 144–145. Worm–Müller, 2:2, 208–210, 212. Knut Utstein Kloster, *Den norske stormakt, Vår skipsfart gjennom tusen år* (Oslo, 1946), 122.

[38]The numbers of Norwegian ships in the harbor are calculated from the annual reports of the Swedish–Norwegian Consul General in New York. The quotation comes from Worm–Müller, *Sjøfarts historie*, 2:2, 209.

[39]For statistics on the number of Norwegian seamen arriving, see the tables on Norwegian shipping in Chapter 3. The quotation and reasons for lengthy stays are found in Worm–Müller, *Den norske sjøfarts historie*, 2:2, 209–210.

[40]Hodne, *Norges økonomiske historie*, 136–141. Fischer and Nordvik, "The Price of Labor," 31–34.

[41]Hodne, *Norges økonomiske historie*. Worm–Müller, *Den norske sjøfarts historie*, 2:2, 213–214, 218–221.

[42]Hodne, *Norges økonomiske historie*, 28–34, 139–142, 158–172. See also Hodne's subtopic "Colonial Past," in the preliminary version of the above work, *An Economic History of Norway, 1815–1970*, 254–258. For an evaluation of shipowners' leading role in movements for Norwegian independence throughout the nineteenth century, see Kloster, *Den norske stormakt*, 66–72, 114–118.

[43]Worm–Müller, *Den norske sjøfarts historie*, 214–215. Tønnessen, "Rømning 1850–1914 fra Norske Skip," 148, 150.

[44]The quotation comes from Moland, *Vår gamle kystkultur*, 2:159.

[45]According to the part–time seamen's pastor, 1,140 Norwegian sailors came to the city in 1870. See "New York," manuscript annual report for 1870, in Seamen's Mission Archives.

[46]M. Andersen, *70 års tilbakeblikk*, 72. Rygg, *Norwegians*, 28, 37, 66–67. Semmingsen, *Veien mot vest, 1865–1915*, 279–283, 269. The quotation comes from Johannes Aardal, "Sjømannskirken i Brooklyn 1878–1953," in *Festskrift i anledning sjømannskirkens 75 års jubileum* (Brooklyn, 1953), 9.

[47]See Table 1 in the appendix. Blegen, *Norwegian Migration to America, 1825–1860*, 18. Semmingsen, *Veien mot vest, 1865–1915*, 366–370, 373. Ordahl, "Emigration from Agder to America," 313–318. Latimer, *Brooklyn Almanac*, 22.

[48]Rygg, *Norwegians*, 28, 66, 80, 97–98.

[49]This and the following paragraphs about Gabriel Ueland, Theodore Kartevold, and the other immigrants who arrived together in 1881 build mainly on a collection of Kartevold's letters home, his diaries from 1881 through 1889, and his father's "Brudstykker av brev fra Theodore Kartevold til foreldre," all of which are in the possession of Gudrun and Bertha Kartevold, 436–75th Street, Brooklyn. A number of details come from interviews with the Kartevold sisters between late April and early June, 1986. See also, Rygg, *Norwegians*, 79, 173, and *Nordisk Tidende*, September 23, 1892.

[50]"Dødens høst. General–Agent Simon W. Flood," in *Nordisk Tidende*, November 22, 1895. "Gavmildhed i det Stille," *Nordisk Tidende*, August 10, 1895. Address list, "Kopibok etter Carsten Hansteen," in Norsk Historisk Kjeldeskrift Institutt archives. Rygg, *Norwegians*, 111.

[51]The main source for the paragraphs about the Fedde family is Fedde, "Pennestrøg – Oplevelser," 28–33, 36, 39–70, 86–109. See also Rygg, *Norwegians*, 88, 95, 97.

[52]M. Andersen, *70 års tilbakeblikk*, "Rulleblad" and 17–23, 35–42.

[53]M. Andersen, *70 års tilbakeblikk*, 35–40, 46.

[54]M. Andersen, *70 års tilbakeblikk*, 52–67, 70–73. Rygg, *Norwegians*, 49, 139.

[55]Latimer, *Two Cities*, 26. Rygg, *Norwegians*, 22–23. Carsten Hansteen, "Hovelbestyrelsen for 'Foreningen til evangeliets forkyndelse for skandinaviske sømænd i fremmede havne'," report from Brooklyn's Seamen's Pastor, in Seamen's Mission Archives file "New York, 1887," September, 16, 1887, 6.

[56]Hansteen, "Hovedbestyrelsen for 'Foreningen'," September 16, 1887, 2–3, 1889. M. Andersen, *Tilbakeblikk*, 72, 77–79.

[57]Rygg, *Norwegians*, 22, 31–32, 66–67, 103–107. Billings, *Vital Statistics*, 171–172, 182–183. Syrett, *The City of Brooklyn*, 138–140, 233–235, 242–243. Kessner, *The Golden Door*, 144–145.

[58]The information about newcomers and the quotations in this and the next paragraph come from R. S. N. Sartz, "Fra Washington, D. C.," in *Normands–Forbundets Tidsskrift*, 2 (Kristiania, 1909), 181–186. See also Rygg, *Norwegians*, 88–92, and Rygg, *The Norwegian Sailors' Home of Brooklyn, N. Y., A Condensed History of the Institution From Its Start in 1887 to the Present Time* (Brooklyn, 1939), 19.

**Chapter 5**

[1]A. Anderson, *The Salt of the Earth: A History of Norwegian–Danish Methodism in America* (Nashville, 1962), 12, 23–26, 29. H. A. Preus, *Syv foredrag, de kirkelige forholde blandt de Norske i Amerika* (Christiania, 1867), 66–75. For an English version of that book, see Herman Amberg Preus, *Vivacious Daughter: Seven Lectures on the Religious Situation Among Norwegians in America,* ed. and trans. by Todd W. Nichol, (Northfield, Minn., 1990), 101–103, 107–108, 111–113. Juul, *Erindringer,* 16–17.

[2]A. Anderson, *Salt of the Earth*, 183–185. Kverndal, "Pionerspor i verdenshavnen," in *Den norske sjømannsmisjon i New York 1878–1978, 100 år,* ed. Sigurd Daasvand (Brooklyn, 1978), 13–14.

[3]Kverndal, "Pionerspor i verdenshavnen," 9–11.

[4]Latimer, *Brooklyn Almanac*, 22. Worm–Müller, *Den norske sjøfarts historie*, 2:1, 569, 571–572, provides the statistics from which the percentage of Norwegians entering via Quebec, 94.0, was calculated.

[5]Gjerset, *Norwegian Sailors in American Waters*, 66–68. Tønnessen, "Rømning 1850–1914 fra Norske Skip," 149.

[6]Worm–Müller, *Den norske sjøfarts historie*, 2:1, 570–572; 2:2, 212–214, 218.

[7]Kverndal, "Pionerspor i verdenshavnen," 12–14. Harriet Terdal, "Norwegian–American Churches in the New York Area," partially published manuscript prepared for *Nordisk Tidende* (Brooklyn, 1975). *Nordisk Tidende*, December 2, 1892. A. Andersen, *Salt of the Earth*, 184–187, 189.

[8]For the quoted material, see the typescript version of letters from "Kopibok etter Carsten Hansteen," in Norsk Historisk Kjeldeskrift–Institutt archives, letters dated April 28 and August 20, 1887.

[9]For the quotation see Juul, *Erindringer*, 16–17. Both Juul and the first seamen's pastors felt that Brooklyn Methodists had the upper hand. See "New York," Manuscript Yearly Reports to the Seamen's Mission Society in Bergen, for 1877–1878, in Seamen's Mission archives.

[10]Juul, *Erindringer*, 13–15. See the Reverend C. S. Everson, "Fra New York," manuscript report to the Seamen's Mission Society, October 23, 1877, Seamen's Mission archives, for the quotation in the text.

[11]Kverndal, "Pionerspor i verdenshavnen," 15–17. Nichol, *Vivacious Daughter*, 100–107. The analysis of the situation is original, based on Kverndal, Nichol, Juul's *Erindringer*, and the manuscript reports of the first seamen's pastors, 1868, 1870, 1877–1878. See also Consul Christian Børs, letter to Director N. Aars Nicholaysen of the Norwegian Seamen's Mission, in "New York, 1878," September 24, 1878, Seamen's Mission archives, 4.

[12]Preus, *Syv foredrag*, 66–75. See also Nichol, *Vivacious Daughter*, 100–107.

[13]Preus, *Syv foredrag*, 67, 75.

[14]Preus, *Syv foredrag*, 67, 75. Kverndal, "Pionerspor," 17–18. Frederik Knudsen, "Arbeidet hjemme," in *Den norske sjømannsmisjon i 75 år, 1864–1939, Festskrift utgitt av foreningens hovedstyre* (Bergen, 1939), 5, 8, 10–11.

[15]Kverndal, "Pionerspor," 17–20, 24. Letter from Assistant Peder B. Larson to Nicolaysen, January 18, 1877, in "New York, 1877," 1–2. Juul, *Erindringer*, 46.

[16]Letter from Everson to the Seamen's Mission's executive board, January 10, 1877, 1; letter from consul Børs to the Mission's board, January 12, 1877, 1–3, and Everson, "Fra New York," May 5, 1877, all in "New York, 1877," Seamen's Mission archives.

[17]Kverndal, "Pionerspor," 21. *Who's Who Among Pastors in all the Norwegian Lutheran Synods of America, 1843–1927* (Minneapolis, 1928), third editon of *Norsk luterske prester i Amerika*, translated and revised by Rasmus Malmin, O. M. Norlie, and O. A. Tingelstad, 32. Ole Asperheim, "Brooklyn, 5te September, 1878," 1, and "Fra New York," October 19, 1878, 1–3, both in "New York, 1878," Seamen's Mission archives.

[18]Kverndal, "Pionerspor," 24. Knudsen, "Arbeidet hjemme," 3–6, 11–12, 22–25, 33, 52–59. The Norwegian Seamen's Mission grew out of state–church circles but remained perforce both officially and financially independent. Its founders, a small group of

merchants, captains, school administrators, and state–church ministers, appealed to the Norwegian parliament for funds and asked for official affiliation with the state church. When these applications were rejected, however, the group managed to develop another institutional base. The state church compromised by allowing individual parish organizations to take collections and contribute the work of women's circles to the mission. Pious captains and crew members canvassed for additional funds. When faced with the need for large expenditures, the mission of necessity turned to the businessmen who were most concerned with the merchant marine, the leaders of the shipping industry.

[19]All citations hereafter, unless otherwise identified, refer to the Seamen's Mission Society Archives in Bergen. Asperheim, "Fra New York," October 19, 1878, 1–5. Andreas Mortensen, "Fra New York," December 30, 1880, 12–13, 21. Aardal, "Sjømannskirken i Brooklyn," 10. Letter dated June 8, 1882, private collection of America letters, names withheld.

[20]Asperheim, "Brooklyn 5te September, 1878," 1–2. The circulars are also in the "New York, 1878" file.

[21]On the executive board's handling of Asperheim's assistant, see the board's marginal notes in "5te September 1878," 3. For the Brooklyn priest's apologies, see "P.S." and "Fra New York," October 19, 1878, 5.

[22]"Til hovedbestyrelsen for for. til ev's forsk. for skandinaviske sømænd i fremmede havne," no date.

[23]Asperheim, "Brooklyn 5te Marts 1879," 2, 6–8; and "Brooklyn 7 Marts 1879," 5–6.

[24]For evidence of the pastors' opposition to drink, desertion, and emigration as well as the station's dependence on contributions from the shipping industry, see the following: Asperheim, "Til hovedbestyrelsen for for. til ev's forsk. for skandinaviske sømænd i fremmede havne," no date, 3, and "Brooklyn 7 Marts 1879," 5–6. Mortensen, "Fra New York," December 30, 1880, 2, 5. Hansteen, "Hovedbestyrelsen for foreningen," September 16, 1887, 2–3, 6. Kristen Sårheim, "Til hovedbestyrelsen for den norske sømandsmission," September 29, 1887, 7–8.

[25]Asperheim, "Til hovedbestyrelsen for for. til ev's forsk," 1; Mortensen, "Fra New York," 3–4; Hansteen, "Hovedbestyrelsen for Foreningen," 6–7; Sårheim, "Norske sømandsmission," 3–4; and M. Andersen, 70 års tilbakeblikk, 72–73.

[26]Asperheim, "Brooklyn 5te September 1878," 1–2. See Worm–Müller, Den norske sjøfarts historie, 2:3, 182–184, on religious awakenings among seamen.

[27]Hansteen, letters dated April 28 and August 20, 1887, in "Kopibok etter Carsten Hansteen," Norsk Historisk Kjeldeskrift–Institutt archives, and Asperheim, "Brooklyn 5te September 1878," 1–2. For the claim that the station's pastors had become Methodists, see Fedde, "Pennestrøg – Oplevelser," 118.

[28]Asperheim, "Brooklyn 7 Marts," 5–6. Rygg, The Norwegian Seamen's Church, Brooklyn, 1867–1948 (Brooklyn, 1948), 18–20, 24. "Sjømannskirkens styre," in Festskrift i anledning sjømannskirkens 75 års jubileum, 30–31. On the Norwegian nationality of Swedish–Norwegian consuls in New York and the consulate's service to shipping interests, see for example, "Høiremanden og konsulen. Det er af sine egne, man skal ha' det," in Nordisk Tidende, November 5, 1897. Any random selection of the consul's annual reports gives abundant evidence of his service to shippers in describing local market and harbor conditions.

[29]Asperheim, "Fra New York," October 19, 1878, 4, and "Brooklyn, 4 Mai 1879," 3. Mortensen, "Fra New York," 4–5.

[30]For the mission's official position on settled immigrants, see Kverndal, "Pionerspor," 23–25. Asperheim, "Brooklyn 5de September 1878," 7, "Fra New York," 3–4, and "Brooklyn 7 Marts," 2–5; Mortensen, "Fra New York," 2–3, 5. See Børs, letter to Nicholaysen, dated September 24, 1878, 4, on the poverty of the settled population.

[31]Asperheim, "Fra New York," October 19, 1878, 3.

[32]Asperheim, "Brooklyn 7 Marts," 2–5.

[33]Asperheim, "Brooklyn 7 Marts," 2–4.

[34]The Relief Society eventually became the Norwegian Deaconess Home and Hospital. Mortensen, "Fra New York," 1–3. Beulah Folkedal, untitled typescript biography of Sister Elizabeth Fedde, in NAHA Archives. Rygg, The Norwegian Seamen's Church, 25. "Elizabeth Fedde's Diary, 1883–1888," Folkedal, ed. and trans., in Norwegian–American Studies and Records, 20 (Northfield, Minn., 1959), 170–175.

[35]Folkedal, typescript biography of Sister Elizabeth Fedde, 1, 8. "Søster Elisabeths optegnelser: Ankomsten til Amerika, de første opgaver," in *Nordisk Tidende*, February 28, 1933.

[36]Folkedal, typescript biography, 1, 3, 13, 19. "Elizabeth Fedde's Diary, 1883–1888," 172, 180–181. *The Norwegian Lutheran Deaconesses' Home and Hospital, A Brief History,* (Brooklyn, 1923), 9.

[37]"Søster Elisabeth's optegnelser," in *Nordisk Tidende*, February 28, March 7 and 14, 1933. "Elizabeth Fedde's Diary, 1883–1888," 176–181.

[38]"Søster Elisabeths optegnelser," February 28 and March 14, 1933. "Elizabeth Fedde's Diary, 1883–1888," 172.

[39]"Søster Elisabeths optegnelser," March 14 and 21, 1933. "Elizabeth Fedde's Diary," 185, 186n.

[40]"Søster Elisabeths optegnelser," March 21, 1933. "Kopibok etter Carsten Hansteen," typescript letters dated March 14 and 30, 1887. Rygg, *Seamen's Church, 1867–1948,* 25.

[41]"Eldre kvinneforening," in *Festskrift i anledning sjømannskirkens 75 års jubileum,* 40, 42. Sårheim, "Norske sømannsmission," 8. Worm–Müller, *Den norske sjøfarts historie,* II:2, 215–216. Rygg, *Seamen's Church, 1867–1948,* 22–25. "New York," in *Uddrag af aarsberetninger fra de forenede rigers konsuler for aaret 1883* (Kristiania, 1884), 241–245.

[42]Mortensen, "Fra New York." "Gjenpart af en skrivelse fra de forenede rigers consulat i New York til departementet for det indre dateret den 3die Januar 1882," in State Church Archives, Oslo.

[43]Folkedal, typescript biography of Sister Elizabeth Fedde, 1. Mortensen, "Fra New York."

[44]This and the succeeding paragraphs on Hansteen's personality and social background build mainly on the "Kopibok etter Carsten Hansteen." See especially the typescript copies of his letters to Mrs. Børs and to his family in Norway.

[45]Folkedal, typescript biography, 8, 16, and Elizabeth Fedde, untitled autobiography, 3, both in NAHA Archives.

[46]Typescript letters from Hansteen's "Kopibok" to "Fru Konsul Børs," April, May 5, and June 6, 1886; March 11, 14, and 30, April 13, 1887.

[47]Folkedal, typescript biography, 17–18. "Søster Elisabeth's optegnelser," March 28, 1933.

[48]This and the next paragraph build on the Relief Society's minutes for April 17, 1883. The Lutheran Medical Center in Brooklyn, successor to the Deaconess Home and Hospital, has the original journals of the board in its archives. Folkedal, typescript biography of Sister Elizabeth Fedde, 1, 14, includes extensive translations of the minutes from the first meeting.

[49]Anne–Lise Seip, *Sosialhjelpstaten blir til: norsk sosialpolitikk, 1740–1920* (Oslo, 1984), 81, 83–84, 178–180. Folkedal, "Elizabeth Fedde's Diary," 170–171, 175, 185n, 191n–192n. Typescript biography of Elizabeth Fedde, 3–4, 7–8, 14, 21. *The Deaconesses' Home and Hospital, A Brief History,* 7–9. "Søster Elisabeths optegnelser," March 21, 1933. "Kopibok etter Carsten Hansteen," typescript letters dated March 14 and 30, 1887.

[50]"Elizabeth Fedde's Diary," 188. *A Brief History,* 35–37.

[51]For Mrs. Børs's term as president of the board, see *A Brief History,* 37. The voting factions on the board are evident from both the minutes of its meetings in 1886–1887 preserved at the Lutheran Medical Center in Brooklyn and Hansteen's "Kopibok," especially the typescript letters dated March 11, March 14, March 30, and August 19, 1887.

[52]Hansteen, typescript copy of letters to Mrs. Børs, April 1886, and May 11, 1886. "Søster Elisabeths optegnelser," March 21 and 28, 1933. Home and Hospital board minutes for meetings from March 1886 through January 1887. Folkedal, typescript biography, 25. "Elizabeth Fedde's Diary," 189–194.

[53]Home and Hospital secretary's minutes for February 8, 1887. Folkedal, "Elizabeth Fedde's Diary," 193–194. Folkedal's typescript biography, 18–19, 25–26. The quotation comes from "Søster Elisabeths optegnelser," March 28, 1933. Not until 1902 did the Home and Hospital's board learn that Alfred Corning Clark had set up this arrangement in honor of his Norwegian friend, Lauritz Skougaard Severini, who had died in 1886. During visits to the Børs home in Manhattan after his friend's death, Corning Clark and his banker friend had set up the conditions for the fund in discussion with the Børses. At

the February meeting, the other board members knew nothing of these specifics, although some may have guessed because of these men's earlier generosity.

[54]Except where otherwise noted, the sources for the analysis of further developments in the Hospital controversy are the following: Minutes of the board meetings, March–August 1887; "Søster Elisabeths optegnelser," March 28 and April 4, 1933; Folkedal, typescript biography, 18–19; "Sister Elizabeth's Diary," 194–196n; *Deaconesses' Home and Hospital, A Brief History*, 10–12, 37–39; and "Kopibok etter Carsten Hansteen," typescript letters dated March 11, 14, 30, April 13 and 28, and August 19, 1887.

[55]"Kopibok," typescript copy of Hansteen's letter to Assistant Seamen's Pastor Kristen Sårheim, August 19, 1887.

[56]"Søster Elisabeths optegnelser," April 4, 1933. *A Brief History*, 10–12. Folkedal, "Sister Elizabeth's Diary," 196n.

[1]Hodne, *Norges økonomiske historie,* 152–158. According to the tenth and eleventh U.S. censuses, the Norwegian–born population of Brooklyn grew from 874 to 4,508 during the 1880s. For the increase in seamen recorded in the emigrant protocols, see Semmingsen, *Veien mot vest,* 282–283; Tønnessen, *Norsk sjøfarts historie,* 2:3, 149; and Løvland, "Utvandringen fra Arendal/Barbu," 66–69. For the contemporary estimate of 400 settlers attending services at the station, see Sårheim, "Meddelelsen til de fastboende," 1–2, enclosed with "Brooklyn N.Y., 1 October 1889," in Seamen's Mission archives. As early as 1887 Hansteen reported the necessity of placing 130 new seats in the station church because of the large numbers in the congregation. See the typescript of his letter home, "Kjære alle hjemme," April 28, 1887, in "Kopibok etter Carsten Hansteen," 1.

[2]Hansteen, "Brooklyn, New York," March 19, 1889, 3. Consul Børs reported the same trends as Hansteen, but limited his remarks to the migration of Scandinavian seamen to the American merchant marine, where the "number of Scandinavian seamen . . . grows each year." In 1887 Børs estimated that at least 25 percent of America's deep–water sailors and a "much higher portion" of her coastal seamen and yacht crews were Scandinavians. Given the fact that Norway's fleet was very much larger than Sweden's or Denmark's, it is fair to assume that most of these men were Norwegians. See *Uddrag av aarsberetninger fra de forenede rigers consuler for aaret 1887,* 525.

[3]Hansteen, "Hovedbestyrelsen for 'foreningen til evangeliets forkyndelse for skandinaviske sømænd i fremmede haven,'" September 16, 1887, in Seamen's Mission archives. All citations hereafter in this chapter without other identification refer to the Seamen's Mission's archives in Bergen, Norway.

[4]Hansteen, "Hovedbestyrelsen for 'foreningen,'" 4–5. See also the typescript of his private letter to mission director Nicolaysen, January 19, 1886, in "Kopibok etter Carsten Hansteen," for his view that the station ought to work for the financial independence of the immigrants.

[5]Hansteen, "Hovedbestyrelsen for 'foreningen,'" 5–6. For the station's income from immigrants, see Sårheim, "Til hovedbestyrelsen for den norske sømannsmission," September 22, 1887, 8.

[6]Hansteen, "Brooklyn, New York," March 19, 1889, 5. In 1887 the pastor wrote his sister that an "invasion" of laymen's groups was infinitely preferable to having settlers tricked by fly–by–night evangelists. See the typescript letter "Kjære alle hjemme," 2–3.

[7]Olsen, *Trinity through the Years,* 6–8. Fedde, "Pennestrøg – Oplevelser," 116, 123.

[8]Asperheim, "Brooklyn 7 marts," 2–4.

[9]*Vor frelsers norsk evangelisk lutherske menighet, 60–aars jubilæum, 1866–1926* (Brooklyn, 1926), 4–5. *Our Savior's Ev. Lutheran Church, 1866–1956* (Brooklyn, 1956), n.p. "A Short History of Our Church," in *Our Savior's Lutheran Church, 237 East 123rd Street, New York* (New York, 1933), 5.

[10]*60–aars jubilæum,* 4. Our Savior's Ev. Lutheran Church.

[11]Hansteen, typescript copies of his letters in "Kopibok etter Carsten Hansteen": to his brother Peter, April 15, 1886, 3; to his family in Norway, October 11, 1886, 5; and to his friend, D. C. Rensch, March 30, 1887, 1. Sårheim, "Til hovedbestyrelsen," 2.

[12]Typescript letters from Hansteen's "Kopibok": to former Seamen's Pastor Mortensen, March 11, 1887, 1–2; to his family, March 13, 1884, 1–2; to D. C. Rensch, March 30, 1887, 1; to Mrs. Børs, April 13, 1887, 1; to Sårheim, August 19, 1887, 2. "Nogle ord til venner af den luterske kirke bandt herværende landsmænd," the circular from Our Savior's, is included in Sårheim, "Til hovedbestyrelsen."

**Chapter 6**

[13]Typescript letters from Hansteen's "Kopibok": to Mrs. Børs, May, 1886, 1–4; to Mortensen, March 11, 1887, 2; to his family, March 14, 1887, 1. Manuscript letter from the "Kopibok," to his family, November 18, 1887, 1–2. Fedde, "Pennestrøg – Oplevelser," 118. "Søster Elisabeths optegnelser V," in *Nordisk Tidende*'s series of excerpts from her diary, 1933. Sårheim, "Til hovedbestyrelsen," 6.

[14]Typescript letter from Hansteen's "Kopibok" to Sårheim, August 18, 1887, 1–2. Manuscript letter from the "Kopibok," to his family, November 18, 1887, 2. Fedde, "Pennestrøg," 114–118. Hansteen, "Hovedbestyrelsen for foreningen," September 16, 1887, 3–4, 6.

[15]Hansteen, "Hovedbestyrelsen for 'foreningen,'" 2, 4. Sårheim, "Til hovedbestyrelsen," 1–3, 5.

[16]Hansteen, "Hovedbestyrelsen for 'foreningen,'" 4. Sårheim, "Til hovedbestyrelsen," 7–8.

[17]Sårheim, "Til hovedbestyrelsen," 6.

[18]Manuscript copies from Hansteen's "Kopibok," to his family, November 18, 1887, 4, and February 2, 1888, 1; to Consul Børs, February 3, 1888, 2–3; to his brother Peter, March 14, 1888, 1.

[19]Hansteen, "Hovedbestyrelsen for 'foreningen,'" 2.

[20]"New York," *Uddrag af de forenede rigers konsuler for 1887*, 523–526, and *Uddrag . . . for 1888*, 184–188.

[21]Typescript letter, Hansteen to his family in Norway, April 28, 1887, 1, in "Kopibok."

[22]Hansteen, "Hovedbestyrelse for . . . skandinaviske sømænd," 6.

[23]For early descriptions of how runners and boarding masters entrapped seamen, see Asperheim, "Fra New York," October 19, 1878, 2–3; and Mortensen, "Fra New York," December 18, 1880, 5–6. Hansteen, "Hovedbestyrelsen for 'foreningen,'" September 16, 1887, 6; and "Til Hovedbestyrelsen," July 9, 1889, 1–2, describe sailortown's activities nearer the time of the pastor's campaign. See also Sårheim, "Sømandens kår," July 7, 1889, 2, 5–6; and "New York," in *Uddrag af aarsberetninger fra de forende rigers konsuler for 1881*, 145–146.

[24]Hansteen, "Hovedbestyrelsen for 'foreningen,'" 3. "Sømandshjemmets forudsætninger," in *Bud og Hilsen* (Bergen, Norway), No. 3 and 4, March 1889, 132–141.

[25]This and the following paragraph derive from the attitudes expressed in the pastor's reports cited in notes 23 and 24; Mortensen, "Fra New York," December 30, 1880, 5–6; and "New York," in *Uddrag av aarsberetninger for aaret 1887*, 532.

[26]The following paragraphs build on M. Andersen, *70 aars tilbakeblikk på mitt virke på sjø og i land*, 71–72; Hansteen, "Hovedbestyrelsen for 'foreningen,'" 2–3; and Rygg, *Fifty Years of Service: The Norwegian Sailors' Home of Brooklyn, N.Y.* (Brooklyn, 1939), 16–17.

[27]Hansteen, "Hovedbestyrelsen for 'foreningen,'" 2.

[28]Rygg, *Fifty Years of Service,* 27.

[29]Hansteen, "Hovedbestyrelsen for 'foreningen,'" 2–3.

[30]M. Andersen, *Tilbakeblikk*, 72.

[31]M. Andersen, *Tilbakeblikk*, 72–73.

[32]Hansteen, "Hovedbestyrelsen for 'foreningen,'" 3.

[33]Hansteen, "Hovedbestyrelsen for 'foreningen,'", 3. See also Rygg, *Fifty Years of Service,* 17, 19, 23.

[34]M. Andersen, *Tilbakeblikk*, 74, 81. Rygg, *Fifty Years,* 23, 27.

[35]Rygg, *Fifty Years*, 19 and 27. M. Andersen, *Tilbakeblikk*, 73–74, 77, 84.

[36]M. Andersen, *Tilbakeblikk*, 77–80.

[37]Hansteen, "Hovedbestyrelsen for 'foreningen,'" 3. "Til Hovedbestyrelsen," July 9, 1889, 1, 3.

[38]Hansteen, "Hovedbestyrelsen for 'foreningen,'" 2. "Til Hovedbestyrelsen," 1.

[39]Hansteen, "Hovedbestyrelsen for 'foreningen,'" 3. M. Andersen, *Tilbakeblikk*, 74.

[40]Hansteen, "Hovedbestyrelsen for 'foreningen,'" 5, 7, and "Brooklyn, New York," 4–5.

[41]Hansteen, "Brooklyn, New York," 3–5.

[42]On Hansteen's audiences to win royal patronage, see the government notes and letters dated October 4, 15, and 19, 1888, in "Om oprettelsen av skandinaviske sjømannshjem . . . i New York," in State Church Archives, Oslo. For his fund raising, see Rygg, *Fifty Years of Service,* 23.

[43]M. Andersen, *Tilbakeblikk*, 80–82. The home's original by–laws (adopted on October 1, 1889) were regularly printed in its annual reports. See, for example, the "Thirty–first Annual Report and By–laws" for 1920. Article I states the general purpose assumed to be the home's main work from the start, that of assisting transient Scandinavian sailors who "may be found within the Port of New York." Article VIII gives the superintendent of the home discretionary powers to extend aid to men in need, which put the stamp of official approval on Andersen's actions during 1888 when many immigrant seamen found berths through the home.

[44]"Den norsk–amerikanske sjømandsforenings 20–aars fest. Lidt om dens historie," *Nordisk Tidende*, April 15, 1909. M. Andersen, *Tilbakeblikk*, 83.

[45]M. Andersen, *Tilbakeblikk*, 78–80.

[46]M. Andersen, *Tilbakeblikk*, 79. Hansteen, "Til hovedbestyrelsen," July 9, 1889, 1. Both men describe the article in the *Herald*, which is enclosed in the Seamen's Society's 1889 journal for New York at the Seamen's Mission archives in Bergen.

[47]Hansteen, "Til hovedbestyrelsen," July 9, 1889, 1.

[48]Hansteen, "Brooklyn, New York," 1; and manuscript letters to Sofie Hansteen, November 2, 1888, and March 1, 1889, 280–282 and 416–418 respectively, in "Kopibok."

[49]Hansteen, manuscript letter to Nicolaysen, January 23, 1889, " in Kopibok," 375–381.

[50]Hansteen, manuscript letter to Nicolaysen, 377, and "Brooklyn, New York," 2. See Fedde, "Pennestrøg – Oplevelser," 127–128, for the new sect's identification with electric lighting.

[51]Hansteen, "Brooklyn, New York," 1–2, 4–6.

[52]"Sjømandsforenings 20–aars fest," in *Nordisk Tidende*, April 15, 1909. Hansteen, "Fra New York," manuscript version of an article for the Mission Society's magazine *Bud og Hilsen*, 1–2.

[53]M. Andersen, *Tilbakeblikk*, 78.

[54]Hansteen, "Til hovedbestyrelsen," July 9, 1889, 5; "Fra New York," 2–3; and manuscript letter to his parents, July 24, 1889, in "Kopibok," 448–449.

[55]For Hansteen's description of the attack, see "Fra New York," 3–8.

[56]Hansteen, "Fra New York," 8, and "Til hovedbestyrelsen," 3.

[57]This and the following three paragraphs are based on Hansteen, "Til hovedbestyrelsen," July 9, 1889, 1–3.

[58]Rygg, *Fifty Years*, 27–28. The quoted material comes from Hansteen, "Til hovedbestyrelsen," July 9, 1889, 2–3.

[59]Hansteen, "Til hovedbestyrelsen," July 9, 1889, 3.

[60]Sårheim, "Til hovedbestyrelsen," July 4, 1889, 2. Hansteen, "Til hovedbestyrelsen," July 9, 1889, 4.

[61]The information in this and the next paragraph (including two articles in no longer extant issues of *Nordiske Blade* ) comes from Hansteen, "Til hovedbestyrelsen," July 8, 1889, 4; Sårheim, "Hr. Cand. Theol. Aars–Nicolaysen!" July 8, 1889, 1–4, and "Brooklyn, N. Y., 1 Oktober 1889," 2. See also Fedde, "Pennestrøg," 115–116.

[62]Hansteen, "Brooklyn, New York," March 19, 1889, 5. Sårheim, "Brooklyn, N.Y., 1 Oktober 1889," 1. Olsen, *Trinity through the Years*, 8–10.

[63]Fedde, "Pennestrøg," 117–119, 121, 123–124, 127–132. Olsen, *Trinity through the Years*, 8–10.

[64]Fedde, "Pennestrøg," 122.

[65]"New York," *Uddrag af aarsberetninger fra de forenede rigers konsuler for 1890*, 83, 85. Semmingsen, *Veien mot vest, 1865–1915*, 183–184, 282–283, 503. Gjerset, *Norwegian Sailors in American Waters* 72, 75–76, cites the figures from *Nordisk Tidende* (February 7, 1893) on Scandinavians in the coastal trade and the nationality of seamen entering the harbor.

[66]Sårheim, "Brooklyn, N. Y., 1 Oktober 1889," 3, and "Til hovedbestyrelsen," January 1890, 5. Kverndal, "Pionerspor i verdenshavnen," 24–25.

[67]M. Andersen, *Tilbakeblikk*, 72–73, 80–82, 84.

[68]"New York," *Uddrag af aarsberetninger fra de forenede rigers konsuler for 1886*, 210. M. Andersen, *Tilbakeblikk*, 72–73, 80–82.

[69]The sources for this and the next two paragraphs are Rygg, *Fifty Years*, 27–29; and Sårheim, "Til hovedbestyrelsen," January 1890, 1, 4–5.

**Chapter 7**

[1]Roedder, *Av en utvandrer–avis' saga*, 1:14–21. Nielsen hired three different "managers" or editors in quick succession but set the tone and determined the goals of the newspaper himself. Officially, at least, he also kept the titles of owner and editor. For Nielsen's comments on launching the newspaper, see his first two editorials, "Et Godt Nytt År," *Nordisk Tidende*, January 2, 1891; and "Vore Foreninger," January 9, 1891.

[2]See the editorials cited above and "Vore Foreninger, II," January 23; "Hvad Vi Bør Arbeide For," January 30; "Vore Foreninger, III," February 6; and "17de Mai," February 20, 1891. Roedder, *Av en utvandrer–avis' saga*, 1: 25–26, 28–30.

[3]The description of the settlements in Wards 1 and 17 is based on an examination of manuscript schedules in the New York State Census of 1892 for those areas. See Mauk, "The Colony," Appendix, for an explanation of the data collected on all Norwegian–born adults in those wards; Table 1 after the Appendix gives the adult population of the northern settlements. On the Greenpoint settlement's decreased size and religious goals, see *Nordisk Tidende*, June 29, 1894.

[4]See Mauk, "The Colony," Appendix and Table 1. Those Norwegians recorded in the New York State Census of 1892 are assumed to be the more settled population, that is, immigrants. One can calculate the transient maritime population from Norway's fleet in 1892 as follows: Statistisk Sentralbyrå (*NOS*), *Beretninger om handel og skipsfart. uddrag af aarsberetninger fra de forenede rigers konsuler for 1892* (Kristiania, 1893), third series, No. 96, 849, gives the number of arriving Norwegian ships as 339. Following the same procedure used in Chapter 3, that number was multiplied by a factor of five to estimate the number of Norwegian sailors on these ships (5 x 339 = 1695). The seamen's pastors expected 23,000 to 25,000 *Scandinavian* sailors to arrive on these ships. Since Norway had by far the largest deep–water merchant marine at the time, it is probable that more than 20,000 of these men were Norwegians. Unfortunately, *NOS* kept no record of desertions in 1892.

[5]State census maps for 1896 (with handwritten notes to indicate boundaries in 1892) provided information for describing the physical outline of the colony. The maps include lines for wards and election districts, the political divisions within wards. Because exact street addresses were infrequently given for areas of Norwegian settlement, the boundaries of the colony could not be more specific than the street limits of election districts showing larger numbers of Norwegians than those outside the colony. A concentration of at least twenty–nine adult Norwegians, including a minimum of seven families, was the standard for "entering" the colony. The information about population density in different sections of the city comes from Billings, *Vital Statistics of New York City and Brooklyn,* Map 7, after page 228.

[6]See Mauk, "The Colony," Appendix and Table 1.

[7]The description of changes in the topography of the Red Hook–Gowanus section of the city in this and following paragraphs derives from Dripps' 1873 map. The state census maps are stored in the documents room of the Kings County Clerk's offices in Brooklyn.

[8]See *Nordisk Tidende* (1892): April 8; September 14, 20.

[9]The collection of Theodore Kartevold's America letters, diaries, and datebooks (which his elderly daughters graciously allowed to be copied and used for this study) includes a number of details that complete the description in the text. Kartevold and many of the oldest people interviewed in the 1980s told about arriving by the Hamilton Avenue Ferry or related their parents' accounts of arrival.

[10]Interviews, the Kartevold collection, and a private collection of America letters preserved in Norway also describe the wharves, commuters from Manhattan, and maritime workers' daily routines.

[11]Interviews with Paul Nord and Hans Berggren on watchmen on boats. For reports of religious revivals on Hamilton Avenue and the reception they got, see *Nordisk Tidende*, April 21, 1893, and Jonassen, "The Norwegian Heritage in Urban America: Conflict and Cooperation in a Norwegian Immigrant Community," in *Norwegian-American Studies*, 31 (Northfield, Minn., 1986), 79–80.

[12]See Mauk, "The Colony," Appendix and Tables 7, 8, and 11 A.

[13]See Mauk, "The Colony," Appendix, for an explanation of how the number of families and adult Norwegians was tabulated.

[14]See Mauk, "The Colony," Appendix and Tables 2–7, 11 A. The Deaconess

Home and Hospital was found on page 24 of the manuscript schedules for Ward 8, Election District 24, which was at 46th Street and Fourth Avenue.

[15]Interviews with Lina Logan, Lulu Lawrence, and Former Domestics 2 and 3. Mrs. Logan said she tried office work but went back to being a maid because she found that when she had to pay for food and lodgings she had less money to spend on herself. Room and board formed part of the "perks" of being in service, according to former domestics in the colony. Logan also described how her female employer periodically laid out clothes she no longer wanted and allowed Logan to choose among them. Later, Logan impressed both colony residents and, on a trip to her hometown in Norway, "everybody" with her wardrobe. These and other former domestics were unanimous in reporting that rich families' chauffeurs drove them to the colony for social affairs on their days off.

[16]See Mauk, "The Colony," Appendix, Table 7, for the major male occupations in Little Norway. Because they were prominent socioeconomic and organizational leaders in the colony, the elite often figured in the pages of *Nordisk Tidende*, which often included the addresses of their businesses as well as their homes in its notices and articles.

[17]Interviews with Erling Rosand, Stanley Solaas, Ole Jensen, Paul Nord, Hans Berggren, Alice and Daniel Fjelldal.

[18]Billings, *Vital Statistics*, 176–177, 197–201, describes the character of the Hamilton Avenue commercial district. During a series of interviews with the daughters of the immigrant watchmaker, optician, and jeweler Theodore Kartevold, Gudrun and Bertha (Gudrun herself a second–generation immigrant entrepreneur), the economic advantanges of the area for immigrant business people became clear.

[19]For samples of *Nordisk Tidende*'s articles on colony businessmen, see 1891, June 19 (on Captain Blix, shipowner) and September 4 (Enoch Olsen, metal ceilings; Johan G. Normann, tobacconist; Theodore Kartevold, watchmaker; and J. F. Iversen, tobacconist and stationer); 1892, March 18 (Edwin O. Lee, ticket office and Scandinavian bank), May 27 (Johan Engelsen, barber), June 3 (John Anson, ship chandler and hardware store owner), July 15 (J. T. Tengelsen, druggist), and August 9 (Thor Halvorsen, undertaker).

[20]Billings, *Vital Statistics*, 165, 171–173, 185–187. See Mauk, "The Colony," Appendix, Table 8. Asperheim, "Til Hovedbestyrelsen for 'Ev's Forkyndelse for Skand. Sømænd i Fremmede Havne,'" in Seamen's Mission archives (Bergen, Norway). Translation by the author.

[21]See Mauk, "The Colony," Appendix, Table 8. Note that in election districts where they were the largest nationality group, "Norwegian" is italicized.

[22]See Mauk, "The Colony," Appendix, Table 8. *Nordisk Tidende*, 1892, April 1 and August 2, 19, and 26.

[23]See Mauk, "The Colony," Appendix, Table 8.

[24]Interviews with Hjørdis Mortensen, John and Liva Nordskog, Sivert Strøm, Paul Igeland, and Gus Tallaksen.

[25]For samples of notices of rooms for rent and articles or announcements about boardinghouses, see *Nordisk Tidende*, 1892, January 22, September 20, September 23, October 28.

[26]See Mauk, "The Colony," Appendix and Tables 9 A–C, 10, and 11.

[27]See Mauk, "The Colony," Appendix, Table 10. Interviews with Solveig Salvesen, Helen Livingstone, Gyda Andersen, Cecilia Tessdal Felt and George Joa, Hannah Simonsen, Birgit Rasmussen, Sigurd Rosseland, Rolf Broun, Inge Berge, Eileen Johansen, and Elsie, Kitty, and Bjørn Jacobsen.

[28]The Kartevold Collection and the series of interviews with Gudrun and Bertha Kartevold inform much of this and the next paragraph.

[29]Men comprised over six–tenths of those living with close relatives, according to the census schedules.

[30]See Mauk, "The Colony," Appendix. The following list gives the locations of small occupational groups that clustered together in families: stovemen (12th Ward, 7th Election District, hereafter, 12w, 7 ed), bakers (12w, 4ed), tailors (12w, 9 & 15 eds); machinists (12w, 1 & 17 eds). The following give examples of common "family" occupations or tradesmen sharing the same residence: dressmakers (6w, 23 & 25 eds); laborers (12w, 4ed); carpenters (6w, 22 ed; 12w, 14 ed); sailors (6w, 25 ed); "boat people" on barges and lighters (12w, 12 & 13 eds); tugboat men and boatman sharing rooms (12w, 3ed); two

sets of sibling sailors (6w, 24ed); three sibling dressmakers (6w, 23ed); lightermen sharing rooms (12w, 4 & 11 eds).

[31]The state census manuscript schedules give information about Ueland and family on page 10 of Ward 6, Election District 25.

[32]"Se Her!" *Nordisk Tidende*, October 28, 1892. The manuscript schedules for Election District 25 and surrounding districts contain the information on other Norwegian immigrant businessmen and professionals.

[33]See Table 10 in Mauk, "The Colony," Appendix. The count of nonfamily lodgers is undoubtedly inflated, because some hallboys and hallgirls were cousins, nephews, and nieces who could not be identified in the census schedules. The portion of lodgers in private families who were hallboys was 41.7 percent, or 43.5 if one includes hall*girls*. Interviews with Solveig Salvesen, Hjørdis and John Mortensen, Paul Nord, Sigurd Rosseland, Rolf Broun, Inge Berge, Eileen Johansen, Paul Igeland, and Elsie, Kitty, and Bjørn Jacobsen. No printed sources the author can find use the term "hallboy," even though the veterans interviewed commonly employed that local coinage. "Tableboard," however, does appear in three instances: *Nordisk Tidende*, December 13, uses the word in the text of an advertisement for rooms. *IOGT Jubilæumsskrift i Anledning Stiftelsen av Loge Dovre, No. 20* (Brooklyn, 1910), 31, shows a photograph of a Red Hook row house bearing a large sign with the text "Oslo Tableboard," and the picture including the sign for Killand's Tableboard on Henry Street, Red Hook, which Erik Aalvik Evensen used on page 71 in his edited collection of America letters, *Amerika–brevene* (Grimstad, Norway, 1996) and generously offered as an illustration for this book.

[34]The age–group analysis is based on the 167 hallboys and hallgirls and 57 household heads who rented room to such non–family lodgers in Wards 6 and 12 at the time of the 1892 census. The average age of household heads with hallboys was 38.3 years, and the mean age classificaion for the same group was 34–39. The average age of hallboys (including hall*girls*) was 24 years, and their mean age classification was 20–24. The range of ages for household heads was 25 to 70. For hallboys the range was 15 to 70.

[35]Including hallgirls, the census showed 167 nonfamily lodgers in private households. From January 1891 through January 1894, *Nordisk Tidende* advertised rooms at twenty–seven addresses that were private homes rather than boardinghouses according to the maps, block indexes, and deeds at the Brooklyn office of the New York City Register.

[36]The quotation comes from an interview with Sigurd Rosseland. Many of those interviewed agreed about using word–of–mouth among family and friends to find hallboys.

[37]For the machinists (father, 2 sons, and 1 hallboy), see 12w, 1ed. A hallboy working as a porter lived with a household head who had the same occupation in 12w, 15ed.

[38]The examples of an almost preindustrial solution to housing for subordinates or employees can be found in the following parts of the manuscript schedules: In Ward 6: the bookkeeper and 6 clerks (11ed); the boat captain and 3 sailor hallboys (24ed); the contractor, 4 framers, all of whom were siblings, and carpenter (25ed). In Ward 12, the grocer with a deliveryman as hallboy (15ed).

[39]See Ward 12, 15ed, for the boatman with 3 hallboys, 2 sailors and 1 dockbuilder.

[40]See, for example, *Nordisk Tidende*, August 14, 1891; November 25, 1892; March 17, 1893. The single, unattached men included uncles (8%), grown sons (15.4%), and hallboys (41.7%), making a total of 65.1%.

[41]*Nordisk Tidende*, September 3, 1897. The translations are the author's.

[42]The distribution patterns of hallboys, siblings, and friends in Wards 6 and 12, when compared to census maps, showed where people most felt the need for family substitutes. In Ward 6, Districts 21–27 were along Hamilton Avenue, in other words, in sailortown. In Ward 12, the highest concentrations of cohabiting siblings, friends, and hallboys appeared in the area of the Atlantic Docks (Districts 4, 6, 7), near the Erie Basin (District 9), and along the Avenue (Districts 11, 14 15). Interviews with Hans Berggren, Paul Nord, and Lulu Lawrence. These and other old–timers who preferred not to be named told of Norwegian sailors with families in Norway who became bigamists in Brooklyn. *Nordisk Tidende* reported on such a case on the front page of its January 4, 1895 issue. Some seamen far from home and family became lonely and resorted to bigamy rather than remain loners.

[43]Rygg, *Norwegians in New York*, 107. Roedder, *Av en utvandrer–avis' saga*, 1:30–31.

Syrett, *The City of Brooklyn, 1865–1898*, 14, documents New York's ownership of Brooklyn's shoreline.

[44]Syrett, *The City of Brooklyn, 1865–1898*, 216–222, 224–225, 230–232. The quoted phrase comes from Rygg, *Norwegians*, 107.

[45]For early advertisements of bars and saloons, see *Nordisk Tidende*, January 9, 1891. *Nordisk Tidende*, August 26, 1892, contains the article on Georg Hansen. Roedder, *Av en utvandrer–avis' saga*, 1:25, 39–41, reports Nielsen's acceptance of payment in kind. The elderly seamen who commented on the story in *Nordisk Tidende* were Per Christiansen and Hans Berggren.

[46]*Nordisk Tidende*, 1892; March 18; June 3; July 8; August 12. On Johan G. Normann's tobacco shop and hiring office for yachtsmen, see Gjerset, *Norwegian Sailors in American Waters*, 104–105. Jenswold, "'I Live Well, But . . .'," 121–123, describes the importance of Edwin O. Lee's Scandinavian bank for Norwegian immigrants.

[47]See Mauk, "The Colony," Appendix and Tables 9 C and 11 A. Amundsen, *Hjemløse fugle*, published by N. Jensen's Book Press, 544 Atlantic Avenue. "Indtryk fra Spredte Felter i Gamlelandet efter 47 Aars Fravær," *Norgesposten* (Brooklyn), December 22, 1931, describes the details of Amundsen's career and the stages in the development of his book.

[48]Amundsen, *Hjemløse fugle*, 21. This and all subsequent passages come from the final book form. Translations by David Mauk.

[49]See Mauk, "The Colony," Table 11 A in the Appendix.

[50]Amundsen, *Hjemløse fugle*, 11. Interviews with John Rønnevik, Tom Svennevik, Carsten Hansen, and four men at Gjoa Sporting Club.

[51]Amundsen, *Hjemløse fugle*, 8–9, 10–13, 26.

[52]Amundsen, *Hjemløse fugle*, 8–9, 10–13, 26. Sartz, "Fra Washington, D. C.," in *Normands–Forbundet* (Kristiania, 1900), 2:181–186. For an example of common advice from the Consul, see *Uddrag av aarsberetninger fra de forenede rigers konsuler for aaret 1887*, *NOS*, third series, No. 60, 549–550.

[53]The teller of the Lista riddle would not give his name, because "I don't want it to get around. There's still lots of those people here." He told his story on Fifth Avenue, Brooklyn, outside Fredricksen's and Johannesen's Scandinavian Specialities store on May 23, 1986.

[54]*Nordisk Tidende*, July 15, 1892, 4.

[55]Amundsen, *Hjemløse fugle*, 22.

[56]The number of boardinghouses with Norwegian lodgers was undoubtedly much greater, when one remembers that the analysis of residential patterns builds on a 10 percent sample of the Norwegians in Wards 10 and 12. The data registered on all adult Norwegians included only marital status, occupation, and the ward and election district in which they lived. Nonetheless, the 216 Norwegian lodgers (the eight boardinghouse operators are excluded) at twenty–eight boardinghouses compiled in the sample are probably representative. See Mauk, "Colony," Table 11 B, for the location of the boardinghouses. For the exception, see 6w, 11ed, which was six blocks north of Hamilton Avenue in an area bounded by Clinton, President, Court, Degraw and Harrison streets.

[57]Amundsen, *Hjemløse fugle*, 21, 40, 45.

[58]For the four boardinghouses with other nationalities see the manuscript schedules for Ward 6, 18ed and 22ed; Ward 12, 4ed and 15ed. A Scottish woman operated the boardinghouse in District 22 of Ward 6, which ran along the Avenue. Even that house had one obvious tie to Norway. The landlady's twelve–year–old son is listed as Norwegian–born. The other nationalities lodging there were, from largest to smallest group, American (32), Irish (25), German (5), and English (2).

[59]The boardinghouses with a mix of occupations were as follows: Ward 6, ed22 and ed26; Ward 12, ed4 and ed7. Those with one or two large occupational groups were Ward 6: ed18, one with laborers; two with marine trades, mostly seamen; and one with marine trades and construction workers. Ed22, one laborers. Ed23, one marine. Ed25, one marine and construction. Ed26, one marine. Ward 12: ed3, two marine. Ed4, one clerks, one laborers, one construction, two marine, and two laborers and marine. Ed6, one marine. Ed7, two marine. Ed9, two marine. Ed15, two marine.

[60]Amundsen, *Hjemløse fugle*, 21.

[61]This and the previous paragraph build on Amundsen, *Hjemløse fugle*, 22–25, 37–46, 47–52, 66–93.

[62]Interviews with Erling Rosand, Carsten Hansen, and Hans Berggren. Billings, *Vital Statistics*, Map 7 and 176–178, 215–219.

[63]New York State Census of 1892, Manuscript Schedules for Ward 22. Domestics were the only Norwegians in election districts 8–9, 13–15, and 18–19. The Norwegian working–class settlement in election districts 2, 11–12, and 16 contained two captains and one lighterman with families, but fourteen carpenters and two masons, nine of them with families. Eight metal workers (six families) also lived in the settlement. On Harry Christian, see "Hans S. Christiansen," *Nordisk Tidende*, January 4, 1895.

[64]Interviews with Tom Svennevik, Paul Nord, Hans Berggren, Daniel and Alice Fjelldal, Sigurd Rosseland, Gudrun and Bertha Kartevold.

[65]*Nordisk Tidende*, September, 1892. Interviews with Kristoffer Henricksen, Erling Rosand, Ole Jensen, and Stanley Solaas. Henricksen and Rosand told about the distribution of jobs after church on Sundays.

[66]Maps, block indexes, and deeds at the Brooklyn Office of the New York City Register confirmed the household structure observed in the census schedules.

[67]Billings, *Vital Statistics*, Map 7, 176–178. New York State Census of 1892, Manuscript Schedules for Ward 8, all Election Districts. The tables of occupations in the appendix show number of Norwegian carpenters in relation to other occupational groups in the colony.

[68]See Mauk, "Colony," Table 12 in the Appendix. Interviews with Kristoffer Henricksen, Hans Berggren, Carsten Hansen, and four men at the Norwegian Marine Veterans Association (*Norsk Krigsseiler Forening*).

[69]See Mauk, "Colony," Table 12. The married men among the workers on the docks, on coastal or deep–sea vessels, and in the harbor or at sea were, according to the men interviewed, very likely "settled." The pressure on married men to go on land that was general around the turn of the century supports their conclusion. On lighters, see "Lighterage—Its Function" in *Pilot Tales and Historical Sketches*, ed. Edward L. Allen (New York, 1922). On the construction and use of wooden harbor craft at the time, see Brouwer, "The Port of New York, 42–47.

[70]For the development of Bush Terminal, see "Maritime Acquisition is Scandinavian Line," *Brooklyn Daily Eagle*, August 16, 1903. On Thomas Olsen, see *Nordisk Tidende*, July 15, 1892. Fedde, "Pennestrøg – Oplevelser," describes his barge–building career late in life.

[71]Amundsen, *Hjemløse fugle*, 47–52.

[72]See Tables 7 and 12 in Mauk, "The Colony," Appendix.

[73]Interviews. See Moland, *Vår gamle kystkultur*, 2:158–159, and Try, *To kulturer, en stat,* 11:139–151.

[74]Manuscript schedules of Wards 8 and 22 in the 1892 state census.

[75]Fedde, "Pennestrøg – Oplevelser," 105, 108–111. The quoted material is on page 11. Translation by the author. On the tailor, see *Nordisk Tidende*, August 29, 1892.

[76]On the Workmen's Association, see *Nordisk Tidende*, April 8, 1892, 4, which contains the quoted material. Translation by the author.

[77]The New York State Census of 1892, Manuscript Schedules for Election Districts 16 and 24. Olsen, *Trinity through the Years*, 9–10, 13–15. *The Norwegian Lutheran Deaconesses' Home and Hospital*, 8–12.

[78]*Nordisk Tidende*, July 4, 1893. Interviews with John and Hjørdis Mortensen, Solveig Salvesen, Gudrun and Bertha Kartevold.

[79]Ferdinand Tönnes, *Community and Association*, trans. Charles P. Loomis (London, 1955), 74–75, 262–272.

## Chapter 8

[1]The phrase "vår egen lille verden" (our own little world) is commonly used in Norway today to describe a complete and close–knit social milieu. Several colony veterans (Paul Nord, Hans Berggren, Solveig Salvesen, and Bjørn Jacobsen, among others) used it to describe what they had heard about the associational life of the colony.

[2]Rygg, *Norwegians in New York*, 60–61. "Søster Elisabeths Optegnelser, VI," and "Søster Elisabeths Optegnelser, VII," *Nordisk Tidende*, April 4 and 11, 1933. M. Andersen, *70 års tilbakeblikk,* 84–85. On Christopher Ravn, see *NT*, July 10, 1891.

[3]For details about the campaign to have Ravn appointed as consul and local leaders' treatment of the man appointed, Karl Woxen, see *NT*, January 2; January 16; Febru-

ary 27; July 10, August 14; September 18, 1891; January 5 and February 5, 1894; May 5 and 12, 1898.

[4]On Pastor Sårheim's changes at the Seamen's Church, see: *NT*, February 13, 1891; Rygg, *The Norwegian Seamen's Church*, 27; Sårheim, "Fra New York, a Report Dated 1ste August, 1890," in *Bud og Hilsen* (Bergen, Norway), No. 9, September, 1890, 155–162. On the Church's lack of representation at the Sailors' Home and the Deaconess Home and Hospital, see *NT*, February 27, 1892; April 1, 1892; "Board of Managers," in *Annual Report of the Norwegian Lutheran Deaconesses' Home and Hospital* (Brooklyn, 1891–1896), 8th through 13th reports, n. p.; Scandinavian Sailors' Temperance Home, "Directors," *Annual Report and By–Laws*, (Brooklyn, 1890–1895), 1st through 5th reports, n. p.; and M. Andersen, *70-års tilbakeblikk*, 84.

[5]Folkedal, typescript biography of Sister Elizabeth Fedde, 28; "Søster Elisabeths Optegnelser, VIII," *NT*, April 18, 1933.

[6]Rygg, *Fifty Years of Service,* 27–29, 35, 39. The title comes from *NT*, November 25, 1892. See also *NT*, June 12, 1891; August 5 and November 29, 1892.

[7]On the expelled settlers' and Sårheim's lasting bitterness, see Fedde, "Pennestrøg – Oplevelser," 122; and *NT*, February 13; March 18; September 27; September 30, 1892.

[8]U. S. Censuses of 1880 and 1890, *Population*, 386 and 676, respectively.

[9]See Ordahl, "Emigration from Agder to America," 314, 317–318, 324–325, 332–333, 335–336, for the exceptionally high emigration rates in southern coastal Norway between the mid–1880s and 1910 and the tendency of these immigrants to settle in urban areas, notably Brooklyn. Svalestuen, "Utvandringen fra Norges Fogderier og Byer 1866–1914, Statistikk utarbeidet for Nordisk Emigrasjonsatlas 1970," unpublished statistical tables at the Norwegian National Archives in Oslo, 1970, 2, 4, shows similar emigration patterns in many parts of southwestern and southern Norway between 1880 and 1910. The following list of absolute totals and percentage increases for Brooklyn's Norwegian–born population between 1870 and 1930 is based on the Ninth through Fifteenth United States Censuses of Population: 1870—301; 1880—874 (190%); 1890—4,508 (416%); 1900—7,969 (77%); 1910—15,150 (90%); 1920—17,505 (16%); 1930—26,142 (49%).

[10]United States Census, 1900 and 1910, *Population*, 773 and 948, respectively. For *NT*'s comments about the effects of the depression of the 1890s on immigration, see September 15, 1893; July 27, 1894; January 11, 1895; July 30 and August 6, 1897. Qualey, *Norwegian Settlement in the United States*, 5–7, gives a concise summary and chart of the variations in emigration from Norway between 1880 and 1914.

[11]Rygg, *Norwegians in New York,* 77–78, contains the quoted phrase and anecdote about Irish–sponsored Constitution Day celebrations. See the chronologically listed register of Little Norway's institutions and associations in the Appendix. In 1889, the colony's organizations included the Seamen's Church, the Deaconess Home and Hospital, the Sailors' Home, Our Savior's Lutheran Church, Bethelship Methodist Church, the Norwegian–American Seamen's Association, the South Brooklyn Sick Benefit Society, and the Norwegian Brotherhood Club.

[12]See the registers of associations in Mauk, "The Colony," Appendix. For *Nordiske Blade*'s founding and relation to the Manhattan colony, see P. S. Christensen, "Lidt Aviskrønike: Skandinaviske Blade i Østen," in *Symra,* 10 (Decorah, Iowa, 1914), 261–265; and Roedder, *Av en utvandrer–avis' saga*, 1:12–16. *Nordiske Blade*'s location was advertised as 92 Hamilton Avenue, next door to *Nordisk Tidende*, in *Norge, Maanedsblad for Lodge Norge No. 26, av IOGT* (Brooklyn) January 5, 1904, 4. Because only slightly more than a year of *Nordiske Blade* is extant, *Nordisk Tidende* is the main newspaper source used for this period. Fortunately, *NT*'s editors often reported the *Blade*'s views or quoted from its articles extensively. See Rygg, *Norwegians*, 134, and Oivind M. Hovde and Martha E. Hanzler, *Norwegian–American Newspapers in Luther College Library* (Decorah, Iowa, 1975), 26.

[13]For documentation on the colony's temperance organizations, see Temperance Orders in the Appendix in the register of Institutions and Associations in Little Norway, Mauk, "The Colony," Appendix. *Jubilæums–skrift i anledning stiftelsen av Lodge Dovre No. 20, 1900–1910* (Brooklyn, 1910), 50, makes the claim that Brooklyn's IOGT lodges had almost 750 members.

[14]Fuglum, *Kampen om alkoholen i Norge, 1816–1904* (Oslo, 1972), 409, 486, 525, documents regional differences in support for Norway's temperance movements. In Red

Hook, Gabriel Ueland, Theodore Kartevold, Julius Selliken, and Sigurd Arnesen were among the temperance leaders who had emigrated from south and southwestern coastal Norway. *IOGT jubilæums–skrift* often states the regional origins of its leaders and indicates the lodges they belonged to in Norway before emigrating. See 8–9, 45–46, 53, 57, 60, and 68 for men from the Agder counties and Rogaland. In *NT*, see, for example, "Vore Foreninger II," January 23, 1891; "Distriktsloge 'Eidsvold' Nr. 4 af IOGT," August 26; and "Temperance Fanatisme," September 2, 1909.

[15]N. S. Stovby, *Skandinavisk temperance–kalender* (Brooklyn, 1896), 26–28. *Jubilæums–skrift*, 20. *NT*, January 7, 1909.

[16]See register of churches in the Appendix, Mauk, "The Colony." Fuglum, *Kampen om alkoholen*, 276–279. Interviews with Erik Friis, John E. Carlson, Johannes Aardal, Paul Qualben, and Gudrun Kartevold.

[17]On Norwegian Lutheranism's opposition to prohibition, see Fuglum, *Kampen*, 525. The characterization of colony churches in this and the next paragraph builds on the sum of comments gathered through 68 interviews and 16 written responses to questionnaries. See the list of people interviewed and/or surveyed in the Appendix.

[18]See the regional associations, mutual benefit societies, temperance orders, and labor societies in the list of institutions and associations in the Appendix.

[19]On the Assistance Association for Unemployed Emigrants, see *NT*, 1891: March 6; August 28; and November 27. Information on soup kitchens operated by religious groups came from interviews with Paul Nord, Hjørdis Mortensen, Kristoffer Oftedal, and Paul Qualben; Amundsen, *Hjemløse fugle*, 42–45; and Terdal, "De Norsk– Amerikanske Kirker i Brooklyn," a series of articles written for *NT* but never published, 58–60, 80. On the other relief efforts during the depression, see *NT*, 1894: October 19; and November 9; 1895: January 5; January 18; February 8; February 22; March 1; March 8.

[20]Lovoll, *A Century of Urban Life,* 189. Kenneth Bjork, *Saga in Steel and Concrete* (Northfield, 1947), 3–4, 20–21, 24–25, 69–75, 83. Rygg, "The Norwegian Club: A History of the Club, 1904–1944," in *Det Norske Selskab, New York: Jubileumsskrift, 1904–1944* (Brooklyn, 1944), 32–36, 41. "By–laws of the Norwegian Club," in *The 50th Anniversary Book of the Norwegian Club– 1904–1954* (Brooklyn, 1954), 100–101.

[21]For lists of the Norwegian Club's members and guests, see *Det Norske Selskab, New York,* 36, 41, 68–71. "A Brief History of Norsemen Lodge No. 878, F. & A. M," in *Thirtieth Anniversary, 1910–1940: Norsemen Lodge* (Brooklyn, 1940), 5–9, gives information about the membership and activities of the Norwegian Masons' Lodge. On the co-operation among the leaders of these two groups in establishing a children's home and a monument to Grieg, see *NT*, May 6; June 10; June 24; July 8, 1909. During interviews Paul Nord, Hans Berggren, Helen Livingstone, and Einar Bredland described the differences between the Club and the Lodge that printed sources confirmed.

[22]Rygg, *Norwegians*, 81–82. *NT*, 1891: March 6; August 21 and 28; 1892: February 5; May 20; 1893: February 21 and 24; March 3 and 10; 1894: May 18, 19, and 21; 1897: September 17; October 8 and 29; 1898: August 18; 1905: May 11; November 16; 1909: February 4; February 25; May 6; May 13; May 27; June 3; August 6.

[23]The quoted phrase comes from Rygg, *Norwegians*, 28. See that page and 269 for his view that the Red Hook colony was unique because of the prevalence of maritime occupations and social networks.

[24]The quotation comes from the interview with Carsten Hansen, but Paul Nord, Hans Berggren, Erik Friis, Einar Bredland, Bjørn Jacobsen, Erling Rosand, Daniel Fjelldal, and many others shared his interpretation of events. A ten–percent sample of Norwegian–born men's occupations (N = 4,457) from the New York State Census for Brooklyn in 1905 showed that 28.6 percent were maritime workers. A similar sample for the state's 1925 census (N = 5820) showed 29.5 percent maritime workers. Including the 1892 New York State Census, the percentage of seamen declined from 16.2 to 5.7 to 3.4, while the percentage of carpenters rose from 16.9 to 20.1 to 29.6. For the number of transient seamen in 1905, see "New York," *Konsulatberetninger, 1905* (Oslo, 1906), 89, 93.

[25]Interviews with Daniel and Alice Fjelldal, Finn Gjertsen, Walter Thorsen, Freddie Fredricksen, Ole Jensen, George Joa, Fred Løken, Paul Nord, John Nersten, and Stanley Solaas. Prominent leaders with maritime backgrounds appear in nearly all the anniversary booklets and annual reports of Little Norway's institutions and associations. Rygg, *Norwegians*, 64–65, 76–79, 109, 114–116, mentions many of these.

[26]Fedde, "Pennestrøg – Oplevelser," 133–136. Terdal, "De Norsk–Amerikanske Kirker i Brooklyn," 15–16, 28–29. *NT*, January 9, 1891; November 2, 1905; August 5, August 12, 1909.

[27]This and the following paragraphs build primarily on "Den Norsk–Amerikanske Sjømandsforenings 20–Aars Fest, Lidt om dens Historie," *NT*, April 15, 1909. See also Rygg, *Norwegians*, 78–80; and *NT*, 1891: January 9; January 23; February 27; March 27; 1892: January 8, January 22; April 1; July 8; July 29; and 1894: January 5.

[28]The quoted and translated phrase comes from the interview with Hans Berggren. For an example of the patronizing tone that runs through much of records of the Seamen's Mission and the Sailors' Home, see "Fra New York," in *Bud og Hilsen* (Bergen, 1897), 99–100, 108–110, 301–302. The founders of the Association were Magnus Andersen, August Reymert, Nils Olsen, Helmin Johnsen, and Oscar Røyen. Reymert practiced law from an office in Manhattan's financial district. His "villa" was in Woodside, Long Island, a fashionable new suburb in the 1890s. Olsen resided near the New York Yacht Club on Manhattan's upper west side, where he was employed as superintendent of the Club. The other two, Johnsen and Røyen, lived in the colony. Johnsen ran a furniture store on Hamilton Avenue and Røyen worked as a harbor captain. Magnus Andersen returned to Norway in 1889.

[29]This and the next paragraph build on the following: Interviews with Hans Berggren, Finn Gjertsen; questionnaire response from Karl K. Kjendal; letter from Per Christiansen, September 20, 1980; *NT*, April 15, 1909. See also *NT*, 1891: January, 16; February 13; February 27; April 10; May 8; June 5; August 14; and "Livlig Foreningsliv i kolonien: Sjømannsforeningen," Nordisk Tidende's World Exhibition number, 1939; *NT*, no date given, 1939, 46.

[30]The percentage of the Association's income for its first twenty years that was paid out in benefits was calculated from statistics reported in *NT*, April 15, 1909. Total income $29,751.15: dispensed in sick benefits, $21,141.54; in funeral benefits, $6,963.30.

[31]Questionnaire response from Karl K. Kjendal; letter from Per Christiansen. America letters in the Kartevold Collection, December 17, 1888; November 9, 1889. Private Collection of America Letters (names withheld), January 23, 1890. See also *NT*, 1891: January 2; January 23; March 9.

[32]America letter in the Kartevold Collection, November 9, 1889. Private Collection of America Letters (names withheld), January 23, 1890. Roedder, *Av en utvandreravis' saga*, 1:13–14. The quoted phrase and paraphrase from Boyesen's speech are based on a transcription made by Professor Per Seyersted at the University of Oslo and sent to the author in a letter from Seyersted dated September 9, 1986. The original Norwegian-language speech is in the Boyesen Papers at the Columbia University Library. For information about Boyesen's career at Columbia and his reputation as an American critic, novelist, and short–story writer, see Per Seyersted, *From Norwegian Romantic to American Realist: Studies in the Life and Writings of Hjalmar Hjorth Boyesen* (Oslo, 1984), 7–19, 21–22, 84–89, 101–104; and Clarence A. Glasrud, *Hjalmar Hjorth Boyesen* (Northfield, Minnesota, 1963), 95n–101, 114–116, 125–126.

[33]On the Leif Erikson Day parade and Rasmus B. Andersen, see *NT*, October 2, 1891; October 5, 1894; and Lloyd Hustvedt, *Rasmus Bjørn Anderson: Pioneer Scholar* (Northfield, Minn., 1966), vii and 311. The statement of Anderson's importance for Norwegian–American culture is on page vii. Roedder, *Utvandreravis' saga*, 1:14–15, 18–20, 23–24. *NT*, 1891: January 2; January 16; February 13; March 31; April 10; April 17; September 4; September 11. See also Theodore Kartevold, "Da Skyskraperne Manglet i New York," in "Nordisk Tidendes Jubilæumsnummer, 1825–1925," *NT*, October 8, 1925, 45. For private correspondance showing the Seamen's Church's reactions to *NT*, see "Korrespondanse og Årsberetninger," Gruppe I: Stasjonene, New York 1901–1910," letters from the seamen's pastor and Sigurd Folkestad explaining Folkestad's decision to start a newspaper in opposition to *NT*, in Seamen's Mission archives (Bergen, Norway).

[34]*NT*, 1894: January 5; January 12; January 17. The quoted phrases come from the January 17 issue. For *NT*'s coverage of other Association initiatives, see August 21, 1891; October 2, 1891; January 8, 1892; February 5, 1892; November 9, 1894; March 1, 1895.

[35]Rygg, *Norwegians*, 80–81, 143–144. *NT*, 1891: March 27; April 10; May 17; May 29; 1892: March 18; May 20; September 27; September 30; October 4; 1893: February 24; May 30; September 15; 1897: May 18, 19, and 21; 1905: May 11; November 16.

[36]*NT*, October 2, 1891; November 9, 1894.

[37]Rygg, *Norwegians*, 80, 82. In 1909, the Association's representatives at the Norwegian National League included the League's president, Gabriel Ueland, and two more prominent community leaders, Juell Bie and Louis M. Johnsen. Together these three contributed much to League decisions during the year. See *NT*, 1909: January 28; February 4; February 25; April 8; August 5. For the Association's donations to the Children's Home Association and the Grieg Monument, see May 27 and June 3. The Seamen's Association's own sports club (Gjøa), choral, and theatrical interests are evident in the program of the "7th of June" celebrations, which it had instituted four years earlier on behalf of the whole colony. See June 7, June 10, June 17. For the tux–and–tie affairs, see April 10 and December 23.

[38]Olaf Morgan Norlie, *The United Church Home Missions* (Minneapolis, 1909), 18–19, 34–36. Lovoll, *A Century of Urban Life*, 118, 220. Lovoll notes, however, that Lutheran churches played a larger role than membership figures might indicate because Norwegian immigrants who were reluctant to take on the responsibilities of voluntary membership often participated in these congregations. Carl H. Chrislock, *Ethnicity Challenged, The Upper Midwest Norwegian–American Experience in World War I* (Northfield, Minn., 1981), 24–26. In *A Folk Epic: The Bygdelag in America* (Boston, 1975), 67, Lovoll estimates that 15 percent of Norwegian Americans may have been "directly touched" by the regional associations he studied.

[39]Interviews with Einar Bredland, Erik Friis, Arne Larsen, Ruth and Paul Qualben, Bjørn and Kitty Jacobsen, Elsie Thorsen Rosvold, and Carsten Hansen. The quoted comment comes from Hansen, who arrived in 1904 with his mother and siblings, four years after his father settled in Red Hook. U. S. Census of Population, 1890 and 1910.

[40]Jenswold, "'I Live Well, But . . .'," 117–118, 121–123, discusses how the search for work drove Norwegian immigrants to become birds of passage in American cities. On the demographic and occupational characteristics of Norwegian immigrants at the turn of the century see Svalestuen, "Nordisk Emigrasjon en Komparativ Oversikt," in *Emigrationen fra Norden indtil 1. verdenskrig, Rapporter til det nordiske historikermøde i København* (Copenhagen, 1971), 42–43, 46–50; and Semmingsen, *Veien mot vest 1865–1915*, 362–364.

[41]"Diary, 1901," handwritten record of a young immigrant's contacts and daily activities, in NAHA Archives.

[42]Interviews with Stanley Solaas, Walter Lee, Bernie Reinertsen, Charles Turgesen, Helen and George Nielsen, Hans Berggren, Ole Jensen, Erling Rosand, and Fred Løken provided information on working conditions, industrial accidents, and the seasonal nature of seamen's and carpenters' work. For a sample of articles in *NT* on the same topics, see 1891: January 23; March 31; April 17. 1892: January 22; February 5, August 5, August 9; 1895: November 22; December 6; 1909: January 7; February 4; March 4; July 29; August 12; September 23; September 30.

[43]The quotations in this paragraph and the next come from a private collection of America letters covering the period from May 7, 1889, to November 28, 1906. All the information in the text comes from the dates cited there.

[44]Quoted in Jonassen, "The Norwegians in Bay Ridge," 257–258.

[45]Interviews with Hans Berggren, Einar Bredland, Tom Svennevik, Paul Nord, Paul and Ruth Qualben, Bjørn and Kitty Jacobsen, and Erling Lande. Rygg, *Norwegians*, 15–16, and *NT*, January 4, 1895, and January 11, 1900. Chrislock, *Ethnicity Challenged*, 24, indicates the likelihood that many successful businessmen and professionals were among those who did not participate in ethnic associations.

[46]The factual information and quoted material in this and the next two paragraphs come from *NT*, January 4, 1895.

[47]See Chrislock, *Ethnicity Challenged*, 24, for support for this view.

[48]Colony veterans first alerted the author to the situation described in this paragraph during interviews with Hans Berggren, Kari Alice Hesthag, Bjørn and Kitty Jacobsen, Gudrun Kartevold, Hjørdis Mortensen, and Kristoffer Oftedal.

[49]Much of the extensive correspondence in the Reymert Papers, in the NAHA Archives, testifies to August Reymert's business connections with firms and shipowners in Norway. Also included in the papers, however, are numerous newspaper clippings from Norwegian, Norwegian–American, and American newspapers that reported his aid to Scandinavian greenhorns and involvement in the Brooklyn colony's associational life.

[50]The annual reports and manuscript archives of the organizations listed in the text

(for 1890–1910), which are currently stored at scattered locations in Brooklyn as well as in Norway and the Midwest, give the best evidence of Reymert's legal aid to both transplanted and immigrant institutions. "Nordmænd i New York," *NT*, December 1, 1921; and "Dengang den Norske Indvandring var i sin Barndom av Advokat Reymerts Mindeoptegnelser," *Norgesposten* (Brooklyn), December 11, 1924, include most of the facts related in this and the remaining paragraphs on Reymert in the text. See also Rygg, *Norwegians*, 9, 62–63, 75, 79, 106, 138.

[51]This view was expressed during interviews with Hans Berggren, Bjørn and Kitty Jacobsen, Eileen Johansen, Erling Lande, Hjørdis Mortensen, and Paul Nord. "New York, N. Y.," in *Norske utvandrere og forretningsdrivende i Amerika,* ed., Johannes Wong (New York, 1925), 49–99, gives many examples of prominent leaders in Manhattan who arrived as representatives of Norwegian shipping interests.

[52]In 1892, only 18.8 percent of adult Norwegian–born women (267 of 1,421) were employed outside the home. In 1905, 19.3 percent (507 of 2,069) of the women included in a ten–percent sample of Norwegian–born adults in three Assembly Districts had jobs.

[53]The quoted phrases come from interviews with Gudrun and Bertha Kartevold and Gyda Andersen. For a sample of bazaars reported in *NT*, see Norwegian–American Seamen's Association bazaar (April 10, 1891), the Scandinavian Seamen's Temperance Home (December 18, 1891), bazaar for the victims of the city fire in Kristiansand, Norway (September 16, 1892), and the Hospice for Unemployed Emigrants (March 1, 1895). Ingrid Hartviksen and Bjørn Jakobsen, "Highlights of 100 Years, 1890–1990: Official Minutes of the Norwegian Singing Society," in *100th Anniversary: Norwegian Singing Society, 1890–1990* (Brooklyn, 1990), n.p.

[54]Interviews with Hjørdis Mortensen, Bjørn and Kitty Jacobsen, Elsie Thorsen Rosvold, Tom Svennevik; questionnaire responses from Einar Bredland, Myrtle Smith Berntsen, and Arne D. Larsen. "Eldre Kvinneforening," in *Den norske sjømannsmisjon i New York 100 år* (Brooklyn, 1978), 66. "Søster Elisabeths Optegnelser," *NT,* February 28, 1933. For *NT*'s complaint about the financial drain caused by the multitude of colony bazaars, see "Bazarerne i Anmarsch, en Uretferdig Beskatning, Bør Indskrænkes," October 15, 1897.

[55]A count of bazaars mentioned in anniversary booklets and *NT* articles for 1905 and 1910 produced the following totals, 25 (1905) and 43 (1910). An issue–by–issue perusal of any full year of *NT* gives ample proof of bazaars' prevalence as a fund–raising technique in the colony.

[56]Interviews with Birgit Rasmussen, Solveig Salvesen, Hannah Simonsen, Hjørdis Mortensen, Bjørn and Kitty Jacobsen, and Eileen Johansen. See the Register of Institutions and Associations in the Appendix for the various activities. Hartviksen and Jakobsen, "Highlights of 100 Years," *100th Anniversary: Norwegian Singing Society, 1890–1990,* first through third pages (no page numbers). *NT*, March 13; October, 16; December 11, 1891; February 2, 1892; February 23; April 5, 1895; April 13, 1896.

[57]*NT*, January 2, 1891; September 30, 1892. Eleventh U. S. Census, *Population*, 1: 675–676. In 1909, *NT* estimated the participation of between 1,200 and 2,000 at three different patriotic celebrations (the 17th of May, June 7th, and Leif Ericson Day) and another 1,500 attending the Leif Ericson society's Ulmer Park Fest in August. See *NT*, May 20; June 10; August 5; September 30.

[58]Interviews with Paul Nord, Tom Svennevik, Hans Berggren, Erling Rosand, Serene Sortland, Carsten Hansen, Alice and Daniel Fjelldal, Ralph and Geta Berntsen, Inge Berge, former domestics 2 and 3, and Lulu Lawrence. The quotation comes from the interview with Nord. On the Seamen's Association's masked ball, see *NT*, January 2, 1892.

[59]Interviews with Gudrun and Bertha Kartevold, Eileen Johansen, Helen and George Nielsen, Ruth and Paul Qualben, Kristoffer Oftedal, Johannes Aardal, Kjell Jordheim, Hannah Simonsen, George Joa, Hjørdis Mortensen, and Hans Berggren.

[60]Gudrun Kartevold made the remark about all immigrant ministers, "even the high–church one at Our Savior's," needing to court financial support and an "audience," as she called it.

[61]The quotation comes from Mrs. C. Zachiariasen's answer to a survey of readers' interests that *Nordisk Tidende* mailed to its subscribers in 1951. Mrs. Zachiariasen described the costume competition as a reply to this question: "Can you recall a memory

from your years in America or other places in connection with *Nordisk Tidende*?" See *NT*, September 4, 1891; February 5, 1892; May 18 and 19, 1894; November 16, 1905, for the complaints of commercial exploitation of patriotic celebrations.

[62]See the notes on individual businesses in "Street Registry of Little Norway's Business District" in Appendix 3 of Mauk, "The Colony," which include founding dates for many enterprises and additional information about many. During interviews Bertha and Gudrun Kartevold, Tom Svennevik, George Joa, Hannah Simonsen, Mrs. Ruth Arnesen Qualben, and others commented on the usefulness of Little Norway's business district as an informal social center. All the 68 people interviewed agreed about Sørlandet's popular reputation. See also Jonassen, "The Norwegian Heritage in Urban America: Conflict and Cooperation in a Norwegian Immigrant Community" in *Norwegian–American Studies*, 31 (Northfield, Minn., 1986), 73–95, especially page 80.

[63]On Hammerstad's bar and Helmin Johnsen's furniture store, see Mauk, "Colony," Appendix 3, Register of Businesses, 118 Hamilton Avenue and 240 Columbia Street. On *Nordisk Tidende*'s involvement with local ethnic theater, see *NT*, January 30; February 27; March 6; and March 13, 1891. Interviews with Inge Berge, Hans Berggren (who is quoted in the text), Rolf Broun, Daniel Fjelldal, Finn Gjertsen, Kristoffer and Mrs. Henricksen, Bjørn and Kitty Jacobsen, Erling Rosand, Sigurd Rosseland, and Tom Svennevik indicated common meeting places for men and attitudes toward people from coastal southern Norway. After 1910 regional associations for immigrants from these areas appear. See *NT*, May 10, 1917; February 4, 1926; and *Norgesposten* (Brooklyn), October 30, 1924. Many veterans claimed that 'Southerners' did not need to form their own clubs until later when other regional groups did. Until then, it had been enough for Southerners to outnumber other Norwegian groups in most churches and bars.

[64]Interviews with Gyda Andersen, Sophie Jarnes, Gudrun and Bertha Kartevold, Lulu Lawrence, Helen Livingstone, Hjørdis Mortensen, Birgit Rasmussen, Solveig Salvesen, Hannah Simonsen, and Serene Sortland. The Street Directory of Businesses in Appendix 3 of Mauk, "Colony," gives the locations of Little Norway's laundresses, dressmakers, seamstresses, and midwives. On the women who organized an octet to raise money for the Norwegian Singing Society, see *NT*, August 28; September 11; October 9; October 16, 1891.

[65]The quoted material comes from an interview with Gudrun Kartevold. See Mauk, "Colony," Appendix 3, for documentation on this and the next paragraph.

[66]For examples, see the references to *NT* and anniversary booklets in Mauk, "Colony," Appendix 3, "Institutions and Associations in Little Norway."

[67]Such remarks were nearly universal in interviews with working–class immigrants who had not held offices in ethnic associations but were also frequent in talks with well–known leaders.

[68]The following people represent a cross–section of colony members who reported the common practice of associating almost exclusively with Norwegians: Gyda Andersen, Domestics 2 and 3, Cecilia Tessdal Felt, Daniel and Alice Fjelldal, Erik Friis about his parents, Mr. and Mrs. Kristoffer Henricksen, Bjørn and Kitty Jacobsen, Ole Jensen, Eileen Johansen about her parents, Joy Edwardsen Kotrch about her parents, Hjørdis Mortensen about her parents, Paul Nord, John and Liva Nordskog, Erling Rosand, Mr. and Mrs. Reinert Reinertsen, Elsie Thorsen Rosvold, Solveig Salvesen, Hannah Simonsen, Tom Svennevik, Charles Turgesen about his parents and grandparents. The following people who arrived as adults were exceptional in their association with non–Norwegians: Ralph and Geta Berntsen, John E. Carlson, Lulu Lawrence, Helen Livingstone, Paul and Ruth Qualben.

[69]Serene Sortland's daughter told the anecdote about her first day at school. "Naar Norske Mødes i Amerika," the anonymous poem, appeared in *Nordisk Tidende* on October 13, 1904. The following second–generation immigrants (or people who arrived as children) spoke of moving between a Norwegian and a wider milieu: Einar Bredland, Joy Edwardsen Kotrch, Harold E. Jansen, Alice Fjelldal, Erik Friis, Kitty Jacobsen, Eileen Johansen, John Nersten, Ruth Arnesen Qualben, Solveig Salvesen's daughter, Stanley Solaas.

[70]The quotations come (respectively) from the interview with Carsten Hansen and the questionnaire filled out by Karl K. Kjendal. Even the individuals with regular social contacts outside the colony asserted that Little Norway's clannish cooperation had created a complete and separate social milieu. Many of the 68 people interviewed talked

of inner strife in the colony when asked directly, but although they universally agreed that it weakened joint efforts, they all also insisted on the loyalty and cooperation within the colony's many sub–groupings of views, interests, and organizations.

NOTES

Chapter 9

[1]Bertram Jensenius, "Bølgene ruller, selv i Chicago, efter 'Ymse betraktninger,'" *NT*, n.d.; found in Carl Søyland Papers, NAHA Archives. For a description of the survey, article series, and reactions to Søyland's "Ymse Betraktninger," see Roedder, *Av en utvandrer–avis' saga*, II:101–108, 113, 117–120, 125–128, 132–133.

[2]Lovoll, *Det løfterike landet* (Oslo, 1997), 172.

[3]See Kverndal, "Pionerspor i Verdenshavnen," 9–11.

[4]Sidney Smith, *Red Hook: A Community Study and Report* (Brooklyn, 1942), 44–47.

[5]"Maritime Acquisition is Scandinavian Line," *The Brooklyn Daily Eagle*, August 16, 1903.

[6]Norlie, *History of the Norwegian People in America* (Minneapolis, Minn., 1925), 235, contains a table ranking Norwegian–born populations by county based on the U. S. Census of 1890. Cook county, Illinois, had a population of 22,365. Seamen's pastors Carsten Hansteen and Kristen Sårheim estimated that at the end of the 1880s, between 23,000 and 25,000 Scandinavian sailors would enter the Port of New York annually on non–Norwegian ships alone. Further, they claimed that four–fifths of these men would be Norwegian. See Hansteen, "Brooklyn, New York," March 19, 1889, Seamen's Mission archives (Bergen), 3.

[7]The quoted phrase comes from the interview with Rolf Broun. Inge Berge, Hans Berggren, Astrid Heggeland, Paul Nord, Erling Rosand, and Sigurd Rosseland, among others, supported the view that boardinghouse residents banded together to help each other.

[8]For the rising number of visiting crews and deserters between 1910 and 1920, see Table 3, Chapter 3. For the revival of Norwegian shipping see Hodne, *Norges Økonomiske Historie*, 158–172; Gjerset, *Norwegian Sailors in American Waters*, 75–78, 92–96. For seamen's pleas for assistance and comments on their questions in the 1920s, see Consul General Hans Fay, "Sjøfolkene og Indvandringsloven, Sterkt Skjærpede Bestemmelser," *Norgesposten* (Brooklyn), October 16, 1924, and H. Sundby–Hansen, "En Bona Fida Sjømand Blir Ikke Vist ut av Amerika," *Norgesposten*, September 4, 1924. In *Nordisk Tidende*, "Om den Norske Sjømand," April 7, 1921; "Immigrationsloven," March 18, 1926; "Fra Sjømandskirken i Brooklyn, Naar Man Seiler paa Hamilton Avenue," January 6, 1927; and "Spørsmål og Svar," a standard editorial page column for questions that ran for several years in the 1920s. For a representative sample, see the newspaper's February issues for 1926. On the effects of World War II on Norwegian shipping and the colony, see Rygg, *Norwegians in New York*, 276–278; and Roedder, *Av en utvandrer–avis' saga*, II:9, 82–83, 93–99.

Appendix

[1]Mauk, "The Colony," 55–59 and 516, provides an explanation of the methodology and definitions used for analysis of the data in the 1904 emigrant protocols from Bergen, Kristiansand, and Trondheim.

[2]Appendix 1, 504–506, in Mauk, "The Colony," explains the aims, methods, and schedule of questions involved in the interviews and questionnaires listed.

[3]Mauk, "Colony," 527–557, provides tables and much fuller information about the methodology used with New York State census materials.

# Index

Aanonsen, Aanon (Anson), 79, 80
African Americans, 69–70
Agder counties: farmers could supplement incomes by fishing, 22; earliest emigrants mostly farmers, 29; crisis in Norwegian shipping encouraged emigration, 31; dominant among Norwegian immigrants in Brooklyn, 34, 190, 214; women used to managing when husbands at sea, 39; ship's carpenters did well in Brooklyn, 181; low-church background, 193
Alcohol, 128, 146, 172, 190–191, 197–198
"America fever," 28, 79
"America letters," 33, 39, 77, 162
*America Not Discovered by Columbus* (R. B. Anderson), 198
American Seamen's Church, 140, 143, 150
American Seamen's Friend Society, 95, 136
Amundsen, Helge, 173–174, 177–178, 181
Amundsen, Roald, 194
Andersen, Anton, 129, 133, 138, 140, 149
Andersen, Magnus, 130 (ill.); history before "going on land," 90–91; chosen to manage

Seamen's Home, 129–134; he and Hansteen differ on what it should be, 132–134, 136–139; founded the Norwegian-American Seamen's Association, 137–138, 140; his idea about the Seamen's Home triumphed, 146, 150; returned to Norway, 188
Anderson, Rasmus B., 198
Anson, Aanon. See Aanonsen, Aanon
Anson, John, 79, 172
Anson, Tom, 79
Arctic Norway, 23–24, 214
Asperheim, Rev. Ole, 100, 101–106, 109, 110, 160
Atlantic Docks: built, on landfill, 44, 72, 154; ethnic rivalry among dockworkers, 71; early Norwegian settlement in vicinity, 74; area's rapid development in size and population, 81, 84, 87, 158; most Norwegian crews landed there, 96; was area's main business, 157

Balling, Hans, 65